Public Secrets

Published January 1997 by the Bureau of Public Secrets
P.O. Box 1044, Berkeley, CA 94701

Printed in USA

ISBN 0-939682-03-6
Library of Congress Catalog No. 96-95067

Special thanks to Andy, Christian,
Gretchen, Jim, Lora and Robert

CONTENTS

THE JOY OF REVOLUTION

CONFESSIONS OF A MILD-MANNERED ENEMY OF THE STATE

PREVIOUS PUBLICATIONS

THE JOY OF REVOLUTION

1. Some Facts of Life

> *"We can comprehend this world only by contesting it as a whole. . . .*
> *The root of the prevailing* lack of imagination *cannot be grasped unless*
> *one is able to* imagine what is lacking, *that is, what is missing,*
> *hidden, forbidden, and yet possible, in modern life."*
>
> —Situationist International*

Never in history has there been such a glaring contrast between what could be and what actually exists.

It's hardly necessary to go into all the problems in the world today —most of them are widely known, and to dwell on them usually does little more than dull us to their reality. But even if we are "stoic enough to endure the misfortunes of others," the present social deterioration ultimately impinges on us all. Those who don't face direct physical repression still have to face the mental repressions imposed by an increasingly mean, stressful, ignorant and ugly world. Those who escape economic poverty cannot escape the general impoverishment of life.

And even life at this pitiful level cannot continue for long. The ravaging of the planet by the global development of capitalism has brought us to the point where humanity may become extinct within a few decades.

Yet this same development has made it possible to abolish the system of hierarchy and exploitation that was previously based on material scarcity and to inaugurate a new, genuinely liberated form of society.

---

*Ken Knabb (ed. and trans.), *Situationist International Anthology* (Bureau of Public Secrets, 1981), p. 81. Here and elsewhere I have sometimes slightly modified my original *SI Anthology* translations.

Plunging from one disaster to another on its way to mass insanity and ecological apocalypse, this system has developed a momentum that is out of control, even by its supposed masters. As we approach a world in which we won't be able to leave our fortified ghettoes without armed guards, or even go outdoors without applying sunscreen lest we get skin cancer, it's hard to take seriously those who advise us to beg for a few reforms.

What is needed, I believe, is a worldwide participatory-democracy revolution that would abolish both capitalism and the state. This is admittedly a big order, but I'm afraid that nothing less can get to the root of our problems. It may seem absurd to talk about revolution; but all the alternatives assume the continuation of the present system, which is even more absurd.

* * *

Before going into what this revolution would involve and responding to some typical objections, it should be stressed that it has nothing to do with the repugnant stereotypes that are usually evoked by the word (terrorism, revenge, political coups, manipulative leaders preaching self-sacrifice, zombie followers chanting politically correct slogans). In particular, it should not be confused with the two principal failures of modern social change, Stalinist "communism" and reformist "socialism."

After decades in power, first in Russia and later in many other countries, it has become obvious that Stalinism is the total opposite of a liberated society. The origin of this grotesque phenomenon is less obvious. Trotskyists and others have tried to distinguish Stalinism from the earlier Bolshevism of Lenin and Trotsky. There *are* differences, but they are more of degree than of kind. Lenin's *The State and Revolution,* for example, presents a more coherent critique of the state than can be found in most anarchist writings; the problem is that the radical aspects of Lenin's thought merely ended up camouflaging the Bolsheviks' actual authoritarian practice. Placing itself above the masses it claimed to represent, and with a corresponding internal hierarchy between party militants and their leaders, the Bolshevik Party was already well on its way toward creating the conditions for the development of Stalinism while Lenin and Trotsky were still firmly in control.*

But we have to be clear about what failed if we are ever going to

---

*See Maurice Brinton's *The Bolsheviks and Workers' Control: 1917–1921,* Voline's *The Unknown Revolution,* Ida Mett's *The Kronstadt Uprising,* Paul Avrich's *Kronstadt 1921,* Peter Arshinov's *History of the Makhnovist Movement,* and Guy Debord's *The Society of the Spectacle* §§98–113. (These and most of the other texts cited in this book can be obtained through the distributors listed on page 383.)

do any better. If socialism means people's full participation in the social decisions that affect their own lives, it has existed neither in the Stalinist regimes of the East nor in the welfare states of the West. The recent collapse of Stalinism is neither a vindication of capitalism nor proof of the failure of "Marxist communism." Anyone who has ever bothered to read Marx (most of his glib critics obviously have not) is aware that Leninism represents a severe distortion of Marx's thought and that Stalinism is a total parody of it. Nor does government ownership have anything to do with communism in its authentic sense of common, communal ownership; it is merely a different type of capitalism in which state-bureaucratic ownership replaces (or merges with) private-corporate ownership.

The long spectacle of opposition between these two varieties of capitalism hid their mutual reinforcement. Serious conflicts were confined to proxy battles in the Third World (Vietnam, Angola, Afghanistan, etc.). Neither side ever made any real attempt to overthrow the enemy in its own heartland. (The French Communist Party sabotaged the May 1968 revolt; the Western powers, which intervened massively in countries where they were not wanted, refused to send so much as the few antitank weapons desperately needed by the 1956 Hungarian insurgents.) Guy Debord noted in 1967 that Stalinist state-capitalism had already revealed itself as merely a "poor cousin" of classical Western capitalism, and that its decline was beginning to deprive Western rulers of the pseudo-opposition that reinforced them by seeming to represent the sole alternative to their system. "The bourgeoisie is in the process of losing the adversary that objectively supported it by providing an illusory unification of all opposition to the existing order" (*The Society of the Spectacle,* §§110–111).

Although Western leaders pretended to welcome the recent Stalinist collapse as a natural victory for their own system, none of them had seen it coming and they now obviously have no idea what to do about all the problems it poses except to cash in on the situation before it totally falls apart. The monopolistic multinational corporations that proclaim "free enterprise" as a panacea are quite aware that free-market capitalism would long ago have exploded from its own contradictions had it not been saved despite itself by a few New Deal–style pseudosocialist reforms.

Those reforms (public services, social insurance, the eight-hour day, etc.) may have ameliorated some of the more glaring defects of the system, but in no way have they led beyond it. In recent years they have not even kept up with its accelerating crises. The most significant improvements were in any case won only by long and often violent popular struggles that eventually forced the hands of the bureaucrats: the leftist parties and labor unions that pretended to lead those struggles have functioned primarily as safety valves, coopting radical tendencies and greasing the wheels of the social machine.

3

As the situationists have shown, the bureaucratization of radical movements, which has degraded people into followers constantly "betrayed" by their leaders, is linked to the increasing *spectacularization* of modern capitalist society, which has degraded people into spectators of a world over which they have no control—a development that has become increasingly glaring, though it is usually only superficially understood.

Taken together, all these considerations point to the conclusion that a liberated society can be created only by the active participation of the people as a whole, not by hierarchical organizations supposedly acting on their behalf. The point is not to choose more honest or "responsive" leaders, but to avoid granting independent power to any leaders whatsoever. Individuals or groups may initiate radical actions, but a substantial and rapidly expanding portion of the population must take part if a movement is to lead to a new society and not simply to a coup installing new rulers.

* * *

I won't repeat all the classic socialist and anarchist critiques of capitalism and the state; they are already widely known, or at least widely accessible. But in order to cut through some of the confusions of traditional political rhetoric, it may be helpful to summarize the basic types of social organization. For the sake of clarity, I will start out by examining the "political" and "economic" aspects separately, though they are obviously interlinked. It is as futile to try to equalize people's economic conditions through a state bureaucracy as it is to try to democratize society while the power of money enables the wealthy few to control the institutions that determine people's awareness of social realities. Since the system functions as a whole it can be fundamentally changed only as a whole.

To begin with the political aspect, roughly speaking we can distinguish five degrees of "government":

(1) Unrestricted freedom

(2) Direct democracy
   a) consensus
   b) majority rule

(3) Delegate democracy

(4) Representative democracy

(5) Overt minority dictatorship

The present society oscillates between (4) and (5), i.e. between overt minority rule and covert minority rule camouflaged by a façade of token democracy. A liberated society would eliminate (4) and (5) and would progressively reduce the need for (2) and (3).

I'll discuss the two types of (2) later on. But the crucial distinction is between (3) and (4).

In representative democracy people abdicate their power to elected officials. The candidates' stated policies are limited to a few vague generalities, and once they are elected there is little control over their actual decisions on hundreds of issues—apart from the feeble threat of changing one's vote, a few years later, to some equally uncontrollable rival politician. Representatives are dependent on the wealthy for bribes and campaign contributions; they are subordinate to the owners of the mass media, who decide which issues get the publicity; and they are almost as ignorant and powerless as the general public regarding many important matters that are determined by unelected bureaucrats and independent secret agencies. Overt dictators may sometimes be overthrown, but the real rulers in "democratic" regimes, the tiny minority who own or control virtually everything, are never voted in and never voted out. Most people don't even know who they are.

In delegate democracy, delegates are elected for specific purposes with very specific limitations. They may be strictly mandated (ordered to vote in a certain way on a certain issue) or the mandate may be left open (delegates being free to vote as they think best) with the people who have elected them reserving the right to confirm or reject any decision thus taken. Delegates are generally elected for very short periods and are subject to recall at any time.

In the context of radical struggles, delegate assemblies have usually been termed "councils." The council form was invented by striking workers during the 1905 Russian revolution (*soviet* is the Russian word for council). When soviets reappeared in 1917, they were successively supported, manipulated, dominated and coopted by the Bolsheviks, who soon succeeded in transforming them into parodies of themselves: rubber stamps of the "Soviet State" (the last surviving independent soviet, that of the Kronstadt sailors, was crushed in 1921). Councils have nevertheless continued to reappear spontaneously at the most radical moments in subsequent history, in Germany, Italy, Spain, Hungary and elsewhere, because they represent the obvious solution to the need for a practical form of nonhierarchical popular self-organization. And they continue to be opposed by all hierarchical organizations, because they threaten the rule of specialized elites by pointing to the possibility of a society of *generalized self-management:* not self-management of a few details of the present setup, but self-management extended to all regions of the globe and all aspects of life.

But as noted above, the question of democratic forms cannot be separated from their economic context.

* * *

Economic organization can be looked at from the angle of work:

   (1) Totally voluntary

   (2) Cooperative (collective self-management)

   (3) Forced and exploitive
        a) overt (slave labor)
        b) disguised (wage labor)

And from the angle of distribution:

   (1) True communism (totally free accessibility)

   (2) True socialism (collective ownership and regulation)

   (3) Capitalism (private and/or state ownership)

Though it's possible for goods or services produced by wage labor to be given away, or for those produced by volunteer or cooperative labor to be turned into commodities for sale, for the most part these levels of work and distribution tend to correspond with each other. The present society is predominately (3): the forced production and consumption of commodities. A liberated society would eliminate (3) and as far as possible reduce (2) in favor of (1).

Capitalism is based on commodity production (production of goods for profit) and wage labor (labor power itself bought and sold as a commodity). As Marx pointed out, there is less difference between the slave and the "free" worker than appears. Slaves, though they seem to be paid nothing, are provided with the means of their survival and reproduction, for which workers (who become temporary slaves during their hours of labor) are compelled to pay most of their wages. The fact that some jobs are less unpleasant than others, and that individual workers have the nominal right to switch jobs, start their own business, buy stocks or win a lottery, disguises the fact that the vast majority of people are collectively enslaved.

How did we get in this absurd position? If we go back far enough, we find that at some point people were forcibly dispossessed: driven off the land and otherwise deprived of the means for producing the goods necessary for life. (The famous chapters on "primitive accumulation" in *Capital* vividly describe this process in England.) As long as people accept this dispossession as legitimate, they are forced into unequal bargains with the "owners" (those who have robbed them, or who have subsequently obtained titles of "ownership" from the original robbers) in which they exchange their labor for a fraction of what it actually produces, the surplus being retained by the owners. This surplus (capital) can then be reinvested in order to generate continually greater surpluses in the same way.

As for distribution, a public water fountain is a simple example of true communism (unlimited accessibility). A public library is an example of true socialism (free but regulated accessibility).

In a rational society, accessibility would depend on abundance. During a drought, water might have to be rationed. Conversely, once libraries are put entirely online they could become totally communistic: anyone could have free instant access to any number of texts with no more need to bother with checking out and returning, security against theft, etc.

But this rational relation is impeded by the persistence of separate economic interests. To take the latter example, it will soon be technically possible to create a global "library" in which every book ever written, every film ever made and every musical performance ever recorded could be put online, potentially enabling anyone to freely tap in and obtain a copy (no more need for stores, sales, advertising, packaging, shipping, etc.). But since this would also eliminate the profits from present-day publishing, recording and film businesses, far more energy is spent concocting complicated methods to prevent or charge for copying (while others devote corresponding energy devising ways to get around such methods) than on developing a technology that could potentially benefit everyone.

One of Marx's merits was to have cut through the hollowness of political discourses based on abstract philosophical or ethical principles ("human nature" is such and such, all people have a "natural right" to this or that) by showing how social possibilities and social awareness are to a great degree limited and shaped by material conditions. Freedom in the abstract means little if almost everybody has to work all the time simply to assure their survival. It's unrealistic to expect people to be generous and cooperative when there is barely enough to go around (leaving aside the drastically different conditions under which "primitive communism" flourished). But a sufficiently large surplus opens up wider possibilities. The hope of Marx and other revolutionaries of his time was based on the fact that the technological potentials developed by the Industrial Revolution had finally provided an adequate material basis for a classless society. It was no longer a matter of declaring that things "should" be different, but of pointing out that they *could* be different; that class domination was not only unjust, it was now *unnecessary*.

Was it ever really necessary? Was Marx right in seeing the development of capitalism and the state as inevitable stages, or might a liberated society have been possible without this painful detour? Fortunately, we no longer have to worry about this question. Whatever possibilities there may or may not have been in the past, present material conditions are more than sufficient to sustain a global classless society.

The most serious drawback of capitalism is not its quantitative unfairness—the mere fact that wealth is unequally distributed, that workers are not paid the full "value" of their labor. The problem is that this margin of exploitation (even if relatively small) makes possible the private accumulation of capital, which eventually reorients everything to its own ends, dominating and warping all aspects of life.

The more alienation the system produces, the more social energy must be diverted just to keep it going—more advertising to sell superfluous commodities, more ideologies to keep people bamboozled, more spectacles to keep them pacified, more police and more prisons to repress crime and rebellion, more arms to compete with rival states—all of which produces more frustrations and antagonisms, which must be repressed by more spectacles, more prisons, etc. As this vicious circle continues, real human needs are fulfilled only incidentally, if at all, while virtually all labor is channeled into absurd, redundant or destructive projects that serve no purpose except to maintain the system.

If this system were abolished and modern technological potentials were appropriately transformed and redirected, the labor necessary to meet real human needs would be reduced to such a trivial level that it could easily be taken care of voluntarily and cooperatively, without requiring economic incentives or state enforcement.

It's not too hard to grasp the idea of superseding overt hierarchical power. Self-management can be seen as the fulfillment of the freedom and democracy that are the official values of Western societies. Despite people's submissive conditioning, everyone has had moments when they rejected domination and began speaking or acting for themselves.

It's much harder to grasp the idea of superseding the economic system. The domination of capital is more subtle and self-regulating. Questions of work, production, goods, services, exchange and coordination in the modern world seem so complicated that most people take for granted the necessity of money as a universal mediation, finding it difficult to imagine any change beyond apportioning money in some more equitable way.

For this reason I will postpone more extensive discussion of the economic aspects till later in this text, when it will be possible to go into more detail.

* * *

Is such a revolution likely? The odds are probably against it. The main problem is that there is not much time. In previous eras it was possible to imagine that, despite all humanity's follies and disasters, we would somehow muddle through and perhaps eventually learn from past mistakes. But now that social policies and technological developments have irrevocable global ecological ramifications, blundering trial and error is not enough. We have only a few decades to turn things around.

And as time passes, the task becomes more difficult: the fact that basic social problems are scarcely even faced, much less resolved, encourages increasingly desperate and delirious tendencies toward war, fascism, ethnic antagonism, religious fanaticism and other forms of mass irrationality, deflecting those who might potentially work toward a new society into merely defensive and ultimately futile holding actions.

But most revolutions have been preceded by periods when everyone scoffed at the idea that things could ever change. Despite the many discouraging trends in the world, there are also some encouraging signs, not least of which is the widespread disillusionment with previous false alternatives. Many popular revolts in this century have already moved spontaneously in the right direction. I am not referring to the "successful" revolutions, which are without exception frauds, but to less known, more radical efforts. Some of the most notable examples are Russia 1905, Germany 1918–19, Italy 1920, Asturias 1934, Spain 1936–37, Hungary 1956, France 1968, Czechoslovakia 1968, Portugal 1974–75 and Poland 1980–81; many other movements, from the Mexican revolution of 1910 to the recent anti-apartheid struggle in South Africa, have also contained exemplary moments of popular experimentation before they were brought under bureaucratic control.

No one is in any position to dismiss the prospect of revolution who has not carefully examined these movements. To ignore them because of their "failure" is missing the point.* Modern revolution is all or nothing: individual revolts are bound to fail until an international

---

*"The journalists' and governments' superficial references to the 'success' or 'failure' of a revolution mean nothing for the simple reason that since the bourgeois revolutions *no revolution has yet succeeded:* not one has abolished classes. Proletarian revolution has not yet been victorious anywhere, but the practical process through which its project manifests itself has already created at least ten revolutionary moments of historic importance that can appropriately be termed revolutions. In none of these moments was the *total content* of proletarian revolution fully developed, but in each case there was a fundamental interruption of the ruling socioeconomic order and the appearance of new forms and conceptions of real life—variegated phenomena that can be understood and evaluated only in their overall significance, including their potential future significance. . . . The revolution of 1905 did not bring down the Czarist regime, it only obtained a few temporary concessions from it. The Spanish revolution of 1936 did not formally suppress the existing political power: it arose, in fact, out of a proletarian uprising initiated in order to defend the Republic against Franco. And the Hungarian revolution of 1956 did not abolish Nagy's liberal-bureaucratic government. Among other regrettable limitations, the Hungarian movement had many aspects of a national uprising against foreign domination; and this national-resistance aspect also played a certain, though less important, role in the origin of the Paris Commune. The Commune supplanted Thiers's power only within the limits of Paris. And the St. Petersburg Soviet of 1905 never even took control of the capital. All the crises mentioned here as examples, though deficient in their practical achievements and even in their perspectives, nevertheless produced enough radical innovations and put their societies severely enough in check to be legitimately termed revolutions." (*SI Anthology,* pp. 235–236.)

chain reaction is triggered that spreads faster than repression can close in. It's hardly surprising that these revolts did not go farther; what is inspiring is that they went as far as they did. A new revolutionary movement will undoubtedly take new and unpredictable forms; but these earlier efforts remain full of examples of what can be done, as well as of what must be avoided.

* * *

It's often said that a stateless society might work if everyone were angels, but due to the perversity of human nature some hierarchy is necessary to keep people in line. It would be truer to say that if everyone were angels the *present* system might work tolerably well (bureaucrats would function honestly, capitalists would refrain from socially harmful ventures even if they were profitable). It is precisely because people are not angels that it's necessary to eliminate the setup that enables some of them to become very efficient devils. Lock a hundred people in a small room with only one air hole and they will claw each other to death to get to it. Let them out and they may manifest a rather different nature. As one of the May 1968 graffiti put it, "Man is neither Rousseau's noble savage nor the Church's depraved sinner. He is violent when oppressed, gentle when free."

Others contend that, whatever the ultimate causes may be, people are now so screwed up that they need to be psychologically or spiritually healed before they can even conceive of creating a liberated society. In his later years Wilhelm Reich came to feel that an "emotional plague" was so firmly embedded in the population that it would take generations of healthily raised children before people would become capable of a libertarian social transformation; and that meanwhile one should avoid confronting the system head-on since this would stir up a hornet's nest of ignorant popular reaction.

Irrational popular tendencies do sometimes call for discretion. But powerful though they may be, they are not irresistible forces. They contain their own contradictions. Clinging to some absolute authority is not necessarily a sign of faith in authority; it may be a desperate attempt to overcome one's increasing doubts (the convulsive tightening of a slipping grip). People who join gangs or reactionary groups, or who get caught up in religious cults or patriotic hysteria, are also seeking a sense of liberation, connection, purpose, participation, empowerment. As Reich himself showed, fascism gives a particularly vigorous and dramatic expression to these basic aspirations, which is why it often has a deeper appeal than the vacillations, compromises and hypocrisies of liberalism and leftism.

In the long run the only way to defeat reaction is to present more forthright expressions of these aspirations, and more authentic opportunities to fulfill them. When basic issues are forced into the open, irrationalities that flourished under the cover of psychological repression tend to be weakened, like disease germs exposed to sunlight and fresh air. In any case, even if we don't prevail, there is at least some satisfaction in fighting for what we really believe, rather than being defeated in a posture of hesitancy and hypocrisy.

There are limits on how far one can liberate oneself (or raise liberated children) within a sick society. But if Reich was right to note that psychologically repressed people are less capable of envisioning social liberation, he failed to realize how much the process of social revolt can be psychologically liberating. (French psychiatrists are said to have complained about a significant drop in the number of their customers in the aftermath of May 1968!)

The notion of total democracy raises the specter of a "tyranny of the majority." Majorities *can* be ignorant and bigoted, there's no getting around it. The only real solution is to confront and attempt to overcome that ignorance and bigotry. Keeping the masses in the dark (relying on liberal judges to protect civil liberties or liberal legislators to sneak through progressive reforms) only leads to popular backlashes when sensitive issues eventually do come to the surface.

Examined more closely, however, most instances of majority oppression of minorities turn out to be due not to majority rule, but to disguised minority rule in which the ruling elite plays on whatever racial or cultural antagonisms there may be in order to turn the exploited masses' frustrations against each other. When people get real power over their own lives they will have more interesting things to do than to persecute minorities.

So many potential abuses or disasters are evoked at any suggestion of a nonhierarchical society that it would be impossible to answer them all. People who resignedly accept a system that condemns millions of their fellow human beings to death every year in wars and famines, and millions of others to prison and torture, suddenly let their imagination and their indignation run wild at the thought that in a self-managed society there might be *some* abuses, some violence or coercion or injustice, or even merely some temporary inconvenience. They forget that it is not up to a new social system to solve all our problems; it merely has to deal with them better than the *present* system does—not a very big order.

If history followed the complacent opinions of official commentators, there would never have been any revolutions. In any given situation there are always plenty of ideologists ready to declare that no radical change is possible. If the economy is functioning well, they will claim that revolution depends on economic crises; if there is an economic crisis, others will just as confidently declare that revolution is impossible because people are too busy worrying about making ends meet. The former types, surprised by the May 1968 revolt, tried to retrospectively uncover the invisible crisis that their ideology insists must have been there. The latter contend that the situationist perspective has been refuted by the worsened economic conditions since that time.

Actually, the situationists simply noted that the widespread achievement of capitalist abundance had demonstrated that guaranteed survival was no substitute for real life. The periodic ups and downs of the economy have no bearing on that conclusion. The fact that a few people at the top have recently managed to siphon off a yet larger portion of the social wealth, driving increasing numbers of people into the streets and terrorizing the rest of the population lest they succumb to the same fate, makes the feasibility of a postscarcity society less evident; but the material prerequisites are still present.

The economic crises held up as evidence that we need to "lower our expectations" are actually caused by *over*-production and *lack* of work. The ultimate absurdity of the present system is that unemployment is seen as a problem, with potentially labor-saving technologies being directed toward creating new jobs to replace the old ones they render unnecessary. The problem is not that so many people don't have jobs, but that so many people still do. We need to raise our expectations, not lower them.*

Far more serious than this spectacle of our supposed powerlessness in the face of the economy is the greatly increased power of the spectacle itself, which in recent years has developed to the point of repressing virtually any awareness of pre-spectacle history or anti-spectacle possibilities. Debord's *Comments on the Society of the Spectacle* (1988) goes into this new development in detail:

> In all that has happened over the last twenty years, the most important change lies in the very continuity of the spectacle. What is significant is not the refinements of the spectacle's media instrumentation, which had already attained a highly advanced stage of development; it is quite simply that spectacular domination has succeeded in raising an entire generation molded to its laws. . . . Spectacular domination's first priority was to eradicate historical knowledge in general, beginning with virtually all information and rational commentary on the most recent past. . . . The spectacle makes sure that people are unaware of what is happening, or at least that they quickly forget whatever they may have become aware of. The more important something is, the more it is hidden. Nothing in the last twenty years has been so thoroughly shrouded with official lies as May 1968. . . . The flow of images carries everything before it, and it is always someone else who controls this simplified digest of the perceptible world, who decides

---

*"We're not interested in hearing about the exploiters' economic problems. If the capitalist economy is not capable of fulfilling workers' demands, that is simply one more reason to struggle for a new society, one in which we ourselves have the decisionmaking power over the whole economy and all social life." (Portuguese airline workers, 27 October 1974.)

where the flow will lead, who programs the rhythm of what is shown into an endless series of arbitrary surprises that leaves no time for reflection . . . . isolating whatever is presented from its context, its past, its intentions and its consequences. . . . It is thus hardly surprising that children are now starting their education with an enthusiastic introduction to the Absolute Knowledge of computer language while becoming increasingly incapable of reading. Because reading requires making judgments at every line; and since conversation is almost dead (as will soon be most of those who knew how to converse) reading is the only remaining gateway to the vast realms of pre-spectacle human experience.

In the present text I have tried to recapitulate some basic points that have been buried under this intensive spectacular repression. If these matters seem banal to some or obscure to others, they may at least serve to recall what once was possible, in those primitive times a few decades ago when people had the quaint, old-fashioned notion that they could understand and affect their own history.

While there is no question that things have changed considerably since the sixties (mostly for the worse), our situation may not be quite as hopeless as it seems to those who swallow whatever the spectacle feeds them. Sometimes it only takes a little jolt to break through the stupor.

Even if we have no guarantee of ultimate victory, such breakthroughs are already a pleasure. Is there any greater game around?

13

2. Foreplay

"An individual cannot know what he really is until he has realized himself through action. . . . The interest the individual finds in something is already the answer to the question of whether he should act and what should be done."
—Hegel, *The Phenomenology of Spirit*

Later on I will try to answer some more of the perennial objections. But as long as the objectors remain passive, all the arguments in the world will never faze them, and they will continue to sing the old refrain: "It's a nice idea, but it's not realistic, it goes against human nature, it's always been this way. . . ." Those who don't realize their own potential are unlikely to recognize the potential of others.

To paraphrase that very sensible old prayer, we need the initiative to solve the problems we can, the patience to endure the ones we can't, and the wisdom to know the difference. But we also need to bear in mind that some problems that can't be solved by isolated individuals can be solved collectively. Discovering that others share the same problem is often the beginning of a solution.

Some problems can, of course, be solved individually, through a variety of methods ranging from elaborate therapies or spiritual practices to simple commonsense decisions to correct some mistake, break some harmful habit, try something new, etc. But my concern here is not with purely personal makeshifts, worthwhile though they may be within their limits, but with moments where people move "outward" in deliberately subversive ventures.

There are more possibilities than appear at first sight. Once you refuse to be intimidated, some of them are quite simple. You can begin anywhere. And you have to begin somewhere—do you think you can learn to swim if you never go in the water?

Sometimes a little action is needed to cut through excessive verbiage and reestablish a concrete perspective. It needn't be anything momentous; if nothing else comes to mind, some rather arbitrary venture may suffice—just enough to shake things up a bit and wake yourself up.

At other times it's necessary to stop, to break the chain of compulsive actions and reactions. To clear the air, to create a little space free from the cacophony of the spectacle. Just about everyone does this to some degree, out of instinctive psychological self-defense, whether by practicing some form of meditation, or by periodically engaging in some activity that effectively serves the same purpose (working in one's garden, taking a walk, going fishing), or simply by pausing to take a deep breath amid their daily round, coming back for a moment to the "quiet center." Without such a space it is difficult to get a sane perspective on the world, or even simply to keep one's own sanity.

One of the methods I have found most useful is to put things in writing. The advantage is partly psychological (some problems lose their power over us by being set out where we can see them more objectively), partly a matter of organizing our thoughts so as to see the different factors and choices more clearly. We often maintain inconsistent notions without becoming aware of their contradictions until we try putting them down on paper.

I have sometimes been criticized for exaggerating the importance of writing. Many matters can, of course, be dealt with more directly. But even nonverbal actions require thinking about, talking about, and usually writing about, if they are to be effectively carried out, communicated, debated, corrected.

(In any case, I don't claim to cover everything; I am merely discussing certain points about which I feel I have something to say. If you think I have failed to address some important topic, why don't you do it yourself?)

Writing enables you to work out your ideas at your own pace, without worrying about oratorical skills or stage fright. You can make a point once and for all instead of having to constantly repeat yourself. If discretion is necessary, a text can be issued anonymously. People can read it at *their* own pace, stop and think about it, go back and check specific points, reproduce it, adapt it, refer others to it. Talking may generate quicker and more detailed feedback, but it can also disperse your energy, prevent you from focusing and implementing your ideas. Those in the same rut as you may resist your efforts to escape because your success would challenge their own passivity.

Sometimes you can best provoke such people by simply leaving them behind and pursuing your own course. ("Hey, wait for me!") Or by shifting the dialogue to a different level. A letter forces both writer and addressee to work out their ideas more clearly. Copies to others concerned may enliven the discussion. An open letter draws in even more people.

If you succeed in creating a chain reaction in which more and more people read your text because they see others reading it and heatedly discussing it, it will no longer be possible for anyone to pretend to be unaware of the issues you have raised.*

---

*The SI's dissemination of a text denouncing an international gathering of art critics in Belgium was a fine example of this: "Copies were mailed to a large number of critics or given to them personally. Others were telephoned and read all or part of the text. A group forced its way into the Press Club where the critics were being received and threw the leaflets among the audience. Others were tossed onto the sidewalks from upstairs windows or from a car. . . . In short, all steps were taken to leave the critics no chance of being unaware of the text." (*SI Anthology,* p. 49.)

Suppose, for example, that you criticize a group for being hierarchical, for allowing a leader to have power over members (or followers or fans). A private talk with one of the members might merely meet with a series of contradictory defensive reactions with which it is fruitless to argue. ("No, he's not really our leader. . . . And even if he is, he's not authoritarian. . . . And besides, what right do you have to criticize?") But a public critique forces such contradictions into the open and puts people in a crossfire. While one member denies that the group is hierarchical, a second may admit that it is and attempt to justify this by attributing superior insight to the leader. This may cause a third member to start thinking.

At first, annoyed that you have disturbed their cozy little scene, the group is likely to close ranks around the leader and denounce you for your "negativity" or "elitist arrogance." But if your intervention has been acute enough, it may continue to sink in and have a delayed impact. The leader now has to watch his step since everyone is more sensitive to anything that might seem to confirm your critique. In order to demonstrate how unjustified you are, the members may insist on greater democratization. Even if the particular group proves impervious to change, its example may serve as an object lesson for a wider public. Outsiders who might otherwise have made similar mistakes can more easily see the pertinence of your critique because they have less emotional investment.

It's usually more effective to criticize institutions and ideologies than to attack individuals who merely happen to be caught up in them —not only because the machine is more crucial than its replaceable parts, but because this approach makes it easier for individuals to save face while dissociating themselves from the machine.

But however tactful you may be, there's no getting around the fact that virtually any significant critique will provoke irrational defensive reactions, ranging from personal attacks on you to invocations of one or another of the many fashionable ideologies that seem to demonstrate the impossibility of any rational consideration of social problems. Reason is denounced as cold and abstract by demagogues who find it easier to play on people's feelings; theory is scorned in the name of practice. . . .

To theorize is simply to try to understand what we are doing. We are all theorists whenever we honestly discuss what has happened, distinguish between the significant and the irrelevant, see through fallacious explanations, recognize what worked and what didn't, consider how something might be done better next time. Radical theorizing is simply talking or writing to more people about more general issues in more abstract (i.e. more widely applicable) terms. Even those who claim to reject theory theorize—they merely do so more unconsciously and capriciously, and thus more inaccurately.

Theory without particulars is empty, but particulars without theory are blind. Practice tests theory, but theory also inspires new practice.

Radical theory has nothing to respect and nothing to lose. It criticizes itself along with everything else. It is not a doctrine to be accepted on faith, but a tentative generalization that people must constantly test and correct for themselves, a practical simplification indispensible for dealing with the complexities of reality.

But hopefully not an oversimplification. Any theory can turn into an ideology, become rigidified into a dogma, be twisted to hierarchical ends. A sophisticated ideology may be relatively accurate in certain respects; what differentiates it from theory is that it lacks a dynamic relation to practice. Theory is when you have ideas; ideology is when ideas have you. "Seek simplicity, and distrust it."

We have to face the fact that there are no foolproof gimmicks, that no radical tactic is invariably appropriate. Something that is collectively possible during a revolt may not be a sensible option for an isolated individual. In certain urgent situations it may be necessary to urge people to take some specific action; but in most cases it is best simply to elucidate relevant factors that people should take into account when making their own decisions. (If I occasionally presume to offer direct advice here, this is for convenience of expression. "Do this" should be understood as "In some circumstances it may be a good idea to do this.")

A social analysis need not be long or detailed. Simply "dividing one into two" (pointing out contradictory tendencies within a given phenomenon or group or ideology) or "combining two into one" (revealing a commonality between two apparently distinct entities) may be useful, especially if communicated to those most directly involved. More than enough information is already available on most issues; what is needed is to cut through the glut in order to reveal the essential. Once this is done, other people, including knowledgeable insiders, will be spurred to more thorough investigations if these are necessary.

When confronted with a given topic, the first thing is to determine whether it is indeed a single topic. It's impossible to have any meaningful discussion of "Marxism" or "violence" or "technology" without distinguishing the diverse senses that are lumped under such labels.

On the other hand, it can also be useful to take some broad, abstract category and show its predominant tendencies, even though such a pure type does not actually exist. The situationists' *Student Poverty* pamphlet, for example, scathingly enumerates all sorts of stupidities and pretensions of "the student." Obviously not every student is guilty of all these faults, but the stereotype serves as a focus around which to organize a systematic critique of general tendencies. By stressing qualities most students have in common, the pamphlet also implicitly challenges those who claim to be exceptions to prove it. The same applies to the critique of "the pro-situ" in Debord and Sanguinetti's *The Real Split in the International*—a challenging rebuff

17

of followers perhaps unique in the history of radical movements.

"Everyone is asked their opinion about every detail in order to prevent them from forming one about the totality" (Vaneigem). Many issues are such emotionally loaded tar-babies that anyone who reacts to them becomes entangled in false choices. The fact that two sides are in conflict, for example, does not mean that you must support one or the other. If you cannot do anything about a particular problem, it is best to clearly acknowledge this fact and move on to something that does present practical possibilities.*

If you do decide to choose a lesser evil, admit it; don't add to the confusion by whitewashing your choice or demonizing the enemy. If anything, it's better to do the opposite: to play devil's advocate and neutralize compulsive polemical delirium by calmly examining the strong points of the opposing position and the weaknesses in your own. "A very popular error: having the courage of one's convictions; the point is to have the courage for an *attack* on one's convictions!" (Nietzsche).

Combine modesty with audacity. Remember that if you happen to accomplish anything it is on the foundation of the efforts of countless others, many of whom have faced horrors that would make you or me crumple into submission. But don't forget that what you say can make a difference: within a world of pacified spectators even a little autonomous expression will stand out.

Since there are no longer any material obstacles to inaugurating a classless society, the problem has been essentially reduced to a question of consciousness: the only thing that really stands in the way is people's unawareness of their own collective power. (Physical repression is effective against radical minorities only so long as social conditioning keeps the rest of the population docile.) Hence a large

---

*"The absence of a revolutionary movement in Europe has reduced the Left to its simplest expression: a mass of spectators who swoon with rapture each time the exploited in the colonies take up arms against their masters, and who cannot help seeing these uprisings as the epitome of revolution. . . . Wherever there is conflict they always see Good fighting Evil, 'total revolution' versus 'total reaction.' . . . Revolutionary criticism begins beyond good and evil; it is rooted in history and operates on the totality of the existing world. In no case can it applaud a belligerent *state* or support the bureaucracy of an exploitive state in the process of formation. . . . It is obviously impossible at present to seek a *revolutionary* solution to the Vietnam war. It is first of all necessary to put an end to the American aggression in order to allow real social struggle in Vietnam to develop in a *natural* way, i.e. to enable the Vietnamese workers and peasants to rediscover their enemies at home: the bureaucracy of the North and the propertied and ruling strata of the South. Once the Americans withdraw, the Stalinist bureaucracy will seize control of the whole country—there's no getting around this. . . . The point is not to give unconditional (or even conditional) support to the Vietcong, but to struggle consistently and uncompromisingly against American imperialism." (*SI Anthology*, pp. 195–196, 203.)

element of radical practice is *negative:* attacking the various forms of false consciousness that prevent people from realizing their positive potentialities.

Both Marx and the situationists have often been ignorantly denounced for such negativity, because they concentrated primarily on critical clarification and deliberately avoided promoting any positive ideology to which people could passively cling. Because Marx pointed out how capitalism reduces our lives to an economic rat-race, "idealistic" apologists for this state of affairs accuse *him* of "reducing life to materialistic concerns"—as if the whole point of Marx's work was not to help us get beyond our economic slavery so that our more creative potentials can flower. "To call on people to give up their illusions about their condition is to call on them to give up a condition that requires illusions. . . . Criticism plucks the imaginary flowers from the chain not in order that man shall continue to bear that chain without fantasy or consolation, but so that he will throw off the chain and pluck the living flower" ("Introduction to a Critique of Hegel's Philosophy of Right").

Accurately expressing a key issue often has a surprisingly powerful effect. Bringing things out into the open forces people to stop hedging their bets and take a position. Like the dexterous butcher in the Taoist fable whose knife never needed sharpening because he always cut between the joints, the most effective radical polarization comes not from strident protest, but from simply revealing the divisions that already exist, elucidating the different tendencies, contradictions, choices. Much of the situationists' impact stemmed from the fact that they articulated things that most people had already experienced but were unable or afraid to express until someone else broke the ice. ("Our ideas are in everybody's mind.")

If some situationist texts nevertheless seem difficult at first, this is because their dialectical structure goes against the grain of our conditioning. When this conditioning is broken they don't seem so obscure (they were the source of some of the most popular May 1968 graffiti). Many academic spectators have floundered around trying unsuccessfully to resolve the various "contradictory" descriptions of the spectacle in *The Society of the Spectacle* into some single, "scientifically consistent" definition; but anyone engaged in contesting this society will find Debord's examination of it from different angles eminently clear and useful, and come to appreciate the fact that he never wastes a word in academic inanities or pointless expressions of outrage.

The dialectical method that runs from Hegel and Marx to the situationists is not a magic formula for churning out correct predictions, it is a tool for grappling with the dynamic processes of social change. It reminds us that social concepts are not eternal; that they contain their own contradictions, interacting with and transforming each other, even into their opposites; that what is true or progressive

19

in one context may become false or regressive in another.*

A dialectical text may require careful study, but each new reading brings new discoveries. Even if it influences only a few people directly, it tends to influence them so profoundly that many of them end up influencing others in the same way, leading to a qualitative chain reaction. The nondialectical language of leftist propaganda is easier to understand, but its effect is usually superficial and ephemeral; offering no challenge, it soon ends up boring even the stupefied spectators for whom it is designed.

As Debord put it in his last film, those who find what he says too difficult would do better to blame their own ignorance and passivity, and the schools and society that have made them that way, than to complain about his obscurity. Those who don't have enough initiative to reread crucial texts or to do a little exploration or a little experimentation for themselves are unlikely to accomplish anything if they are spoonfed by someone else.

* * *

Debord is in fact virtually the only person who has made a truly dialectical and antispectacular use of film. Although would-be radical filmmakers often give lip service to Brechtian "distanciation"—the notion of encouraging spectators to think and act for themselves rather than sucking them into passive identification with hero or plot—most radical films still play to the audience as if it were made up of morons. The dimwitted protagonist gradually "discovers oppression" and becomes "radicalized" to the point where he is ready to become a fervent supporter of "progressive" politicians or a loyal militant in some bureaucratic leftist group. Distanciation is limited to a few token gimmicks that allow the spectator to think: "Ah, a Brechtian touch! What a clever fellow that filmmaker is! And how clever am I to recog-

---

*"In its mystified form, dialectics became the fashion in Germany because it seemed to transfigure and glorify the existing state of things. In its rational form it is a scandal and abomination to bourgeois society and its doctrinaire professors, because in comprehending the existing state of things it simultaneously recognizes the negation of that state, its inevitable breaking up; because it sees the fluid movement of every historically developed social form, and therefore takes into account its transience as well as its momentary existence; because it lets nothing impose on it, and is in its essence critical and revolutionary." (Marx, *Capital*.)

The split between Marxism and anarchism crippled both sides. The anarchists rightly criticized the authoritarian and narrowly economistic tendencies in Marxism, but they generally did so in an undialectical, moralistic, ahistorical manner, contraposing various absolute dualisms (Freedom versus Authority, Individualism versus Collectivism, Centralization versus Decentralization, etc.) and leaving Marx and a few of the more radical Marxists with a virtual monopoly on coherent dialectical analysis—until the situationists finally brought the libertarian and dialectical aspects back together again. On the merits and flaws of Marxism and anarchism see *The Society of the Spectacle* §§78–94.

nize such subtleties!" The radical message is usually so banal that it is obvious to virtually anyone who would ever go to see such a film in the first place; but the spectator gets the gratifying impression that *other* people might be brought up to his level of awareness if only they could be got to see it.

If the spectator has any uneasiness about the quality of what he is consuming, it is assuaged by the critics, whose main function is to read profound radical meanings into practically any film. As with the Emperor's New Clothes, no one is likely to admit that he wasn't aware of these supposed meanings until informed of them, for fear that this would reveal him as less sophisticated than the rest of the audience.

Certain films may help expose some deplorable condition or convey some sense of the feel of a radical situation. But there is little point in presenting images of a struggle if both the images and the struggle are not criticized. Spectators sometimes complain that a film portrays some social category (e.g. women) inaccurately. This may be true insofar as the film reproduces certain false stereotypes; but the usually implied alternative—that the filmmaker "should have presented images of women struggling against oppression"—would in most cases be equally false to reality. Women (like men or any other oppressed group) have in fact usually been passive and submissive—that's precisely the problem we have to face. Catering to people's self-satisfaction by presenting spectacles of triumphant radical heroism only reinforces this bondage.

* * *

To rely on oppressive conditions to radicalize people is unwise; to intentionally worsen them in order to accelerate this process is unacceptable. The repression of certain radical projects may incidentally expose the absurdity of the ruling order; but such projects should be worthwhile for their own sake—they lose their credibility if they are merely pretexts designed to provoke repression. Even in the most "privileged" milieus there are usually more than enough problems without needing to add to them. The point is to reveal the *contrast* between present conditions and present *possibilities;* to give people enough taste of real life that they'll want more.

Leftists often imply that a lot of simplification, exaggeration and repetition is necessary in order to counteract all the ruling propaganda in the other direction. This is like saying that a boxer who has been made groggy by a right hook will be restored to lucidity by a left hook.

People's consciousness is not "raised" by burying them under an avalanche of horror stories, or even under an avalanche of information. Information that is not critically assimilated and used is soon forgotten. Mental as well as physical health requires some balance between what we take in and what we do with it. It may sometimes be necessary to force complacent people to face some outrage they are unaware of, but even in such cases harping on the same thing ad nauseam usually accomplishes nothing more than driving them to escape to less boring and depressing spectacles.

One of the main things that keeps us from understanding our situation is the spectacle of other people's apparent happiness, which makes us see our own unhappiness as a shameful sign of failure. But an omnipresent spectacle of misery also keeps us from seeing our positive potentials. The constant broadcasting of delirious ideas and nauseating atrocities paralyzes us, turns us into paranoids and compulsive cynics.

Strident leftist propaganda, fixating on the insidiousness and loathsomeness of "oppressors," often feeds this delirium, appealing to the most morbid and mean-spirited side of people. If we get caught up in brooding on evils, if we let the sickness and ugliness of this society pervade even our rebellion against it, we forget what we are fighting for and end up losing the very capacity to love, to create, to enjoy.

The best "radical art" cuts both ways. If it attacks the alienation of modern life, it simultaneously reminds us of the poetic potentialities hidden within it. Rather than reinforcing our tendency to wallow in self-pity, it encourages our resilience, enables us to laugh at our own troubles as well as at the asininities of the forces of "order." Some of the old IWW songs and comic strips are good examples, even if the IWW ideology is by now a bit musty. Or the ironic, bittersweet songs of Brecht and Weill. The hilarity of *The Good Soldier Švejk* is probably a more effective antidote to war than the moral outrage of the typical antiwar tract.

Nothing undermines authority like holding it up to ridicule. The most effective argument against a repressive regime is not that it is evil, but that it is silly. The protagonists of Albert Cosséry's novel *La violence et la dérision,* living under a Middle-Eastern dictatorship, plaster the walls of the capital with an official-looking poster that praises the dictator to such a preposterous degree that he becomes a laughingstock and is forced to resign out of embarrassment. Cosséry's pranksters are apolitical and their success is perhaps too good to be true, but somewhat similar parodies have been used with more radical aims (e.g. the Li I-Che coup mentioned on page 304). At demonstrations in Italy in the 1970s the Metropolitan Indians (inspired perhaps by the opening chapter of Lewis Carroll's *Sylvie and Bruno:* "Less Bread! More Taxes!") carried banners and chanted slogans such as "Power to the Bosses!" and "More work! Less pay!" Everyone recognized the irony, but it was harder to dismiss with the usual pigeonholing.

Humor is a healthy antidote to all types of orthodoxy, left as well as right. It's highly contagious and it reminds us not to take ourselves too seriously. But it can easily become a mere safety valve, channeling dissatisfaction into glib, passive cynicism. Spectacle society thrives on delirious reactions against its most delirious aspects. Satirists often have a dependent, love-hate relation with their targets; parodies become indistinguishable from what they are parodying, giving the impression that everything is equally bizarre, meaningless and hopeless.

In a society based on artificially maintained confusion, the first task is not to add to it. Chaotic disruptions usually generate nothing but annoyance or panic, provoking people to support whatever measures the government takes to restore order. A radical intervention may at first seem strange and incomprehensible; but if it has been worked out with sufficient lucidity, people will soon understand it well enough.

Imagine being at Strasbourg University at the opening of the school year in fall 1966, among the students, faculty and distinguished guests filing into an auditorium to hear President de Gaulle's commencement address. You find a little pamphlet placed on each seat. A program? No, something about "the poverty of student life." You idly open it up and start to read: "It is pretty safe to say that the student is the most universally despised creature in France, apart from the policeman and the priest. . . ." You look around and see that everyone else is also reading it, reactions ranging from puzzlement or amusement to shock and outrage. Who is responsible for this? The title page reveals that it is published by the Strasbourg Student Union, but it also refers to "the Situationist International," whatever that might be. . . .

What made the Strasbourg scandal different from some college prank, or from the confused and confusing capers of groups like the Yippies, was that its scandalous form conveyed an equally scandalous content. At a moment when students were being proclaimed as the most radical sector of society, this text was the only one that put things into perspective. But the particular poverties of students just happened to be the point of departure; equally scathing texts could and should be written on the poverty of every other segment of society (preferably by those who know them from inside). Some have in fact been attempted, but none have approached the lucidity and coherence of the situationist pamphlet, so concise yet so comprehensive, so provocative yet so accurate, moving so methodically from a specific situation through increasingly general ramifications that the final chapter presents the most pithy existing summary of the modern revolutionary project. (See *SI Anthology*, pp. 204–212, 319–337.)

The situationists never claimed to have single-handedly provoked May 1968—as they said, they predicted the content of the revolt, not the date or location. But without the Strasbourg scandal and the subsequent agitation by the SI-influenced Enragés group (of which the more well known March 22nd Movement was only a belated and confused imitation) the revolt might never have happened. There was no economic or governmental crisis, no war or racial antagonism destabilizing the country, nor any other particular issue that might have fostered such a revolt. There were more radical worker struggles going on in Italy and England, more militant student struggles in Germany and Japan, more widespread countercultural movements in the United States and the Netherlands. But only in France was there a perspective that tied them all together.

Carefully calculated interventions like the Strasbourg scandal must be distinguished not only from confusionistic disruptions, but also from merely spectacular exposés. As long as social critics confine themselves to contesting this or that detail, the spectacle-spectator relation continually reconstitutes itself: if such critics succeed in discrediting existing political leaders, they themselves often become new stars (Ralph Nader, Noam Chomsky, etc.) whom slightly more aware spectators admiringly rely on for a continuing flow of shocking information that they rarely do anything about. The milder exposés get the audience to root for this or that faction in intragovernmental power struggles; the more sensational ones feed people's morbid curiosity, sucking them into consuming more articles, news programs and docudramas, and into interminable debates about various conspiracy theories. Most such theories are obviously nothing but delirious reflections of the lack of critical historical sense produced by the modern spectacle, desperate attempts to find some coherent meaning in an increasingly incoherent and absurd society. In any case, as long as things remain on the spectacular terrain it hardly matters whether any of these theories are true: *those who keep watching to see what comes next never affect what comes next.*

Certain revelations are more interesting because they not only open up significant issues to public debate, but do so in a manner that draws lots of people into the game. A charming example is the 1963 "Spies for Peace" scandal in England, in which a few unknown persons publicized the location of a secret bomb shelter reserved for members of the government. The more vehemently the government threatened to prosecute anyone who reproduced this "state secret" information which was no longer secret from anyone, the more creatively and playfully it was disseminated by thousands of groups and individuals (who also proceeded to discover and invade several other secret shelters). Not only did the asininity of the government and the insanity of the nuclear war spectacle became evident to everyone, the spontaneous human chain reaction provided a taste of a quite different social potential.

* * *

"Since 1814 no Liberal government had come in except by violence. Cánovas was too intelligent not to see the inconvenience and the danger of that. He therefore arranged that Conservative governments should be succeeded regularly by Liberal governments. The plan he followed was, whenever an economic crisis or a serious strike came along, to resign and let the Liberals deal with it. This explains why most of the repressive legislation passed during the rest of the century was passed by them."

—Gerald Brenan, *The Spanish Labyrinth*

The best argument in favor of radical electoral politics was made by Eugene Debs, the American socialist leader who in 1920 received nearly a million votes for president while in prison for opposing World War I: "If the people don't know enough to know who to vote for, they're not going to know who to shoot at." On the other hand, the workers during the 1918–19 German revolution were confused about who to shoot at precisely by the presence of "socialist" leaders in the government who were working overtime to repress the revolution.

In itself, voting is of no great significance one way or the other (those who make a big deal about refusing to vote are only revealing their own fetishism). The problem is that it tends to lull people into relying on others to act for them, distracting them from more significant possibilities. A few people who take some creative initiative (think of the first civil rights sit-ins) may ultimately have a far greater effect than if they had put their energy into campaigning for lesser-evil politicians. At best, legislators rarely do more than what they have been forced to do by popular movements. A conservative regime under pressure from independent radical movements often concedes more than a liberal regime that knows it can count on radical support. If people invariably rally to lesser evils, all the rulers have to do in any situation that threatens their power is to conjure up a threat of some greater evil.

Even in the rare case when a "radical" politician has a realistic chance of winning an election, all the tedious campaign efforts of thousands of people may go down the drain in one day because of some trivial scandal discovered in his personal life, or because he inadvertently says something intelligent. If he manages to avoid these pitfalls and it looks like he might win, he tends to evade controversial issues for fear of antagonizing swing voters. If he actually gets elected he is almost never in a position to implement the reforms he has promised, except perhaps after years of wheeling and dealing with his new colleagues; which gives him a good excuse to see his first priority as making whatever compromises are necessary to keep himself in office indefinitely. Hobnobbing with the rich and powerful, he develops new interests and new tastes, which he justifies by telling himself that he deserves a few perks after all his years of working for good causes. Worst of all, if he does eventually manage to get a few "progressive" measures passed, this exceptional and usually trivial success is held up as evidence of the value of relying on electoral politics, luring many more people into wasting their energy on similar campaigns to come.

As one of the May 1968 graffiti put it, "It's painful to submit to our bosses; it's even more stupid to choose them."

Referendums on particular issues are less susceptible to the precariousness of personalities; but the results are often no better since the issues tend to be posed very simplistically, and any measure that threatens powerful interests can usually be defeated by the influence of money and mass media.

Local elections sometimes offer people a more realistic chance to affect policies and keep tabs on elected officials. But even the most enlightened communities cannot insulate themselves from the deterioration of the rest of the world. If a city manages to preserve desirable cultural or environmental features, these very advantages put it under increasing economic pressure. The fact that human values have been given precedence over property values ultimately causes enormous increases in the latter (more people will want to invest or move there). Sooner or later this property-value increase overpowers the human values: local policies are overruled by high courts or by state or national governments, outside money is poured into municipal elections, city officials are bribed, residential neighborhoods are demolished to make room for highrises and freeways, rents skyrocket, the poorer classes are forced out (including the diverse ethnic groups and artistic bohemians who contributed to the city's original liveliness and appeal), and all that remains of the earlier community are a few isolated sites of "historical interest" for tourist consumption.

* * *

Still, "acting locally" may be a good place to start. People who feel that the global situation is hopeless or incomprehensible may nevertheless see a chance to affect some specific local matter. Block clubs, co-ops, switchboards, study groups, alternative schools, free health clinics, community theaters, neighborhood newspapers, public-access radio and television stations and many other kinds of alternative institutions are worthwhile for their own sake, and if they are sufficiently participatory they may lead to broader movements. Even if they don't last very long, they provide a temporary terrain for radical experimentation.

But always within limits. Capitalism was able to develop gradually within feudal society, so that by the time the capitalist revolution cast off the last vestiges of feudalism, most of the mechanisms of the new bourgeois order were already firmly in place. An anticapitalist revolution, in contrast, cannot really build its new society "within the shell of the old." Capitalism is far more flexible and all-pervading than was feudalism, and tends to coopt any oppositional organization.

Nineteenth-century radical theorists could still see enough surviving remnants of traditional communal forms to suppose that, once the overarching exploitive structure was eliminated, they might be revived and expanded to form the foundation of a new society. But the global penetration of spectacular capitalism in the present century has destroyed virtually all forms of popular control and direct human interaction. Even the more modern efforts of the sixties counterculture have long been integrated into the system. Co-ops, crafts, organic farming and other marginal enterprises may produce better quality goods under better working conditions, but those goods still have to function as commodities on the market. The few successful ventures tend to evolve into ordinary businesses, with the founding members gradually assuming an ownership or managerial role over the newer workers and dealing with all sorts of routine commercial and bureaucratic matters that have nothing to do with "preparing the ground for a new society."

The longer an alternative institution lasts, the more it tends to lose its volunteer, experimental, nothing-to-lose character. Permanent paid staffs develop a vested interest in the status quo and avoid rocking the boat for fear of offending supporters or losing their government or foundation funding. Alternative institutions also tend to demand too much of the limited free time people have, bogging them down, robbing them of the energy and imagination to confront more general issues. After a brief period of participation most people get burned out, leaving the work to the dutiful types or to leftists trying to make an ideological point. It may sound nice to hear about people forming block clubs, etc., but unless a real local emergency comes up you may not *want* to attend interminable meetings to listen to your neighbors' complaints, or otherwise commit yourself to matters you don't really care about.

In the name of realism, reformists limit themselves to pursuing "winnable" objectives, yet even when they win some little adjustment in the system it is usually offset by some other development at another level. This doesn't mean that reforms are irrelevant, merely that they are insufficient. We have to keep resisting particular evils, but we also have to recognize that the system will keep generating new ones until we put an end to it. To suppose that a series of reforms will eventually add up to a qualitative change is like thinking we can get across a ten-foot chasm by a series of one-foot hops.

People tend to assume that because revolution involves much greater change than reforms, it must be more difficult to bring about. In the long run it may actually be easier, because in one stroke it cuts through so many petty complications and arouses a much greater enthusiasm. At a certain point it becomes more practical to start fresh than to keep trying to replaster a rotten structure.

Meanwhile, until a revolutionary situation enables us to be truly constructive, the best we can do is be *creatively negative*—concentrating on critical clarification, leaving people to pursue whatever positive projects may appeal to them but without the illusion that a new society is being "built" by the gradual accumulation of such projects.

Purely negative projects (e.g. abolition of laws against drug use, consensual sex and other victimless crimes) have the advantage of simplicity, immediately benefiting virtually everyone (except for that symbiotic duo, organized crime and the crime-control industry) while requiring little if any followup work once they are successful. On the other hand, they provide little opportunity for creative participation.

The best projects are those that are worthwhile for their own sake while simultaneously containing an implicit challenge to some fundamental aspect of the system; projects that enable people to participate in significant issues according to their own degree of interest, while tending to open the way to more radical possibilities.

Less interesting, but still worthwhile, are demands for improved conditions or more equal rights. Even if such projects are not in themselves very participatory, they may remove impediments to participation.

Least desirable are mere zero-sum struggles, where one group's gain is another's loss.

Even in the latter case the point is not to tell people what they should do, but to get them to realize what they are doing. If they are promoting some issue in order to recruit people, it is appropriate to expose their manipulative motives. If they believe they are contributing to radical change, it may be useful to show them how their activity is actually reinforcing the system in some way. But if they are really interested in their project for its own sake, let them go for it.

Even if we disagree with their priorities (fundraising for the opera, say, while the streets are filled with homeless people) we should be wary of any strategy that merely appeals to people's guilt, not only because such appeals generally have a negligible effect but because such moralism represses healthy positive aspirations. To refrain from contesting "quality of life" issues because the system continues to present us with survival emergencies is to submit to a blackmail that no longer has any justification. "Bread and roses" are no longer mutually exclusive.*

---

*"What surfaced this spring in Zurich as a demonstration against the closing of a youth center has crept across Switzerland, feeding on the restlessness of a young generation anxious to break out of what they see as a suffocating society. 'We don't want a world where the guarantee of not dying of hunger is paid for by the certainty of dying of boredom,' proclaim banners and spray-painted storefronts in Lausanne." (*Christian Science Monitor*, 28 October 1980.) The slogan is from Vaneigem's *The Revolution of Everyday Life.*

"Quality of life" projects are in fact often more inspiring than routine political and economic demands because they awaken people to richer perspectives. Paul Goodman's books are full of imaginative and often amusing examples. If his proposals are "reformist," they are so in a lively, provocative way that provides a refreshing contrast to the cringing defensive posture of most present-day reformists, who confine themselves to reacting to the reactionaries' agenda. ("We agree that it is essential to create jobs, fight crime, keep our country strong; but moderate methods will accomplish this better than the conservatives' extremist proposals.")

Other things being equal, it makes sense to concentrate one's energy on issues that are not already receiving public attention; and to prefer projects that can be done cleanly and directly, as opposed to those that require compromises, such as working through government agencies. Even if such compromises don't seem too serious, they set a bad precedent. Reliance on the state almost always backfires (commissions designed to root out bureaucratic corruption themselves develop into new corrupt bureaucracies; laws designed to thwart armed reactionary groups end up being used primarily to harass unarmed radicals).

The system is able to kill two birds with one stone by maneuvering its opponents into offering "constructive solutions" to its own crises. It in fact needs a certain amount of opposition to warn it of problems, to force it to rationalize itself, to enable it to test its instruments of control, and to provide excuses to impose new forms of control. Emergency measures imperceptibly become standard procedures as regulations that might ordinarily be resisted are introduced during situations of panic. The slow, steady rape of the human personality by all the institutions of alienated society, from school and factory to advertising and urbanism, is made to seem normal as the spectacle focuses obsessively on sensational individual crimes, manipulating people into law-and-order hysteria.

Above all, the system thrives when it can deflect social contestation into squabbles over privileged positions within it.

This is a particularly thorny area. All social inequalities need to be challenged, not only because they are unfair, but because as long as they remain they can be used to divide people. But attaining equal wage slavery or equal opportunity to become a bureaucrat or a capitalist hardly amounts to any victory over bureaucratic capitalism.

It is both natural and necessary that people defend their own interests; but if they try do so by identifying too exclusively with some particular social group they tend to lose sight of the larger picture. As increasingly fragmented categories scramble over the crumbs allotted to them, they get caught up in petty mutual-blame games and the notion of abolishing the whole hierarchical structure is forgotten. People who are normally quick to denounce the slightest hint of derogatory stereotyping get carried away into lumping all men or all whites as "oppressors," then wonder why they run up against such powerful backlashes among the vast majority of the latter, who are quite aware that they have little real power over their own lives, much less over anyone else's.

Aside from the reactionary demagogues (who are pleasantly surprised to find "progressives" providing them with such easy targets for ridicule) the only people who actually benefit from these internecine squabbles are a few careerists struggling for bureaucratic posts, government grants, academic tenure, publishing contracts, commercial clienteles or political constituencies at a time when there is increasingly limited space at the trough. Sniffing out "political incorrectness" enables them to bash rivals and critics and reinforce their own positions as recognized specialists or spokespeople of their particular fragment. The various oppressed groups that are foolish enough to accept such spokespeople get nothing but the bittersweet thrill of self-righteous resentment and a ludicrous official terminology reminiscent of Orwell's Newspeak.*

There is a crucial, though sometimes subtle, distinction between fighting social evils and *feeding* on them. People are not empowered by being encouraged to wallow in their own victimhood. Individual autonomy is not developed by taking refuge is some group identity. Equal intelligence is not demonstrated by dismissing logical reasoning as a "typical white male tactic." Radical dialogue is not fostered by harassing people who don't conform to some political orthodoxy, much less by striving to get such orthodoxy legally enforced.

Nor is history made by rewriting it. We do need to free ourselves from uncritical respect for the past and to become aware of the ways it has been distorted. But we have to recognize that despite our disapproval of past prejudices and injustices, it is unlikely that we would have done any better had we ourselves lived under the same conditions. Applying present-day standards retroactively (smugly correcting earlier authors every time they use the formerly conventional masculine forms, or trying to censor *Huckleberry Finn* because Huck doesn't refer to Jim as a "person of color") only reinforces the historical ignorance that the modern spectacle has been so successful in fostering.

A lot of this nonsense stems from the false assumption that being radical implies living up to some moral "principle"—as if no one could

---

*For some hilarious examples see Henry Beard and Christopher Cerf's *The Official Politically Correct Dictionary and Handbook* (Villard, 1992): it's often hard to tell which of the Correctspeak terms are satirical and which have actually been seriously proposed or even officially adopted and enforced. The only antidote to such delirium is a lot of healthy guffaws.

work for peace without being a total pacifist, or advocate the abolition of capitalism without giving away all their money. Most people have too much common sense to actually follow such simplistic ideals, but they often feel vaguely guilty that they don't. This guilt paralyzes them and makes them more susceptible to blackmail by leftist manipulators (who tell us that if we don't have the courage to martyrize ourselves, we must uncritically support those who do). Or they try to repress their guilt by disparaging others who seem even more compromised: a manual laborer may take pride in not selling out mentally like a professor; who perhaps feels superior to an ad designer; who may in turn look down on someone who works in the arms industry. . . .

Turning social problems into personal moral issues deflects attention from their potential solution. Trying to change social conditions by charity is like trying to raise the sea level by dumping buckets of water in the ocean. Even if some good is accomplished by altruistic actions, to rely on them as a general strategy is futile because they will always be the exception. Most people naturally look out first for themselves and for those closest to them. One of the merits of the situationists was to have cut through the traditional leftist appeal to guilt and self-sacrifice by stressing that the primary reason to make a revolution is for ourselves.

"Going to the people" in order to "serve" or "organize" or "radicalize" them usually leads to manipulation and often meets with apathy or hostility. The example of others' independent actions is a far stronger and healthier means of inspiration. Once people begin to act on their own they are in a better position to exchange experiences, to collaborate on equal terms and, if necessary, to *ask* for specific assistance. And when they win their own freedom it's much harder to take it back from them. One of the May 1968 graffitists wrote: "I'm not a servant of the people (much less of their self-appointed leaders)—let the people serve themselves." Another put it even more succinctly: "Don't liberate me—I'll take care of that."

A total critique means that everything is called into question, not that everything must be totally opposed. Radicals often forget this and get caught up in outbidding each other with increasingly extremist assertions, implying that any compromise amounts to selling out or even that any enjoyment amounts to complicity with the system. Actually, being "for" or "against" some political position is just as easy, and usually just as meaningless, as being for or against some sports team. Those who proudly proclaim their "total opposition" to all compromise, all authority, all organization, all theory, all technology, etc., usually turn out to have no *revolutionary* perspective whatsoever—no practical conception of how the present system might be overthrown or how a postrevolutionary society might work. Some even attempt to justify this lack by declaring that a mere revolution could never be radical enough to satisfy their eternal ontological rebelliousness.

Such all-or-nothing bombast may temporarily impress a few spectators, but its ultimate effect is simply to make people blasé. Sooner or later the contradictions and hypocrisies lead to disillusionment and resignation. Projecting their own disappointed delusions onto the world, the former extremists conclude that all radical change is hopeless and repress the whole experience; or perhaps even flip to some equally silly reactionary position.

If every radical had to be a Durruti we might as well forget it and devote ourselves to more realizable concerns. But being radical does not mean being the most extreme. In its original sense it simply means going to the root. The reason it is necessary to strive for the abolition of capitalism and the state is not because this is the most extreme goal imaginable, but because it has unfortunately become evident that nothing less will do.

We need to find out what is both necessary and sufficient; to seek projects that we are actually capable of doing and realistically likely to do. Anything beyond this is just hot air. Many of the oldest and still most effective radical tactics—debates, critiques, boycotts, strikes, sit-ins, workers councils—caught on precisely because they are at once simple, relatively safe, widely applicable, and open-ended enough to lead to broader possibilities.

Simplistic extremism naturally seeks the most extremist foil for itself. If all problems can be attributed to a sinister clique of "total fascists," everything else will seem comfortingly progressive by comparison. Meanwhile the actual forms of modern domination, which are usually more subtle, proceed unnoticed and unopposed.

Fixating on reactionaries only reinforces them, makes them seem more powerful and more fascinating. "It matters little if our opponents mock us or insult us, if they represent us as clowns or criminals; the essential thing is that they talk of us, preoccupy themselves with us" (Hitler). Reich pointed out that "by drilling people to hate the police one only strengthens police authority and invests it with mystic power in the eyes of the poor and the helpless. The strong are hated but also feared and envied and followed. This fear and envy felt by the 'have-nots' accounts for a portion of the political reactionaries' power. One of the main objectives of the rational struggle for freedom is to disarm reactionaries by exposing the illusionary character of their power" (*People in Trouble*).

The main problem with compromising is not so much moral as practical: it's difficult to attack something when we ourselves are implicated in it. We hedge our critiques lest others criticize us in turn. It becomes harder to think big, to act boldly. As has often been noted, many of the German people acquiesced to Nazi oppression because it began fairly gradually and was at first directed mainly at unpopular minorities (Jews, Gypsies, Communists, homosexuals); by the time it began affecting the general population, they had become incapable of doing anything about it.

In hindsight it's easy to condemn those who capitulated to fascism or Stalinism, but it's unlikely that most of us would have done any better had we been in the same position. In our daydreams, picturing ourself as a dramatic personage faced with a clear-cut choice in front of an appreciative audience, we imagine that we would have no trouble making the right decision. But the situations we actually face are usually more complex and obscure. It's not always easy to know where to draw the line.

The point is to draw it *somewhere,* stop worrying about guilt and blame and self-justification, and take the offensive.

This spirit is well exemplified by those Italian workers who have gone on strike without making any demands whatsoever. Such strikes are not only more interesting than the usual bureaucratic union negotiations, they may even be more effective: the bosses, uncertain of how far they have to go, frequently end up offering much more than the strikers would have dared to demand. The latter can then decide on their next move without having committed themselves to anything in return.

A defensive reaction against this or that social symptom at best wins some temporary concession on the specific issue. Aggressive agitation that refuses to limit itself exerts far more pressure. Faced with widespread, unpredictable movements like the sixties counterculture or the May 1968 revolt—movements calling everything in question, generating autonomous contestations on many fronts, threatening to spread throughout the whole society and too vast to be controlled by cooptable leaders—rulers hasten to clean up their image, pass reforms, raise wages, release prisoners, declare amnesties, initiate peace talks—anything in the hope of preempting the movement and reestablishing their control. (The sheer unmanageability of the American counterculture, which was spreading deeply into the army itself, probably played as great a role as the explicit antiwar movement in forcing the end of the Vietnam war.)

The side that takes the initiative defines the terms of the struggle. As long as it keeps innovating, it also retains the element of surprise. "Boldness is virtually a creative power.... Whenever boldness meets hesitation it already has a significant advantage because the very state of hesitation implies a loss of equilibrium. It is only when it encounters cautious foresight that it is at a disadvantage" (Clausewitz, *On War*). But cautious foresight is quite rare among those who run this society. Most of the system's processes of commodification, spectacularization and hierarchization are blind and automatic: merchants, media and leaders merely follow their natural tendencies to make money or grab audiences or recruit followers.

Spectacle society is often the victim of its own falsifications. As each level of bureaucracy tries to cover for itself with padded statistics, as each "information source" outbids the others with more sensational stories, and as competing states, governmental departments and private companies each launch their own independent disinformation operations (see chapters 16 and 30 of Debord's *Comments on the Society of the Spectacle*), even the exceptional ruler who may have some lucidity has a hard time finding out what is really happening. As Debord observes elsewhere in the same book, a state that ends up repressing its own historical knowledge can no longer conduct itself strategically.

* * *

> "The whole history of the progress of human liberty shows that all concessions yet made to her august claims have been born of struggle. . . . If there is no struggle there is no progress. Those who profess to favor freedom and yet deprecate agitation, are men who want crops without plowing up the ground. They want rain without thunder and lightning. They want the ocean without the awful roar of its many waters. The struggle may be a moral one; or it may be a physical one; or it may be both moral and physical, but it must be a struggle. Power concedes nothing without a demand. It never did and it never will."
> —Frederick Douglass

Anyone with any knowledge of history is aware that societies do not change without stubborn and often savage resistance by those in power. If our ancestors had not resorted to violent revolt, most of those who now self-righteously deplore it would still be serfs or slaves.

The routine functioning of this society is far more violent than any reaction against it could ever be. Imagine the outrage that would greet a radical movement that executed 20,000 opponents; that's a conservative estimate of the number of children that the present system allows to starve to death *each day*. Vacillations and compromises allow this ongoing violence to drag on indefinitely, ultimately causing a thousand times more suffering than a single decisive revolution.

Fortunately a modern, genuinely majority revolution would have relatively little need for violence except to neutralize those elements of the ruling minority who try to violently maintain their own power.

Violence is not only undesirable in itself, it generates panic (and thus manipulability) and promotes militaristic (and thus hierarchical) organization. Nonviolence entails more open and democratic organization; it tends to foster composure and compassion and to break the miserable cycle of hatred and revenge.

But we have to avoid making a fetish out of it. The common retort, "How can you work for peace with violent methods?" is no more logical than it would be to tell a drowning man that if he wants to get to dry land he must avoid touching water. Striving to resolve "misunderstandings" through dialogue, pacifists forget that some problems are based on objective conflicts of interest. They tend to underestimate the malice of enemies while exaggerating their own guilt, berating themselves even for their "violent feelings." The seemingly personal practice of "bearing witness" actually reduces the activist to a passive object, "another person for peace" who (like a soldier) puts her body on the line while abdicating personal investigation or experimentation. Those who want to undermine the notion of war as exciting and heroic must get beyond such a cringing, beggarly notion of peace. Defining their objective as survival, peace activists have had little to say to those who are fascinated by global annihilation precisely because they are sick of an everyday life reduced to mere survival, who see war not as a threat but as a welcome deliverance from a life of boredom and constant petty anxiety.

Sensing that their purism would not hold up under the test of reality, pacifists usually remain deliberately ignorant about past and present social struggles. Though often capable of intensive study and stoic self-discipline in their personal spiritual practices, they seem to feel that a *Reader's Digest* level of historical and strategical knowledge will suffice for their ventures into "social engagement." Like someone hoping to eliminate injurious falls by abolishing the law of gravity, they find it simpler to envision a never-ending moral struggle against "greed," "hatred," "ignorance," "bigotry," than to challenge the specific social structures that actually reinforce such qualities. If pressed, they sometimes complain that radical contestation is a very stressful terrain. It is indeed, but this is a strange objection to hear from those whose spiritual practices claim to enable people to confront problems with detachment and equanimity.

There's a wonderful moment in *Uncle Tom's Cabin:* As a Quaker family is helping some slaves escape to Canada, a Southern slave catcher appears. One of the Quakers points a shotgun at him and says, "Friend, thee isn't wanted here." I think that's just the right tone: not caught up in hatred, or even contempt, but ready to do what is necessary in a given situation.

Reactions against oppressors are understandable, but those who get too caught up in them risk becoming mentally as well as materially enslaved, chained to their masters by "bonds of hate." Hatred of bosses is partly a projection of people's self-hatred for all the humiliations and compromises they have accepted, stemming from their secret awareness that bosses ultimately exist only because the bossed put up with them. Even if there is some tendency for the scum to rise to the top, most people in positions of power don't act much differently than would anyone else who happened to find themselves in the same position, with the same new interests, temptations and fears.

Vigorous retaliation may teach enemy forces to respect you, but it also tends to perpetuate antagonisms. Forgiveness sometimes wins

35

over enemies, but in other cases it simply gives them a chance to recover and strike again. It's not always easy to determine which policy is best in which circumstances. People who have suffered under particularly vicious regimes naturally want to see the perpetrators punished; but too much revenge sends a message to other present and future oppressors that they may as well fight to the death since they have nothing to lose.

But most people, even those who have been most blamably complicitous with the system, will tend to go whichever way the wind blows. The best defense against counterrevolution is not to be preoccupied with sniffing out people's past offenses or potential future betrayals, but to deepen the insurgence to the point that everyone is drawn in.

3. Climaxes

> *"As soon as the relations of exploitation and the violence that underlies them are no longer concealed by the mystical veil, there is a breakthrough, a moment of clarity, the struggle against alienation is suddenly revealed as a ruthless hand-to-hand fight against naked power, power exposed in its brute force and its weakness, a vulnerable giant . . . . sublime moment when the complexity of the world becomes tangible, transparent, within everyone's grasp."*
> —Raoul Vaneigem, "Basic Banalities" (*SI Anthology*, p. 93)

It's hard to generalize about the immediate causes of radical breakthroughs. There have always been plenty of good reasons to revolt, and sooner or later instabilities will arise where something has to give. But why at one moment and not another? Revolts have often occurred during periods of social improvement, while worse conditions have been endured with resignation. If some have been provoked by sheer desperation, others have been touched off by relatively trivial incidents. Grievances that have been patiently accepted as long as they seemed inevitable may suddenly seem intolerable once it appears possible to remove them. The meanness of some repressive measure or the asininity of some bureaucratic blunder may bring home the absurdity of the system more clearly than a steady accumulation of oppressions.

The system's power is based on people's belief in their powerlessness to oppose it. Normally this belief is well founded (transgress the rules and you are punished). But when for one reason or another enough people begin to ignore the rules that they can do so with impunity, the whole illusion collapses. What was thought to be natural and inevitable is seen to be arbitrary and absurd. "When no one obeys, no one commands."

The problem is how to reach this point. If only a few disobey, they can easily be isolated and repressed. People often fantasize about wonderful things that might be achieved "if only everyone would agree to do such and such all at once." Unfortunately, social movements don't usually work that way. One person with a six-gun can hold off a hundred unarmed people because each one knows that the first six to attack will be killed.

Of course some people may be so infuriated that they attack regardless of risk; and their apparent determination may even save them by convincing those in power that it's wiser to give in peacefully than to be overwhelmed after arousing even more hatred against themselves. But it is obviously preferable not to depend on acts of desperation, but to seek forms of struggle that minimize risk until a movement has spread so far that repression is no longer feasible.

People living under particularly repressive regimes naturally begin by taking advantage of whatever rallying points already exist. In 1978 the Iranian mosques were the only place people could get away with criticizing the Shah's regime. Then the huge demonstrations called by Khomeini at 40-day intervals began providing the safety of numbers. Khomeini thus became recognized as a general symbol of opposition, even by those who were not his followers. But tolerating any leader, even as a mere figurehead, is at best a temporary measure that should be abandoned as soon as more independent action becomes possible—as did those Iranian oil workers who by fall 1978 felt they had enough leverage to strike on days different from those called for by Khomeini.

The Catholic Church in Stalinist Poland played a similarly ambiguous role: the state used the Church to help control the people, but the people also used the Church to help them get around the state.

Fanatical orthodoxy is sometimes the first step toward more radical self-expression. Islamic fundamentalists may be extremely reactionary, but by getting used to taking events in their own hands they complicate any return to "order" and may even, if disillusioned, become genuinely radical—as happened with some of the similarly fanatical Red Guards during the Chinese "Cultural Revolution," when what was originally a mere ploy by Mao to lever out some of his bureaucratic rivals eventually led to uncontrolled insurgency by millions of young people who took his antibureaucratic rhetoric seriously.*

If someone proclaimed: "I am the greatest, strongest, noblest, cleverest, and most peace-loving person in the world," he would be considered obnoxious, if not insane. But if he says precisely the same things about his country he is looked upon as an admirably patriotic citizen. Patriotism is extremely seductive because it enables even the most miserable individual to indulge in a vicarious collective narcissism. The natural nostalgic fondness for one's home and surroundings is transformed into a mindless cult of the state. People's fears and resentments are projected onto foreigners while their frustrated aspirations for authentic community are mystically projected onto their

---

*On the Cultural Revolution, see *SI Anthology,* pp. 185–194, and Simon Leys's *The Chairman's New Clothes.*

own nation, which is seen as somehow essentially wonderful despite all its defects. ("Yes, America has its problems; but what we are fighting for is the *real* America, what America really stands for.") This mystical herd-consciousness becomes almost irresistible during war, smothering virtually all radical tendencies.

Yet patriotism has sometimes played a role in triggering radical struggles (e.g. Hungary 1956). And even wars have sometimes led to revolts in the aftermath. Those who have borne the greatest share of the military burden, supposedly in the name of freedom and democracy, may return home to demand a fairer share for themselves. Seeing historic struggle in action and acquiring the habit of dealing with obstacles by destroying them, they may be less inclined to believe in a changeless status quo.

The dislocations and disillusionments produced by World War I led to uprisings all over Europe. If World War II did not do the same, it was because genuine radicalism had since been destroyed by Stalinism, fascism and reformism; because the victors' rationales for the war, though full of lies as always, were more credible than usual (the defeated enemies were more obvious villains); and because this time the victors had taken care to work out the postwar reestablishment of order in advance (eastern Europe was handed over to Stalin in exchange for his guaranteeing the docility of the French and Italian Communist Parties and his abandonment of the insurgent Greek CP). Nevertheless the global jolt of the war was sufficient to open the way for an autonomous Stalinist revolution in China (which Stalin had not wanted, as this threatened his exclusive domination of the "socialist camp") and to give a new impetus to the anticolonial movements (which the European colonial powers naturally did not want, though they were eventually able to retain the more profitable aspects of their domination through the sort of economic neocolonialism that the United States was already practicing).

Faced with the prospect of a postwar power vacuum, rulers often collaborate with their ostensible enemies in order to repress their own people. At the end of the Franco-German war of 1870–71 the victorious German army helped surround the Paris Commune, enabling the French rulers to crush it more easily. As Stalin's army approached Warsaw in 1944 it called on the people of the city to rise against the Nazi occupiers, then waited outside the city for several days while the Nazis wiped out the thus-exposed independent elements which might later have resisted the imposition of Stalinism. We have recently seen a similar scenario in the de facto Bush-Saddam alliance in the aftermath of the Gulf war, when, after calling on the Iraqi people to rise against Saddam, the American military systematically massacred Iraqi conscripts retreating from Kuwait (who, if they had regained their country, would have been ripe for revolt) while leaving Saddam's elite Republican Guards intact and free to crush the immense radical uprisings in northern and southern Iraq.*

In totalitarian societies the grievances are obvious but revolt is difficult. In "democratic" societies struggles are easier, but the goals are less clear. Controlled largely by subconscious conditioning or by vast, seemingly incomprehensible forces ("the state of the economy") and offered a wide range of apparently free choices, it's difficult for us to grasp our situation. Like a flock of sheep, we're herded in the desired direction, but allowed enough room for individual variations to enable us to preserve an illusion of independence.

Impulses toward vandalism or violent confrontation can often be seen as attempts to break through this frustrating abstractness and come to grips with something concrete.

> Just as the first organization of the classical proletariat was preceded, during the end of the eighteenth century and the beginning of the nineteenth, by a period of isolated "criminal" acts aimed at destroying the machines of production that were depriving people of their jobs, we are presently witnessing the first appearance of a wave of vandalism against the *machines of consumption* that are just as certainly depriving us of our life. In both cases the significance obviously does not lie in the destruction itself, but in the rebelliousness which could potentially develop into a positive project going to the point of reconverting the machines in a way that increases people's real power over their lives. [*SI Anthology*, p. 82.]

(Note that last sentence, incidentally: To point out a symptom of social crisis, or even to defend it as an understandable reaction, does not necessary imply recommending it as a tactic.)

Many other triggers of radical situations could be enumerated. A strike may spread (Russia 1905); popular resistance to some reactionary threat may overflow official bounds (Spain 1936); people may take advantage of token liberalization in order to push further (Hungary 1956, Czechoslovakia 1968); exemplary small group actions may catalyze a mass movement (the early civil rights sit-ins, May 1968); a particular outrage may be seen as the last straw (Watts 1965, Los

---

*"As Shiites and Kurds battle the regime of Saddam Hussein and Iraqi opposition parties try to patch together a democratic future, the United States finds itself in the awkward position of, in effect, supporting continuing one-party rule in Iraq. US government statements, including those of President Bush, have stressed the desire to see Saddam Hussein overthrown, but not to see Iraq broken apart by civil strife. At the same time, Bush administration officials have insisted that democracy is not currently a viable alternative for Iraq. . . . This may account for the fact that thus far, the administration has refused to meet with Iraqi opposition leaders in exile . . . . 'The Arabs and the US have the same agenda,' says a coalition diplomat. 'We want Iraq in the same borders and Saddam to disappear. But we will accept Saddam in Baghdad in order to have Iraq as one state.' " (*Christian Science Monitor*, 20 March 1991.)

Angeles 1992); the sudden collapse of a regime may leave a power vacuum (Portugal 1974); some special occasion may bring people together in such numbers that it's impossible to prevent them from expressing their grievances and aspirations (Tiananmen Square 1976 and 1989); etc.

But social crises involve so many imponderables that it is rarely possible to predict them, much less provoke them. In general it seems best to pursue projects we are personally most drawn to, while trying to remain aware enough to quickly recognize significant new developments (dangers, urgent tasks, favorable opportunities) that call for new tactics.

Meanwhile, we can move on to examine some of the crucial stages in radical situations once they do get started.

* * *

A radical situation is a collective awakening. At one extreme it may involve a few dozen people in a neighborhood or workplace; at the other it shades into a full-fledged revolutionary situation involving millions of people. It's not a matter of numbers, but of open-ended public dialogue and participation. The incident at the beginning of the 1964 Free Speech Movement (FSM) is a classic and particularly beautiful example. As police were about to take away an arrested civil rights activist on the university campus in Berkeley, a few students sat down in front of the police car; within a few minutes hundreds of others spontaneously followed their example, surrounding the car so it could not move. For the next 32 hours the car roof was turned into a platform for freewheeling debate. The May 1968 occupation of the Sorbonne created an even more radical situation by drawing in much of the nonstudent Parisian population; the workers' occupation of factories throughout France then turned it into a revolutionary situation.

In such situations people become much more open to new perspectives, readier to question previous assumptions, quicker to see through the usual cons. Every day *some* people go through experiences that lead them to question the meaning of their lives; but during a radical situation practically everyone does so all at once. When the machine grinds to a halt, the cogs themselves begin wondering about their function.

Bosses are ridiculed. Orders are ignored. Separations are broken down. Personal problems are transformed into public issues; public issues that seemed distant and abstract become immediate practical matters. The old order is analyzed, criticized, satirized. People learn more about society in a week than in years of academic "social studies" or leftist "consciousness raising." Long repressed experiences are re-

41

vived.* Everything seems possible—and much more *is* possible. People can hardly believe what they used to put up with in "the old days." Even if the outcome is uncertain, the experience is often seen as worthwhile for its own sake. "If we only have enough time . . ." wrote one May 1968 graffitist; to which a couple others responded: "In any case, no regrets!" and "Already ten days of happiness."

As work comes to a halt, rat-race commuting is replaced by leisurely circulation, passive consumption by active communication. Strangers strike up lively discussions on street corners. Debates continue round the clock, new arrivals constantly replacing those who depart for other activities or to try to catch a few hours of sleep, though they are usually too excited to sleep very long. While some people succumb to demagogues, others start making their own proposals and taking their own initiatives. Bystanders get drawn into the vortex, and go through astonishingly rapid changes. (A beautiful example from May 1968: The director of the national Odéon Theater was at first dismayed at its being taken over by the radical crowds; but after taking in the situation for a few minutes, he came forward and exclaimed: "Yes! Now that you have it, keep it, never give it up—burn it rather than do that!")

Of course, not everyone is immediately won over. Some people simply lay low, anticipating the time when the movement will subside and they can recover their possessions or their positions, and take their revenge. Others waver, torn between desire for change and fear of change. An opening of a few days may not be enough to break a lifetime of hierarchical conditioning. The disruption of habits and routines can be disorienting as well as liberating. Everything happens so fast it's easy to panic. Even if you manage to keep calm, it's not easy to grasp all the factors in play quickly enough to determine the best thing to do, which may appear obvious in hindsight. One of the main purposes of the present text is to point out certain typical recurring patterns so that people can be prepared to recognize and exploit such opportunities before it's too late.

Radical situations are the rare moments when qualitative change

---

*"I am flabbergasted at the memory people retain of their own revolutionary past. Present events have shaken that memory. Dates never learned at school, songs never sung openly, are recalled in their totality. . . . The noise, the noise, the noise is still ringing in my ears. The horns tooting in joy, the shouting, the slogans, the singing and dancing. The doors of revolution seem open again, after forty-eight years of repression. In that single day everything was replaced in perspective. Nothing was god-given, all was man-made. People could see their misery and their problems in a historical setting. . . . A week has passed, although it already feels like many months. Every hour has been lived to the full. It is already difficult to remember what the papers looked like before, or what people had then said. Hadn't there always been a revolution?" (Phil Mailer, *Portugal: The Impossible Revolution?*)

really becomes possible. Far from being abnormal, they reveal how abnormally repressed we usually are; they make our "normal" life seem like sleepwalking. Yet of the vast number of books that have been written about revolutions, few have much to say about such moments. Those dealing with the most radical modern revolts are usually merely descriptive, perhaps giving a hint of what such experiences feel like but seldom providing any useful tactical insights. Studies of bourgeois and bureaucratic revolutions are generally even less relevant. In such revolutions, where the "masses" played only a temporary supporting role for one leadership or another, their behavior could to a large degree be analyzed like the motions of physical masses, in terms of the familiar metaphors of rising and ebbing tides, pendulum swings from radicality to reaction, etc. But an antihierarchical revolution requires people to cease being homogenous, manipulable masses, to get beyond the subservience and unconsciousness that make them subject to this sort of mechanistic predictability.

During the sixties it was widely felt that the best way to foster such demassification was to form "affinity groups": small associations of close friends with compatible lifestyles and perspectives. Such groups do have many obvious advantages. They can decide on a project and immediately carry it out; they are difficult to infiltrate; and when necessary they can link up with others. But even leaving aside the various pitfalls to which most of the sixties affinity groups soon succumbed, there's no getting around the fact that some matters require large-scale organization. And large groups will soon revert to accepting some sort of hierarchy unless they manage to organize themselves in a manner that renders leaders unnecessary.

One of the simplest ways for a large gathering to *begin* organizing itself is for those who have something to say to line up or sign up, with each person allowed a certain time within which they can talk about anything they want. (The Sorbonne assembly and the FSM gathering around the police car each established a three-minute limit, occasionally extended by popular acclaim.) Some of the speakers will propose specific projects that will precipitate smaller, more workable groups. ("I and some others intend to do such and such; anyone who wants to take part can join us at such and such time and place.") Others will raise issues involving the general aims or ongoing functioning of the assembly itself. (Whom does it include? When will it meet again? How will urgent new developments be dealt with in the interim? Who will be delegated to deal with specific tasks? With what degree of accountability?) In this process the participants will soon see what works and what doesn't—how strictly delegates need to be mandated, whether a chairperson is needed to facilitate discussion so that everyone isn't talking at once, etc. Many modes of organization are possible; what is essential is that things remain open, democratic and participatory, that any tendency toward hierarchy or manipulation is immediately exposed and rejected.

Despite its naïveté and confusions and lack of rigorous delegate accountability, the FSM is a good example of the spontaneous tendencies toward practical self-organization that arise in a radical situation. Some two dozen "centrals" were formed to coordinate printing, press releases, legal assistance, to rustle up food, speaker systems and other necessary supplies, or to locate volunteers who had indicated their skills and availability for different tasks. Phone trees made it possible to contact over twenty thousand students on short notice.

But beyond mere questions of practical efficiency, and even beyond the ostensible political issues, the insurgents were breaking through the whole spectacular façade and getting a taste of real life, real community. One participant estimated that within a few months he had come to know, at least as a nodding acquaintance, two or three thousand people—this at a university that was notorious for "turning people into numbers." Another movingly wrote: "Confronting an institution apparently and frustratingly designed to depersonalize and block communication, neither humane nor graceful nor responsive, we found flowering in ourselves the presence whose absence we were at heart protesting."*

A radical situation must spread or fail. In exceptional cases a particular location may serve as a more or less permanent base, a focus for coordination and a refuge from outside repression. (Sanrizuka, a rural region near Tokyo that was occupied by local farmers during the 1970s in an effort to block the construction of a new airport, was so stubbornly and successfully defended for so many years that it came to be used as a headquarters for diverse struggles all over Japan.) But a fixed location facilitates manipulation, surveillance and repression, and being stuck with defending it inhibits people's freedom to move around. Radical situations are always characterized by a lot of circulation: while some people converge to key locations to see what's happening, others fan out to spread the contestation to other areas.

A simple but essential step in any radical action is for people to *communicate what they are actually doing and why*. Even if what they have done is very limited, such communication is in itself exemplary:

---

*One of the most powerful moments was when the sitdowners around the police car averted a potentially violent confrontation with a mob of fraternity hecklers by remaining *totally silent for half an hour*. With the wind taken out of their sails, the hecklers became bored and embarrassed, and eventually dispersed. Such collective silence has the advantage of dissolving compulsive reactions on both sides; yet because it is nonspecific it does this without the dubious content of many slogans and songs. (Singing "We Shall Overcome" has also served to calm people in difficult situations, but at the cost of sentimentalizing reality.)

The best account of the FSM is David Lance Goines's *The Free Speech Movement* (Ten Speed Press, 1993).

besides spreading the game to a wider field and inciting others to join in, it cuts through the usual reliance on rumors, news media and self-appointed spokespeople.

It's also a crucial step in self-clarification. A proposal to issue a collective communiqué presents concrete alternatives: Who do we want to communicate with? For what purpose? Who is interested in this project? Who agrees with this statement? Who disagrees? With which points? This may lead to a polarization as people see the different possibilities of the situation, sort out their own views, and regroup with like-minded persons to pursue diverse projects.

Such polarization clarifies matters for everyone. Each tendency remains free to express itself and to test its ideas in practice, and the results can be discerned more clearly than if contradictory strategies were mixed together in some lowest-common-denominator compromise. When people see a practical need for coordination, they will coordinate; in the mean time, the proliferation of autonomous individuals is far more fruitful than the superficial, top-down "unity" for which bureaucrats are always appealing.

Large crowds sometimes enable people to do things that would be imprudent if undertaken by isolated individuals; and certain collective actions, such as strikes or boycotts, require people to act in concert, or at least not to go against a majority decision. But many other matters can be dealt with directly by individuals or small groups. Better to strike while the iron is hot than to waste time trying to argue away the objections of masses of spectators who are still under the sway of manipulators.

Small groups have every right to choose their own collaborators: specific projects may require specific abilities or close accord among the participants. A radical situation opens up broader possibilities among a broader range of people. By simplifying basic issues and cutting through habitual separations, it renders masses of ordinary people capable of carrying out tasks they could not even have imagined the week before. In any case, the self-organized masses are the only ones who can carry out those tasks—no one else can do it on their behalf.

What is the role of individual radicals in such a situation? It is clear that they must not claim to represent or lead the people. On the other hand, it is absurd to declare, in the name of avoiding hierarchy, that they should immediately "dissolve into the masses" and cease putting forward their own views or initiating their own projects. They should hardly do less than the ordinary "mass" individuals, who have to express *their* views and initiate *their* projects or nothing at all would happen. In practice those radicals who claim to be afraid of "telling people what to do" or of "acting in place of the workers" generally end up either doing nothing or disguising their endless reiterations of their ideology as "reports of discussions among some workers."

The situationists and Enragés had a considerably more lucid and forthright practice during May 1968. During the first three or four days of the Sorbonne occupation (14–17 May) they openly expressed their views on the tasks of the assembly and of the general movement. On the basis of those views one of the Enragés, René Riesel, was elected to the first Sorbonne Occupation Committee, and he and his fellow delegates were reelected the following day.

Riesel and one other delegate (the rest apparently slipped away without fulfilling any of their responsibilities) endeavored to carry out the two policies he had advocated: maintaining total democracy in the Sorbonne and disseminating the most widespread appeals for occupying the factories and forming workers councils. But when the assembly repeatedly allowed its Occupation Committee to be overridden by various unelected leftist bureaucracies and failed to affirm the call for workers councils (thereby denying the workers the encouragement to do what the assembly itself was doing in the Sorbonne), the Enragés and situationists left the assembly and continued their agitation independently.

There was nothing undemocratic about this departure: the Sorbonne assembly remained free to do whatever it wanted. But when it failed to respond to the urgent tasks of the situation and even contradicted its own pretensions of democracy, the situationists felt that it had no further claim to be considered a focal point of the most radical possibilities of the movement. Their diagnosis was confirmed by the subsequent collapse of any pretense of participatory democracy at the Sorbonne: after their departure the assembly had no more elections and reverted to the typical leftist form of self-appointed bureaucrats running things over the heads of passive masses.

While this was going on among a few thousand people in the Sorbonne, millions of workers were occupying their factories throughout the country. (Hence the absurdity of characterizing May 1968 as a "student movement.") The situationists, the Enragés and a few dozen other councilist revolutionaries formed the Council for Maintaining the Occupations (CMDO) with the aim of encouraging those workers to bypass the union bureaucrats and directly link up with each other in order to realize the radical possibilities their action had already opened up.*

* * *

---

*On May 1968 see *SI Anthology*, pp. 225–256, 343–352, and René Viénet's *Enragés and Situationists in the Occupation Movement*. Also recommended is Roger Grégoire and Fredy Perlman's *Worker-Student Action Committees, France May '68* (Black & Red, 1969).

"Virtuous indignation is a powerful stimulant, but a dangerous diet. Keep in mind the old proverb: anger is a bad counsellor. . . . Whenever your sympathies are strongly stirred on behalf of some cruelly ill used person or persons of whom you know nothing except that they are ill used, your generous indignation attributes all sorts of virtues to them, and all sorts of vices to those who oppress them. But the blunt truth is that ill used people are worse than well used people."

—George Bernard Shaw, *The Intelligent Woman's Guide to Socialism and Capitalism*

"We shall abolish slaves because we can't stand the sight of them."

—Nietzsche

Fighting for liberation does not imply applauding the traits of the oppressed. The ultimate injustice of social oppression is that it is more likely to debase the victims than to ennoble them.

A lot of traditional leftist rhetoric stemmed from obsolete work-ethic notions: the bourgeois were bad because they didn't do productive work, whereas the worthy proletarians deserved the fruits of their labor, etc. As labor has become increasingly unnecessary and directed to increasingly absurd ends, this perspective has lost whatever sense it may once have had. The point is not to praise the proletariat, but to abolish it.

Class domination hasn't gone away just because a century of leftist demagogy has made some of the old radical terminology sound pretty corny. While phasing out certain kinds of traditional blue-collar labor and throwing whole sectors of the population into permanent unemployment, modern capitalism has proletarianized almost everyone else. White-collar workers, technicians, and even middle-class professionals who formerly prided themselves on their independence (doctors, scientists, scholars) are increasingly subject to the crassest commercialization and even to virtually assembly-line style regimentation.

Less than 1% of the global population owns 80% of the world's land. Even in the supposedly more egalitarian United States, economic disparity is extreme and constantly growing more extreme. Twenty years ago the average CEO salary was 35 times that of the average production worker; today it's 120 times as much. Twenty years ago the richest half-percent of the American population owned 14% of the total private wealth; they now own 30% of it. But such figures do not convey the full extent of this elite's power. The "wealth" of the lower and middle classes is almost entirely devoted to covering their day-to-day expenses, leaving little or nothing for investment at any significant, socially empowering level. A magnate who owns as little as five or ten percent of a corporation will usually be able to *control* it (due to the apathy of the unorganized mass of small stockholders), thus wielding as much power as if he owned the whole thing. And it only takes a few major corporations (whose directorates are closely interlinked with each other and with upper government bureaucracies) to buy out, wipe out or marginalize smaller independent competitors and effectively control the key politicians and media.

The omnipresent spectacle of middle-class prosperity has concealed this reality, especially in the United States where, because of its particular history (and despite the violence of many of its past class conflicts), people are more naïvely oblivious to class divisions than anywhere else in the world. The wide variety of ethnicities and the multitude of complex intermediate gradations has buffered and blurred the fundamental distinction between top and bottom. Americans own so many commodities that they fail to notice that someone else owns the whole society. Except for those at the very bottom, who can't help knowing better, they generally assume that poverty is the fault of the poor, that any enterprising person has plenty of opportunity, that if you can't make a satisfactory living in one place you can always make a fresh start somewhere else. A century ago, when people could just pick up and head further west, this belief had some foundation; the persistence of nostalgic frontier spectacles obscures the fact that present conditions are quite different and that we no longer have anywhere else to go.

The situationists sometimes used the term *proletariat* (or more precisely, *the new proletariat*) in a broadened sense, to refer to "all those who have no power over their own lives and know it." This usage may be rather loose, but it has the merit of stressing the fact that society is still divided into classes, and that the fundamental division is still between the few who own and control everything and the rest who have little or nothing to exchange but their own labor power. In some contexts it may be preferable to use other terms, such as "the people"; but not when this amounts to indiscriminately lumping exploiters with exploited.

The point is not to romanticize wage laborers, who, not surprisingly, considering that the spectacle is designed above all to keep them deluded, are often among the most ignorant and reactionary sectors of society. Nor is it a matter of scoring points to see who is most oppressed. All forms of oppression must be contested, and everyone can contribute to this contestation—women, youth, unemployed, minorities, lumpens, bohemians, peasants, middle classes, even renegades from the ruling elite. But none of these groups can achieve a definitive liberation without abolishing the material foundation of all these oppressions: the system of commodity production and wage labor. And this abolition can be achieved only through the collective *self-abolition* of wage laborers. They alone have the leverage not only to directly bring the whole system to a stop, but to start things up again in a fundamentally different way.*

Nor is it a matter of giving anyone special privileges. Workers in essential sectors (food, transportation, communications, etc.) who have rejected their capitalist and union bosses and begun to self-manage their own activities will obviously have no interest in holding on to the "privilege" of doing all the work and every interest in inviting everyone else, whether nonworkers or workers from obsolete sectors (law, military, sales, advertising, etc.), to join them in the project of reducing and transforming it. Everyone who takes part will share in the decisionmaking; the only ones left out will be those who remain on the sidelines claiming special privileges.

Traditional syndicalism and councilism have tended to take the existing division of labor too much for granted, as if people's lives in a postrevolutionary society would continue to center around fixed jobs and workplaces. Even within the present society such a perspective is becoming increasingly obsolete: as most people work at absurd and frequently only temporary jobs without in any way identifying with them, while many others don't work on the wage market at all, work-related issues become merely one aspect of a more general struggle.

At the beginning of a movement it may be appropriate for workers to identify themselves as such. ("We, the workers of such and such company, have occupied our workplace with such and such aims; we urge workers in other sectors to do likewise.") The ultimate goal, however, is not the self-management of existing enterprises. For, say, media workers to have control over the media just because they happen to work there would be almost as arbitrary as the present control by whoever happens to own them. Workers' management of the particular conditions of their work will need to be combined with community management of matters of general concern. Housewives and others working in relatively separated conditions will need to develop their own forms of organization to enable them to express their own particular interests. But potential conflicts of interest between "producers" and "consumers" will be quickly superseded when everyone becomes directly involved in both aspects; when workers councils interlink with neighborhood and community councils; and when fixed work positions fade through the obsoleting of most jobs and the

---

*"Labor will not only SHUT DOWN the industries, but Labor will REOPEN, under the management of the appropriate trades, such activities as are needed to preserve public health and public peace. If the strike continues, Labor may feel led to avoid public suffering by reopening more and more activities. UNDER ITS OWN MANAGEMENT. And that is why we say that we are starting on a road that leads—NO ONE KNOWS WHERE!" (Announcement on the eve of the 1919 Seattle general strike.) See Jeremy Brecher's *Strike!* (South End, 1972), pp. 101–114. More extensive accounts are included in *Root & Branch: The Rise of the Workers' Movements* and in Harvey O'Connor's *Revolution in Seattle*, both currently out of print.

reorganization and rotation of those that remain (including housework and child care).

The situationists were certainly right to strive for the formation of workers councils during the May 1968 factory occupations. But it should be noted that those occupations were triggered by actions of largely nonworker youth. The post-1968 situationists tended to fall into a sort of workerism (though a resolutely anti-work-ethic one), seeing the proliferation of wildcat strikes as the major indicator of revolutionary possibilities while paying less attention to developments on other terrains. Actually, blatant union sellouts often force into wildcat struggles workers who are in other respects not particularly radical; and on the other hand, people can resist the system in many other ways besides strikes (including avoiding wage labor as much as possible in the first place). The situationists rightly recognized collective self-management and individual "radical subjectivity" as complementary and equally essential aspects of the revolutionary project, but without quite succeeding in bringing them together (though they certainly came closer than did the surrealists, who tried to link cultural and political revolt simply by declaring their fervent adhesion to one or another version of Bolshevik ideology).*

Wildcat strikes do present interesting possibilities, especially if the strikers occupy their workplace. Not only does this make their position more secure (it prevents lockouts and scabbing, and the machines and products serve as hostages against repression), it brings everyone together, virtually guaranteeing collective self-management of the struggle and hinting at the idea of self-managing the whole society.

Once the usual operation has been stopped, everything takes on a different ambience. A drab workplace may be transfigured into an almost sacred space that is jealously guarded against the profane intrusion of bosses or police. An observer of the 1937 sitdown strike in Flint, Michigan, described the strikers as "children playing at a new and fascinating game. They had made a palace out of what had been their prison." (Quoted in Sidney Fine's *Sit-Down: The General Motors Strike of 1936–1937.*) Though the aim of the strike was simply to win

---

*Raoul Vaneigem (who incidentally wrote a good brief critical history of surrealism) represented the clearest expression of both aspects. His little book *De la grève sauvage à l'autogestion généralisée* (literally "From Wildcat Strike to Generalized Self-Management," but partially translated as *Contributions to the Revolutionary Struggle*) usefully recapitulates a number of basic tactics during wildcat strikes and other radical situations as well as various possibilities of postrevolutionary social organization. Unfortunately it is also padded with the inflated verbiage characteristic of Vaneigem's post-SI writings, attributing to worker struggles a Vaneigemist content that is neither justified nor necessary. The radical-subjectivity aspect was rigidified into a tediously repeated ideology of hedonism in Vaneigem's later books (*The Book of Pleasures*, etc.), which read like cotton-candy parodies of the ideas he dealt with so trenchantly in his earlier works.

the right to unionize, its organization was virtually councilist. During the six weeks that they lived in their factory (using car seats for beds and cars for closets) a general assembly of all 1200 workers met twice daily to determine policies regarding food, sanitation, information, education, complaints, communication, security, defense, sports and recreation, and to elect accountable and frequently rotated committees to implement them. There was even a Rumor Committee, whose purpose was to counteract disinformation by tracking down the source and checking the validity of every rumor. Outside the factory, strikers' wives took care of rounding up food and organizing pickets, publicity, and liaison with workers in other cities. Some of the bolder ones organized a Women's Emergency Brigade which had a contingency plan to form a buffer zone in case of a police attack on the factories. "If the police want to fire then they'll just have to fire into us."

Unfortunately, although workers retain a pivotal position in some crucial areas (utilities, communication, transportation), workers in many other sectors have less leverage than they used to. Multinational companies usually have large reserves and can wait it out or shift operations to other countries, while workers have a hard time holding out without wages coming in. Far from threatening anything essential, many present-day strikes are mere appeals to postpone shutting down obsolete industries that are losing money. Thus, while the strike remains the most basic worker tactic, workers must also devise other forms of on-the-job struggle and find ways to link up with struggles on other terrains.

Like worker strikes, consumer strikes (boycotts) depend on both the leverage they can exert and the support they can enlist. There are so many boycotts in favor of so many causes that, except for a few based on some glaringly clear moral issue, most of them fail. As is so often the case in social struggles, the most fruitful consumer strikes are those in which people are fighting directly for themselves, such as the early civil rights boycotts in the South or the "self-reduction" movements in Italy and elsewhere in which whole communities have decided to pay only a certain percentage of utility bills or mass transit fares. A rent strike is a particularly simple and powerful action, but it's difficult to achieve the degree of unity necessary to get one started except among those who have nothing to lose; which is why the most exemplary challenges to the fetish of private property are being made by homeless squatters.

In what might be called reverse boycotts, people sometimes join in *supporting* some popular institution that is threatened. Raising money for a local school or library or alternative institution is usually fairly banal, but such movements occasionally generate a salutary public debate. In 1974 striking reporters took over a major South Korean newspaper and began publishing exposés of government lies and repression. In an effort to bankrupt the paper without having to openly

51

suppress it, the government pressured all the advertisers to remove their ads from the paper. The public responded by buying thousands of individual ads, using their space for personal statements, poems, quotations from Tom Paine, etc. The "Freedom of Speech Support Column" soon filled several pages of each issue and circulation increased significantly before the paper was finally suppressed.

But consumer struggles are limited by the fact that consumers are at the receiving end of the economic cycle: they may exert a certain amount of pressure through protests or boycotts or riots, but they don't control the mechanisms of production. In the above-mentioned Korean incident, for example, the public participation was only made possible by the workers' takeover of the paper.

A particularly interesting and exemplary form of worker struggle is what is sometimes called a "social strike" or "giveaway strike," in which people carry on with their jobs but in ways that prefigure a free social order: workers giving away goods they have produced, clerks undercharging customers, transportation workers letting everyone ride free. In February 1981 11,000 telephone workers occupied exchanges throughout British Columbia and carried on all phone services without charge for six days before being maneuvered out by their union. Besides winning many of their demands, they seem to have had a delightful time.* One can imagine ways of going further and becoming more selective, such as blocking business and government calls while letting personal calls go through free. Postal workers could do likewise with mail; transportation workers could continue to ship necessary goods while refusing to transport police or troops. . . .

But this type of strike would make no sense for that large majority of workers whose jobs serve no sensible purpose. (The best thing that such workers can do is to publicly denounce the absurdity of their own work, as some ad designers nicely did during May 1968.) Moreover, even useful work is often so parcelized that isolated groups of workers can implement few changes on their own. And even the small minority who happen to produce finished and salable products (as did the workers who in 1973 took over the bankrupt Lip watch factory in Besançon, France, and started running it for themselves) usually remain dependent on commercial financing and distribution networks.

---

*"One day into this thing, and I'm tired, but compared to the positive sensations that are passing through this place, fatigue doesn't stand a chance. . . . Who will ever forget the look on management's faces when we tell them we are now in control, and their services are obviously no longer needed. . . . Everything as normal, except we don't collect phone bills. . . . We're also making friends from other departments. Guys from downstairs are coming up to help out and learn our jobs. . . . We're all flying. . . . Sailing on pure adrenalin. It's like we own the bloody thing. . . . The signs on the front door say, CO-OP TEL: UNDER NEW MANAGEMENT—NO MANAGEMENT ALLOWED." (Rosa Collette, "Operators Dial Direct Action," *Open Road*, Vancouver, Spring 1981.)

In the exceptional case where such workers make a go of it on their own, they simply become one more capitalist company; more often, their self-management innovations merely end up rationalizing the operation for the benefit of the owners. A "Strasbourg of the factories" might occur if workers finding themselves in a Lip-type situation use the facilities and publicity it gives them to go farther than the Lip workers (who were struggling simply to save their jobs) by calling on others to join them in superseding the whole system of commodity production and wage labor. But this is unlikely to happen until there is a sufficiently widespread movement to enlarge people's perspectives and offset the risks—as in May 1968, when most of the factories of France were occupied:

> If, in a single large factory, between 16 May and 30 May, a general assembly had constituted itself as a *council* holding all powers of decision and execution, expelling the bureaucrats, organizing its self-defense and calling on the strikers of all the enterprises to link up with it, this qualitative step could have immediately brought the movement to the *ultimate showdown* . . . . A very large number of enterprises would have followed the course thus discovered. This factory could immediately have taken the place of the dubious and in every sense eccentric Sorbonne of the first days and have become the real center of the occupations movement: genuine *delegates* from the numerous councils that already virtually existed in some of the occupied buildings, and from all the councils that could have imposed themselves in all the branches of industry, would have rallied around this base. Such an assembly could then have proclaimed the expropriation of all capital, *including state capital;* announced that all the country's means of production were henceforth the collective property of the proletariat organized in direct democracy; and appealed directly (by finally seizing some of the means of telecommunication, for example) to the workers of the entire world to support this revolution. Some people will say that such a hypothesis is utopian. We answer: It is precisely because the occupations movement was objectively at several moments *only an hour away* from such a result that it spread such terror, visible to everyone at the time in the impotence of the state and the panic of the so-called Communist Party, and since then in the conspiracy of silence concerning its gravity. [*SI Anthology,* pp. 234–235]

What prevented this from happening was above all the labor unions, in particular the largest one in the country: the Communist Party–dominated CGT. Inspired by the rebellious youth who had fought the police in the streets and taken over the Sorbonne and other public buildings, ten million workers ignored their unions and occupied virtually all the factories and many of the offices in the country, launching the first wildcat general strike in history. But most of these workers were unclear enough as to what to do next that they allowed the union bureaucracy to insinuate itself into the movement it had tried to prevent. The bureaucrats did everything they could to brake and fragment the movement: calling brief token strikes; setting up phony "rank-and-file" organizations composed of loyal Party members; seizing control of the loudspeaker systems; rigging elections in favor of returning to work; and most crucially, locking the factory gates in order to keep workers isolated from each other and from the other insurgents (on the pretext of "guarding against outside provocateurs"). The unions then proceeded to negotiate with the employers and the government a package of wage and vacation bonuses. This bribe was emphatically rejected by a large majority of the workers, who had the sense, however confused, that some more radical change was on the agenda. In early June, de Gaulle's presenting the carrot/stick alternative of new elections or civil war finally intimidated many workers into returning to work. There were still numerous holdouts, but their isolation from each other enabled the unions to tell each group that all the others had resumed work, so that they would believe they were alone and give up.

* * *

As in May 1968, when the more developed countries are threatened with a radical situation, they usually rely on confusion, concessions, curfews, distractions, disinformation, fragmentation, preemption, postponement and other methods of diverting, dividing and coopting the opposition, reserving overt physical repression as a last resort. These methods, which range from the subtle to the ludicrous,* are so numerous that it would be impossible here to mention more than a few.

A common method of confusing the issues is to distort the apparent alignment of forces by projecting diverse positions onto a linear, left-versus-right schema, implying that if you are opposed to one side you must be in favor of the other. The communism-versus-capitalism spectacle served this purpose for over half a century. Since the recent collapse of that farce, the tendency has been to declare a centrist pragmatic global consensus, with any opposition being lumped with lunatic-fringe "extremisms" (fascism and religious fanaticism on the right, terrorism and "anarchy" on the left).

One of the classic divide-and-rule methods has been discussed earlier: encouraging the exploited to fragment into a multitude of narrow group identities, which can be manipulated into directing their

---

*"A South African company is selling an anti-riot vehicle that plays disco music through a loudspeaker to soothe the nerves of would-be troublemakers. The vehicle, already bought by one black nation, which the company did not identify, also carries a water cannon and tear gas." (AP, 23 September 1979.)

energies into squabbling with each other. Conversely, opposed classes can be lumped together by patriotic hysteria and other means. Popular fronts, united fronts and similar coalitions serve to obscure fundamental conflicts of interest in the name of joint opposition to a common enemy (bourgeoisie + proletariat versus a reactionary regime; military-bureaucratic strata + peasantry versus foreign domination). In such coalitions the upper group generally has the material and ideological resources to maintain its control over the lower group, which is tricked into postponing self-organized action on its own behalf until it's too late. By the time victory has been attained over the common enemy, the upper group has had time to consolidate its power (often in a new alliance with elements of the defeated enemy) in order to crush the radical elements of the lower group.

Any vestige of hierarchy within a radical movement will be used to divide and undermine it. If there are no cooptable leaders, a few will be created by intensive media exposure. Leaders can be privately bargained with and held responsible for their followers; once they are coopted, they can establish similar chains of command beneath them, enabling a large mass of people to be brought under control without the rulers having to deal with all of them openly and simultaneously.

Cooption of leaders serves not only to separate them from the people, but also divides the people among themselves—some seeing the cooption as a victory, others denouncing it, others hesitating. As attention shifts from participatory actions to the spectacle of distant leader-celebrities debating distant issues, most people become bored and disillusioned. Feeling that matters are out of their hands (perhaps even secretly relieved that somebody else is taking care of them), they return to their previous passivity.

Another method of discouraging popular participation is to emphasize problems that seem to require specialized expertise. A classic instance was the ploy of certain German military leaders in 1918, at the moment when the workers and soldiers councils that emerged in the wake of the German collapse at the end of World War I potentially had the country in their hands.*

---

*"On the evening of November 10, when the Supreme Command was still at Spa, a group of seven enlisted men presented themselves at headquarters. They were the 'Executive Committee' of the Supreme Headquarters Soldiers' Council. Their demands were somewhat unclear, but obviously they expected to play a role in the command of the Army during its retreat. At the very least they wanted the right to countersign the Supreme Command's orders and to insure that the field army was not used for any counterrevolutionary purpose. The seven soldiers were courteously received by a Lieutenant Colonel Wilhelm von Faupel, who had been carefully rehearsed for the occasion. . . . Faupel led the delegates into the Supreme Command's map room. Everything was laid out on a gigantic map which occupied one wall: the huge complex of roads, railway lines, bridges, switching points, pipelines, command posts and supply dumps—the whole an intricate lace of red, green, blue and black lines converging into narrow bottlenecks at the crucial

Terrorism has often served to break the momentum of radical situations. It stuns people, turns them back into spectators anxiously following the latest news and speculations. Far from weakening the state, terrorism seems to confirm the need to strengthen it. If terrorist spectacles fail to spontaneously arise when it needs them, the state itself may produce them by means of provocateurs. (See Sanguinetti's *On Terrorism and the State* and the last half of Debord's *Preface to the Fourth Italian Edition of "The Society of the Spectacle."*)

A popular movement can hardly prevent individuals from carrying out terrorist or other thoughtless actions, actions that may sidetrack and destroy it as surely as if they were the work of a provocateur. The only solution is to create a movement with such consistently forthright and nonmanipulative tactics that everyone will recognize individual stupidities or police provocations for what they are.

An antihierarchical revolution can only be an "open conspiracy." Obviously some things require secrecy, especially under the more repressive regimes. But even in such cases the means should not be inconsistent with the ultimate goal: the supersession of all separate power through the conscious participation of everyone. Secrecy often has the absurd result that the police are the *only* ones who know what is happening, and are thus able to infiltrate and manipulate a radical group without anyone else being aware of it. The best defense against infiltration is to make sure there's nothing of any importance to infiltrate, i.e. that no radical organization wields any separate power. The best safety is in numbers: once thousands of people are openly involved, it hardly matters if a few spies are among them.

Even in small group actions safety often lies in maximum publicity. When some of the Strasbourg scandal participants started to get cold feet and suggested toning things down, Mustapha Khayati (the SI delegate who was the main author of the *Student Poverty* pamphlet) pointed out that the safest course would not be to avoid offending the authorities too much—as if they would be grateful for being only moderately and hesitantly insulted!—but to perpetrate such a widely publicized scandal that they wouldn't dare retaliate.

Rhine bridges. . . . Faupel then turned to them. The Supreme Command had no objection to the soldiers' councils, he said, but did his hearers feel competent to direct the general evacuation of the German Army along these lines of communication? . . . The disconcerted soldiers stared uneasily at the immense map. One of them allowed that this was not what they had really had in mind—'This work can well be left to the officers.' In the end, the seven soldiers willingly gave the officers their support. More than this, they practically begged the officers to retain command. . . . Whenever a soldiers' council delegation appeared at Supreme Headquarters, Colonel Faupel was trotted out to repeat his earlier performance; it always worked." (Richard Watt, *The Kings Depart: Versailles and the German Revolution.*)

* * *

To get back to the May 1968 factory occupations, suppose that the French workers had rejected the bureaucratic maneuvers and established a councilist network throughout the country. What then?

> In such an eventuality, civil war would naturally have been inevitable. ... Armed counterrevolution would certainly have been launched immediately. But it would not have been certain of winning. Some of the troops would obviously have mutinied. The workers would have figured out how to get weapons, and they certainly would not have built any more barricades (a good form of *political* expression at the beginning of the movement, but obviously ridiculous *strategically*). ... Foreign intervention would have inevitably followed . . . probably beginning with NATO forces, but with the direct or indirect support of the Warsaw Pact. But then everything would once again have hinged on the European proletariat: double or nothing. [*SI Anthology*, p. 235]

Roughly speaking, the significance of armed struggle varies inversely with the degree of economic development. In the most underdeveloped countries social struggles tend to be reduced to military struggles, because without arms there is little that the impoverished masses can do that will not hurt them more than the rulers, especially when their traditional self-sufficiency has been destroyed by a one-crop economy geared for export. (But even if they win militarily, they can usually be overpowered by foreign intervention or pressured into compliance with the global economy, unless parallel revolutions elsewhere open up new fronts.)

In more developed countries armed force has relatively less significance, though it can, of course, still be an important factor at certain critical junctures. It is possible, though not very efficient, to force people to do simple manual labor at gunpoint. It is not possible to do this with people who work with paper or computers within a complex industrial society—there are too many opportunities for troublesome yet untraceable "mistakes." Modern capitalism requires a certain amount of cooperation and even semicreative participation from its workers. No large enterprise could function for a day without its workers' spontaneous self-organization, reacting to unforeseen problems, compensating for managers' mistakes, etc. If workers engage in a "work-to-rule" strike in which they do nothing more than strictly follow all the official regulations, the whole operation will be slowed down or even brought to a complete halt (forcing the managers, who are unable to openly condemn such strictness, into the amusingly awkward position of having to hint to the workers that they should get on with their work without being quite so rigorous). The system survives only because most workers are relatively apathetic and, in order not to cause trouble for themselves, cooperate enough to keep things going.

Isolated revolts may be repressed one at a time; but if a movement spreads fast enough, as in May 1968, a few hundred thousand soldiers and police can hardly do anything in the face of ten million striking workers. Such a movement can be destroyed only from the inside. If the people don't know what they need to do, arms can scarcely help them; if they do know, arms can scarcely stop them.

Only at certain moments are people "together" enough to revolt successfully. The more lucid rulers know that they are safe if they can only disperse such threats before they develop too much momentum and self-awareness, whether by direct physical repression or by the various sorts of diversion mentioned above. It hardly matters if the people later find out that they were tricked, that they had victory in their hands if they had only known it: once the opportunity has passed, it's too late.

Ordinary situations are full of confusions, but matters are generally not so urgent. In a radical situation things are both simplified and speeded up: the issues become clearer, but there is less time to resolve them.

The extreme case is dramatized in a famous scene in Eisenstein's *Potemkin.* Mutinous sailors, heads covered by a tarp, have been lined up to be shot. Guards aim their rifles and are given the order to fire. One of the sailors cries out: "Brothers! Do you realize who you are shooting?" The guards waver. The order is given again. After a suspenseful hesitation the guards lower their weapons. They help the sailors to raid the armory, together they turn against the officers, and the battle is soon won.

Note that even in this violent showdown the outcome is more a matter of consciousness than of brute power: once the guards come over to the sailors, the fight is effectively over. (The remainder of Eisenstein's scene—a drawn-out struggle between an officer villain and a martyrized revolutionary hero—is mere melodrama.) In contrast to war, in which two distinct sides consciously oppose each other, "class struggle is not just a battle waged against an external enemy, the bourgeoisie; it is equally the struggle of the proletariat *against itself:* against the devastating and degrading effects of the capitalist system on its class consciousness" (Lukács, *History and Class Consciousness*). Modern revolution has the peculiar quality that the exploited majority automatically wins as soon as it becomes collectively aware of the game it is playing. The proletariat's opponent is ultimately nothing but the product of its own alienated activity, whether in the economic form of capital, the political form of party and union bureaucracies, or the psychological form of spectacular conditioning. The rulers are such a tiny minority that they would be immediately overwhelmed if they had not managed to bamboozle a large portion of the population into identifying with them, or at least into taking their system for granted; and especially into becoming divided against each other.

The tarp, which dehumanizes the mutineers, making it easier for the guards to shoot them, symbolizes this divide-and-rule tactic. The "Brothers!" shout represents the countertactic of *fraternization*.

While fraternization refutes lies about what is happening elsewhere, its greatest power probably stems from the emotional effect of direct human encounter, which reminds soldiers that the insurgents are people not essentially different from themselves. The state naturally tries to prevent such contact by bringing in troops from other regions who are unfamiliar with what has taken place and who, if possible, don't even speak the same language; and by quickly replacing them if they nevertheless become too contaminated by rebellious ideas. (Some of the Russian troops sent in to crush the 1956 Hungarian revolution were told that they were in Germany and that the people confronting them in the streets were resurgent Nazis!)

In order to expose and eliminate the most radical elements, a government sometimes deliberately provokes a situation that will lead to an excuse for violent repression. This is a dangerous game, however, because, as in the *Potemkin* incident, forcing the issue may provoke the armed forces to come over to the people. From the rulers' standpoint, the optimum strategy is to brandish just enough of a threat that there is no need to risk the ultimate showdown. This worked in Poland in 1980–81. The Russian bureaucrats knew that to invade Poland might bring about their own downfall; but the constantly hinted threat of such an invasion successfully intimidated the radical Polish workers, who could easily have overthrown the state, into tolerating the persistence of military-bureaucratic forces within Poland. The latter were eventually able to repress the movement without having to call in the Russians.

* * *

"Those who make revolutions half way only dig their own graves." A revolutionary movement cannot attain some local victory and then expect to peacefully coexist with the system until it's ready to try for a little more. All existing powers will put aside their differences in order to destroy any truly radical popular movement before it spreads. If they can't crush it militarily, they'll strangle it economically (national economies are now so globally interdependent that no country would be immune from such pressure). The only way to defend a revolution is to *extend* it, both qualitatively and geographically. The only guarantee against internal reaction is the most radical liberation of every aspect of life. The only guarantee against external intervention is the most rapid internationalization of the struggle.

The most profound expression of internationalist solidarity is, of course, to make a parallel revolution in one's own country (1848, 1917–1920, 1968). Short of this, the most urgent task is at least to prevent counterrevolutionary intervention *from* one's own country, as when British workers pressured their government not to support the slave states during the American Civil War (even though this meant greater unemployment due to lack of cotton imports); or when Western workers struck and mutinied against their governments' attempts to support the reactionary forces during the civil war following the Russian revolution; or when people in Europe and America opposed their countries' repression of anticolonial revolts.

Unfortunately, even such minimal defensive efforts are few and far between. Positive internationalist support is even more difficult. As long as the rulers remain in control of the most powerful countries, direct personal reinforcement is complicated and limited. Arms and other supplies may be intercepted. Even communications sometimes don't get through until it's too late.

One thing that does get through is an announcement that one group is relinquishing its power or claims over another. The 1936 fascist revolt in Spain, for example, had one of its main bases in Spanish Morocco. Many of Franco's troops were Moroccan and the antifascist forces could have exploited this fact by declaring Morocco independent, thereby encouraging a revolt at Franco's rear and dividing his forces. The probable spread of such a revolt to other Arab countries would at the same time have diverted Mussolini's forces, which were supporting Franco, to defend Italy's North African possessions. But the leaders of the Spanish Popular Front government rejected this idea for fear that such an encouragement of anticolonialism would alarm France and England, from whom they were hoping for aid. Needless to say this aid never came anyway.*

---

*If this question had been openly posed to the Spanish workers (who had already bypassed the vacillating Popular Front government by seizing arms and resisting the fascist coup by themselves, and in the process launched the revolution) they would probably have agreed to grant Moroccan independence. But once they were swayed by political leaders—including even many anarchist leaders—into tolerating that government in the name of antifascist unity, they were kept unaware of such issues.

The Spanish revolution remains the single richest revolutionary experience in history, though it was complicated and obscured by the simultaneous civil war against Franco and by the sharp contradictions within the antifascist camp—which, besides two or three million anarchists and anarchosyndicalists and a considerably smaller contingent of revolutionary Marxists (the POUM), included bourgeois republicans, ethnic autonomists, socialists and Stalinists, with the latter in particular doing everything in their power to repress the revolution. The best comprehensive histories are Pierre Broué and Emile Témime's *Revolution and the War in Spain* and Burnett Bolloten's *The Spanish Revolution* (the latter is also substantially incorporated in Bolloten's monumental final work, *The Spanish Civil War*). Some good first-hand accounts are George Orwell's *Homage to Catalonia,* Franz Borkenau's *The Spanish Cockpit,* and Mary Low and Juan Breá's *Red Spanish Notebook.* Other books worth reading include Vernon

Similarly, if, before the Khomeiniists had been able to consolidate their power, the insurgent Iranians in 1979 had supported total autonomy for the Kurds, Baluchis and Azerbaijans, this would have won them as firm allies of the most radical Iranian tendencies and might have spread the revolution to the adjacent countries where overlapping portions of those peoples live, while simultaneously undermining the Khomeiniist reactionaries in Iran.

Encouraging others' autonomy does not imply supporting any organization or regime that might take advantage of it. It's simply a matter of leaving the Moroccans, the Kurds, or whomever to work out their own affairs. The hope is that the example of an antihierarchical revolution in one country will inspire others to contest their own hierarchies.

It's our only hope, but not an entirely unrealistic one. The contagion of a genuinely liberated movement should never be underestimated.

Richards's *Lessons of the Spanish Revolution,* Murray Bookchin's *To Remember Spain,* Gerald Brenan's *The Spanish Labyrinth,* Sam Dolgoff's *The Anarchist Collectives,* Abel Paz's *Durruti: The People Armed,* and Victor Alba and Stephen Schwartz's *Spanish Marxism versus Soviet Communism: A History of the P.O.U.M.*

4. Rebirth

"It will, of course, be said that such a scheme as is set forth here is quite impractical, and goes against human nature. This is perfectly true. It is impractical, and it goes against human nature. This is why it is worth carrying out, and that is why one proposes it. For what is a practical scheme? A practical scheme is either a scheme that is already in existence, or a scheme that could be carried out under existing conditions. But it is exactly the existing conditions that one objects to; and any scheme that could accept these conditions is wrong and foolish. The conditions will be done away with, and human nature will change. The only thing that one really knows about human nature is that it changes. Change is the one quality we can predicate of it. The systems that fail are those that rely on the permanency of human nature, and not on its growth and development."

—Oscar Wilde, *The Soul of Man Under Socialism*

Marx considered it presumptuous to attempt to predict how people would live in a liberated society. "It will be up to those people to decide if, when and what they want to do about it, and what means to employ. I don't feel qualified to offer them any advice on this matter. They will presumably be at least as clever as we are" (letter to Kautsky, 1 February 1881). His modesty in this regard compares favorably with those who accuse him of arrogance and authoritarianism while themselves not hesitating to project their own fancies into pronouncements as to what such a society can or cannot be.

It is true, however, that if Marx had been a little more explicit about what he envisioned, it would have been that much more difficult for Stalinist bureaucrats to pretend to be implementing his ideas. An exact blueprint of a liberated society is neither possible nor necessary, but people must have some sense of its nature and feasibility. The belief that there is no practical alternative to the present system is one of the things that keeps people resigned.

Utopian speculations can help free us from the habit of taking the status quo for granted, get us thinking about what we really want and what might be possible. What makes them "utopian" in the pejorative sense that Marx and Engels criticized is the failure to take present conditions into consideration. There is usually no serious notion of how we might get from here to there. Ignoring the system's repressive and cooptive powers, utopian authors generally envision some simplistic cumulative change, imagining that, with the spread of utopian communities or utopian ideas, more and more people will be inspired to join in and the old system will simply collapse.

I hope the present text has given some more realistic ideas of how a new society might come about. In any case, at this point I am going to jump ahead and do a little speculating myself.

To simplify matters, let us assume that a victorious revolution has spread throughout the world without too much destruction of basic infrastructures, so that we no longer need to take into consideration problems of civil war, threats of outside intervention, the confusions of disinformation or the delays of massive emergency reconstruction, and can examine some of the issues that might come up in a new, fundamentally transformed society.

Though for clarity of expression I will use the future tense rather than the conditional, the ideas presented here are simply possibilities to consider, not prescriptions or predictions. If such a revolution ever happens, a few years of popular experimentation will change so many of the variables that even the boldest predictions will soon seem laughably timid and unimaginative. All we can reasonably do is try to envision the problems we will confront at the very beginning and some of the main tendencies of further developments. But the more hypotheses we explore, the more possibilities we will be prepared for and the less likely we will be to unconsciously revert to old patterns.

Far from being too extravagant, most fictional utopias are too narrow, generally being limited to a monolithic implementation of the author's pet ideas. As Marie Louise Berneri notes in the best survey of the field (*Journey Through Utopia*), "All utopias are, of course, the expression of personal preferences, but their authors usually have the conceit to assume that their personal tastes should be enacted into laws; if they are early risers the whole of their imaginary community will have to get up at four o'clock in the morning; if they dislike women's make-up, to use it is made a crime; if they are jealous husbands infidelity will be punished by death."

If there is one thing that can be confidently predicted about the new society, it is that it will be *far more diverse* than any one person's imagination or any possible description. Different communities will reflect every sort of taste—aesthetic and scientific, mystical and rationalist, hightech and neoprimitive, solitary and communal, industrious and lazy, Spartan and epicurean, traditional and experimental—continually evolving in all sorts of new and unforeseeable combinations.*

There will be a strong tendency toward decentralization and local autonomy. Small communities promote habits of cooperation, facilitate direct democracy, and make possible the richest social experimentation: if a local experiment fails, only a small group is hurt (and others

---

*P.M.'s *Bolo'bolo* (1983; new edition: Semiotext(e), 1995) has the merit of being one of the few utopias that fully recognize and welcome this diversity. Leaving aside its flippancies and idiosyncrasies and its rather unrealistic notions about how we might get there, it touches on a lot of the basic problems and possibilities of a postrevolutionary society.

can help out); if it succeeds it will be imitated and the advantage will spread. A decentralized system is also less vulnerable to accidental disruption or to sabotage. (The latter danger, however, will probably be negligible in any case: it's unlikely that a liberated society will have anywhere near the immense number of bitter enemies that are constantly produced by the present one.)

But decentralization can also foster hierarchical control by isolating people from each other. And some things can best be organized on a large scale. One big steel factory is more energy-efficient and less damaging to the environment than a smelting furnace in every community. Capitalism has tended to overcentralize in some areas where greater diversity and self-sufficiency would make more sense, but its irrational competition has also fragmented many things that could more sensibly be standardized or centrally coordinated. As Paul Goodman notes in *People or Personnel* (which is full of interesting examples of the pros and cons of decentralization in various present-day contexts), where, how and how much to decentralize are empirical questions that will require experimentation. About all we can say is that the new society will probably decentralize as much as possible, but without making a fetish of it. Most things can be taken care of by small groups or local communities; regional and global councils will be limited to matters with broad ramifications or significant efficiencies of scale, such as environmental restoration, space exploration, dispute resolution, epidemic control, coordination of global production, distribution, transportation and communication, and maintenance of certain specialized facilities (e.g. hightech hospitals or research centers).

It is often said that direct democracy may have worked well enough in the old-fashioned town meeting, but that the size and complexity of modern societies make it impossible. How can millions of people each express their own viewpoint on every issue?

They don't need to. Most practical matters ultimately come down to a limited number of options; once these have been stated and the most significant arguments have been advanced, a decision can be reached without further ado. Observers of the 1905 soviets and the 1956 Hungarian workers councils were struck by the brevity of people's statements and the rapidity with which decisions were arrived at. Those who spoke to the point tended to get delegated; those who spouted hot air got flak for wasting people's time.

For more complicated matters, committees can be elected to look into various possibilities and report back to the assemblies about the ramifications of different options. Once a plan is adopted, smaller committees can continue to monitor developments, notifying the assemblies of any relevant new factors that might suggest modifying it. On controversial issues multiple committees reflecting opposing perspectives (e.g. protech versus antitech) might be set up to facilitate the formulation of alternative proposals and dissenting viewpoints. As always, delegates will not impose any decisions (except regarding the organization of their own work) and will be elected on a rotating and recallable basis, so as to ensure both that they do a good job and that their temporary responsibilities don't go to their heads. Their work will be open to public scrutiny and final decisions will always revert to the assemblies.

Modern computer and telecommunication technologies will make it possible for anyone to instantly check data and projections for themselves, as well as to widely communicate their own proposals. Despite current hype, such technologies do not automatically promote democratic participation; but they have the potential to facilitate it if they are appropriately modified and put under popular control.*

Telecommunications will also render delegates less necessary than during previous radical movements, when they functioned to a great extent as mere bearers of information back and forth. Diverse proposals could be circulated and discussed ahead of time, and if an issue was of sufficient interest council meetings could be hooked up live with local assemblies, enabling the latter to immediately confirm, modify or repudiate delegate decisions.

But when the issues are not particularly controversial, mandating

---

*Although the so-called networking revolution has so far been limited mainly to increased circulation of spectator trivia, modern communications technologies continue to play an important role in undermining totalitarian regimes. Years ago the Stalinist bureaucracies had to cripple their own functioning by restricting the availability of photocopy machines and even typewriters lest they be used to reproduce *samizdat* writings. The newer technologies are proving even more difficult to control:

"The conservative *Guangming Daily* reported new enforcement measures targeted at an estimated 90,000 illegal fax machines in Beijing. Chinese analysts say the regime fears that the proliferation of fax machines is allowing information to flow too freely. Such machines were used extensively during student demonstrations in 1989 that resulted in a military crackdown. . . . In the comfort of their own homes in Western capitals, such as London, oppositionists can tap out messages to activists in Saudi Arabia who, by downloading via Internet in their own homes, no longer have to fear a knock on the door in the middle of the night. . . . Every taboo subject from politics to pornography is spreading through anonymous electronic messages far beyond the government's iron grip. . . . Many Saudis find themselves discussing religion openly for the first time. Atheists and fundamentalists regularly slug it out in Saudi cyberspace, a novelty in a country where the punishment for apostasy is death. . . . But banning the Internet is not possible without removing all computers and telephone lines. . . . Experts claim that for those willing to work hard enough to get it, there is still little any government can do to totally deny access to information on the Internet. Encrypted e-mail and subscribing to out-of-country service providers are two options available to net-savvy individuals for circumventing current Internet controls. . . . If there is one thing repressive East Asian governments fear more than unrestricted access to outside media sources, it is that their nations' competitiveness in the rapidly growing information industry may be compromised. Already, protests have been voiced in the business communities of Singapore, Malaysia, and China that censoring the Internet may, in the end, hamper those nations' aspirations to be the most technologically advanced on the block." (*Christian Science Monitor*, 11 August 1993, 24 August 1995 and 12 November 1996.)

will probably be fairly loose. Having arrived at some general decision (e.g. "This building should be remodeled to serve as a daycare center"), an assembly might simply call for volunteers or elect a committee to implement it without bothering with detailed accountability.

Idle purists can always envision possible abuses. "Aha! Who knows what subtle elitist maneuvers these delegates and technocratic specialists may pull off!" The fact remains that large numbers of people cannot directly oversee every detail at every moment. Any society has to rely to *some* extent on people's good will and common sense. The point is that abuses are far less possible under generalized self-management than under any other form of social organization.

People who have been autonomous enough to inaugurate a self-managed society will naturally be alert to any reemergence of hierarchy. They will note how delegates carry out their mandates, and rotate them as often as practicable. For some purposes they may, like the ancient Athenians, choose delegates by lot so as to eliminate the popularity-contest and deal-making aspects of elections. In matters requiring technical expertise they will keep a wary eye on the experts until the necessary knowledge is more widely disseminated or the technology in question is simplified or phased out. Skeptical observers will be designated to sound the alarm at the first sign of chicanery. A specialist who provides false information will be quickly found out and publicly discredited. The slightest hint of any hierarchical plot or of any exploitive or monopolistic practice will arouse universal outrage and be eliminated by ostracism, confiscation, physical repression or whatever other means are found necessary.

These and other safeguards will always be available to those worried about potential abuses, but I doubt if they will often be necessary. On any serious issue people can insist on as much mandating or monitoring as they want to bother with. But in most cases they will probably give delegates a reasonable amount of leeway to use their own judgment and creativity.

Generalized self-management avoids both the hierarchical forms of the traditional left and the more simplistic forms of anarchism. It is not bound to any ideology, even an "antiauthoritarian" one. If a problem turns out to require some specialized expertise or some degree of "leadership," the people involved will soon find this out and take whatever steps *they* consider appropriate to deal with it, without worrying about whether present-day radical dogmatists would approve. For certain uncontroversial functions they might find it most convenient to appoint specialists for indefinite periods of time, removing them only in the unlikely event that they abuse their position. In certain emergency situations in which quick, authoritative decisions are essential (e.g. fire-fighting) they will naturally grant to designated persons whatever temporary authoritarian powers are needed.

But such cases will be exceptional. The general rule will be consensus when practicable, majority decision when necessary. A character in William Morris's *News from Nowhere* (one of the most sensible, easygoing and down-to-earth utopias) gives the example of whether a metal bridge should be replaced by a stone one. At the next Mote (community assembly) this is proposed. If there is a clear consensus, the issue is settled and they proceed to work out the details of implementation. But

> if a few of the neighbors disagree to it, if they think that the beastly iron bridge will serve a little longer and they don't want to be bothered with building a new one just then, they don't count heads that time, but put off the formal discussion to the next Mote; and meantime arguments pro and con are flying about, and some get printed, so that everybody knows what is going on; and when the Mote comes together again there is a regular discussion and at last a vote by show of hands. If the division is a close one, the question is again put off for further discussion; if the division is a wide one, the minority are asked if they will yield to the more general opinion, which they often, nay, most commonly do. If they refuse, the question is debated a third time, when, if the minority has not perceptibly grown, they always give way; though I believe there is some half-forgotten rule by which they might still carry it on further; but I say, what always happens is that they are convinced, not perhaps that their view is the wrong one, but they cannot persuade or force the community to adopt it.

Note that what enormously simplifies cases like this is that there are no longer any conflicting economic interests—no one has any means or any motive to bribe or bamboozle people into voting one way or the other because he happens to have a lot of money, or to control the media, or to own a construction company or a parcel of land near a proposed site. Without such conflicts of interest, people will naturally incline to cooperation and compromise, if only to placate opponents and make life easier for themselves. Some communities might have formal provisions to accommodate minorities (e.g. if, instead of merely voting no, 20% express a "vehement objection" to some proposal, it must pass by a 60% majority); but neither side will be likely to abuse such formal powers lest it be treated likewise when the situations are reversed. The main solution for repeated irreconcilable conflicts will lie in the wide diversity of cultures: if people who prefer metal bridges, etc., constantly find themselves outvoted by Morris-type arts-and-crafts traditionalists, they can always move to some neighboring community where more congenial tastes prevail.

Insistence on total consensus makes sense only when the number of people involved is relatively small and the issue is not urgent. Among any large number of people complete unanimity is rarely possible. It is absurd, out of worry over possible majority tyranny, to uphold a minority's right to constantly obstruct a majority; or to imagine that such problems will go away if we leave things "unstructured."

As was pointed out in a well-known article many years ago (Jo Freeman's "The Tyranny of Structurelessness"), there's no such thing as a structureless group, there are simply different types of structures. An unstructured group generally ends up being dominated by a clique that does have some effective structure. The unorganized members have no means of controlling such an elite, especially when their anti-authoritarian ideology prevents them from admitting that it exists.

Failing to acknowledge majority rule as a backup when unanimity is not attainable, anarchists and consensists are often unable to arrive at practical decisions except by following those de facto leaders who are skilled at maneuvering people into unanimity (if only by their capacity to endure interminable meetings until all the opposition has got bored and gone home). Fastidiously rejecting workers councils or anything else with any taint of coercion, they themselves usually end up settling for far less radical lowest-common-denominator projects.

It's easy to point out shortcomings in the workers councils of the past, which were, after all, just hurried improvisations by people involved in desperate struggles. But if those brief efforts were not perfect models to blindly imitate, they nevertheless represent the most practical step in the right direction that anyone has come up with so far. Riesel's article on councils (*SI Anthology*, pp. 270–282) discusses the limitations of these old movements, and rightly stresses that council power should be understood as the sovereignty of the popular assemblies as a whole, not merely of the councils of delegates they have elected. Some groups of radical workers in Spain, wishing to avoid any ambiguity on this latter point, have referred to themselves as "assemblyists" rather than "councilists." One of the CMDO leaflets (*SI Anthology*, p. 351) specifies the following essential features of councilist democracy:

- Dissolution of all external power
- Direct and total democracy
- Practical unification of decision and execution
- Delegates who can be revoked at any moment by those who have mandated them
- Abolition of hierarchy and independent specializations
- Conscious management and transformation of all the conditions of liberated life
- Permanent creative mass participation
- Internationalist extension and coordination

Once these features are recognized and implemented, it will make little difference whether people refer to the new form of social organization as "anarchy," "communalism," "communist anarchism," "council communism," "libertarian communism," "libertarian socialism," "participatory democracy" or "generalized self-management," or whether its various overlapping components are termed "workers councils," "anti-work councils," "revolutionary councils," "revolutionary assemblies," "popular assemblies," "popular committees," "communes," "collectives," "kibbutzes," "bolos," "motes," "affinity groups," or anything else. ("Generalized self-management" is unfortunately not very catchy, but it has the advantage of referring to both means and goal while being free of the misleading connotations of terms like "anarchy" or "communism.")

In any case, it's important to remember that large-scale formal organization will be the exception. Most local matters can be handled directly and informally. Individuals or small groups will simply go ahead and do what seemed appropriate in any given situation ("adhocracy"). Majority rule will merely be a *last resort* in the progressively diminishing number of cases in which conflicts of interest cannot otherwise be resolved.

A nonhierarchical society does not mean that everyone magically becomes equally talented or must participate equally in everything; it simply means that *materially based and reinforced* hierarchies have been eliminated. Although differences of abilities will undoubtedly diminish when everyone is encouraged to develop their fullest potentials, the point is that whatever differences remain will no longer be transformed into differences of wealth or power.

People will be able to take part in a far wider range of activities than they do now, but they won't have to rotate all positions all the time if they don't feel like it. If someone has a special taste and knack for a certain task, others will probably be happy to let her do it as much as she wants—at least until someone else wants a shot at it. "Independent specializations" (monopolistic control over socially vital information or technologies) will be abolished; open, nondominating specializations will flourish. People will still ask more knowledgeable persons for advice when they feel the need for it (though if they are curious or suspicious they will always be encouraged to investigate for themselves). They will still be free to voluntarily submit themselves as students to a teacher, apprentices to a master, players to a coach or performers to a director—remaining equally free to discontinue the relation at any time. In some activities, such as group folksinging, anyone can join right in; others, such as performing a classical concerto, may require rigorous training and coherent direction, with some people taking leading roles, others following, and others being happy just to listen. There should be plenty of opportunity for both types. The situationist critique of the spectacle is a critique of an excessive tendency in present society; it does not imply that everyone must be an "active participant" twenty-four hours a day.

Apart from the care necessary for mental incompetents, the only unavoidable enforced hierarchy will be the temporary one involved in raising children until they are capable of managing their own affairs. But in a safer and saner world children could be given considerably more freedom and autonomy than they are now. When it comes to openness to the new playful possibilities of life, adults may learn as much from them as vice versa. Here as elsewhere, the general rule will be to let people find their own level: a ten-year-old who takes part in some project might have as much say in it as her adult co-participants, while a nonparticipating adult will have none.

Self-management does not require that everyone be geniuses, merely that most people not be total morons. It's the *present* system that makes unrealistic demands—pretending that the people it systematically imbecilizes are capable of judging between the programs of rival politicians or the advertising claims of rival commodities, or of engaging in such complex and consequential activities as raising a child or driving a car on a busy freeway. With the supersession of all the political and economic pseudoissues that are now intentionally kept incomprehensible, most matters will turn out not to be all that complicated.

When people first get a chance to run their own lives they will undoubtedly make lots of mistakes; but they will soon discover and correct them because, unlike hierarchs, they will have no interest in covering them up. Self-management does not guarantee that people will always make the right decisions; but any other form of social organization guarantees that someone else will make the decisions for them.

* * *

The abolition of capitalism will eliminate the conflicts of interest that now serve as a pretext for the state. Most present-day wars are ultimately based on economic conflicts; even ostensibly ethnic, religious or ideological antagonisms usually derive much of their real motivation from economic competition, or from psychological frustrations that are ultimately linked to political and economic repression. As long as desperate competition prevails, people can easily be manipulated into reverting to their traditional groupings and squabbling over cultural differences they wouldn't bother about under more comfortable circumstances. War involves far more work, hardship and risk than any form of constructive activity; people with real opportunities for fulfillment will have more interesting things to do.

The same is true for crime. Leaving aside victimless "crimes," the vast majority of crimes are directly or indirectly related to money and will become meaningless with the elimination of the commodity system. Communities will then be free to experiment with various methods for dealing with whatever occasional antisocial acts might still occur.

There are all sorts of possibilities. The persons involved might argue their cases before the local community or a "jury" chosen by lot, which would strive for the most reconciling and rehabilitating solutions. A convicted offender might be "condemned" to some sort of public service—not to intentionally unpleasant and demeaning shitwork administered by petty sadists, which simply produces more anger and resentment, but to meaningful and potentially engaging projects that might introduce him to healthier interests (ecological restoration, for example). A few incorrigible psychotics might have to be humanely restrained in one way or another, but such cases would become increasingly rare. (The present proliferation of "gratuitous" violence is a predictable reaction to social alienation, a way for those who are not treated as real persons to at least get the grim satisfaction of being recognized as real threats.) Ostracism will be a simple and effective deterrent: the thug who laughs at the threat of harsh punishment, which only confirms his macho prestige, will be far more deterred if he knows that everyone will give him the cold shoulder. In the rare case where that proves inadequate, the variety of cultures might make banishment a workable solution: a violent character who was constantly disturbing a quiet community might fit in fine in some more rough-and-tumble, Wild West–type region—or face less gentle retaliation.

Those are just a few of the possibilities. Liberated people will undoubtedly come up with more creative, effective and humane solutions than any we can presently imagine. I don't claim that there will be no problems, only that there will be far fewer problems than there are now, when people who happen to find themselves at the bottom of an absurd social order are harshly punished for their crude efforts to escape, while those at the top loot the planet with impunity.

The barbarity of the present penal system is surpassed only by its stupidity. Draconian punishments have repeatedly been shown to have no significant effect on the crime rate, which is directly linked to levels of poverty and unemployment as well as to less quantifiable but equally obvious factors like racism, the destruction of urban communities, and the general alienation produced by the commodity-spectacle system. The threat of years in prison, which might be a powerful deterrent to someone with a satisfying life, means little to those with no meaningful alternatives. It is hardly very brilliant to slash already pitifully inadequate social programs in the name of economizing, while filling prisons with lifers at a cost of close to a million dollars each; but like so many other irrational social policies, this trend persists because it is reinforced by powerful vested interests.*

* * *

A liberated society must abolish the whole money-commodity economy.
To continue to accept the validity of money would amount to accepting
the continued dominance of those who had previously accumulated it,
or who had the savvy to reaccumulate it after any radical reapportion-
ment. Alternative forms of "economic" reckoning will still be needed for
certain purposes, but their carefully limited scope will tend to diminish
as increasing material abundance and social cooperativity render them
less necessary.

A postrevolutionary society might have a three-tier economic setup
along the following lines:

1) Certain basic goods and services will be freely available
   to everyone without any accounting whatsoever.

2) Others will also be free, but only in limited, rationed
   quantities.

3) Others, classified as "luxuries," will be available in
   exchange for "credits."

Unlike money, credits will be applicable only to certain specified goods,
not to basic communal property such as land, utilities or means of
production. They will also probably have expiration dates to limit any
excessive accumulation.

---

*"In the post–Cold War era politicians have discovered crime-baiting as a substitute for
red-baiting. Just as the fear of communism propelled the unimpeded expansion of the
military-industrial complex, crime-baiting has produced the explosive growth of the
correctional-industrial complex, also known as the crime-control industry. Those who
disagree with its agenda of more prisons are branded criminal sympathizers and victim
betrayers. Since no politician will risk the 'soft on crime' label, an unending spiral of
destructive policies is sweeping the country. . . . Repression and brutalization will be
further promoted by the institutions that are the primary beneficiaries of such policies.
As California increased its prison population from 19,000 to 124,000 over the past 16
years, 19 new prisons were built. With the increase in prisons, the California Correc-
tional Peace Officers Association (CCPOA), the guards' union, emerged as the state's
most powerful lobby. . . . As the percentage of the state budget devoted to higher education has fallen from 14.4 percent to 9.8 percent, the share of the budget for corrections
has risen from 3.9 percent to 9.8 percent. The average salary and benefits for prison
guards in California exceeds $55,000—the highest in the nation. This year the CCPOA,
along with the National Rifle Association, has directed its substantial war chest to
promote the passage of the 'three strikes, you're out' initiative that would triple the
current size of California's prison system. The same dynamics that evolved in California
will certainly result from Clinton's crime bill. As more resources are poured into the
crime-control industry, its power and influence will grow." (Dan Macallair, *Christian
Science Monitor,* 20 September 1994.)

Such a setup will be quite flexible. During the initial transition period the amount of free goods might be fairly minimal—just enough to enable a person to get by—with most goods requiring earning credits through work. As time goes on, less and less work will be necessary and more and more goods will become freely available—the tradeoff between the two factors always remaining up to the councils to determine. Some credits might be generally distributed, each person periodically receiving a certain amount; others might be bonuses for certain types of dangerous or unpleasant work where there is a shortage of volunteers. Councils might set fixed prices for certain luxuries, while letting others follow supply and demand; as a luxury becomes more abundant it will become cheaper, perhaps eventually free. Goods could be shifted from one tier to another depending on material conditions and community preferences.

Those are just some of the possibilities.* Experimenting with different methods, people will soon find out for themselves what forms of ownership, exchange and reckoning are necessary.

In any case, whatever "economic" problems may remain will not be serious because scarcity-imposed limits will be a factor only in the sector of inessential "luxuries." Free universal access to food, clothing, housing, utilities, health care, transportation, communication, education and cultural facilities could be achieved almost immediately in the industrialized regions and within a fairly short period in the less developed ones. Many of these things already exist and merely need to be made more equitably available; those that don't can easily be produced once social energy is diverted from irrational enterprises.

Take housing, for example. Peace activists have frequently pointed out that everyone in the world could be decently housed at less than the cost of a few weeks of global military expenditure. They are no doubt envisioning a fairly minimal sort of dwelling; but if the amount of energy people now waste earning the money to enrich landlords and

---

*Other possibilities are presented in considerable detail in *Workers' Councils and the Economics of a Self-Managed Society* (London Solidarity's edition of a *Socialisme ou Barbarie* article by Cornelius Castoriadis). This text is full of valuable suggestions, but I feel that it assumes more centering around work and workplace than will be necessary. Such an orientation is already somewhat obsolete and will probably become much more so after a revolution.

Michael Albert and Robin Hahnel's *Looking Forward: Participatory Economics for the Twenty First Century* (South End, 1991) also includes a number of useful points on self-managed organization. But the authors assume a society in which there is still a money economy and the workweek is only slightly reduced (to around 30 hours). Their hypothetical examples are largely modeled on present-day worker·co-ops and the "economic participation" envisaged includes voting on marketing issues that will be superseded in a noncapitalist society. As we will see, such a society will also have a far shorter workweek, reducing the need to bother with the complicated schemes for equal rotation among different types of jobs that occupy a large part of the book.

real estate speculators was diverted to building new dwellings, everyone in the world could soon be housed very decently indeed.

To begin with, most people might continue living where they are now and concentrate on making dwellings available for homeless people. Hotels and office buildings could be taken over. Certain outrageously extravagant estates might be requisitioned and turned into dwellings, parks, communal gardens, etc. Seeing this trend, those possessing relatively spacious properties might offer to temporarily quarter homeless people while helping them build homes of their own, if only to deflect potential resentment from themselves.

The next stage will be raising and equalizing the quality of dwellings. Here as in other areas, the aim will probably not be a rigidly uniform equality ("everyone must have a dwelling of such and such specifications"), but people's general sense of fairness, with problems being dealt with on a flexible, case-by-case basis. If someone feels he is getting the short end of the stick he can appeal to the general community, which, if the grievance is not completely absurd, will probably bend over backward to redress it. Compromises will have to be worked out regarding who gets to live in exceptionally desirable areas for how long. (They might be shared around by lot, or leased for limited periods to the highest bidders in credit auctions, etc.) Such problems may not be solved to everyone's complete satisfaction, but they will certainly be dealt with much more fairly than under a system in which accumulation of magic pieces of paper enables one person to claim "ownership" of a hundred buildings while others have to live on the street.

Once basic survival needs are taken care of, the quantitative perspective of labor time will be transformed into a qualitatively new perspective of free creativity. A few friends may work happily building their own home even if it takes them a year to accomplish what a professional crew could do more efficiently in a month. Much more fun and imagination and love will go into such projects, and the resulting dwellings will be far more charming, variegated and personal than what today passes for "decent." A nineteenth-century rural French mailman named Ferdinand Cheval spent all his spare time for several decades constructing his own personal fantasy castle. People like Cheval are considered eccentrics, but the only thing unusual about them is that they continue to exercise the innate creativity we all have but are usually induced to repress after early childhood. A liberated society will have lots of this playful sort of "work": personally chosen projects that will be so intensely engaging that people will no more think of keeping track of their "labor time" than they would of counting caresses during lovemaking or trying to economize on the length of a dance.

Fifty years ago Paul Goodman estimated that less than ten percent of the work then being done would satisfy our basic needs. Whatever the exact figure (it would be even lower now, though it would of course depend on precisely what we consider basic or reasonable needs), it is clear that most present-day labor is absurd and unnecessary. With the abolition of the commodity system, hundreds of millions of people now occupied with producing superfluous commodities, or with advertising them, packaging them, transporting them, selling them, protecting them or profiting from them (salespersons, clerks, foremen, managers, bankers, stockbrokers, landlords, labor leaders, politicians, police, lawyers, judges, jailers, guards, soldiers, economists, ad designers, arms manufacturers, customs inspectors, tax collectors, insurance agents, investment advisers, along with their numerous underlings) will all be freed up to share the relatively few actually necessary tasks.

Add the unemployed, who according to a recent UN report now constitute over 30% of the global population. If this figure seems large it is because it presumably includes prisoners, refugees, and many others who are not usually counted in official unemployment statistics because they have given up trying to look for work, such as those who are incapacitated by alcoholism or drugs, or who are so nauseated by the available job options that they put all their energy into evading work through crimes and scams.

Add millions of old people who would love to engage in worthwhile activities but who are now relegated to a boring, passive retirement. And teenagers and even younger children, who would be excitedly challenged by many useful and educational projects if they weren't confined to worthless schools designed to instill ignorant obedience.

Then consider the large component of waste even in undeniably necessary work. Doctors and nurses, for example, spend a large portion of their time (in addition to filling out insurance forms, billing patients, etc.) trying with limited success to counteract all sorts of socially induced problems such as occupational injuries, auto accidents, psychological ailments and diseases caused by stress, pollution, malnutrition or unsanitary living conditions, to say nothing of wars and the epidemics that often accompany them—problems that will largely disappear in a liberated society, leaving health-care providers free to concentrate on basic preventive medicine.

Then consider the equally large amount of *intentionally* wasted labor: make-work designed to keep people occupied; suppression of labor-saving methods that might put one out of a job; working as slowly as one can get away with; sabotaging machinery to exert pressure on bosses, or out of simple rage and frustration. And don't forget all the absurdities of "Parkinson's Law" (work expands to fill the time available), the "Peter Principle" (people rise to their level of incompetence) and similar tendencies that have been so hilariously satirized by C. Northcote Parkinson and Laurence Peter.

Then consider how much wasted labor will be eliminated once products are made to last instead of being designed to fall apart or go out of style so that people have to keep buying new ones. (After a brief initial period of high production to provide everyone with durable, high-quality goods, many industries could be reduced to very modest levels—just enough to keep those goods in repair, or to occasionally upgrade them whenever some truly significant improvement is developed.)

Taking all these factors into consideration, it's easy to see that in a sanely organized society the amount of necessary labor could be reduced to one or two days per week.

But such a drastic quantitative reduction will produce a qualitative change. As Tom Sawyer discovered, when people are not forced to work, even the most banal task may become novel and intriguing: the problem is no longer how to get people to do it, but how to accommodate all the volunteers. It would be unrealistic to expect people to work full time at unpleasant and largely meaningless jobs without surveillance and economic incentives; but the situation becomes completely different if it's a matter of putting in ten or fifteen hours a week on worthwhile, varied, self-organized tasks of one's choice.

Moreover, many people, once they are engaged in projects that interest them, will not want to limit themselves to the minimum. This will reduce necessary tasks to an even more minuscule level for others who may not have such enthusiasms.

There's no need to quibble about the term *work*. Wage work needs to be abolished; meaningful, freely chosen work can be as much fun as any other kind of play. Our present work usually produces practical results, but not the ones we would have chosen, whereas our free time is mostly confined to trivialities. With the abolition of wage labor, work will become more playful and play more active and creative. When people are no longer driven crazy by their work, they will no longer require mindless, passive amusements to recover from it.

Not that there's anything wrong with enjoying trivial pastimes; it's simply a matter of recognizing that much of their present appeal stems from the absence of more fulfilling activities. Someone whose life lacks real adventure may derive at least a little vicarious exoticism from collecting artifacts from other times and places; someone whose work is abstract and fragmented may go to great lengths to actually produce a whole concrete object, even if that object is no more significant than a model ship in a bottle. These and countless other hobbies reveal the persistence of creative impulses that will really blossom when given free play on a broader scale. Imagine how people who enjoy fixing up their home or cultivating their garden will get into recreating their whole community; or how the thousands of railroad enthusiasts will jump at the chance to rebuild and operate improved versions of the rail networks that will be one of the main ways to reduce automobile traffic.

When people are subjected to suspicion and oppressive regulations, they naturally try to get away with doing as little as possible. In situations of freedom and mutual trust there is a contrary tendency to take pride in doing the best job possible. Although some tasks in the new society will be more popular than others, the few really difficult or unpleasant ones will probably get more than enough volunteers, responding to the thrill of the challenge or the desire for appreciation, if not out of a sense of responsibility. Even now many people are happy to volunteer for worthy projects if they have the time; far more will do so once they no longer have to constantly worry about providing for the basic needs of themselves and their families. At worst, the few totally unpopular tasks will have to be divided up into the briefest practicable shifts and rotated by lot until they can be automated. Or there might be auctions to see if anyone is willing to do them for, say, five hours a week in lieu of the usual workload of ten or fifteen; or for a few extra credits.

Uncooperative characters will probably be so rare that the rest of the population may just let them be, rather than bothering to pressure them into doing their small share. At a certain degree of abundance it becomes simpler not to worry about a few possible abuses than to enlist an army of timekeepers, accountants, inspectors, informers, spies, guards, police, etc., to snoop around checking every detail and punishing every infraction. It's unrealistic to expect people to be generous and cooperative when there isn't much to go around; but a large material surplus will create a large "margin of abuse," so that it won't matter if some people do a little less than their share, or take a little more.

The abolition of money will prevent anyone from taking *much* more than their share. Most misgivings about the feasibility of a liberated society rest on the ingrained assumption that money (and thus also its necessary protector: the state) would still exist. This money-state partnership creates unlimited possibilities for abuses (legislators bribed to sneak loopholes into tax laws, etc.); but once it is abolished both the motives and the means for such abuses will vanish. The abstractness of market relations enables one person to anonymously accumulate wealth by indirectly depriving thousands of others of basic necessities; but with the elimination of money any significant monopolization of goods would be too unwieldy and too visible.

Whatever other forms of exchange there may be in the new society, the simplest and probably most common form will be gift-giving. The general abundance will make it easy to be generous. Giving is fun and satisfying, and it eliminates the bother of accounting. The only calculation is that connected with healthy mutual emulation. "The neighboring community donated such and such to a less well off region; surely we can do the same." "They put on a great party; let's see if we can do an even better one." A little friendly rivalry (who can create the most delicious new recipe, cultivate a superior vegetable, solve a social problem, invent a new game) will benefit everyone, even the losers.

A liberated society will probably function much like a potluck party. Most people enjoy preparing a dish that will be enjoyed by others; but even if a few people don't bring anything there's still plenty to go around. It's not essential that everyone contribute an exactly equal share, because the tasks are so minimal and are spread around so widely that no one is overburdened. Since everyone is openly involved, there's no need for checking up on people or instituting penalties for noncompliance. The only element of "coercion" is the approval or disapproval of the other participants: appreciation provides positive reinforcement, while even the most inconsiderate person realizes that if he consistently fails to contribute he will start getting funny looks and might not be invited again. Organization is necessary only if some problem turns up. (If there are usually too many desserts and not enough main dishes, the group might decide to coordinate who will bring what. If a few generous souls end up bearing an unfair share of the cleanup work, a gentle prodding suffices to embarrass others into volunteering, or else some sort of systematic rotation is worked out.)

Now, of course, such spontaneous cooperation is the exception, found primarily where traditional communal ties have persisted, or among small, self-selected groups of like-minded people in regions where conditions are not too destitute. Out in the dog-eat-dog world people naturally look out for themselves and are suspicious of others. Unless the spectacle happens to stir them with some sentimental human-interest story, they usually have little concern for those outside their immediate circle. Filled with frustrations and resentments, they may even take a malicious pleasure in spoiling other people's enjoyments.

But despite everything that discourages their humanity, most people, if given a chance, still like to feel that they are doing worthy things, and they like to be appreciated for doing them. Note how eagerly they seize the slightest opportunity to create a moment of mutual recognition, even if only by opening a door for someone or exchanging a few banal remarks. If a flood or earthquake or some other emergency arises, even the most selfish and cynical person often plunges right in, working twenty-four hours a day to rescue people, deliver food and first-aid supplies, etc., without any compensation but others' gratitude. This is why people often look back on wars and natural disasters with what might seem like a surprising degree of nostalgia. Like revolution, such events break through the usual social separations, provide everyone with opportunities to do things that really matter, and produce a strong sense of community (even if only by uniting people against a common enemy). In a liberated society these sociable impulses will be able to flourish without requiring such extreme pretexts.

*   *   *

Present-day automation often does little more than throw some people out of work while intensifying the regimentation of those who remain; if any time is actually gained by "labor-saving" devices, it is usually spent in an equally alienated passive consumption. But in a liberated world computers and other modern technologies could be used to eliminate dangerous or boring tasks, freeing everyone to concentrate on more interesting activities.

Disregarding such possibilities, and understandably disgusted by the current misuse of many technologies, some people have come to see "technology" itself as the main problem and advocate a return to a simpler lifestyle. How much simpler is debated—as flaws are discovered in each period, the dividing line keeps getting pushed farther back. Some, considering the Industrial Revolution as the main villain, disseminate computer-printed eulogies of hand craftsmanship. Others, seeing the invention of agriculture as the original sin, feel we should return to a hunter-gatherer society, though they are not entirely clear about what they have in mind for the present human population which could not be sustained by such an economy. Others, not to be outdone, present eloquent arguments proving that the development of language and rational thought was the real origin of our problems. Yet others contend that the whole human race is so incorrigibly evil that it should altruistically extinguish itself in order to save the rest of the global ecosystem.

These fantasies contain so many obvious self-contradictions that it is hardly necessary to criticize them in any detail. They have questionable relevance to actual past societies and virtually no relevance to present possibilities. Even supposing that life was better in one or another previous era, *we have to begin from where we are now*. Modern technology is so interwoven with all aspects of our life that it could not be abruptly discontinued without causing a global chaos that would wipe out billions of people. Postrevolutionary people will probably decide to reduce human population and phase out certain industries, but this can't be done overnight. We need to seriously consider how we will deal with all the practical problems that will be posed in the interim.

If it ever comes down to such a practical matter, I doubt if the technophobes will really want to eliminate motorized wheelchairs; or pull the plug on ingenious computer setups like the one that enables physicist Stephen Hawking to communicate despite being totally paralyzed; or allow a woman to die in childbirth who could be saved by technical procedures; or accept the reemergence of diseases that used to routinely kill or permanently disable a large percentage of the population; or resign themselves to never visiting or communicating with people in other parts of the world unless they're within walking distance; or stand by while people die in famines that could be averted through global food shipments.

The problem is that meanwhile this increasingly fashionable ideology deflects attention from real problems and possibilities. A simplistic Manichean dualism (nature is Good, technology is Bad) enables people to ignore complex historical and dialectical processes; it's so much easier to blame everything on some primordial evil, some sort of devil or original sin. What begins as a valid questioning of excessive faith in science and technology ends up as a desperate and even less justified faith in the return of a primeval paradise, accompanied by a failure to engage the present system in any but an abstract, apocalyptical way.*

Technophiles and technophobes are united in treating technology in isolation from other social factors, differing only in their equally simplistic conclusions that new technologies are automatically empowering or automatically alienating. As long as capitalism alienates all human productions into autonomous ends that escape the control of their creators, technologies will share in that alienation and will be used to reinforce it. But when people free themselves from this domination, they will have no trouble rejecting those technologies that are harmful while adapting others to beneficial uses.

Certain technologies—nuclear power is the most obvious example—are indeed so insanely dangerous that they will no doubt be brought to a prompt halt. Many other industries which produce absurd, obsolete or superfluous commodities will, of course, cease automatically with the disappearance of their commercial rationales. But many technologies (electricity, metallurgy, refrigeration, plumbing, printing, recording, photography, telecommunications, tools, textiles, sewing machines, agricultural equipment, surgical instruments, anesthetics, antibiotics, among dozens of other examples that will come to mind), however they may presently be misused, have few if any *inherent* drawbacks. It's simply a matter of using them more sensibly, bringing them under popular control, introducing a few ecological improvements, and redesigning them for human rather than capitalistic ends.

Other technologies are more problematic. They will still be needed

---

*Fredy Perlman, author of one of the most sweeping expressions of this tendency, *Against His-story, Against Leviathan!* (Black & Red, 1983), provided his own best critique in his earlier book about C. Wright Mills, *The Incoherence of the Intellectual* (Black & Red, 1970): "Yet even though Mills rejects the passivity with which men accept their own fragmentation, he no longer struggles against it. The coherent self-determined man becomes an exotic creature who lived in a distant past and in extremely different material circumstances. . . . The main drift is no longer the program of the right which can be opposed by the program of the left; it is now an external spectacle which follows its course like a disease. . . . The rift between theory and practice, thought and action, widens; political ideals can no longer be translated into practical projects."

to some extent, but their harmful and irrational aspects will be phased out, usually by attrition. If one considers the automobile industry as a whole, including its vast infrastructure (factories, streets, highways, gas stations, oil wells) and all its inconveniences and hidden costs (traffic jams, parking, repairs, insurance, accidents, pollution, urban destruction), it is clear that any number of alternative methods would be preferable. The fact remains that this infrastructure is already there. The new society will thus undoubtedly continue to use existing automobiles and trucks for a few years, while concentrating on developing more sensible modes of transportation to gradually replace them as they wear out. Personal vehicles with nonpolluting engines might continue indefinitely in rural areas, but most present-day urban traffic (with a few exceptions such as delivery trucks, fire engines, ambulances, and taxis for disabled people) could be superseded by various forms of public transit, enabling many freeways and streets to be converted to parks, gardens, plazas and bike paths. Airplanes will be retained for intercontinental travel (rationed if necessary) and for certain kinds of urgent shipments, but the elimination of wage labor will leave people with time for more leisurely modes of travel—boats, trains, biking, hiking.

Here, as in other areas, it will be up to the people involved to experiment with different possibilities to see what works best. Once people are able to determine the aims and conditions of their own work, they will naturally come up with all sorts of ideas that will make that work briefer, safer and more pleasant; and such ideas, no longer patented or jealously guarded as "business secrets," will rapidly spread and inspire further improvements. With the elimination of commercial motives, people will also be able to give appropriate weight to social and environmental factors along with purely quantitative labor-time considerations. If, say, production of computers currently involves some sweatshop labor or causes some pollution (though far less than classic "smokestack" industries), there's no reason to believe that better methods cannot be figured out once people set their minds to it—very likely precisely through a judicious use of computer automation. (Fortunately, the more repetitive the job, the easier it usually is to automate.)

The general rule will be to simplify basic manufactures in ways that facilitate optimum flexibility. Techniques will be made more uniform and understandable, so that people with a minimal general training will be able to carry out construction, repairs, alterations and other operations that formerly required specialized training. Basic tools, appliances, raw materials, machine parts and architectural modules will probably be standardized and mass-produced, leaving tailor-made refinements to small-scale "cottage industries" and the final and potentially most creative aspects to the individual users. Once time is no longer money we may, as William Morris hoped, see a revival of elaborate "labor"-intensive arts and crafts: joyful making and giving by people who care about their creations and the people for whom they are destined.

Some communities might choose to retain a fair amount of (ecologically sanitized) heavy technology; others might opt for simpler lifestyles, though backed up by technical means to facilitate that simplicity or for emergencies. Solar-powered generators and satellite-linked telecommunications, for example, would enable people to live off in the woods with no need for power and telephone lines. If earth-based solar power and other renewable energy sources proved insufficient, immense solar receptors in orbit could beam down a virtually unlimited amount of pollution-free energy.

Most Third World regions, incidentally, lie in the sun belt where solar power can be most effective. Though their poverty will present some initial difficulties, their traditions of cooperative self-sufficiency plus the fact that they are not encumbered with obsolete industrial infrastructures may give them some compensating advantages when it comes to creating new, ecologically appropriate structures. By drawing *selectively* on the developed regions for whatever information and technologies they themselves decide they need, they will be able to skip the horrible "classic" stage of industrialization and capital accumulation and proceed directly to postcapitalist forms of social organization. Nor will the influence necessarily be all one way: some of the most advanced social experimentation in history was carried out during the Spanish revolution by illiterate peasants living under virtually Third World conditions.

Nor will people in developed regions need to accept a drab transitional period of "lowered expectations" in order to enable less developed regions catch up. This common misconception stems from the false assumption that most present-day products are desirable and necessary—implying that more for others means less for ourselves. In reality, a revolution in the developed countries will immediately supersede so many absurd commodities and concerns that even if supplies of certain goods and services are temporarily reduced, people will still be better off than they are now even in material terms (in addition to being far better off in "spiritual" terms). Once their own immediate problems are taken care of, many of them will enthusiastically assist less fortunate people. But this assistance will be voluntary, and most of it will not entail any serious self-sacrifice. To donate labor or building materials or architectural know-how so that others can build homes for themselves, for example, will not require dismantling one's own home. The potential richness of modern society consists not only of material goods, but of knowledge, ideas, techniques, inventiveness, enthusiasm, compassion, and other qualities that are actually *increased* by being shared around.

A self-managed society will naturally implement most present-day ecological demands. Some are essential for the very survival of humanity; but for both aesthetic and ethical reasons, liberated people will undoubtedly choose to go well beyond this minimum and foster a rich biodiversity.

The point is that we can debate such issues open-mindedly only when we have eliminated the profit incentives and economic insecurity that now undermine even the most minimal efforts to defend the environment (loggers afraid of losing their jobs, chronic poverty tempting Third World countries to cash in on their rain forests, etc.).*

When humanity as a species is blamed for environmental destruction, the specific social causes are forgotten. The few who make the decisions are lumped with the powerless majority. Famines are seen as nature's revenge against overpopulation, natural checks that must be allowed to run their course—as if there was anything natural about the World Bank and the International Monetary Fund, which force Third World countries to cultivate products for export rather than food for local consumption. People are made to feel guilty for using cars, ignoring the fact that auto companies (by buying up and sabotaging electric transit systems, lobbying for highway construction and against railroad subsidies, etc.) have created a situation in which most people have to have cars. Spectacular publicity gravely urges everyone to reduce energy consumption (while constantly inciting everyone to consume more of everything), though we could by now have developed more than enough clean and renewable energy sources if the fossil-fuel companies had not successfully lobbied against devoting any significant research funding to that end.

The point is not to blame even the heads of those companies—they too are caught in a grow-or-die system that impels them to make such decisions—but to abolish the setup that continually produces such irresistible pressures.

A liberated world should have room both for human communities and for large enough regions of undisturbed wilderness to satisfy most of the deep ecologists. Between those two extremes I like to think that there will be all sorts of imaginative, yet careful and respectful, human interactions *with* nature. Cooperating with it, working with it, playing with it; creating variegated interminglings of forests, farms, parks, gardens, orchards, creeks, villages, towns.

Large cities will be broken up, spaced out, "greened," and re-arranged in a variety of ways incorporating and surpassing the visions

---

*Isaac Asimov and Frederick Pohl's *Our Angry Earth: A Ticking Ecological Bomb* (Tor, 1991) is among the more cogent summaries of this desperate situation. After demonstrating how inadequate current policies are for dealing with it, the authors propose some drastic reforms that might postpone the worst catastrophes; but such reforms are unlikely to be implemented as long as the world is dominated by the conflicting interests of nation-states and multinational corporations.

of the most imaginative architects and city planners of the past (who were usually limited by their assumption of the permanence of capitalism). Exceptionally, certain major cities, especially those of some aesthetic or historical interest, will retain or even amplify their cosmopolitan features, providing grand centers where diverse cultures and lifestyles can come together.*

Some people, drawing on the situationists' early "psychogeographical" explorations and "unitary urbanism" ideas, will construct elaborate changeable decors designed to facilitate labyrinthine wanderings among diverse ambiences—Ivan Chtcheglov envisioned "assemblages of castles, grottos, lakes," "rooms more conducive to dreams than any drug," and people living in their own personal "cathedrals" (*SI Anthology*, pp. 3–4). Others may incline more to the Far Eastern poet's definition of happiness as living in a hut beside a mountain stream.

If there aren't enough cathedrals or mountain streams to go around, maybe some compromises will have to be worked out. But if places like Chartres or Yosemite are presently overrun, this is only because the rest of the planet has been so uglified. As other natural areas are revitalized and as human habitats are made more beautiful and interesting, it will no longer be necessary for a few exceptional sites to accommodate millions of people desperate to get away from it all. On the contrary, many people may actually gravitate toward the most miserable regions because these will be the "new frontiers" where the most exciting transformations will be taking place (ugly buildings being demolished to make way for experimental reconstruction from scratch).

The liberation of popular creativity will generate lively communities surpassing Athens, Florence, Paris and other famous centers of the past, in which full participation was limited to privileged minorities. While some people may choose to be relatively solitary and self-sufficient (hermits and nomads will be free to keep to themselves except for a few minimal arrangements with nearby communities), most will probably prefer the pleasure and convenience of doing things together, and will set up all sorts of public workshops, libraries, laboratories, laundries, kitchens, bakeries, cafés, health clinics, studios, music rooms, auditoriums, saunas, gyms, playgrounds, fairs, flea markets (without forgetting some quiet spaces to counterbalance all the socializing). City blocks might be converted into more unified complexes, connecting outer buildings with hallways and arcades and

---

*For a wealth of suggestive insights on the advantages and drawbacks of urban communities, past, present and potential, I recommend two books: Paul and Percival Goodman's *Communitas* and Lewis Mumford's *The City in History*. The latter is one of the most penetrating and comprehensive surveys of human society ever written.

removing fences between back yards so as to create larger interior park, garden or nursery areas. People could choose among various types and degrees of participation, e.g. whether to sign up for a couple days per month of cooking, dishwashing or gardening entitling them to eat at a communal cafeteria, or to grow most of their own food and cook for themselves.

In all these hypothetical examples it's important to bear in mind the diversity of cultures that will develop. In one, cooking might be seen as a tedious chore to be minimized as much as possible and precisely apportioned; in another it might be a passion or a valued social ritual that will attract more than enough enthusiastic volunteers.

Some communities, like Paradigm III in *Communitas* (allowing for the fact that the Goodmans' schema still assumes the existence of money), may maintain a sharp distinction between the free sector and the luxury sector. Others may develop more organically integrated social patterns, along the lines of Paradigm II of the same book, striving for maximum unity of production and consumption, manual and intellectual activity, aesthetic and scientific education, social and psychological harmony, even at the cost of purely quantitative efficiency. The Paradigm III style might be most appropriate as a initial transitional form, when people are not yet used to the new perspectives and want some fixed economic frame of reference to give them a sense of security against potential abuses. As people get the bugs out of the new system and develop more mutual trust, they will probably tend more toward the Paradigm II style.

As in Fourier's charming fantasies, but minus his eccentricities and with much more flexibility, people will be able to engage in a variety of pursuits according to elaborately interrelated affinities. A person might be a regular member of certain ongoing groupings (affinity group, council, collective, neighborhood, town, region) while only temporarily taking part in various ad hoc activities (as people do today in clubs, hobbyist networks, mutual-aid associations, political-issue groups and barnraising-type projects). Local assemblies will keep tallies of offers and requests; make known the decisions of other assemblies and the current state of projects in progress or problems yet unresolved; and form libraries, switchboards and computer networks to gather and disseminate information of all kinds and to link up people with common tastes. Media will be accessible to everyone, enabling them to express their own particular projects, problems, proposals, critiques, enthusiasms, desires, visions. Traditional arts and crafts will continue, but merely as one facet of continuously creative lives. People will still take part, with more zest than ever, in sports and games, fairs and festivals, music and dancing, lovemaking and child raising, building and remodeling, teaching and learning, camping and traveling; but new genres and arts of life will also develop that we can now hardly imagine.

More than enough people will gravitate to socially necessary projects, in agronomy, medicine, engineering, educational innovation, environmental restoration and so on, for no other reason than that they find them interesting and satisfying. Others may prefer less utilitarian pursuits. Some will live fairly quiet domestic lives; others will go in for daring adventures, or live it up in feasts and orgies; yet others may devote themselves to bird-watching, or exchanging zines, or collecting quaint memorabilia from prerevolutionary times, or any of a million other pursuits. Everyone can follow their own inclinations. If some sink into a passive spectator existence, they'll probably eventually get bored and try more creative ventures. Even if they don't, that will be their affair; it won't harm anyone else.

For anyone who finds the earthly utopia too insipid and really wants to get away from it all, the exploration and colonization of the solar system—perhaps eventually even migration to other stars—will provide a frontier that will never be exhausted.

But so will explorations of "inner space."

* * *

An antihierarchical revolution will not solve all our problems; it will simply eliminate some of the anachronistic ones, freeing us to tackle *more interesting problems.*

If the present text seems to neglect the "spiritual" aspects of life, this is because I wanted to stress some basic material matters that are often overlooked. But these material matters are only the framework. A liberated society will be based far more on joy and love and spontaneous generosity than on rigid rules or egoistic calculations. We can probably get a more vivid sense of what it might be like from visionaries like Blake or Whitman than from pedantic debates about economic credits and recallable delegates.

I suspect that once people's basic material needs are generously taken care of and they are no longer subjected to a constant barrage of commercial titillation, most of them (after brief binges of overindulgence in things they were previously deprived of) will find the greatest satisfaction in relatively simple and uncluttered lifestyles. The erotic and gustatory arts will undoubtedly be enriched in many ways, but simply as facets of full, rounded lives that also include a wide range of intellectual, aesthetic and spiritual pursuits.

Education, no longer limited to conditioning young people for a narrow role in an irrational economy, will become an enthusiastic lifelong activity. In addition to whatever formal educational institutions there may still be, people will have instant access via books and computers to information on any subject they wish to explore, and they'll be able to get hands-on experience in all sorts of arts and skills, or to seek out anyone for personal instruction or discussion—like the ancient

Greek philosophers debating in the public marketplace, or the medieval Chinese monks wandering the mountains in search of the most inspiring Zen master.

The aspects of religion that now serve as mere psychological escapes from social alienation will fade away, but the basic questions that have found more or less distorted expression in religion will remain. There will still be pains and losses, tragedies and frustrations, people will still face sickness, old age and death. And in the process of trying to figure out what, if anything, it all means, and how to deal with it, some of them will rediscover what Aldous Huxley, in *The Perennial Philosophy*, refers to as the "highest common factor" of human consciousness.

Others may cultivate exquisite aesthetic sensibilities like the characters in Murasaki's *Tale of Genji*, or develop elaborate metacultural genres like the "glass bead games" in Hermann Hesse's novel (freed from the material limits that formerly confined such pursuits to narrow elites).

I like to think that as these diverse pursuits are alternated, combined and developed, there will be a general tendency toward the personal reintegration envisioned by Blake, and toward the genuine "I–Thou" relations envisioned by Martin Buber. A permanent spiritual revolution in which joyous communion does not preclude rich diversity and "generous contention." *Leaves of Grass*, Whitman's wishful thinking about the potentialities of the America of his day, perhaps comes as close as anything to conveying the expansive state of mind of such communities of fulfilled men and women, ecstatically working and playing, loving and loitering, strolling down the never-ending Open Road.

With the proliferation of continually developing and mutating cultures, travel could once again become an unpredictable adventure. The traveler could "see the cities and learn the ways of many different peoples" without the dangers and disappointments faced by the wanderers and explorers of the past. Drifting from scene to scene, from encounter to encounter; but occasionally stopping, like those barely visible human figures in Chinese landscape paintings, just to gaze into the immensity, realizing that all our doings and sayings are just ripples on the surface of a vast, unfathomable universe.

These are just a few hints. We aren't limited to radical sources of inspiration. All sorts of creative spirits of the past have manifested or envisioned some of our almost unlimited possibilities. We can draw on any of them as long as we take care to extricate the relevant aspects from their original alienated context.

The greatest works do not so much tell us something new as remind us of things we have forgotten. We all have intimations of what life can be like at its richest—memories from early childhood, when experiences were still fresh and unrepressed, but also occasional later moments of love or camaraderie or enthusiastic creativity, times when we can't wait to get up in the morning to continue some project, or simply to see what the new day will bring. Extrapolating from these moments probably gives the best idea of what the whole world could be like. A world, as Whitman envisions it,

> Where the men and women think lightly of the laws,
> Where the slave ceases, and the master of slaves ceases,
> Where the populace rise at once against the never-ending
> audacity of elected persons, . . .
> Where children are taught to be laws to themselves, and to
> depend on themselves,
> Where equanimity is illustrated in affairs,
> Where speculations on the soul are encouraged,
> Where women walk in public processions in the streets the
> same as the men,
> Where they enter the public assembly and take places the
> same as the men . . . .
> The main shapes arise!
> Shapes of Democracy total, result of centuries,
> Shapes ever projecting other shapes,
> Shapes of turbulent manly cities,
> Shapes of the friends and home-givers of the whole earth,
> Shapes bracing the earth and braced with the whole earth.

CONFESSIONS OF A
MILD-MANNERED ENEMY
OF THE STATE

"If the world reproaches me for talking too much about myself, I reproach the world for not even thinking about itself."

—Montaigne

I was born in 1945 in Louisiana, where my mother had gone to be with my father at an army camp. While he was overseas we lived on her parents' farm in Minnesota. When he returned a couple years later, we moved to his home town in the Missouri Ozarks.

Moving at a somewhat slower pace than most of the country, Plainstown still maintained much of that small-town, early-twentieth-century, pre-television American life idealized by Norman Rockwell—the world of porch swings and lazy afternoons, Boy Scouts and vacant-lot baseball, square dances and church picnics, county fairs, summer camps, autumn leaves, white Christmases. That way of life has often been disparaged, but it did have some advantages over the plastic suburban lifestyle that was already beginning to replace it. Despite their naïveté in many regards, the inhabitants of the Show-Me State retained some vestiges of Mark Twainian skepticism and common sense. Even the poorest people often owned their own home or farm. Extended families provided a social cushion if anyone fell on hard times. Things were quiet and safe. A kid could grow up without much awareness of the problems in the outside world.

Yearly visits to the Minnesota farm maintained another link with earlier traditions. I still remember burrowing in the huge hayloft in the old barn; exploring the Victorian house, with its old-fashioned furniture and intriguing things like a clothes chute that ran from the second floor all the way down to the musty basement full of strange curios and contraptions left over from the previous century; or traipsing after my grandfather, a spry old guy still working vigorously in the fields in his late eighties.

My father was one of the last of the old-fashioned family doctors—
the kind who used to deliver successive generations of babies and who
charged $5 for a house call, even if it was in the middle of the night—
or sometimes nothing at all if the family was in difficult circumstances.
Like his father before him, he combined full-time doctoring with part-
time farming; he still does a little of the latter, though he retired from
medical practice a couple years ago. My mother was trained as a
physical therapist, but spent most of her time as a homemaker taking
care of me and my two sisters.

My earliest and best friend was Sam Thomas. He was two years
older and lived just around the corner. We played all the typical games
—baseball, basketball, football, badminton, ping pong, kick the can,
marbles, cards, Monopoly, Scrabble; but what I remember enjoying
most of all were the activities that we created for ourselves—elaborate
constructions with Lincoln Logs or erector sets, deployment of little
metal cowboys and Indians among forts and tunnels in a sandbox,
building our own club house and tree house, putting on shows and car-
nivals for the other kids in the neighborhood.

I also have fond memories of grade school. Although the educational system was not particularly "progressive," it was very flexible
and encouraging for me. Once I had demonstrated that the usual lessons were a breeze, the teachers allowed me, and to a lesser extent a
few of my more intelligent classmates, to skip some of the routine
tasks and pursue independently chosen projects—researching geog-
raphy, history, astronomy or atomic physics in the encyclopedias, com-
piling lists and charts, conducting experiments, constructing science
exhibits.

Outside class I read voraciously—science, history and *Pogo* comics
being my main favorites—and learned some new games: tennis, pool,
chess, and above all, bridge (a fascinating game—I still enjoy reading
books on bridge strategy, though I've rarely played it since I left
home). But here again, I remember with particular fondness the activities my friends and I devised for ourselves. Three of us created a little
imaginary island world with extended families of characters cut out of
foam, about whom we composed elaborate genealogies and stories.
Another friend and I invented a game inspired by our fascination with
the history of exploration. (Politically correct types will have a field day
with this one.) He was England and I was France, each out to explore
and colonize the rest of the world during the sixteenth century. We
would close our eyes and point to a spot on a spinning globe, then
throw three coins: the combination of heads and tails would determine
how far we could travel from that spot (the distance depending on
whether we traveled by sea, river or land) and how much territory we
could claim. I think there were additional rules governing fortifications
and battles in disputed territory. Everything was marked in different
colors on a blank world map. On weekends we would often spend the

90

night together and play all evening (until our parents made us go to bed) and much of the next day until the game came to an end through exhaustion or because the whole map was finally divided up between us.

I also had a lot of fun in Boy Scouts, as well as picking up some useful skills—lifesaving, first aid, crafts, nature lore, camping, canoeing (sublime combination of quietude and graceful motion, silently gliding along a winding stream past ancient weathered bluffs, looking down through the crystal clear water at the fish swimming and the crawdads and other critters scrambling on the gravel bottom). Despite its objectionable patriotic and semi-militaristic aspects, scouting put an exemplary stress on ecological principles and fostered what was for the time an unusual respect for the American Indian. My initiation into the "Order of the Arrow" included an entire day of total silence in the woods, modeled loosely on Indian initiatory practices and not all that different from some Zen practices I later went through.

Looking back, I realize how fortunate I was to have all these experiences. Thanks to caring parents and encouraging teachers, I was able to explore things for myself and learn the delights of independent, self-organized activity. I feel sorry for kids nowadays who get so hooked on television and video games that they never realize how much more fun it is to read or to create your own projects. I enjoyed some of the early TV programs, but we got our first set late enough that I had already had a chance to discover that books were a gateway to far richer and more interesting worlds.

The only sore point in my early memories is religion. Like most people in Plainstown, I had a fairly conservative (though not fundamentalist) Protestant upbringing. As a young child I painlessly absorbed the Sunday school version of Christianity; but as I became older and began to understand what the Bible actually said, I became haunted by the possibility of going to hell. Even if I managed to escape this doom, I was horrified at the idea that anyone, no matter how sinful, might be consigned to torture for all eternity. It was hard to understand how a supposedly loving God could be infinitely more cruel than the most sadistic dictator; but it was difficult to question the Biblical dogma when everyone I knew, including presumably intelligent adults, seemed to accept it. Except for vague mentions of "atheistic Communists" on the other side of the world, I had never heard of anyone seriously professing any other perspective.

One day when I was thirteen, I was browsing through James Newman's anthology *The World of Mathematics* and started reading an autobiographical piece by Bertrand Russell. A little ways into it, I came upon a passage where he mentioned how as a teenager he had become an agnostic upon realizing the fallaciousness of one of the classic arguments for the existence of God. I was stunned. Russell only mentioned this in passing, but the mere discovery that an intelligent person could disbelieve in religion was enough to set me thinking. A couple days later I was on the point of saying my usual bedtime prayers when I thought to myself, "What am I doing? I don't believe this stuff anymore!"

Surrounded by virtually unanimous religious belief (at least as far as I could tell), I didn't dare breathe a word about this for over a year. To all appearances I remained a polite, conventional, churchgoing boy, completing my Eagle Scout requirements and going through all the expected social motions. But all the while, I was quietly observing and reconsidering everything I had formerly taken for granted.

When I went to high school a year later, I met some older students who openly questioned religion. That was all it took to bring me out of the closet. The result was a mild scandal. That the boy whom fond teachers had for years praised as the smartest kid in town had suddenly come forth as an outspoken atheist was a shock to everyone. Students would point at me and whisper that I was doomed to hell; teachers hardly knew how to deal with my wise-ass comments; and my poor parents, at an utter loss to understand how such a thing could have happened, sent me to a psychoanalyst.

Once I had seen the absurdity of Christianity, I began to question other commonly accepted beliefs. It was obvious, for example, that "capitalistic Americanism" was also riddled with absurdities. But I had no interest in politics because the amoral, hedonistic philosophy I had adopted made me dismiss any concern with the general welfare unless it happened to bear on my own interests. I was on principle against any morality, although in practice I did scarcely anything more immoral than being obnoxiously sarcastic. I no longer hesitated to express my contempt for every aspect of conventional life, whether popular culture, social mores, or the content of my high school classes.

My real education was already coming from all the outside reading I was doing, and from discussions with a few friends who were reading some of the same books. Though I still enjoyed science and history, I had since junior high become increasingly interested in literature. Over the next two or three years I went through quite a few classic works —Homer, Greek mythology, *The Golden Ass, Arabian Nights*, Omar Khayyam, *The Decameron*, Chaucer, Rabelais, *Don Quixote, Tom Jones, Tristram Shandy*, Poe, Melville, Dostoyevsky, Tolstoy, Bernard Shaw, Aldous Huxley, Durrell's *Alexandria Quartet*, to mention some of my favorites. Given my limited experience of life, I missed many of the nuances of these works, but they at least gave me some idea of the variety of ways people had lived and thought out in the great world. I was of course particularly drawn to those writers who were most radically unconventional. Nietzsche was a special favorite—I delighted in scandalizing teachers and classmates with quotes from his scathing critiques of Christianity. But my supreme idol was James Joyce. I haven't been especially interested in Joyce in a long time, but when I first discovered him I was awed by all his stylistic innovations and multicultural references, and devoured all his works, even *Finnegans Wake,* as well as numerous books about him. I was also already becoming a bit of a francophile: I found Stendhal and Flaubert more interesting than the Victorian novelists, and was fascinated with Baudelaire and Rimbaud before I ever read much British or American poetry.

I learned about more recent literary rebels from J.R. Wunderle, an older student who had grown up in St. Louis and thus had a little more cosmopolitan savvy than my other friends. I had heard vague rumors about the Beats, but J.R. turned me on to the actual writings of Ginsberg and Kerouac, and even affected a certain bohemianism himself, to the very limited degree that this was possible for a high school student in a very square Midwestern town. A year later he and another guy went out to Venice West (near Los Angeles) and actually lived in the thick of the Beat scene for a while.

I doubt if I would have been ready to handle something like that myself. Except for a few family vacations, I had never been out of the Ozarks, nor held any job apart from a little neighborhood lawn mowing. But I sure did want to get out of Plainstown. The prospect of enduring it for two more years until I finished high school was extremely depressing, especially when I saw several of my older friends already going off to college.

A lucky solution turned up. A high school counselor, to whom I will be forever grateful, came across a catalog for Shimer College, a small experimental liberal arts college that accepted exceptional students before they had graduated from high school, and immediately thought of me. It seemed ideal. I would be able to get out of Plainstown and into an intellectually interesting scene without being abruptly thrown on my own; my teachers were no doubt relieved to get me out of their hair; and my parents rightly saw this as the best chance to resolve a situation they had no idea of how to deal with.

I entered Shimer in fall 1961, and I loved it. Located in a small town in northwestern Illinois, Shimer carried on the great books discussion program developed at the University of Chicago in the thirties by Robert Hutchins and Mortimer Adler. The total student body was around three hundred. Average class size was ten. There were no textbooks and virtually no lectures. Factual knowledge was not neglected, but the emphasis was on learning how to think, to question, to test and articulate ideas by participating in round-table discussions of seminal classic texts. The teacher's role was simply to facilitate the discussion with pertinent questions. Unorthodox viewpoints were welcome—but you had to defend them competently; unfounded opinion was not enough.

Shimer was not socially radical, nor was it particularly freeform in ways that some other experimental schools have been before and since. The administration was fairly conventional and the regulations were fairly conservative. The curriculum was Eurocentric and tended perhaps to overemphasize works of systematic philosophical discourse such as those Adler-Hutchins favorites, Aristotle and Aquinas. (Someone quipped that Hutchins's University of Chicago was "a Baptist university where Jewish professors teach Catholic philosophy to atheist students.")

But whatever the flaws of the Shimer system, it was a pretty coherent one. Three out of the four years were taken up with an intricately interrelated course sequence that everyone was required to take, covering humanities, social sciences, natural sciences, history and philosophy, leaving room for only a few electives. (With this basic grounding, most students had little trouble catching up on their eventual subject of specialization in grad school.) Moreover, in contrast to conservative advocates of classical curricula, Adler and Hutchins did not envision their program as destined only for an elite minority: they insisted that the basic issues dealt with in the great books could and should be grappled with by everyone as the foundation of a lifelong education. If they were rather naïve in accepting Western "democratic society" on its own terms, they at least challenged that society to live up to its own pretensions, pointing out that if it was to work it required a citizenry capable of participating in it knowledgeably and critically, and that what presently passes for education does not begin to accomplish this.

While these courses were pretty interesting, I actually learned a lot more from some of my fellow students. My roommate, Michael Beardsley, had a somewhat similar background—he came from a small town in Texas and like me had skipped the last two years of high school. But most of my new friends were Chicago Jews, with a radical, skeptical, humanistic, cosmopolitan culture that was refreshingly new to me. There were also some more apolitical characters, one of the most memorable being a plump, goateed chess prodigy and classical music connoisseur with the manner of an Oriental potentate, who successfully ran for student government with the single campaign promise that if he was elected, it would be gratifying for his ego! There were a few ordinary fraternity/sorority types, but they were definitely in the minority, and even they, like all the rest of us, took a perverse pride in the fact that in its one intercollegiate sport, basketball, Shimer held the national record for number of consecutive losses.

At Shimer, and during breaks in Chicago, my new friends introduced me to booze, jazz, folk and classical music, foreign films, ethnic cuisines, leftist politics, and a lively interracial scene. Although Plainstown was not flagrantly racist like the deep South, it was de facto segregated by neighborhoods, so I had scarcely so much as met a black person there. Shimer itself had only a few blacks, but at my friends' parties in Chicago I met lots of them. It was the heyday of the early civil rights movement and there was a warm, genuine, enthusiastic camaraderie, unlike the uneasy interracial suspicion that was to develop in radical circles a few years later. Though I was still apolitical on principle, I was beginning to discard my stilted amoralism; my new friends and surroundings were helping me to loosen up, to become more human and more humanistic.

Another big influence in this direction was the folk music revival, which was just getting under way. The simplicity and directness of folk music was a refreshing contrast to the inane pop music of the time. Joan Baez's first album was the most popular one on campus; but some of my friends had grown up on Woody Guthrie and Pete Seeger and had already developed more puristic tastes, and they turned me on to earlier, earthier and even more exciting artists—above all the great Leadbelly. I was also inspired by the first folksinger I ever saw in person, Ramblin' Jack Elliott, a performer in the Guthrie tradition who traveled around the country in an old pickup. I wanted nothing better than to play guitar like that. Moreover, such an aspiration was not totally unrealistic. Folk music lent itself to participation—you could easily sing along with it and almost as easily learn to play it, at least at a simple level. Many of my friends were already doing so. I started to learn guitar, and also eventually learned to fiddle some simple tunes.

That winter, after a few amorous relations that had never got beyond the heavy petting stage, I finally found a young woman who said yes. The blessed event took place in the Folklore Society office, which happened to have a convenient couch. (Finding a place for lovemaking was a perennial problem at Shimer until dorm regulations were liberalized several years later. In spring and fall we resorted to the campus golf course, which was never used for anything else, or to the nearby town cemetery; but during winter it was too cold, and all sorts of precarious alternatives were attempted.)

A few weeks later I also lost what you might call my spiritual virginity. This was just 1962 and, outside of a few marginal urban scenes, drugs were still practically unknown. Very few college students had even tried marijuana. As for psychedelics, scarcely anyone had so much as heard of them. They weren't even illegal yet. Mike Beardsley and I ordered a large box of peyote buttons from the Smith Cactus Ranch in Texas, which were duly delivered without the postal service or the school authorities taking the slightest notice. A few days later, without much idea of what we were in for, we ingested some of them.

For an hour or so we endured the peyote nausea, then, as that faded, we began feeling something strange and extremely unsettling happening. At first I thought I was going insane. Finally I managed to relax and settle into it. We spent most of the day in our room, lying

95

down with our eyes closed, watching the shifting patterns evoked by different kinds of music—most unforgettably Prokofiev's first three piano concertos, which we savored for their unique combination of classical lucidity, romantic extravagance and zany trippiness. Everything was fresh, like returning to early childhood or waking up in the Garden of Eden; as if things were suddenly in 3-D color that we had previously seen only in flat black and white. But what really made the experience so overwhelming was not the sensory effects, but the way the whole sense of "self" was shaken. We were not just looking on from outside; we ourselves were part of this vibrant, pulsating world.

With visions of Rimbaud and Kerouac dancing in our heads, we neglected our classes and began dreaming of quitting school and heading out on our own to explore the great world. That spring we both did so. Mike and his girlfriend Nancy went to Berkeley, where she had some friends. I decided to check out Venice West since J.R.'s friend was still out there.

Venice was full of Beat poets, abstract expressionist painters, jazz musicians, sexual nonconformists, junkies, bums, hustlers, petty crooks —and lots of undercover cops. Very exciting, but also very paranoid; far from the relaxed openness and joyousness of the later hippie scene. Without the hippies' economic cushion of easy panhandling, it was also much more down and out. Never knowing where my next meal was coming from or where I might end up spending the night, I scraped by one way and another. . . .

Eventually I was busted for petty theft. Since I was a minor and it was my first offense, I was only in for three days before being shipped back to the custody of my parents in Plainstown.

That, fortunately, has been my only experience of prison. Being confined is bad enough, but what makes it really nauseating is the mean, sick, inhuman ambience. As a white middle-class kid, I was of course just screwing around and was always free to return to more comfortable circumstances; but I never forget those who haven't been so lucky. Thinking of people being locked in there for years makes me angrier than just about anything.

For the next few months I lived with my parents, working at a local bookstore and doing a lot of reading—Blake, Thoreau, Lautréamont, Breton, Céline, Hesse, D.T. Suzuki, Alan Watts, and above all Henry Miller, by then my favorite author. After decades of censorship his two *Tropic* books had just become available in America, and they hit me like a bombshell. Here, I thought, is a real person, talking about real life, beyond all the artifices of literature. I no longer take Miller seriously as a thinker, but I still love the humor and gusto of his autobiographical novels.

Another healthy and even more enduring influence was Gary

Snyder. I already knew about him as "Japhy Ryder," the hero of Kerouac's *The Dharma Bums.* It's a wonderful book, but certain aspects of Snyder were utterly beyond Kerouac's comprehension. Snyder's own writings were more lucid and his life was more inspiring. I had been intrigued by what I had read about Zen Buddhism, but here was someone who had actually studied Oriental languages and gone to Japan for years of rigorous Zen training. I couldn't have been farther from that sort of self-discipline, but I started reading more books on Zen, with the idea that I'd like to explore it in practice if I got a chance.

In addition to Snyder's poetry, I was also struck by his essay "Buddhist Anarchism" (later reprinted in *Earth House Hold* under the title "Buddhism and the Coming Revolution"). Despite my sympathy for civil rights and other dissident causes espoused by some of my Shimer friends, I had until then remained apolitical on principle, feeling (like Henry Miller) that all politics was superficial bullshit and that if any fundamental change was to come about it would have to be through some sort of "revolution of the heart." Instinctively detesting what Rexroth calls the Social Lie, I could never get very excited about the goal of enabling people to have a "normal life" when present-day normal life was precisely what I had despised since I was 13. Snyder's essay did not alter this view, but it showed me how a radical social perspective could be related to spiritual insight. I still didn't pay much attention to political matters, but the way was opened for eventual social engagement when I later confronted issues that seemed meaningful to me.

By January 1963 I had accumulated enough bookstore earnings (supplemented by some winnings from a local poker game) to quit my job and begin venturing out of town again. To begin with, I hitched up to see J.R., now back in St. Louis, hanging out in a biker scene and working, of all things, as an attendant in a state mental hospital. J.R. himself, if not exactly insane, was always a pretty eccentric character. In later years he successively adopted so many intentionally outrageous personas, from W.C. Fieldsian con man to old-time frontiersman to cantankerous reactionary, that I'm not sure even he himself always distinguished the irony from the reality. He died a few years ago of cirrhosis of the liver at the age of 46.

Then I made a second California trip, this time with Sam Thomas. I hadn't seen Sam much since childhood days—we had gone to different schools, and he had remained a rather conventional, popular, outgoing guy while I was already in fervent intellectual revolt. But he got hip once he went to college; by the time I saw him again he had discovered jazz, grown a beard and started writing freeform poetry. During his semester break we picked up a driveaway car from a Missouri dealer, drove to Berkeley, then down to Los Angeles, where we looked up my Venice West buddies and delivered the car, and bussed back to Missouri, all in the space of ten days.

Next, I went down to Texas, where Mike and Nancy Beardsley had moved while she had their baby. This whole period still remains magical for me, though I can dimly recall only a few of our ventures—hopping on a moving freight train just to see what it felt like; trying the poisonous witch drug, belladonna, and finding ourselves in a psychotic nightmare world. . . . Even if some of our escapades were pretty foolish, we were exploring things for ourselves; there were as yet no media-propagated models to imitate. Isolated in Mid-America, occasionally encountering some kindred spirit with whom we would passionately share this or that discovery or aspiration or premonition, groping for the sort of perspective that took shape a few years later in the hip counterculture, we sensed that something new was in the air, but the only thing we knew for certain was that the world in which we found ourselves was fundamentally absurd. That world itself was still utterly oblivious to what was brewing. (Bear in mind that most of the things "the sixties" are known for didn't really get under way, or at least come to public notice, until around 1965–66.)

That spring we all moved to Chicago and got an apartment together in Hyde Park. When I wasn't working at odd jobs (first in a warehouse, then, rather more congenially, in a folk music store) I babysat their baby while they worked, and hung out with a few other old Shimer friends. I also discovered a small Zen center and got my first taste of formal meditation.

This experience, plus the fact that I was getting tired of the hassles of poverty, got me in the mood to get my life organized and move on to other things. As a first step, I decided to go back and finish up my Shimer degree, with the tentative idea (Snyder's example in mind) of going on to Oriental studies in grad school, and then conceivably even going to Japan for Zen monastic training.

Back at Shimer I had two main extracurricular activities. One was making love with my beautiful girlfriend Aili. The other was folk music. Several friends and I played every chance we got, modeling our styles on the oldest and most "authentic" recordings—Appalachian ballads and fiddle tunes, old-timey string bands (Charlie Poole, Gid Tanner, Clarence Ashley, the Carolina Tar Heels), field hollers, jug bands, country blues (Blind Lemon Jefferson, Sleepy John Estes, Charley Patton, Son House, Robert Johnson).

The golden age was the 1920s, when locally popular musicians all over the country were more or less indiscriminately recorded by small commercial companies searching for potential hit material. There was an immense variety of styles—those in one region were often quite different from those in the neighboring state or even county. In the 1930s the Depression wiped out the regional rural markets just as recordings and radio were leading to increasing homogenization, with local performers being influenced by new nationwide stars like Jimmie Rodgers, the Carter Family and the first bluegrass and country-western groups (or analogously in black music, by more citified blues and jazz).

I enjoyed some of the Rodgers and Carter Family songs, but that's about as modern as my tastes ever got. The slickness of bluegrass (to say nothing of the sappiness of country-western) left me cold; it had lost the haunting quality I loved in the old mountain ballads and tunes. For really vintage music, my friends and I turned to reissues of the 1920s recordings, to the field recordings made for the Library of Congress in the 1930s, and to live performances by the few surviving old-time greats who had been rediscovered and brought to play before entranced urban audiences. For purists like ourselves, the annual University of Chicago Folk Festival was the best in the country. I still remember the after-concert parties at my friends' apartments—hundreds of people playing in every room and overflowing into the stairwells from midnight till dawn, then, after a few hours of sleep, excitedly returning to the campus for the next day's concerts and workshops. Considering its far smaller size, Shimer didn't do so badly either: during my two years as president of the Folklore Society, I managed to arrange concerts by Dock Boggs, Son House, Sleepy John Estes and Big Joe Williams, as well as the granddaddy of modern old-timey groups, the New Lost City Ramblers, whose yearly appearances had become a Shimer tradition. J.R. and I also made a sort of field trip of our own, hitching from St. Louis to Memphis to record Gus Cannon and Will Shade, the last surviving members of the great jug bands of the twenties.

I think most real education is self-education, and I have a very low opinion of most educational institutions. But I do want to say that, far from interfering with my education as most schools would have, Shimer actually fostered it in many ways. One of my senior-year courses introduced me to two of my biggest influences. We were examining a number of different philosophies of life (Kierkegaard, Buber, Camus, etc.). For me, Buber's *I and Thou* stood out from all the other readings. Martin Buber was a real man of wisdom, one of the few Western religious thinkers I can stomach. During one of our discussions a classmate pulled out a copy of Kenneth Rexroth's *Bird in the Bush* and read some passages from his essay on Buber. I immediately borrowed it, devoured it, and was never quite the same again.

When I graduated from Shimer (1965) there was no question about where I would go next. Everything I had heard about the Bay Area sounded great, from the San Francisco poetry renaissance of the fifties to the recent Free Speech Movement at the University of California in Berkeley. Adding to the appeal, Sam Thomas (now with a wife and baby) had already moved there to do graduate study in poetry. One of his teachers had been none other than Gary Snyder, just back from several years of Zen study in Japan; and that fall he would be taking a class from—Kenneth Rexroth! After working that summer at a steel mill in East Chicago, I moved to Berkeley. I've lived here ever since.

It was a wonderful time to arrive. You could still feel the invigorating reverberations from the FSM; there were lively, ongoing conversations on campus, on street corners, in cafés, everywhere you went—and not just among hippies and radicals; ordinary liberals and even young conservatives were vividly aware that everything was being called into question and were drawn into debates about every aspect of life.

Over the next year, I took graduate classes at the small and now defunct American Academy of Asian Studies in San Francisco. Apart from that, I spent most of the time tripping around with Sam. Through him, I got in on the lively Bay Area poetry scene, meeting lots of other young poets and going to scads of readings by some of the most vital figures of the previous generation—Rexroth, Snyder, William Everson, Robert Duncan, Lawrence Ferlinghetti, Allen Ginsberg, Philip Whalen, Lew Welch. Though I never wrote much poetry myself, I was immersed in it. Sam and I would read Whitman or Patchen or William Carlos Williams aloud, sometimes with jazz background, or improvise chain poems with each other while driving over the Bay Bridge to San Francisco, where I tagged along with him to Lew Welch's night-school poetry class and to the open-ended discussion "class" given by Rexroth at SF State.

Much as I liked Rexroth, I was at first more excited by Welch. He was a lot younger, more like a peer, sharing our zany sense of humor and youthful enthusiasms for psychedelics and the new rock music. What I remember most was his stress on finding the right word. Feeling that poets had a shamanic vocation to express the crucial realities in the most incisive way, he always denounced any "cheating" in a poem, any sloppy, sentimental, "inaccurate" phrasing.

Rexroth, though also sympathetic to our enthusiasms, was more detached and ironic about them. He pooh-poohed psychedelics, for example. At first I thought this was because he didn't know what he was talking about; but after reading some of his mystical poems I realized that he knew these experiences deeply, whether or not he had used any chemical means to arrive at them. Little by little I came to appreciate his subtle, low-key wisdom and magnanimity.

During my first couple years in Berkeley I took around a dozen psychedelic trips with Sam and other friends. Usually three or four of us would get together in some quiet place where we would not be disturbed, preferably with an experienced nonparticipant on hand who could take care of any necessary errands. Most often we simply listened to music, letting the opening of an Indian raga take us back to the timeless beginning of the universe, or feeling the notes of a Bach harpsichord partita pour through us like a shower of jewels. Sometimes we got into a humor zone in which a sense of universal sacredness was inseparable from a sense of the fundamental zaniness of everything— our cheeks would still be sore the next day from the multiple orgasms of laughter. Sometimes we went out into the woods: I remember two especially lovely psilocybin trips in a tiny cabin in a nearby canyon—in the afterglow I almost felt like founding a nature religion. I found psychedelics overwhelming enough without adding the noise and confusion of large crowds, but I made an exception for a rare Berkeley appearance of Bob Dylan. On another occasion, Sam and I took some acid and went to one of the first major marches against the Vietnam war (October 1965). We knew, of course, that this would hardly be an ideal environment for a calm trip, but we thought that it might be interesting to see how the two realms would go together. (Not that badly. Some of the straight politicos' speechmaking seemed rather jarring, but I enjoyed the general sense of engaged community.)

In fall of 1966 I quit school. There were too many more exciting things going on. The underground hip counterculture, which had just begun to surface a year or so before, was now spreading like wildfire. Haight-Ashbury was overflowing into the streets in virtually a nonstop party. Tens of thousands of young people were coming out to see what was happening, including dozens of my friends from Shimer, Chicago and Missouri.

My little cottage (two 10′ × 10′ rooms plus kitchen and bath for $35 a month) served as a halfway house, sometimes accommodating as many as seven or eight people at once. Now that I'm so used to quietly living alone, it's hard to imagine how I put up with it. But we were all young, sharing many of the same enthusiasms, and when we weren't out at concerts, or cavorting around Telegraph Avenue or Haight-Ashbury or Chinatown or Golden Gate Park, or off camping somewhere, we happily hung around the house reading, rapping, jamming, listening to records and scarfing the delicious homemade bread we baked fresh every day, without minding too much that we hardly had room enough to put down our sleeping bags. And of course being turned on most of the time helped keep everything mellow.

My parents had supported me while I was in school, but after I dropped out I was back on my own. Like so many others during the sixties, I got by quite well on practically nothing, getting food stamps, sharing cheap rent among several people, selling underground papers, picking up very occasional odd jobs. Within a few minutes I could hitch a ride anywhere in Berkeley or across the bay to San Francisco, and often get turned on to boot. If necessary, I could easily panhandle the price of a meal or a concert ticket.

After half a year of this pleasant but somewhat precarious lifestyle, I got a job as a mail carrier, worked six months, then quit and lived on my savings for the next couple years. Just as that was about to run out, I discovered a weekly poker game, and the $100 or so per month which this netted me, supplemented by driving one day a week for a hippie taxi co-op, enabled me to get by for the next few years.

If the heart of the counterculture was psychedelics, its most visible, or rather audible, manifestation was of course the new rock music. When the increasingly sophisticated music of the Beatles and other groups converged with the increasingly sophisticated lyrics of Bob Dylan, who was bringing folk music beyond corny protest songs and rigid attachment to traditional forms, we finally had a popular music that we could relate to, which served as our own folk music. As Dylan, the Beatles and the Rolling Stones were becoming more openly psychedelic, the first *totally* psychedelic bands were taking shape in the Bay Area. Long before they made any records, we could see the Grateful Dead, Country Joe & the Fish, Big Brother & the Holding Company and dozens of other exciting groups almost any day we wanted at the Fillmore or the Avalon or free in the parks.

When they did get around to recording, none of their records came close to conveying what they were like live, as an integral part of a flourishing counterculture. Those early concerts, Trips Festivals, Acid Tests and Be-Ins, corny as such terms may now sound, included lots of improvisation and interaction, off stage as well as on. The music and light shows were clearly subordinate to the tripping within the "audience," less a spectacle than an accompaniment to ecstatic celebration. If there were a few famous people on stage—Leary, Ginsberg, Kesey—they were not inaccessible stars; we knew they were as tripped out as the rest of us, fellow travelers on a journey whose destination none of us could predict, but which was *already* fantastic.

And those large public gatherings were only the tip of the iceberg. The most significant experiences were personal and interpersonal. There was considerably more intellectual substance to the counterculture than appeared to superficial observers. While there were indeed lots of stereotypically naïve and passive flower children (particularly among the second wave of teenagers, who adopted the trappings of an already existing hip lifestyle without ever having to have gone through any independent ventures), many hip people had broader experiences and more critical sense, and were engaged in a variety of creative and radical pursuits.

Some people may be surprised at the contrast between the scathing critiques I made of the counterculture in some of my previous writings and the more favorable picture presented here. It's the context that has changed, not my views. In the early seventies, when everyone was still quite aware of the counterculture's radical aspects, I felt it was necessary to challenge its complacency, to point out its limits and illusions. Now that the radical aspects have been practically forgotten, it seems equally important to recall just how wild and liberating it was. Alongside all the spectacular hype, millions of people were making drastic changes in their own lives, carrying out daring and outrageous experiments they could hardly have dreamed of a few years before.

I don't deny that the counterculture contained a lot of passivity and foolishness. I only want to stress that we were aiming at—and to some extent already experiencing—a fundamental transformation of all aspects of life. We knew how profoundly psychedelics had altered our own outlook. In the early sixties, only a few thousand people had had the experience; five years later the number was over a million. Who was to say that this trend would not continue and finally undermine the whole system?

While it lasted it was remarkably trusting and good-natured. I'd think nothing of hitching with anyone, offering total strangers a joint, or inviting them over to crash at my place if they were new in town. This trust was almost never abused. True, Haight-Ashbury itself didn't last very long. (The turning point was around 1967, when the "Summer of Love" publicity brought a huge influx of less experienced teenagers who were more susceptible to exploitation by the parallel influx of ripoff artists and hard-drug dealers.) But elsewhere the counterculture continued to flourish and spread for several more years.

Personally, I was interested in "mind-expanding" experiences; mere mind-numbing escapist kicks had little appeal for me, and most of the people I hung out with felt the same way. Apart from an occasional beer, we scarcely even drank alcohol—we had a hard time imagining how anyone, unless extremely repressed, could prefer the crude and often obnoxious effects of booze to the benign aesthetic effects of grass. As for hard drugs, we scarcely ever heard of them—with the one notable exception of speed (amphetamine). In moderate doses, speed isn't much different than drinking a lot of coffee, and most of us had occasionally used it to stay up all night to write a school paper or to drive across the country. But it doesn't take much to become dangerous. It ended up killing Sam.

In 1966 he had begun taking a lot of speed, and by 1967 he was becoming increasingly manic and paranoid. This paranoia found expression in his discovery of the Hollow Earth cult, which holds that the inside of the earth is inhabited by some sort of mysterious beings and that (as in the rather similar flying saucer cults) the powers that be are keeping this information secret from the general public. At any mention, say, of the word "underground" Sam would give a sly, knowing nod; in fact, just about anything, whether a line in a poem or a phrase in an advertising jingle, could, with appropriate wordplay, be interpreted as a hint that the author was among those in the know about the Hollow Earth.

One of the most painful experiences of my life was seeing my best friend slowly become more and more insane without any of my attempts to reason with him having the slightest effect. One time he slipped out of the house naked in the middle of the night, and his wife and I ran around the neighborhood for hours before we found him. Another time he was found hitching down the highway so out of it that the Highway Patrol took him to the state mental hospital at Napa. Eventually his wife took him back to Missouri.

Over the next couple years his condition varied considerably. Sometimes his general exuberance and good humor made people think that perhaps his verbal ramblings were not really meant seriously, but were just playful poetic improvisations. At other times he slipped into severe depressions and was hospitalized. When I last saw him, he was calm but pretty wasted looking (probably on tranquilizers); he didn't seem like the Sam I had known since earliest childhood. A couple weeks later I got a call informing me that he had hung himself. He had just turned 27.

Rexroth often remarked that an astonishingly high proportion of twentieth-century American poets have committed suicide. The presumption is that their creative efforts led them to become unbearably sensitive to the ugliness of the society, as well as laying them open to extremes of frustration and disillusionment in their personal life. The fact remains that the Rimbaudian notion of seeking visions through the "systematic derangement of all the senses" has often inspired behavior that is simply foolish and self-destructive. Whatever social or personal factors may have contributed to Sam's insanity, the immediate cause was certainly all the speed he was taking.

Psychedelics may also have been a factor, but I doubt if they were a significant one. Despite a few widely publicized and usually exaggerated instances of people going insane during trips, millions of people took psychedelics during the sixties without suffering the slightest harm. To put things into perspective, the total number of deaths attributable to psychedelics during the entire *decade* was far smaller than those due to alcohol or tobacco on any single *day*. In some cases psychedelics may have brought latent mental problems into the open, but even this was probably more often for the better than for the worse. I suspect that far more people were *saved* from going insane by psychedelics, insofar as the experience loosened them up, opened them up to wider perspectives, made them aware of other possibilities besides blind acceptance of the insane values of the conventional world.

I certainly feel that psychedelics were beneficial for me. I had one truly hellish trip (on DMT), but just about all the others were wonderful, among the most cherished experiences of my life. If I stopped taking them in 1967, it was because I came to realize that they are erratic and that the salutary effects don't last. They just give you a glimpse, a hint of what's there. This is why so many of us eventually went on to Oriental meditational practices, in order to explore such experiences more systematically and try to learn how to integrate them more enduringly into our everyday life.

The practice that continued to appeal to me was Zen Buddhism. I had already discovered the San Francisco Zen Center and occasionally went over there to do zazen or listen to talks by the genial little Zen master, Shunryu Suzuki. When a small branch center opened up in Berkeley in 1967, I started going a little more regularly. But I didn't keep it up—partly because I had some reservations about the traditional religious forms, but mostly because it required getting up at four o'clock in the morning, which was hard to fit in with the lifestyle I was leading at the time. I was into so many different, overlapping trips that it's difficult to narrate them chronologically.

One of the most enthusiastic ones was film. At some point in early 1968 the wonder of the whole medium suddenly hit me and I went through a period of total fascination with it. Over the next couple years I saw close to a thousand films—practically every one of any interest that showed in the Bay Area, including eight or ten a week at the Telegraph Repertory Cinema (I convinced them to let me in free in exchange for distributing their calendars, and would often return for second or third viewings of those I especially liked). Stan Brakhage's experimental films inspired me to play around with an 8mm camera; but mostly I was simply an ecstatic spectator. My favorites were the early European classics—Carl Dreyer, the German and Russian silents, the French films of the thirties (Pagnol, Vigo, Renoir, Carné)—along with a few postwar Japanese films. Apart from the early comics (Chaplin, Keaton, Fields, the Marx Brothers, Laurel & Hardy), who more than made up for their corniness with the sublime moments of poetic hilarity they sometimes achieved, I never cared for most American films. Hollywood has always vulgarized everything it touches, regardless of the quality of the actors and directors or the literary works on which its films are supposedly based; but until its influence came to dominate the whole planet, some of the foreign film industries allowed at least a few creative efforts to slip through.

Eventually, after having seen most of the classics, as well as a pretty wide sampling of modern styles, I got burned out. I've seen very few post-1970 films, and I'm almost invariably disappointed when I do. Practically all of them, including reputedly sophisticated masterpieces, are all to obviously designed for audiences of emotionally disturbed illiterates. About the only recent filmmaker I've found of slightly more than routine interest is Alain Tanner. No doubt there are a few other works of some merit out there, but you have to wade through too much garbage to find them. I'd rather read a good book any day.

The most interesting ones I was reading at the time were by Rexroth or by other authors he had turned me on to. I had liked him very much on first reading him and then meeting him; but it was only gradually, as I myself matured (somewhat) over the next few years, that I really came to appreciate him, to the point that he came to be my dominant influence, eclipsing earlier hero-mentors like Miller, Watts, Ginsberg, Welch, and finally even Buber and Snyder.

At once mystical and radical, earthy and urbane, Rexroth had a breadth of vision I've never seen in anyone else before or since. Oriental philosophy, Amerindian songs, Chinese opera, medieval theology, avant-garde art, classical languages, underground slang, tantric yoga, utopian communities, natural history, jazz, science, architecture, mountaineering—he seemed to know lots of interesting things about just about everything and how it all fit together. Following up his hints for further reading (above all in those incredibly pithy little *Classics Revisited* essays) was a liberal education in itself. Besides giving me illuminating new takes on Homer, Lao Tze, Blake, Baudelaire, Lawrence and Miller, he turned me on to a variety of other gems I might otherwise never have discovered—the modest, meditative journal of the antislavery Quaker John Woolman; the immodest but engrossing autobiography of Restif de la Bretonne (a sort of ultrasentimental eighteenth-century Henry Miller); the subtle magnanimity of Ford Madox Ford's *Parade's End;* the hard-boiled down-and-out narrative of B. Traven's *The Death Ship;* the delightful Finnish folk-epic, *The Kalevala* (get the literal Magoun translation); Finley Peter Dunne's "Mr. Dooley" (a turn-of-the-century Chicago Irish bartender whose monologues are as worldly-wise as Mark Twain, and to my taste even funnier). . . .

I reread two of his essays so often I practically knew them by heart. "The Hasidism of Martin Buber," by presenting a mysticism whose ultimate expression is in dialogue and communion, challenged those countercultural tendencies that saw mysticism primarily in terms of individual experience while tending to play down the social and ethical aspects of life.

"The Chinese Classic Novel in Translation" introduced me to Rexroth's notion of magnanimity, which I consider the central theme of his work. The notion goes back to Aristotle's ideal of the "great-souled" man (the literal sense of the term), but Rexroth enrichens it by linking it with the traditional Chinese ideal of the "human-hearted" sage. His contrasting of magnanimity with various forms of self-indulgence was a revelation to me. It deflated a whole range of self-consciously "profound," wearing-their-soul-on-their-sleeve writers who were fashionable at the time—Kierkegaard, Dostoyevsky, Nietzsche, Proust, Joyce, Pound, the surrealists, the existentialists, the Beats. . . . The list could go on and on: once you grasp Rexroth's perspective it's hard to find any modern writer whose self-indulgence doesn't stick out like a sore thumb.

As always in Rexroth, what might seem to be a mere aesthetic discussion is actually a way of talking about basic approaches to life. That magnanimity/self-indulgence distinction became one of my main touchstones from then on. An autobiographer can hardly claim not to be self-indulgent; but if you think I'm self-indulgent now, imagine what I would have been without Rexroth's tempering influence!

After dropping out of school and losing my student deferment, I avoided the draft for the next couple years on the basis of a letter from the psychoanalyst my parents had sent me to, which stated that I would not make good army material due to my extreme "resentment of authority." By the late sixties, however, the army was getting desperate for more bodies to send to Vietnam and that sort of excuse no longer cut it. When I was called in to the Oakland induction center, the examining psychologist scarcely glanced at the letter, then to my horror checked me off as fit for military service.

I had no intention of going into the army, but I didn't relish the idea of going to jail or going through all the conscientious-objector hassles. Probably I would have gone to Canada if necessary; but I was really annoyed at the idea of having to drop everything and leave the Bay Area. I vowed not to leave the building before I had settled the matter once and for all.

I considered hurling a chair through a window, but concluded that that might be a little too extreme (I didn't want to end up in a strait-jacket). Instead, I decided to concentrate on the psychologist who had passed me. Gearing up for the most crucial acting role of my life, I went back and barged into his office, where he was interviewing another guy, and started screaming at him: "You dumb jerk you think you understand me listen when I get in the army just wait till I get a gun in my hand you think I won't shoot the first fucking officer who gives me an order ha ha and when I do I'd like to see your face when your bosses ask you why you passed me ha ha . . ." (all this was accentuated with infantile grimaces and twitches and shrieks, so I looked and sounded like a kid having a tantrum). Then I slammed the door and sat down outside his office.

When he came out I silently followed him down the hall, determined to stick with him no matter what. He went into another room and soon emerged with an officer, who came over to me and said, "What's the idea of threatening Dr. So-and-So?" I went off on another tirade. The officer told me to come into his office. After a few more minutes of my ranting, he said that he was rejecting me for the army. But he couldn't just let it go at that, he had to save face: "Now, that's probably just what you want to hear. But let me tell you this. I've seen a lot of guys in this business. Some of them were conscientious objectors. I didn't agree with them, but I could respect them. But you! Judging from your disgusting violent behavior we haven't come very far since the cave men! You're not good enough for the army!"

Resisting the impulse to grin, I just sat there glowering at him and gripping the edge of the desk as if I might go into a spasm at any moment, while he filled out and signed the form. I took it without a word, stomped out the door, delivered the form to the appropriate desk, walked out of the building, rounded the corner . . . and went skipping down the street!

Although I had showed up at a few civil rights and antiwar demonstrations during my first couple years in Berkeley, it wasn't until late 1967 that the intensification of the Vietnam war led me to become seriously involved in New Left politics. My first step was joining the newly formed Peace and Freedom Party, which tentatively proposed a Martin Luther King–Benjamin Spock presidential ticket for the following year. Most of the PFP's hundred thousand California members were probably no more politically knowledgeable than I, but had simply registered in it in order to make sure that some antiwar choice was on the ballot. But though the PFP was primarily an electoral party, it did make some effort to get people to participate beyond merely voting. I went to several neighborhood meetings and attended all three days of its March 1968 convention.

There was a lot of good will and enthusiasm among the delegates, but it was also my first experience of witnessing political maneuvers from close up. Totally open and eclectic, the PFP naturally attracted most of the leftist organizations, each jockeying to promote their own lines and candidates. Some of the politicos seemed rather obnoxious, but in general I admired those who had taken part in civil rights struggles or the FSM, and was quite willing to defer to their more experienced and presumably more knowledgeable views. While I might claim to have been an early and fairly independent participant in the counterculture, in the political movement I was nothing but a belated run-of-the-mill follower.

As I became more "active" in the PFP (though never more than in banal subordinate capacities: attending rallies, stuffing envelopes, handing out leaflets) I was progressively "radicalized" by the more experienced politicos, especially the Black Panthers. Looking back, it's embarrassing to realize how easily I was duped by such crude manipulation, in which a handful of individuals appointed themselves the sole authentic representatives of "the black community," then claimed the right to veto power, and in practice to virtual domination, over the PFP and any other groups with which they condescended to form "coalitions." But they were obviously courageous, and unlike the black separatist tendencies they were at least willing to work with whites; so most of us naïvely swallowed the old con: "They're black, and are being jailed, beaten and killed; since we are none of the above, we have no right to criticize them." Practically no one, not even supposedly antiauthoritarian groups like the Diggers, the Motherfuckers and the Yippies, raised any serious objections to this racist double standard, which among other things amounted to relegating all other blacks to the choice of supporting their self-appointed "supreme servants" or being intimidated into silence.

Meanwhile the healthy participatory-democracy tendencies of the early New Left were being smothered by browbeating, spectacularization and ideological delirium. Calls for terrorism and "picking up the gun" were echoed in much of the underground press. Activists who who disdained "theoretical nitpicking" were caught unprepared when SDS was taken over by asinine sects debating which combination of Stalinist regimes to support (China, Cuba, Vietnam, Albania, North Korea). The vast majority of us were certainly not Stalinists (to speak for myself, even as a child, reading about the crushing of the 1956 Hungarian revolution, I had enough sense to know that Stalinism was total bullshit); but in our ignorance of political history it was easy to identify with martyrized heroes like Che Guevara or the Vietcong as long as they were exotic enough that we didn't really know much about them. Fixating on the spectacle of Third World struggles, we had little awareness of the real issues at play in modern society. One of the most militant Berkeley confrontations did indeed begin as a "demonstration of solidarity" with the May 1968 revolt in France, but we had no conception of what the latter was really about—we were under the vague impression that it was some sort of "student protest against de Gaulle" along the narrow lines we were familiar with.

It is common nowadays to blame the collapse of the movement on the FBI's COINTELPRO operation, which included planting disinformation designed to sow suspicion between various radical groups, use of provocateurs to discredit them, and frameups of certain individuals. The fact remains that the authoritarian structure of the Panthers and other hierarchical groups lent itself to this sort of operation. For the most part all the provocateurs had to do was encourage already delirious ideological tendencies or inflame already existing power rivalries.

For me the last straw was the Panthers' "United Front Against Fascism" conference (July 1969). I dutifully attended all three days. But the conference's militaristic orchestration; the frenzied adulation of hero-martyrs; the Pavlovian chanting of mean-spirited slogans; the ranting about "correct lines" and "correct leadership"; the cynical lies and maneuvers of temporarily allied bureaucratic groups; the violent threats against rival groups who had not accepted the current Panther line; the "fraternal" telegram from the North Korean Politburo; the framed picture of Stalin on the Panthers' office wall—all this finally made me sick, and led me to look for a perspective that was more in line with my own feelings.

I thought I knew where to look. One of my Shimer friends who had moved out here was an anarchist, and his occasional wry comments on the movement's bureaucratic tendencies had helped save me from getting too carried away. I went over to his place and borrowed a whole sackful of anarchist literature—classic writings by Bakunin,

Kropotkin, Malatesta, Emma Goldman, Alexander Berkman, pamphlets on Kronstadt, the Spanish revolution, Hungary 1956, France 1968, current journals such as *Solidarity* (London), *Anarchy* (London), *Anarchos* (New York), *Black & Red* (Michigan).

It was a revelation. I had intuitively sympathized with what little I knew about anarchism, but like most people I had assumed that it was not really practicable, that without some government everything would fall apart into chaos. The anarchist texts demolished this misconception, revealing the creative potentials of popular self-organization and showing how societies could function—and in certain situations or in certain respects already had functioned—quite well without authoritarian structures. From this perspective it became easy to see that hierarchical forms of opposition tend to reproduce the dominant hierarchy (the Bolshevik Party's rapid devolution into Stalinism being the most obvious example) and that reliance on any leaders, even supposedly radical ones, tends to reinforce people's passivity instead of encouraging their creativity and autonomy.

"Anarchism" turned out to encompass a wide variety of tactics and tendencies—individualist, syndicalist, collectivist, pacifist, terrorist, reformist, revolutionary. About the only thing on which most anarchists were in agreement was in opposing the state and encouraging popular initiative and control. But this was at least a good beginning. Here was a perspective I could wholeheartedly espouse, that made sense of the current failings of the movement and gave some idea of the right direction to move in. For me it tied in perfectly with the Rexroth-Buber goal of genuine interpersonal community as opposed to impersonal collectivities. Some of Rexroth's recent articles had pointed out the Kropotkin-ecology connection. Rexroth and Snyder had also referred to a "Great Subculture" encompassing various nonauthoritarian currents throughout history, and had expressed the hope that with the current counterculture these tendencies might be on the point of finally becoming fulfilled in a liberated global community. Anarchism seemed to be the political component of such a movement.

Ron Rothbart (a close Shimer friend who had recently moved to Berkeley) soon became an equally enthusiastic convert. We began looking at the movement more critically, and started taking some modest initiatives on our own—talking up anarchism among our friends, ordering anarchist literature for local distribution, carrying black flags at demonstrations. We soon discovered some other local anarchists, with whom we took part in a discussion group, planned to reprint certain anarchist texts, and considered the possibility of opening an anarchist bookstore in Berkeley. My first ever "public" writing was a mimeo leaflet (a few dozen copies circulated among friends and acquaintances) in which I tried to convey the anarchist relevance of Rexroth and Snyder.

In our reading of recent anarchist literature Ron and I came upon several mentions of the Situationist International (SI), a small but notorious group that had played a key role in catalyzing the May 1968 revolt in France. I vaguely remembered having seen some situationist texts a year or so before, but at the time I had put them back on the shelf after a brief glance had given me the impression that this was just one more variant of the European ideological systems (Marxism, surrealism, existentialism, etc.) that seemed so old hat after psychedelics. In December 1969 we again came across some situationist pamphlets in a local bookstore, and this time of course we did read them.

We were immediately struck by how different they were from the simplistic propagandistic style of most anarchist writings. The situationist style seemed rather strange and tortuous, but it was extremely provocative, clearly aimed more at undermining people's habits and illusions than at merely converting them to some vague and more or less passive "libertarian perspective." At first we were bewildered, but as we reread and discussed the texts we gradually began to see how it all fit together. The situationists seemed to be the missing link between different aspects of revolt. Striving for a more radical social revolution than was dreamt of by most of leftists, they simultaneously attacked the absurdities of modern culture and the boredom of everyday life (picking up where the dadaists and surrealists had left off). Total iconoclasts, they rejected all ideologies—including Marxism, anarchism, and even "situationism"—and simply adopted or adapted whatever insights they found pertinent. While carrying on the traditional anarchist opposition to the state, they had developed a more comprehensive analysis of modern society, a more rigorously anti-hierarchical organizational practice, and a more consistent attack on the system's conditioning of people into passive followers and spectators. (Their name came from their original aim of creating open-ended, participatory "situations" as opposed to fixed works of art.) Last but not least, they emphatically rejected the "politics of guilt," the whole idea of basing revolution on self-sacrifice, self-flagellation and martyr worship.

A couple months later Ron and I came across some situationist-style leaflets by a local group with the intriguing name Council for the Eruption of the Marvelous. We wrote to them proposing a meeting. They accepted, and the next day we met two of them. They answered our questions briefly but lucidly, made sharp criticisms of most of our vague projects, and dismissed our anarchism as just another ideology which would inhibit us from doing anything significant. Quick to express their contempt for just about everything that passed as radical, they clearly knew what they were talking about and meant exactly what they said. Yet it was obvious that despite their seriousness they were having a lot of fun. Their own agitational practice, consisting primarily of critical interventions in various situations, seemed to combine careful calculation with a delightful sense of mischievousness.

Having made it quite clear that they did not intend to waste their time with any additional efforts to convince us, they left.

We were stunned, but also aroused. Even if we were not sure we agreed with them on some points, their autonomy was a practical challenge. If they could put out leaflets expressing their own views, why couldn't we?

We went back to Ron's place, turned on, and each wrote one. Mine was a collage of anarchist and situationist slogans followed by a list of recommended books; his was a satire of the way revolution was being turned into a trite spectacle. We mimeoed 1500 copies of each and handed them out on Telegraph Avenue near the University. Abstract though this action was, just creating something and getting it out there was an exciting breakthrough.

Over the next couple months we carried out several other leaflet experiments. I wrote one on the theme that people should never relinquish their power to leaders, which I distributed at the apropos film *Viva Zapata*, and put together a comic on the mindless, ritualistic nature of militant street fighting in Berkeley. Ron wrote a review of Buber's *Paths in Utopia* and a critique of an inept classroom disruption carried out by some of our anarchist acquaintances. These interventions were all pretty rudimentary, but by noting the various reactions they provoked we gradually got a better feel for confronting issues publicly. There was a progression toward greater incisiveness and criticality.

During this same period we attempted to find some viable compromise between our hangloose countercultural milieu and the rigorous extremism of the situationists (at least as we somewhat confusedly understood it). We had numerous discussions with friends aimed at inciting them to some sort of radical experimentation, but though some of them were vaguely intrigued by our "new trip," virtually none of them responded with any initiative. If nothing else, these confrontations at least served as good self-clarifications. We were becoming so involved in our new ventures that we had little interest in continuing relations on the old terms.

As for the anarchists we had been hanging around with, just as they had made no demands on us, they expected us to make none on them. When we offered a few mild critiques (far milder than the CEM had made of us) they reacted defensively. We began to see that despite its pertinent insights, anarchism functioned as just one more ideology, complete with its own set of fetishized ideas and heroes. After months of discussions and study groups, the grouping had not proved capable even of carrying out any of the reprinting projects, much less of starting a bookstore. We concluded that if we wanted anything done we'd better do it ourselves; and that autonomous interventions were more likely to strike a chord than distributing a few more copies of anarchist classics.

112

We rarely saw the CEM, but were occasionally informed of some of their delightfully scandalous interventions, whose combination of the situationist tactic of *détournement* with a dash of surrealist and William Burroughs influence was theorized in their pamphlet *On Wielding the Subversive Scalpel:* lampooning the spectacular role of sacrificial militants with a leaflet showing the Chicago Eight being crucified; going from door to door in a plastic suburb, dressed in suit and tie, delivering a tract exhorting the recipients to drop everything and get a life; disrupting a local Godard appearance with rotten tomatoes and bilingual leaflets; handing out packets of trading cards featuring stereotypical roles (housewife, sparechange artist, hip merchant, etc.) and "Great Moments in the Void" (traffic jam, supermarket shopping, watching TV).

We also met two emissaries of another situationist-influenced group from Massachusetts, the Council for Conscious Existence. The CCE was less humorous and surrealistic than the CEM, but equally intense, intransigent and iconoclastic. Their example reinforced the CEM challenge to call in question everything out of our past, including all our previous idols.

One of my few remaining heroes was Gary Snyder. I could agree that most of the movement and counterculture leaders were hierarchical manipulators or spectacular confusionists, but Snyder still seemed to me almost totally admirable. In any case I had the common misconception that in order to have the right to criticize someone I should myself be better, and I scarcely thought I could compare myself with Snyder.

Then one day I learned that he was coming to Berkeley to give a reading of his poetry. Previously this would have been one of the high points of my year. Now I was uncertain. Did I still think such an event was a good thing? Or was it "spectacular"—did it contribute toward people's passivity, complacency, star worship? After a little thought I decided that the most appropriate way to come to terms with this question would be to compose a leaflet to distribute at the event— thereby at the same time challenging others involved. The time limit was also a good challenge: the reading was in three days.

In making notes I started out with rather moderate criticism. But the more I considered the whole situation, the more radically I began to question it. Up till this time I had accepted Snyder as a spectacular package—his life and writings were "inspirational" to me, but only in a vague, general sort of way. Now I realized that if he had said something I thought was useful, the point was to use it. If he said something I felt was mistaken, I should point it out. It seemed particularly appropriate if I could turn some of his most valid remarks against other aspects of his practice that fell short.

Each little step opened the way for more. It went against the grain to "ruin" my prized picture of Snyder and his friends by cutting it out

113

and pasting it on the leaflet; but once I had "detourned" it by adding the comic balloons, my fetishism disappeared. Now it was just an image, interesting only because I could use it to undermine other people's fetishism. I laughed at myself as I broke through my own psychological resistances, just as I laughed to think how this or that aspect of the leaflet would meet with uneasy puzzlement on the part of the people who received it. If what I came up with seemed bizarre or awkward, so what? I was creating my own genre, and there were no rules but the desire to get to the root of the situation and expose it in the most challenging way possible.

I finished the leaflet (see page 161) just before the reading and had a hundred copies printed. As I approached the auditorium, nervously clutching them under my arm, I became hesitant. Wasn't this too extreme? How did I dare attack Gary Snyder this way? He himself was more or less an anarchist; he wasn't trying to recruit anyone to anything; he wasn't even charging any money. Had I gone off the deep end? I decided to sit down and listen to the beginning and see what it felt like.

There was an audience of several hundred people. Snyder started off by saying that before he got under way with the poetry he'd like to "say a few words about the revolution." He made a few remarks on that topic which were a bit vague, but not bad. When he finished, the audience *applauded*.

That did it. Nothing could have made the spectacular nature of the whole occasion more clear. The applause was the glaring sign that his words would not be taken up practically, but would merely serve as one more tidbit for passive titillation. (People would probably go home after the reading and tell their friends, "He not only read a lot of great poems, but he even said some far out stuff about revolution!") I was outraged at the situation. The most insulting aspects of my leaflet were only too appropriate. I took them out, threw them into the crowd and ran away. I had no further interest in anything Snyder might say, and I did not wish the incisiveness of my act to be diluted by a debate with the audience as to what alternatives I had to propose. That was their problem.

People sometimes ask if situationists "do" anything or if they "just write." I had had this same misconception—I had felt that I wasn't sure what to do, but that meanwhile it might be helpful to write the leaflet in order to clarify matters. It was only afterwards that I realized I *had* done something. If a critique really stirs even a few people to stop and think, to see through some illusion, to reconsider some practice, perhaps even provokes them to new ventures of their own, this is already a very worthwhile and practical effect—how many "actions" do as much? I saw that the insistence on being "constructive" was just a shuck that intimidated people from confronting their own condition; and that a critique (as opposed to a self-righteous moral condemnation) need not imply one's own superiority. If we had to be better than others before criticizing them, the "best" people would never be criticized at all (and hierarchs tend to define the issues in such a way that they remain on top). It didn't matter how talented or wise or well-intentioned Snyder was. If the purpose of poetry is to "change life," I felt there was more poetry in my act than in any poem he might read that evening.

I will be the first to admit that this particular intervention was inept and probably had no notable effect on anyone but myself. Though the leaflet was clear enough in attacking passive consumership of culture, the social perspective on which this attack was based was only vaguely implied. (The "Ode on the Absence of Real Poetry" that I put out a few months later was more explicit on this score, but also more stodgy.)

The action was also a flop as a disruption. I had searched in vain for some balcony-type place from which I could drop the leaflets over the whole audience, so as to create a "critical mass" situation in which everyone would be intrigued into reading them at the same time. I could have achieved the same result a little less dramatically by barging through all sections of the audience. Nowadays I would think nothing of doing that, but back then I was new at the game and didn't have the nerve. As a result of my more timid distribution, only a fraction of the people got the leaflets, and (as I was later told by some friends who were there) after a few seconds' pause the reading continued, with most of the rest of the audience probably assuming that it was merely some run-of-the-mill leaflet about Black Studies or the Vietnam war.

But whatever effect my action had on the audience, it was very illuminating for me. As I ran from the auditorium I felt like a child again, as excited as a grade school kid playing a prank. My real breakthrough in grasping the situationist perspective dates from that moment. I had already learned a lot from reading situationist texts; and from the example of the CEM (who after sharply criticizing my previous confusions had wisely *left me on my own* to work out what I was going to do next); and from my experiments over the previous months. But pulling the rug out from under my own passivity and star-worship had the most liberating effect of all. The fact that I had picked what was for me just about the hardest conceivable target made the experience the biggest turning point of my life.

The CEM members were aware of my admiration for Snyder. When I later showed them the leaflet, one of them said, "Hmm. I see you've been subverting yourself as well as others!" We all grinned.

In June the CEM broke up. The group had contained divergent tendencies, some of the members were not as autonomous or committed as others, and some of their ideological contradictions could never in any case have lasted very long before exploding. After the breakup two of the ex-members, Isaac Cronin and Dan Hammer, went to Paris and New York to meet members of the SI.

Meanwhile Ron and I formed our own two-person group (later referred to as "1044" after our P.O. box number). He moved in with me in July and for the next few months we lived communally, in accordance with the mistaken impression we had derived from the CCE and CEM that this was *de rigueur* for a situationist-type organization. Actually, although the SI was very strict about internal group democracy and avoidance of hierarchy, SI membership did not imply any such economic pooling or any sacrifice of privacy or independence in other personal affairs. We soon found that our puristic misconception was not very workable, though the experience of living and working together more closely than usual was interesting in some ways.

Our mystification about coherent organization was linked with a rather apocalyptic notion of coherent practice. Our little "In This Theater" text, with its evocation of Vaneigem's "unitary triad" of participation, communication and realization (see *The Revolution of Everyday Life,* chapter 23), hints at our state of mind at the time. We knew that the separations in our lives could not be definitively overcome short of a revolution, but we felt we could make a significant breakthrough by attacking the separations in a unitary manner. The Snyder disruption had been such a revelation to me that I, in particular, tended to overemphasize such experience as the "one thing needful," imagining that if others could only make a similar qualitative leap they too would discover the whole new world of possibilities of the "reversal of perspective." In my eagerness to incite people into such ventures I often became too pedagoguish, a bad habit that has persisted to this day. I still think that people need to take autonomous initiatives if they are ever going to break out of their conditioning, but as a practical matter being preachy and pushy seldom leads them to do so. As I noted above, one of the merits of the CEM was that they did not hang over our shoulders with wise advice, but simply made a few incisive critiques and then left us on our own. After a number of mostly fruitless efforts to arouse our friends, Ron and I learned to do likewise.

At our first encounter with the CEM delegates they had brought along a cassette recorder and taped our entire conversation. This was partly so that the other members of their group could listen to it later, but also because they found it useful to constantly review their own practice. Ron and I tried recording some of our own talks with friends, noting where we had talked too much, become stilted, responded inadequately, etc. The general idea was to become more conscious of whatever we were doing, to recognize and break up undesirable habits by altering habitual forms. Other methods we used included doing "circle talks" (three or more people sit in a circle and each person talks

116

only in turn); putting more things in writing (challenging ourselves to better organize our ideas); and detourning comics (taking comics from which we had whited out the original words and filling in the balloons with new ones—composing a new story on a given theme, or copying in randomly selected passages from situationist or other writings). In our most extensive venture of this sort we set aside one entire day for an intensively and arbitrarily scheduled series of activities (successive brief periods of reading, letter writing, brainstorming, drawing, cooking, eating, automatic writing, dancing, house cleaning, translating, play acting, leaflet composing, comic altering, gardening, meditation, exercise, rest, discussion, jamming), then spent the next week writing up a ten-page account of the experience, which we printed in a private edition of a dozen copies to give to a few friends.

Lest this add to the many misconceptions of "what situationists do," I should stress that this was only a one-time experiment and that the various other activities mentioned here were not necessarily typical of the situ milieu in general.* While SI-influenced groups tended to be fairly experimental in both everyday life and political agitation, the types of experimentation varied considerably. Some of our ventures reflected our American countercultural background more than would have been typical of our European counterparts. We were, of course, quite aware of the limits of such experiments. But liberating even a little space for even a brief period of time gives you a taste for more. You develop the knack of playing with different possibilities instead of assuming that the status quo is inevitable, and you get a more concrete sense of the social and psychological obstacles that stand in your way. The advantage of private experiments is that within their limits you can try anything without any risk but the salutary one of embarrassing your ego. The same principles apply, but obviously with more need for caution, in public activity.

Our public ventures included several experiments with *détournement,* the situationist tactic of diverting cultural fragments to new subversive uses. One of my creations was a comic balloon printed on stickum paper, designed to be pasted over ad posters so that the usual stereotypically beautiful woman model would be making a critique of the manipulative function of her image: "Hello, men! I'm a picture of a woman that doesn't exist. But my body corresponds to a stereotype you have been conditioned to desire. Since your wife or girlfriend is unlikely to look as I do, you are naturally frustrated. The people who

---

*Although the term *situationist* originally referred specifically to members of the SI, it later also came to be used in a broader sense to designate others in the "situ milieu" carrying on more or less similar activities. Here and in my other writings the context should usually make clear in which sense I am using the term. (Past tense usually refers to the SI; present tense—as in much of "The Society of Situationism" and "The Realization and Suppression of Religion"—usually indicates the broad sense.)

117

put me up here have got you just where they want you—by the balls. With your 'manhood' challenged, you're putty in their hands. . . ." (If I may say so myself, I think this way of turning spectacular manipulation against itself is more illuminating than the usual merely reactive complaints such as "This ad exploits women"—as if such ads didn't also exploit and manipulate men.) I also took advantage of the openness of an open poetry reading to read a lengthy critique of the limits of merely literary poetry, "Ode on the Absence of Real Poetry Here This Afternoon," to the puzzlement and disgruntlement of the other poets present, who by the rules of the game had to sit there and listen politely to my "poem" without interrupting.

Ron wrote a pamphlet analyzing a recent Chicano riot in Los Angeles, and on a lark signed it "by Herbert Marcuse." This resulted in the pamphlet's getting a wider readership, both at first, when people assumed that Marcuse was really the author, then after Marcuse had been forced to publicly disavow it, when even more people became intrigued by all the speculations as to who could have perpetrated such a strange prank. To add to the fun we wrote a series of pseudonymous letters to the editors of various local papers denouncing, and thereby further publicizing, the pamphlet. (This tactic of putting out falsely attributed texts, which we later termed "counterfeitism," subsequently became rather sloppily used by other groups in ways that often produced more confusion than clarity. We ourselves soon abandoned it, and that fall Isaac and I collaborated on a critique of those aspects of the *Subversive Scalpel* pamphlet that gave the impression that détournement meant throwing random confusion into the spectacle.)

Taking our cue from the situationists, we also began to fill in the enormous gaps in our knowledge of previous radical efforts, exploring the history of past revolts and checking out seminal figures like Hegel (a hard nut to crack, but even a little familiarization helped us get a better feel for dialectical processes); Charles Fourier (whose delightful though somewhat loony utopia is based on encouraging the interplay, rather than the repression, of the variety of human passions); Wilhelm Reich (his early social-psychological analyses, not his later "orgone" theories); and some of the more radical Marxist thinkers: Rosa Luxemburg, Anton Pannekoek, Karl Korsch, early Lukács.

And Marx himself. Like most anarchists, we knew virtually nothing about him except for a few platitudes about his supposed authoritarianism. When we discovered that many of the situationists' most pertinent insights, and even some of their most striking phrases, were derived from Marx, we started reexamining him more carefully. We soon realized that it was simply ignorant to uncritically lump Marx with Bolshevism, much less with Stalinism; and that, while there were undoubtedly significant flaws in Marx's perspective, his insights on so many aspects of capitalist society are so penetrating that trying to develop a coherent social analysis while ignoring him is about as silly

118

as it would be to try to develop a coherent theory of biology while ignoring Darwin.*

Above all, of course, we read everything of the SI that we could get our hands on. Unfortunately, most of the situationist texts were available only in French. Apart from half a dozen pamphlets and a few leaflets, the only things in English were a few rough manuscript translations done by people who in some cases knew scarcely more French than we did. I still remember the excitement, but also the frustration, upon first obtaining a copy of Vaneigem's *Treatise on Living* (a.k.a. *The Revolution of Everyday Life*), which we struggled to read in a dim photocopy of a photocopy of a photocopy of a poor manuscript translation. When I realized how much I was missing, I started brushing up my rudimentary and long-forgotten college French. I had always imagined it would be great to get proficient enough to read my favorite French writers in the original, but such a goal was too vague to inspire me to do the necessary study. The situationists provided the incentive. Just about everyone else I knew who became seriously interested in them eventually picked up at least enough French to piece out the most important texts. When we later met comrades from other countries, French was as likely as English to be our common language.

That summer Ron and I met Michael Lucas, who had moved to the Bay Area after having collaborated and become dissatisfied with Murray Bookchin's *Anarchos* group in New York. In October Sydney Lewis (one of the CCE emissaries we had met the preceding spring) arrived in town, having left the CCE in disillusionment with some of its more extravagant ideological rigidities. Soon afterward Dan and Isaac returned from Paris and New York. Comparing the positive and negative conclusions from our diverse experiences, we found a significant convergence of views.

Two tentative group projects developed: a study group devoted to Guy Debord's *The Society of the Spectacle* (the other main situationist book, which had just been translated by Black & Red) and a critique of the American radical movement and counterculture. The study group didn't last very long—we soon found that we got a better grasp of Debord's theses by the experience of using them (in graffiti, in leaflets and in our movement drafts) than by merely discussing them in the abstract. The preliminary stages of the movement critique meanwhile confirmed an increasing degree of accord among the six of

---

*I should mention one other important influence whom we discovered independently of the SI: Josef Weber. He was the leading spirit of *Contemporary Issues,* a little-known but remarkably high quality radical journal that was published in London from 1948–1970. We picked up a lot of basic knowledge of recent history from the sober, well-researched articles in the *CI* back issues and a lot of provocative ideas from the brilliant, if sometimes rather eccentric, pieces by Weber.

us, while eliminating three or four other people who had attended the study group but had not followed up with any autonomous initiatives. In December Dan, Isaac, Michael, Ron and I formed the group Contradiction. Besides our movement critique, we envisaged publishing an SI-type journal and carrying out various other critical agitations.

Sydney would almost certainly have been the sixth member of the new group if he had not returned to the East Coast just before its formation; but once out of town he drifted into somewhat different perspectives, and we eventually discontinued the relation. Meanwhile we had discovered a new comrade in Berkeley. I was strolling around on campus one day and happened to overhear two people talking, one of whom was making an intelligent critique of bureaucratic leftism. After listening a moment I interrupted to say that he was absolutely right, but that he was wasting his time since the person he was talking to was obviously incapable of seeing his points. He gave me a surprised look, stopped and thought for a moment, realized I was right, took his leave of the other person, and we went off to talk. At first I let him do most of the talking, merely nodding and asking a few questions. Though he had never read a word of the situationists, he had independently arrived at virtually all their positions. Then I pulled some pamphlets out of my bag and read him a few passages that expressed the same things he had been saying. You could have pushed him over with a feather! He began working with us on our movement critique and eventually became the sixth member of Contradiction. I always think of this encounter with John Adams as a striking confirmation of the situationists' claim that they were not propagating an ideology, but simply expressing the realities that were already present.

The first Contradiction publication was my poster "Bureaucratic Comix," inspired by the recent revolt in Poland. Now that we've become used to the idea of the collapse of Stalinism it may be necessary to recall how much people used to take its permanence for granted, and just how uncomprehending the New Left was when it came to the issues raised by such a rebellion. While a few leftist groups tried to distinguish between "revisionist" East European regimes and "revolutionary" Third World ones, most of the underground papers, unable to figure out how to fit such an event into their Guevarist fantasy world, did not even *mention* the uprising. Thus the poster's détournement of various movement heroes, which may seem only mildly amusing to present-day readers, had a far more traumatic effect on their habitual admirers (as some of them later admitted to me).

While we had been experimenting with methods inspired by the SI, the SI itself had been going through crises which were eventually to lead to its dissolution.

In March 1971 I went to New York to meet Jon Horelick and Tony Verlaan, the two remaining members of the American section of the SI, and learned that they had recently split from the Europeans. They presented me with a fat stack of correspondence and internal documents, mostly in French, which I began to struggle through in a generally unsuccessful effort to figure out what it was all about. Then I flew to Paris.

The first people I looked up were Roger Grégoire and Linda Lanphear, ex-participants in Black & Red. We had read with interest the B&R publications (especially Grégoire and Perlman's excellent booklet on their activities during May 1968), which combined some situationist features with a more traditional anarcho-Marxist orientation; but our interest had faded as the group began to settle into an ultraleftist eclecticism. Roger and Linda's recent open-letter critique, "To the Readers of Black & Red," demonstrated that they, like us, were moving in the direction of a more rigorous, situationist-style practice. We hit it off fine and I ended up staying at their apartment for most of my trip.

I wasn't able to see the remaining members of the SI, but I did meet a number of other people in the Parisian situ milieu, including Vaneigem and a couple other ex-SI members. The discussions were a mixture of genuinely interesting exchange of information and ideas with the exaggerated hopes and illusions that sprung up in the heady aftermath of May 1968.

Of course just being in Paris was exciting—taking in all the new sights and sounds and smells, losing myself in the labyrinthine street layout, wandering for hours through cobblestone alleys among centuries-old buildings and obscure little shops; stopping at outdoor cafés and watching all the passersby, catching tantalizing fragments of the strange language I was just beginning to be able to understand; shopping in the little open-air markets that used to be on practically every street corner; savoring those tasty multi-course French meals and excellent wines and liqueurs that we would linger over during hours of lively conversation. . . .

After a month and a half in Paris, plus brief visits to London and Amsterdam, I flew back to New York and stayed a couple weeks with Tony Verlaan. He and Jon Horelick had just had a falling out, and Jon more or less disappeared until two years later, when he came out with his journal *Diversion*. Tony and Arnaud Chastel had meanwhile formed Create Situations, and were in the middle of translating some SI articles, which I helped with. Then I returned to Berkeley.

Over the next few months we had quite a few visitors: Tony and Arnaud (after a couple weeks of tumultuous interaction we broke with them); Point-Blank (a group of teenagers from Santa Cruz, with whom we also eventually broke after working with them for some time); Roger and Linda; one or two contacts from England; and a young Spanish couple, Javier and Tita. Tita and I hit it off right away, although our verbal communication was at first limited to pidgin French.

When Javier returned to Europe a few weeks later, she stayed with me.

During all this time we were continuing to work on the movement critique and other articles for our projected journal. Unfortunately, except for a few incidental leaflets none of this work was destined to materialize. There were lots of good ideas in our drafts, but also many insufficiencies, and we proved incapable of bringing the project to completion. Partly this was because we undertook too much, partly it was due to poor organization, leading to duplication of effort. One person might put in a lot of work on a certain topic, then find that his draft had to be drastically reorganized to fit in with changes in other articles; which themselves had been altered by the next meeting, necessitating yet further changes. Meetings became a headache.

(In retrospect, we might have done better to delegate one or two people to draft the movement piece as a whole, drawing on individual contributions but without worrying about sticking to them in detail. It might also have been a good idea to issue short preliminary versions of some of the chapters, produced and signed by different members, both to get something out there for feedback and to develop more individual autonomy.)

Meanwhile the various fragments of the movement were self-destructing from the very contradictions we had been analyzing. There was less and less to attack that was not already widely discredited. By early 1972 about all that might have remained for us was to make a more lucid postmortem. Even that would have been worth doing (you have to understand what went wrong if you're ever going to do better); but by this time we were so sick of the whole project that we no longer had the necessary enthusiasm, and had already started drifting into other pursuits. Michael and I had gotten into classical music and were spending a lot of our time listening to records and going to concerts and operas. Dan and Isaac were spending most of their time in San Jose working with Jimmy Carr (Dan's ex–Black Panther brother-in-law) on his prison memoirs.* Our abandonment of the movement critique in April 1972 marked the effective end of the group, though we didn't formally dissolve it till September.

A general exodus followed. John and Michael both moved out of town. Dan, Isaac and his girlfriend Jeanne went to Europe, where Tita had returned shortly before. I still saw Ron occasionally, but scarcely anyone else. Relations with many of my older friends had cooled since our 1970 confrontations, and some of the ones I was still close to had recently moved back to the Midwest as the counterculture began to

---

*After Jimmy's 1972 assassination (which may have been caused by a COINTELPRO setup) they completed and published the book under the title *Bad: The Autobiography of James Carr* (1975; reissued by Carroll & Graf, 1995).

wind down. About the only bright spot during the whole year was a reunion with a former girlfriend, who flew out from New England for a brief visit; unfortunately there were too many obstacles to continuing the relation.

Lonely, depressed and frustrated by the *coitus interruptus* of Contradiction, I didn't have the spirit for anything but reading, listening to classical music, and trying to maintain my survival with poker.

The private game I had been playing in had disbanded, and I had shifted to playing lowball at the casinos in nearby Emeryville. This was a tougher proposition: not only was the competition keener, but you also had to pay an hourly fee to the house. I plugged away practically full time for several months, to the point where I was becoming addicted. Clustered around a brightly lit green felt table, insulated from the outside world, you become jaded. The thought of going back to some humdrum job seems intolerable when you remember the night you walked home with several hundred dollars after a few hours' play. (You tend to forget all the losses, or attribute them to temporary back luck.) I had hoped that with experience I might gradually improve and win enough to move to the higher stakes games, but my records showed that my net winnings were barely holding steady at around 75 cents an hour. In November I finally gave it up.

That was a good step, but I wasn't sure what to do next. Inspired by reading Montaigne, I tried writing some self-exploratory essays. This might not have been a bad idea in other circumstances (writing the present text has included a lot of this type of self-exploration via confronting diverse topics), but at the time nothing came of it because practically any topic I started to write about sooner or later led to some connection with the Contradiction experience, and I had gotten so depressed about the latter that I could hardly bear to think about it. Yet I felt equally uncomfortable about evading the issue.

In December Dan, Isaac, Jeanne and Tita all returned from Europe. As I recounted in my "Case Study" (see pages 282–287), their return helped spur me back to life. I began experimenting once again, reassessed my relations (which led to some traumatic breaks), and after having repressed the whole Contradiction experience for months, finally got the idea of confronting it in a pamphlet. As with my earlier Snyder leaflet, I saw this as a way to bring things together: for my own sake I wanted to figure out what went wrong, but I wanted at the same time to force others to face these issues, both those who were directly concerned and those who might be involved in similar ventures in the future.

Later on I'll say a little about the situationist practice of breaks. For the moment I will only mention that I now regret the first letter quoted in the "Case Study," which was to Ron's girlfriend C—. The faults I criticized her for were not really anything more than the sort of white lies and mild social hypocrisies of which practically everyone

123

is guilty. It would probably have sufficed, and been much easier on everybody concerned, to have simply politely distanced myself from her, as people usually do in such cases and as I myself would undoubtedly do now. But at the time I was desperate to break out of the rut I had fallen into.

The letter certainly did accomplish this, for both good and bad. On one hand, it helped clear the way for the personal revival I described; on the other, it ended my relation not only with C— but also with Ron, and ultimately with John and Michael as well. I was deeply saddened by this, but I had known the risk I was taking. Ironically, I ran into C— a few years later and we "renormalized" our relation to a limited but amicable level; whereas the estrangement with Ron lasted twenty years, ending only recently when (as a result of reconsidering the incident in the process of writing this autobiography) it finally occurred to me to write him a letter of apology.

(We've both lost touch with Michael Lucas—last heard of living in Germany—and John Adams. Does anyone know where they are?)

The second critical letter quoted in the "Case Study" (which I feel was more justified; for one thing, it wasn't even a break letter, merely a sharp challenge) was directed to one of Dan, Isaac and Jeanne's friends, thus putting some of my other close relations at risk. But after some initial uncertainty, they soon came around to agreeing with it. The appearance of *Remarks on Contradiction* and the surprising changes I was making in my life began to inspire them to similar ventures, bringing us closer together than ever.

The next two or three months saw a flurry of self-analyses, neo-Reichian exercises, recording of dreams, reassessments of our pasts, and other challenges to ingrained character traits and petrified relations. This was all to the good; but after a while, beginning to feel that we were getting too narrowly internal and psychoanalytical, I wrote them a letter stressing the social context of our experiments and the need to continually supersede our situation so as to avoid falling into yet another rut.

To my great delight they answered my challenge by shifting the dialogue to another level. Three days later they turned up with a draft of a large poster:

WE'RE TIRED OF PLAYING WITH OURSELVES

Truly Voluptuous Spirits,

. . . We are three people much like yourselves . . . . We had some common perspectives toward daily life, concerning what we did and didn't want from society as it is now organized. We worked as little as possible, . . . read all the best books (*Capital, The Maltese Falcon*, etc.), listened to the best music, ate at the best cheap restaurants, got drunk, went for hikes and trips to the beach and Paris. . . .

We were anti-spectators of the spectacle of decomposition. We read the *Chronicle* just like you do, which is to say "critically," which is to say that the very chic cynicism which appeared to add spice to our lives actually helped drain the life out of us. We had plenty of clever remarks about the lacks and excesses of the bourgeois world, but despite the fact that we were reproached by others for being too bold we were actually too timid. . . .

The sky didn't open up one day. But since we weren't quite dead yet, enough was soon too much. We received a terrific kick in the ass from Jean-Pierre Voyer's *Use of Reich* and from our friend Ken Knabb's use of Voyer in *Remarks on Contradiction and Its Failure.* The work of Voyer was the first since Debord that concretely shed light on our alienation. We realized that we were to a great extent accomplices in the ruling spectacle, and that character is the form of this complicity. We began the strategically crucial task of character assassination—after some tentatives which either over-psychologized the attack on character (Isaac and Jeanne) or defended against this attack by criticizing psychology (Dan)—including in that attack those traits of our own and of each other which we had previously accepted as "part of the package," which we'd patronizingly accepted as immutable, which we'd timidly considered "too personal" to criticize except when they became unavoidably excessive. This negative task begun, positivity was release from the chains of repression. . . .

Our attack on this rot has made external restraints—especially our inability to meet you—all the more unbearable. The enrichment of our relations with each other has underscored the poverty of our relations with the rest of the city. . . .

We expect this address to help us break some of the barriers to meeting you. . . . But whether or not you even see this, we're coming after you.

> For days without chains and nights without armor,
> Dan Hammer, Jeanne Smith, Isaac Cronin

Since the comic poster announcing my Voyer translation was going to be ready at the same time, we decided to distribute the two posters together. Over the next few days we pasted up several hundred copies around the Bay Area.

Fresh and audacious though their poster was, the responses revealed that it was not as clear as it might have been. The dozens of letters they received certainly showed that a sympathetic chord had been struck, but most of the responders had the impression that this was simply a matter of overcoming individual isolation by meeting more people, with little grasp of the implied connection to social critique.

Nevertheless, the two posters led us to meet a much larger variety of people than usual—not only those who wrote to us, but many others we ran into on the street or in cafés who were intrigued by our lively and mischievous manner and by the fact that we were obviously having so much fun. My new "Special Investigator" business card (see page 279) added to the mixture of amusement and intrigue when people got around to the inevitable "Just what is it that you do?"

That fall we all returned to Europe, though not all at the same times and places. I was in Paris for three months, staying at Roger and Linda's again and spending most of my time among their circle of friends, which now included Jean-Pierre Voyer. I had been inspired by the amusingly audacious style of Voyer's early activity (the name "Bureau of Public Secrets" was partly suggested by his notion of *publicité*). In person I found him to be intellectually provocative, but he had a tendency to get carried away with his theoretical insights, harping on them to the point that they became ideological. I was also disappointed to learn that he was not following up some of the embryonic ideas that had most interested me in his Reich text. I realized that if I wanted to see these ideas developed, I would have to do it myself—which I later did to a certain extent in *Double-Reflection* and the "Case Study."

During my first weeks in Paris there was a lot of excited discussion centering around Voyer's ideas and our recent Bay Area ventures. I soon came to feel that this talk was leading nowhere and that there remained a lot of rigidities and repressions in our relations, and wrote a letter to Voyer and the others criticizing both the scene in general and each of the particular individuals involved. This stirred up a flurry of self-questioning for a few days, but ultimately things reverted to how they were before. From this point on my relations with all of them cooled.

Part of my impatience with them was due to the contrast with Daniel Denevert, whom I met around this same time. He had discovered a copy of *Remarks on Contradiction* at a Paris store and decided to translate it; then he happened to hear through the grapevine that I was in town and hunted me up. It turned out that he, in turn, was the author of a earlier pamphlet that I had greatly appreciated (*Pour l'intelligence de quelques aspects du moment*). This independent accord made for an exciting encounter. I spent most of the rest of my stay seeing him and the other members of his recently formed group, the Centre de Recherche sur la Question Sociale (CRQS): his wife Françoise Denevert (pseudonym: Jeanne Charles), Nadine Bloch and Joël Cornuault.

When I returned to California in December I was already working on *Double-Reflection*. Dan and Isaac were each working on small newsletters. Tita had just published a Spanish version of Voyer's Reich article and was going on to translate Vaneigem's "Basic Banalities." Robert Cooperstein (a friend we had met the year before) was working on a comic-illustrated pamphlet about children. In March 1974 we got an exciting and unexpected vindication of our perspectives when Chris Shutes and Gina Rosenberg came out with *Disinterest Compounded Daily,* a detailed critique of Point-Blank from the inside (Chris was an ex-member and Gina a sometime collaborator) that had been inspired in part by our recent publications.

Over the next several months there were quite a few collaborations among us and the CRQS. Once I had completed *Double-Reflection* (which Joël immediately started translating into French), I joined Dan and Robert in translating Daniel's recent pamphlet, *Théorie de la misère, misère de la théorie,* along with a couple other CRQS texts; the chapter on "behindism" in *Double-Reflection* inspired Chris to follow up with a whole pamphlet on the subject; he and Isaac wrote a critique of Jon Horelick's journal *Diversion,* then began working on their own journal, *Implications;* Isaac and Gina translated Debord's article on dérives; Isaac and Dan composed a leaflet on a baseball riot in Cleveland, which they distributed at a local Oakland A's game. . . .

Not surprisingly we began to be considered as a de facto organization. People would write to us as a group or assume that a letter from one of us represented the views of the others. We thought it might be interesting to try to work out a joint public statement in order to see just what degree of accord we did have. Eventually we came up with a text along the lines of the CRQS's "Declaration," but specifying that though we shared certain perspectives, we were each acting only in our own name. This "Notice Concerning the Reigning Society and Those Who Contest It" was issued in November 1974, along with a second poster advertising our publications.

Despite the "Notice's" statement to the contrary, putting out the two posters paradoxically tended to reinforce the idea (among us as well as others) that we formed a unified tendency, whose activity was objectified as a collection of mutually approved texts. There was indeed a considerable accord among us, but it was probably a mistake to stress this commonality at the expense of neglecting the diversity of our views and interests. We were more careful about preserving individual responsibility than Contradiction had been, but on the other hand Contradiction had had a substantial common project that gave more reason for adopting an explicit organization. Formulating a collective statement can be a fruitful way to work out where you stand, but it also involves some risks; speaking in the name of a collectivity makes it easier to get carried away in extravagant rhetoric that you might be less likely to use if speaking only for yourself. The "arrogance" of the "Notice" was, of course, an intentional effort to challenge others—far from being "elitist," it obviously undermined whatever tendencies we might have had to accommodate passive followers. Nevertheless, this kind of style does tend to become habitual and encourage a pompous attitude. We would probably have done better to have kept things looser, more autonomous and more modest.

Anyway, over the next three years we were all pretty close, socially as well as politically. We even worked together—Jeanne, Dan and I at *Rolling Stone* magazine in San Francisco, most of the others as a house-painting team.

While I was at *Rolling Stone* I vaguely considered perpetrating some sort of détournement, such as replacing one of the pages with an alternative text critiquing the magazine and its readership; but this turned out to be technically unfeasible. More innocuously, just for the in-joke amusement of my fellow workers, one deadline night while I was waiting for copy to come in I typeset a takeoff on the *RS* table of contents, modeled on Dan's wonderful "Great Moments in the Void" trading cards:

The Rolling Stone Interview: Jeanne Jambu
by Ben Fong-Torres   40

Many of our readers may be more familiar with artist Jeanne Jambu under her former name, Jeanne Smith. (See mastheads, *RS* Nos. 174-186.) Senior Editor Ben Fong-Torres seeks Ms. Jambu's reasons for the change, probing behind her enigmatic "I didn't like the name 'Smith.'" Throughout the interview Jambu comes through as a woman who knows what she wants: witness her bringing her own (European) coffee to the Production Department this issue. But Jambu retains a sense of proportion: she modestly noted that fellow artist Roger Carpenter had actually introduced the practice with his frequent and popular "French Roast" contributions.

Personalities   23

With this issue *ROLLING STONE* introduces a dynamic new staff member, Dan ("Danny") Hammer. Hammer's has been a varied career, with work ranging from the book to the trading card fields, but he has made the shift to *ROLLING STONE* with ease. His main trip here is typesetting, but, as he noted in a recent conversation, "I also sometimes do a little opaquing when they need me."

The Missing Tapes: Four Views • by Samuel Beckett, Norman
Mailer, Henry Miller and Alexander Solzhenitsyn   27

Shortly after dinner, Art Assistant Suzy Rice had trouble locating some typeset corrections. Senior Typesetter Ken Knabb said he had put them in the proofreading room, but Rice, finding that they were no longer there, grew frantic. Later it turned out that the missing tapes had already been picked up by Art Director Tony Lane.

We asked four prominent writers what *they* thought about the incident. The responses were lively and varied. Perhaps Alexander Solzhenitsyn's was the most penetrating comment: "I guess things like that are bound to happen every now and then."

I quit my job in summer 1975 and got back to work on notes I had put on hold the year before. The first and only issue of my journal, *Bureau of Public Secrets,* was completed the following January. As soon as it was printed and mailed out I went to Paris.

Apart from brief side trips to London and Bordeaux, I stayed with the Deneverts for the next three months. For the most part we got on very well. (Here as elsewhere I'm skipping many encounters, collaborations and general good times, and focusing on a few turning points.) But despite our closeness in most regards, a divergence began to become evident on the question of breaks. While I was there they broke with several people on what seemed to me rather subtle grounds. This divergence became more problematic when such breaks involved people with whom I had substantial relations. Joël Cornuault had been excluded from the CRQS a few months before, and Nadine Bloch was in a rather uncertain position between him and the Deneverts. The fact that I was seeing her frequently while the Deneverts were not made for an uneasy and sometimes delicate situation. At one time there might seem to be a rapprochement in the making; then it would be broken off because of some seemingly trivial matter. Though I could by now understand French pretty well, some of the nuances were still over my head—one side might explain to me that such and such a phrase in a letter contained a snide irony, only to have the other deny this. . . .

Soon after I returned to Berkeley I got a letter from Daniel announcing a "chain break" with Nadine—i.e. that he was not only breaking with Nadine, but would also break with anyone else who maintained any relation with her. I was not really any more enlightened about the whole business than I had been before (he justified this ultimatum by the *tone* of a recent letter from her), but after much agonizing I finally decided to rely on the trust and respect I had for his judgment. Such reliance might have been appropriate regarding some third party I didn't know, but in the present case I should have refused to go along with his demand. Though this would have ended my relation with him, it might have brought the whole issue of breaks to a head earlier and in a cleaner way than later developed. Once I had capitulated in this way, it became that much more difficult for me to take a clear stand on related issues that came up a few months later.

Upsetting as this affair was, its impact on me was diminished by the fact that, for the moment, it concerned only my relations in France. Things seemed to be going well enough in Berkeley. I had started making notes for *The Realization and Suppression of Religion* in Paris, and now plunged into the project full time. I also began taking night-school courses in Spanish and Japanese. A guy in Spain was preparing a small anthology of BPS and CRQS texts and I wanted to learn enough Spanish to be able to check his translations (he eventually abandoned the project, however). I had also been corresponding with Tommy Haruki, a Japanese anarchist who was manifesting a lot of interest in the situationists, and I had begun to think about visiting Japan. Besides the political motivation, I still retained a certain interest in Zen and Japanese culture. I was doing a little zazen every morning and having a lot of fun going to a karate class with Robert and Tita. Relations with them and my other "Notice" friends still seemed pretty good.

But not for long. Within a few months there was a traumatic breakup—ironically, just as I was completing the religion pamphlet, which was in part concerned with questioning aspects of the situ scene that tended to give rise to this sort of hostility and delirium.

In January 1977 Chris wrote a letter to the Deneverts questioning the manner of their breaks with Joël and Nadine. They responded with a scathing letter to all the "Notice" signers en bloc, not only taking issue with several of Chris's points, but considering his letter as exemplifying various incoherences that all of us had been manifesting or tolerating. After much discussion of these issues, the rest of us decided to break with Chris—not so much because of the points objected to by the Deneverts (on some of those we were in at least partial agreement with Chris) as because of our reconsideration of some recurring tendencies in his activity over the previous years.

The Deneverts concluded that we were using him as a scapegoat and broke with us in April. A few weeks later Gina came around to a similar position, and demanded that each of us "(1) denounce thoroughly and publicly the break with Chris and the break letter to him; (2) . . . thereby announce the project of future public disclosure(s) giving, as one moment of his return to revolutionary practice, . . . a written form to the practical truth he has grasped in his struggle to be seizing his point-of-view in the aftermath of the Notice days (which have ended); (3) sever relations with any one of the Notice signers who has not seen fit to carry out these two criteria." Over the next month Chris, Isaac, Robert and Tita declared their acceptance of these three demands. Dan and I refused them.

I now think the break with Chris was inappropriate, especially considering the situation in which it took place. The Deneverts had challenged us to clarify our individual and collective activity. We should first of all have confronted these matters to the point where each of us knew where we stood, instead of getting carried away exaggerating the significance of Chris's faults, which in retrospect do not seem to me to have been all that serious. At the time, however, I did not feel that the break was so totally unjustified as to call for a "thorough denunciation"; and in any case I had no intention of "announcing" a public accounting of the affair before I felt I had anything definite to say about it.

It turned out that, except for Isaac, none of those who rallied to

Gina's position ever fulfilled her second demand either. And Isaac's bilious piece ("The American Situationists: 1972–77") contained so many distortions and self-contradictions that he himself soon became dissatisfied with it and stopped circulating it, though he never bothered to publicly repudiate it.

I started drafting a critique of Isaac's text, which among other things projected onto me various pretensions and illusions that I had in fact vehemently opposed whenever they had been manifested (most often by Isaac and Chris); but I eventually concluded that it was such a gross distortion of reality that it would take an equally extensive text to adequately deal with it. There seemed little point in getting embroiled in such a dismal project when I would have had nothing to offer but denunciations of his misrepresentations or reiterations of points I had already made in other publications.

Daniel circulated a more serious and cogent analysis of his position on the affair ("Sur les fonds d'un divorce"). There were a few aspects of his account that I might have debated, but his main point was simply that he and Françoise had a more rigorous position on breaks and relations than we did, and this was true enough. Without wishing to play down the significance of our other differences, I believe that some of them merely reflected our geographical separation. Thus my unsuccessful effort to get Debord's films circulated in America, where situationist theory was still almost unknown and they might have had a significant impact, was viewed by Daniel as contradicting his efforts (notably expressed in his December 1976 text, *Suggestions relatives au légitime éloge de l'I.S.*) to criticize the development of a "Debordist" orthodoxy in the quite different conditions of France.

Why didn't I respond to the mess by getting it out in public, like I did in *Remarks on Contradiction*? First of all, my frustration with the fizzling out of Contradiction had been due to the fact that so much promising effort had gone unfulfilled. In the present case we had already communicated the main things we had to say in numerous publications. Secondly, while I had had several points to make regarding the reasons for Contradiction's failure, I had not arrived at any clear conclusions about the reasons for the current debacle. About the only thing I had derived from the whole miserable affair was a personal determination never again to yield to pressure regarding breaks.

Probably I would nevertheless have done better to issue *some* public statement rather than letting the affair linger on in unanswered rumors. But at this distance in time, when all the persons involved have long abandoned their old positions, there would be little point in going any more into the details in contention, which in my view were as unedifying as they were convoluted.

This may, however, be a good place to make some remarks about the whole vexed issue of situationist-type breaks.

First of all, just to keep things in perspective, it's important to remember that in breaking with people the situationists were doing nothing more than choosing their own company—deciding whom they wished to associate with and making clear, in cases where there might otherwise have been some confusion, whom they did not wish to be associated with. There's nothing elitist about such a practice; those who want to recruit devoted followers employ tact, not insults. The situationists strove to provoke others to carry out their own autonomous activities. If the "victims" of their breaks proved incapable of doing so, they only confirmed the appropriateness of the break.

Different types of projects call for different criteria. Beginning by criticizing the avant-garde cultural milieu in which they found themselves in the 1950s and moving toward a more general critique of the global system, the situationists' project was at once extremely ambitious and quite specific to their own situation. It would have been absurd for them to accept collaboration with those who did not even grasp what this project was, or who clung to practices that were inconsistent with it. If, say, the SI wanted to carry out a boycott of some cultural institution, this boycott would obviously lose its punch if some SI members continued to maintain relations with the institution in question. An early SI article pointed out the danger of losing one's radical coherence by blurring into the ambiguity of the cultural milieu:

> Within such a community people have neither the need nor the objective possibility for any sort of collective discipline. Everyone always politely agrees about the same things and nothing ever changes. . . . The "terrorism" of the SI's exclusions can in no way be compared to the same practices in political movements by power-wielding bureaucracies. It is, on the contrary, the extreme ambiguity of the situation of artists, who are constantly tempted to integrate themselves into the modest sphere of social power reserved for them, that makes some discipline necessary in order to clearly define an incorruptible platform. Otherwise there would be a rapid and irremediable osmosis between this platform and the dominant cultural milieu because of the number of people going back and forth. [SI Anthology, p. 60. For other articles relating to breaks, see pp. 47–48, 177–79, 216–19 in the same book.]

One need only recall how many radical cultural and political movements have lost their original audacity, and eventually their very identity, by becoming habituated to little deals and compromises, settling into comfortable niches in academia, hobnobbing with the rich and famous, becoming dependent on government or foundation grants, pandering to audiences, catering to reviewers and interviewers, and otherwise accommodating themselves to the status quo. It is safe to say that if the SI had not had a rigorous policy of breaks and exclusions,

132

it would have ended up as one more amorphous and innocuous avant-garde group of the sort that come and go every year and are remembered only in the footnotes of cultural histories.

This is a practical question, not a moral one. It's not just that it would have seemed hypocritical for the situationists to have written *On the Poverty of Student Life* if they had been academics; if they had been academics they would not have been *capable* of writing it. The lucidity of the SI texts was directly linked to the authors' intransigence. You don't get on the cutting edge without cutting yourself free from the routines and compromises around you.

But what was perhaps appropriate for the SI is not necessarily essential for others in other circumstances. When the situationists were isolated and practically unknown, they did well to make sure that their unique perspective was not compromised. Now that that perspective has spread among thousands of people around the world and could not possibly be repressed (though it can, of course, still be coopted in various ways), there would seem to be less justification for the old SI-style bluster. A radical group may still decide to dissociate itself from certain individuals or institutions, but it has less reason to act as if everything hinges on its own purity, much less to imply that its own particular standards should be adopted by everyone else.

The situationist practice of public polarization has had the merit of fostering radical autonomy; but (in part, I believe, because of some of the factors I discussed in my religion pamphlet) this practice ultimately developed its own irrational autonomous momentum. Increasingly trivial personal antagonisms came to be treated as serious political differences. However justified some of the breaks may have been, the whole situ scene ended up looking pretty silly when virtually every individual had disdainfully split from virtually all the others. Many participants finally got so traumatized that they ended up repressing the whole experience.

I never went that far. I never renounced my radical and (apart from a few nuances) still basically situationist perspective, and have no plans to. But I was certainly disheartened by our 1977 breakup. For years I mulled it over, trying to come to terms with what had happened. As long as it hung over me it was difficult to be as audacious as I had sometimes been before. I continued to make notes on various topics, but except for two or three relatively short and specific projects I was unable to bring them to completion. Besides objective difficulties in the topics themselves (including the relative ebbing of radical activity in the late seventies) there would inevitably be ramifications that would relate back to the old trauma.

Anyway, in the immediate aftermath of the breakup, finding myself suddenly estranged from several of my closest friends and unsure of what to do next, I figured this was as good a time as any to go to Japan. That summer I took an intensive three-month Japanese course at the University, and in September I flew to Tokyo.

I was in Japan for two months, based in Fujinomiya, a quiet country town at the foot of Mt. Fuji where Tommy Haruki and his family lived, enough off the beaten track that some of the neighborhood children had never seen a foreigner.

After a week or two I returned to Tokyo to meet some young anarchists who were translating my "Society of Situationism." It was interesting to try to come up with Japanese equivalents for what I had written; but due to the absence of situationist activity in Japan they naturally had no conception of many of the nuances of ideologization that my text is largely concerned with, so I doubt if the translation ever met with much understanding.

I met a number of other anarchists in Tokyo, but for the most part I did not find the scene of much interest. Just to see if I could stir things up a bit, I wrote a sharply critical open letter to one of the groups, which Haruki translated and circulated to anarchist addresses throughout Japan. The group reprinted it along with a couple responses on the "If you can't say anything nice, don't say anything" theme.

In November I made a three-week trip to Hong Kong to meet the "'70s," an anarchist group that was disseminating information on dissident tendencies in China at a time when such information was very hard to come by and many people still had illusions about Mao and the "Cultural Revolution." I later put out a critical appreciation of the group and its publications. To my surprise and disappointment, this text did not receive any public response from the 70s, though it apparently stirred up some internal debate. "Although some overseas comrades have criticised your 'A Radical Group in Hong Kong' as supercilious there are a number of us here (people including myself who have not met you) who *do very much* agree with you in your criticisms of the 70's to the finest details," wrote one correspondent, who unfortunately ended up rallying to the stale dogmatism of the International Communist Current, which hardly represents any improvement. The 70s group itself dissolved in the early 1980s.

Back in Japan, I visited some other anarchists in Kyoto and Osaka; helped Haruki reprint a Japanese translation of *On the Poverty of Student Life* that we had discovered; savored a few final dictionary-aided conversations, accompanied with cups of hot saké (particularly pleasant as the December cold began to penetrate the uninsulated houses); and returned to Berkeley.

I had mixed feelings about Japan. I disliked the conformism, the work ethic, and the persistence of traditional hierarchies and gender divisions. (There are even different grammatical forms depending on whether you're a man or a woman, or are speaking to a superior or an inferior—I found it hard to take that sort of thing seriously.) But I

134

liked some aspects of the culture very much—the traditional architecture and decor; the polite, modest comportment; the delicious cuisine; the almost fanatical neatness. (The practice of taking off your shoes before entering someone's home seemed so sensible and comfortable that I've adopted it ever since in my own home.) And the language, though difficult, is fascinating to work with. Back in Berkeley I continued to study it, with the idea that I might go back and live there for a while. But I never ended up doing so, primarily because I didn't hear of any interesting new radical developments there or any new contacts I wanted to meet. After a year I discontinued the study, and have since forgotten almost everything I knew. But it was fun while it lasted.

Apart from Japanese study, most of 1978 was taken up with proofreading work. For the last two decades I've gotten by on various freelance proofreading and editing jobs—not very exciting, but it allows me flexible hours and a lot of free time. Having fairly simple tastes and no family to support, I've been able to live my entire adult life in modest comfort on an income below the official poverty level. Of my only two apparent extravagances, my publications have almost paid for themselves (if you don't count my "labor" on them, which has mostly been fun) and even my occasional foreign trips have been relatively cheap because I generally only go to places where there are friends or contacts I can stay with.

That fall I started closely following the revolt in Iran, reading daily press accounts as well as exploring a lot of background history. In March 1979 I issued a poster, "The Opening in Iran," several hundred copies of which were distributed to radical Iranian student groups in America. It was my hope that a few copies, or at least some of the ideas, might find their way to Iran, but I don't know if this ever happened. Some of the individual Iranians I met were vaguely sympathetic, but most were too caught up in the momentum of events and too attached to Islam or to one or another variety of Leninism to comprehend any truly radical perspective. A few even threatened to beat me up for disparaging Khomeini.

My text has been criticized for underestimating the preponderance of the religious element in the uprising. I assumed that both the strength of the Khomeiniist movement and its reactionary nature were obvious. In any case, though Khomeini's eventual victory seemed likely, I did not believe it was a foregone conclusion—as it was, it took him several months to really consolidate his power. Leaving aside the admittedly overenthusiastic opening sentence, which was added on a last-minute impulse, my text was simply an attempt to cut through the prevalent confusions and distinguish the various forces and factors in play; it presented possibilities, not probabilities or predictions. For whatever it may be worth, someone later wrote to me: "I was in Iran shortly after the revolution. I hitchhiked from the Pakistan border to the Turkish border. I can tell of dozens of examples where ordinary people had taken power. Your analysis of the situation in Iran and its possibilities is *the only* bit of information I have seen that even remotely resembles the truth." I know nothing about the reliability of this person, but every statement in my text was based on documented sources, most of them no more radical than *Le Monde* or the *Christian Science Monitor*.

The *Monitor*, incidentally, is the only mainstream news publication I read with any regularity: I've subscribed to it ever since I discovered it while researching my Iran piece. It is, of course, far from radical, but I find it less obnoxious than other American papers, and within its moderate, more or less liberal-humanistic limits (the paper's religious perspective rarely obtrudes) it gives more international news and wastes less space on the latest moronic sensations.

In fall 1979 I went to Europe for four months. Several weeks were taken up in side trips to meet contacts in Mannheim, Nantes, Bordeaux, Barcelona, Athens and Thessaloniki. The rest of the time I stayed in Paris, hosted by Nadine and Joël, with whom I was back on excellent terms (they had visited me in California the year before). I also saw the Deneverts a few times. After the 1977 break they too had gone through a traumatic period that had eventually led them to question the sort of hostility and delirium that had frequently accompanied breaks in the situ milieu, and had initiated some degree of reconciliation with some of the people they had previously broken with. This did not mean that they were resigned to settling back into the usual superficial social relations. A year later they sent out a set of "Lettres sur l'amitié" in which they discussed their recent experiences on the terrain of political and personal relationships and declared a "friendship strike" of indefinite duration. That was the last I ever heard of them. The next time I tried to get in touch with them they had moved and left no address. (Does anyone know where they are?)

While I was in Paris I drafted a leaflet, apropos of nothing in particular (I envisioned handing it out at random in the Métro, etc.). What with one thing or another I never got around to printing it up. Here it is for the first time, seventeen years later:

PARIS SPLEEN

In Paris more than anywhere else, especially since the situationists, everything has been said but few have taken advantage of it. Because theory is in itself commonplace it can only be of value to people who are not. Radical texts have become as routine as the work and consumption they denounce. Yes, we know it's necessary to abolish the state and wage labor, to liberate our everyday lives, etc. But we become blasé. It becomes difficult to think for ourselves. Revolution is contained by overexposure.

Only exceptionally are our struggles open and clear. Usually we are entangled, implicated in what we want to fight. It's easy, and comforting, to blame the capitalists or the bureaucrats or the police; but it's only thanks to the passive complicity of the "masses" that those small minorities have any power. It's not so much the "fault" of the unions or the mass media for falsifying workers' struggles— after all, that's their function—as of the workers who fail to themselves assure the communication of their own experiences and perspectives.

Bad enough that the system exploits us and hurts us and keeps us in ignorance. Worse is that it *warps* us, turns us into mean, petty, spiteful, cowardly creatures. Were we confronted with a single gross temptation to self-betrayal we might well refuse it. But little by little a thousand compromises wear away our resistance. We become incapable of any experimentation, for fear of disturbing the defenses we have built up to repress our shame. Even when we arrive at considering a critical action, we hesitate; we find so many objections—we are afraid of seeming foolish, afraid of being mistaken, afraid that our idea won't work, or that if it does it won't amount to anything.

Hypocrite reader, your blasé expression doesn't hide the fact that you know very well what I'm talking about. You go from ideology to ideology, each containing just enough truth to keep you hanging on but fragmentary enough to keep you from confronting the totality concretely. Successively disillusioned, you end up believing in nothing but the illusory nature of everything. Cynical spectator, like everyone else you pride yourself on being "different." You console yourself by despising the naïve, the provincial, the yokel, the person who still believes in God or in his job—whose caricatured submission is presented as a foil precisely to make you forget your own submission. You are even telling yourself right now that this applies to most people but not to you; while the person next to you thinks that it applies to you but not to him.

You vaguely imagine that somehow your life may get better. Do you really have any reason to believe that? Are you going to continue as you have until you die? Have you nothing to say? Have you no audacity, no imagination?

Dialogue must concern itself with the suppression of the conditions that suppress dialogue!

Let's resolve the anachronistic "social question" so we can tackle more interesting problems!

Pettiness is always counterrevolutionary!

Back in Berkeley I started working on my *Situationist International Anthology.* For years I had been frustrated by the lack of SI translations. Most of those that had appeared were inaccurate, and the few relatively good ones were usually out of print. It was difficult for people to get a sense of the overall situationist perspective and how it had developed by reading just a few scattered articles, and the only general collection, Christopher Gray's *Leaving the Twentieth Century*, was inadequate in several respects. I had already considered doing some translations myself, but my 1975 proposal (in the "Blind Men and the Elephant" poster) had failed to interest any publishers, and the thought of self-publishing a large collection seemed too overwhelming. Delay was also caused by two projected commercial editions of Vaneigem's *Treatise* that proved abortive: those of us who might have gone ahead to translate and publish situationist texts ourselves were misled by these publishers' firm assurance that their editions would soon be out—which, if true, would probably have led to other situationist books being issued by major publishers.

Eventually, after yet other rumors of new translations proved unfounded, I concluded that if I wanted a competent collection I would have to do it myself. Though not totally fluent in French, I did by this time have a pretty thorough understanding of the texts and I was able to enlist Joël and Nadine's help in clarifying any obscurities that remained.

As soon as I had worked out a fairly specific idea of the contents of the *Anthology* I sent out a prospectus to some thirty publishers, but ran into the usual presumption that situationist writings were too difficult or obscure. In retrospect this was probably fortunate. Had I succeeded, I might have had to worry about the publisher arguing about my choice of texts, insisting on a preface by some radical celebrity, adding blurbs by reviewers who didn't know what they were talking about, delaying publication, letting the book go out of print, etc. By self-publishing I was able to control the whole project. Among other things this meant that I could maintain the SI's original non-copyright policy and that I was able to keep the price down and send large quantities of free copies to prisoners and to indigent comrades in East Europe and the Third World.

The project took up most of the next two years. This was just before the advent of cheap desktop publishing; with present-day equipment I could have saved hundreds of hours and thousands of dollars on typesetting, indexing, pasteup, etc. But believing that these texts are the most important body of social critique in this century, I was quite happy to do whatever was necessary to present them as accurately as possible.

I don't believe there are any significant errors in my translation, though I might have been able to render some of the passages a bit more clearly and idiomatically (as I did in the new version of the Watts article I recently issued). A few people have questioned my decision to anglicize *dérive* and *détournement*, but I have yet to see any alternatives that are not more confusing. (On the other hand, I now feel that the one other French term I anglicized, *récupération*, can be most clearly translated by "cooption," despite the slightly different connotations of the two words.)

As happens with any anthology, some readers disagreed with the choice of articles. Michel Prigent, who seems never to have forgiven me for having pointed out that his own translations of situationist texts (published under the names Piranha and Chronos) are clumsily over-literal, accused me of shaping the selection to accord with my own "ideological perspectives"; but aside from apparently implying that I should have included one or two texts that he himself had already translated, the only alternative he suggested was a complete English edition of the French journals. I hope someone will eventually publish such an edition, but this would have tripled the time and expense of what was already a pretty overwhelming project.

A few other critics claimed that I "concealed" the earlier, more cultural phase of the SI. The *Anthology* is admittedly weighted somewhat toward the situationists' later, more "political" period (without which no one but a few specialists in obscure avant-garde movements would have ever heard of them), but the main features of the earlier phase could hardly escape anyone who reads the first dozen articles of the book. I probably would have included more selections from *Potlatch* and other pre-SI material if it had been available at the time; but if I didn't go into the subsequent history of the "Nashists" and other artistic tendencies this is because I think they are of little interest and have little to do with the situationists' most original and vital contributions. Since the book's appearance these critics have had fifteen years to publish the vital texts I supposedly concealed; so far what they have come up with has not been overwhelming.

Other readers wished there were more annotations explaining obscure references. Actually the supposed obscurity of situationist texts is greatly exaggerated. They usually assume little more than a minimal acquaintance with a few basic works and major historical events that anyone with a serious desire to understand and change the world should certainly find out about for themselves if they don't already know about them. The context usually makes the sense pretty clear even if you are not familiar, say, with some particular European ideologue being denounced, just as you can learn a lot from Marx and Engels without knowing anything about the particular philosophers and economists they criticized.

Others wished I had included some of the original SI illustrations. I like them as much as anyone. But many of the best ones (particularly the detourned comics) were already so widely reprinted and imitated that they were tending to distract from the writings and reinforce the popular misconception that situationist publications consisted of zappy collages designed to blow people's minds. I felt that it wouldn't hurt the image addicts to pay attention to the simple unadorned texts for a change.

There were also, of course, many more comments about the texts themselves. In the last few years books and articles on the SI have become even more numerous than in the immediate aftermath of May 1968, and the SI has become more intriguingly notorious than ever.

A little of the aura has even rubbed off on me. Since the original SI members have generally remained unavailable, I have sometimes been considered the next best thing, and have been asked to do book-signings, to grant interviews, to give talks, to be videotaped, to contribute to various publications, to provide information for graduate theses, to take part in radical conferences and academic symposiums, to be a "visiting artist" at an art institute, and even to furnish background material for a television program. I have refused all these requests.

This isn't a matter of rigid principle. Someday, if I'm ever in the mood and am given sufficiently free conditions, I may decide to detourn one of these situations, as Debord once did when he gave a talk at a conference on "everyday life" which among other things criticized the inherent limits and biases of such conferences (see *SI Anthology*, pp. 68–75). But on the whole I think people are fooling themselves if they believe that the radical effect of this sort of publicity outweighs all the trivializing and neutralizing effects (including the subtle temptations to accentuate one's own trendy or sensational qualities while refraining from offending anyone, in order to ensure that one will be invited again). In any case, although I'm somewhat less rigorous in these matters than was the SI, when I am asked to present or represent "the situationist perspective" I feel I convey that perspective most incisively by refusing the kinds of things the situationists themselves consistently refused.

Anyone is free to reprint, adapt or comment on the *SI Anthology* or any of my other publications. I can't take seriously those who never do so while seeking some personal encounter or scoop designed to give spectators the impression they have gotten some inside dope about texts they often haven't even bothered to read, much less put into practice. It seems to me that maintaining this distance puts things on the clearest basis. Shortly after the publication of the *Anthology*, for example, a certain professional writer wanted to interview me to obtain information for an article he had been asked to write on the situationists for the weekly *East Bay Express*. I refused to have anything to do with him, and the projected article never appeared. Around the same time I also refused to meet Greil Marcus when he was preparing a review of the *Anthology* for the *Village Voice*, but to his credit he did not let this stop him from writing a lengthy and very laudatory article. There was, after all, plenty of information in the SI texts themselves, and because he read them carefully he was able to get most of his facts right. Though limited in some regards,* his article was an honest expression of his take on the situationists, done out of his own enthusiastic interest, not because someone assigned him to do it or because I sucked up to him. Everything is so much clearer this way.

By the early 1980s I had reestablished friendly relations with most of the other "Notice" signers. They had gone their various ways and, except for Chris and Isaac, who had each put out two or three pamphlets in the interim, none of them had carried on any notable radical activity since our 1977 breakup. In 1982 Isaac and his wife Terrel Seltzer also put out *Call It Sleep,* a 45-minute videotape roughly in the style of Debord's films. Not long afterwards Isaac renounced his previous radical perspective, justifying his subsequent devotion to primarily financial pursuits with what seems to be a sort of neo-laissez-faire ideology in a bizarre book he co-authored with Paul Béland, *Money: Myths and Realities* (1986).

I've made some criticisms of Isaac because he expressed viewpoints from which I felt obliged to dissociate myself. But I would like to acknowledge my debt to him and to many other former comrades. We went through a lot of exciting times together. All the polemics have tended to overemphasize the problems of the situ milieu. For me, at any rate, the ventures recounted here so tersely contained many valued relationships, lots of good times, and an immense amount of laughs; even the fiascos were often amusing. I hope my old friends haven't entirely forgotten them.

---

*To put it briefly, in both his *Village Voice* article and his subsequent book, *Lipstick Traces,* Marcus relates to the situationists *aesthetically,* as a fascinated *spectator.* For all his awe of their extremist ideas, he shows little interest in the carefully calculated tactics and organizational forms through which they tried to *implement* those ideas instead of merely impulsively "expressing" them like his other heroes, the dadaists and the punks. His personal, impressionistic approach is more illuminating than the fatuous accounts of most academic and cultural critics, but he shares the latter's main blind spot: preferring the situationists' early, more intriguingly exotic phase, while seeing their later revolutionary perspective as an embarrassing anachronism. Such critics invariably assure us that, whatever revolutions may have happened in the past, it's all over now and will never happen again. After ridiculing the SI's advocacy of workers councils (which was far less simplistic than he implies), Marcus blasély concludes: "If the situationist idea of general contestation was realized in May 1968, the idea also realized its limits. The theory of the exemplary act . . . may have gone as far as such a theory or such an act can go"—ignoring how close the May movement came to going much farther (see the passages cited on pages 53 and 57 of the present book) and never mentioning subsequent movements such as Portugal 1974 or Poland 1980 (which in some respects did go farther) or any of the individual currents attempting to actually use and develop the situationists' achievements. I myself am oddly pigeonholed as a "student" of the SI, as if there was nothing left for any of us latecomers but to produce learned dissertations or wistful elegies on the heroic ventures of bygone times.

Once the *SI Anthology* was published I felt less obliged to devote so much time and energy to explaining the situationist perspective, correcting misconceptions, etc. The most significant questions were dealt with quite lucidly by the situationists themselves in the texts that were now available. Over the next few years, apart from carrying on more or less routine correspondence and distribution and making occasional notes, I began to explore other things.

My first new venture turned out to be rock climbing, one of the last things I would ever have imagined myself getting into. Like almost everyone, I was very afraid of heights; but during recent outings I had begun to find myself more and more intrigued by the idea of climbing, feeling a sort of primal, primate allure whenever I saw cliffs or rock formations. Eventually I suppressed my terror and signed up for a beginning rock climbing class. We spent a couple hours learning the basic principles, then went to some outcrops in the Berkeley Hills and actually climbed. A few weeks later I took a more advanced class in Yosemite and did my first really high climbs on the granite cliffs, hundreds of feet straight up.

For the next two years rock climbing was my passion. When possible I went on trips in Yosemite and elsewhere in the Sierras; but most of the time I climbed right in town, biking several times a week up to Indian Rock for bouldering (practicing difficult moves near the ground). With the right kind of shoes (made with high-friction rubber soles and worn supertight so your foot becomes one firm, scrunched-up unit like a mountain goat's hoof) it's amazing what meager indentations in the rock can accommodate your toe or finger—a pea-sized bump will do if you orient your body just right, gauging the right balance of opposing forces, moving carefully but with relaxed confidence (if you tremble you're more likely to slip).

If you pay attention and use the ropes properly, rock climbing isn't as dangerous as it might seem. Still, there's obviously some risk. At first I loved it so much that I felt the risk was acceptable; but after a couple years I decided to quit while I was ahead. In Aldous Huxley's utopian novel *Island* it's part of the education of every adolescent to have at least one psychedelic trip and one rock climbing trip (though not at the same time!). Considering their risks I would hesitate to recommend either one unreservedly, but both experiences have certainly meant a lot to me.

I still occasionally do a little bouldering and hiking (most often over the hills, through the woods and along the beach at nearby Point Reyes), but my main exercise in recent years has been basketball and tennis. Playing basketball with the black teenagers in my neighborhood was an interesting cultural as well as physical challenge: I felt like I had accomplished something when I finally became accepted as more or less one of the guys. More recently I've shifted to tennis. It's also virtually the only thing I ever watch on television: I lug my set out of storage three or four times a year for Wimbledon and other major tournaments.

In fall 1984 I made another trip to France, staying most of the time in Paris with my friend Christian Camous. We had originally met in a situ context during my previous trip, but by this time his focus had shifted to experimenting with ways to enliven his own immediate milieu. That's fine with me: if I have to choose, I prefer intellectually alive people who do interesting things with their life over those who do nothing but regurgitate political platitudes and gripe all the time. Full of playful irony, provocative banter and jokes in several languages, and possessing a keen insight into people's games and scripts (in Eric Berne's sense), Christian keeps me on my toes when I start becoming too stodgy and pedantic.

There were two side trips: to the Dordogne region in southwest France where Joël and Nadine were now living, and to Germany to revisit my Mannheim friends and briefly meet another group in West Berlin.

Back in Berkeley I began work on two Rexroth projects. During the early seventies my interest in Rexroth had waned. In the light of the situationist perspectives his political analysis seemed insufficient, his notion of subversion through art and poetry seemed dubious, and some of his activities, such as writing newspaper columns or dabbling in Catholicism, seemed unacceptably compromising.

In less direct ways, however, his influence persisted. Recalling his skeptical magnanimity helped me keep things in perspective during some of the more traumatic situ affairs. In my 1977 religion pamphlet I was already trying to figure out to what extent these two major influences of my life could be reconciled; since that time, my enthusiasm for him had fully revived. Besides rereading all his books, I hunted up and photocopied as many of his uncollected articles as I could locate in the old magazine files at the University library, including all of the 800+ columns he wrote for the San Francisco *Examiner*.

On a lark, I sent out a proposal to edit an anthology of the columns. There was enough tentative interest on the part of a few publishers that I spent several months going through the columns in order to prepare a representative sampling. Ultimately only one small publisher made an offer, and it was so unsatisfactory that I rejected it and decided to put the project on the shelf. I would have been happy to put in a lot of time editing the columns for a modest royalty, but I didn't feel like publishing them myself.

It had meanwhile occurred to me that it was more to the point to express my own perspective on Rexroth, to try to convey just what it was that I thought was so great about him as well as to clarify the points where I disagreed with him. Besides hopefully turning people on to him, this would be a good way for me to work out my own views on all sorts of topics.

This project turned out to occupy me on and off over the next five years. I could, of course, have written most of what I had to say in a much shorter period; but since I had no deadline I took my time and indulged myself, reading his works over and over, gleaning favorite quotes, accumulating masses of notes, and following out all sorts of tangents. It might occur to me, say, that it would be interesting to compare Rexroth with other freewheeling writers such as H. L. Mencken, Edmund Wilson, George Orwell or Paul Goodman; this would be a good excuse to reread several of their books, even if I ended up making little if any use of them in my text.

In 1985 I also began a regular Zen practice. Over the years I had occasionally done a little zazen at home, but I had scarcely taken part in any formal group practice since the sixties. As I mentioned earlier, in addition to laziness and involvement in other things, I had reservations about some of the traditional forms. Although Zen is less dogmatic and more intellectually sophisticated than most religions, traditional Zen practice is quite strict and formal. I could recognize the need for certain forms to facilitate concentration and self-discipline, but I was dubious about others that seemed to be mere vestiges of Oriental social hierarchy. I was quite aware of the deplorable role religion has played in reinforcing acquiescence in the established order, and of people's remarkable capacity for self-deception.*

---

*Before going on, I should stress that my Zen practice has nothing to do with any supernatural beliefs. To my understanding, Zen does not invalidate science or reason, it simply tries to break the habit of excessive, compulsive intellectualizing. Without *some* logical discrimination people could not survive for a day—or even understand what I'm saying well enough to disagree with it.

Though science is often accused of arrogance, it is virtually the only field of human endeavor that takes into account its own fallibility, that consistently tests itself and corrects its own errors through rigorously objective methods designed to counteract people's natural tendencies toward fallacious reasoning, unconscious biases and selective memory (remembering the hits and forgetting all the misses). To really test the claims of astrology, for example, requires checking a statistically large sampling of people to see if, say, a disproportionate number of scientists are born under signs supposed to indicate rationalistic tendencies. Such tests have been carried out many times and in no case has there turned out to be any such correlation. Similar investigations of many other supposed paranormal phenomena have been described in books by James Randi, Martin Gardner and others and in numerous articles in the *Skeptical Inquirer* (journal of the Committee for the Scientific Investigation of Claims of the Paranormal). Over and over such claims have been shown to be based on rumors that turn out to be false, misinterpretations of otherwise explainable events, insufficiently rigorous conditions of experimentation, or hoaxes and charlatanism.

There may turn out to be kernels of truth in a few of these areas, but considering how susceptible people are to fooling themselves (and to clinging to their beliefs rather

Rexroth used to say, "Religion is not something you believe, it's something you do." I don't know if this can justly be said of the major Western religions, which very emphatically insist on belief in certain dogmas, but it's at least partially true of some of the Eastern ones. The Eastern religions probably contain as much bullshit as the Western ones (the more superstitious or obnoxious aspects are usually discreetly omitted in Western popularizations), but they do tend to be more tolerant and ecumenical. Their myths are often explicitly presented as mere spiritual metaphors and there is relatively little insistence on beliefs. Zen in particular is more a practice than a belief system. Verbal teachings are considered meaningless unless you test and assimilate them for yourself. The most vital teachings are by living example. Despite an element of guru-disciple hierarchy (which has been considerably attenuated as Zen has been adapted in the West), the emphasis is not on worship of superior beings but on the practice of meditation and mindfulness in one's own day-to-day activity.

In my Rexroth book I implied where I personally draw the line: "It is one thing to practice some type of meditation or take part in some ritual or festival that everyone understands is simply an arbitrary form to focus one's life or celebrate communion; it is another to seem to lend credibility to repugnant institutions and to sick dogmas that are still widely believed." I suppose this is mainly a matter of taste. I have friends who have fewer qualms than I, and others who wouldn't be caught dead taking part in any formal religious practice whatsoever. Personally I like most of the Zen rituals, the silence, the bells, the incense, the neat Japanese-style decor, the ultraconsiderate etiquette. And practicing with a group offers many advantages in the way of instruction, camaraderie and mutual encouragement.

Anyway, I was in a mood to suspend my relatively mild objections and try out a more regular practice. The Berkeley center I had gone to in the sixties had quietly carried on the Soto Zen practice brought to America by Shunryu Suzuki. The teacher, Mel Weitsman, one of Suzuki's students whom I had known in the sixties, was both solid and low-key, and the members, a varied and generally congenial assortment of laypeople trying to integrate Zen practice into their everyday lives, seemed to have kept their sense of humor and to have avoided any excessive cultishness. And I didn't even have to get up early: they now had afternoon as well as morning sittings.

---

than admitting that they've been made fools of) I intend to reserve judgment until I see some good evidence. For years Randi and others have made a standing offer of $100,000 to anyone who can demonstrate any paranormal power whatsoever under scientifically controlled conditions (including observation by professional magicians like Randi, who are capable of recognizing the sorts of tricks often used by charlatans). Hundreds of self-proclaimed psychics, dowsers, astrologers, etc., have tried to do so. So far not a single one has succeeded.

I started going for a forty-minute period of zazen every weekday afternoon.

In zazen (sitting meditation) we sit cross-legged on a firm cushion, facing a blank wall. The belly is pushed slightly forward so that the spine is erect and the body is stably balanced on buttocks and knees. Mouth closed. Eyes lowered but open. Shoulders relaxed. Hands in lap, left on right, thumb tips lightly touching. If sitting cross-legged is too difficult other postures, such as sitting over one's heels or even sitting on a chair, are okay as long as the back is straight; but the cross-legged lotus position (both feet resting on opposite thighs) or some easier variation thereof (one foot on opposite thigh or calf) provides optimum groundedness.

In Soto-style zazen we generally concentrate on maintaining our posture (constantly correcting the tendencies to slump or to tense up) and following our breath—breathing from the abdomen and silently counting exhalations: "O-n-n-n-e . . ., t-w-o-o-o . . ." If you get to ten you just start all over again. The numbers simply provide an arbitrary nonemotive focus to help maintain concentration. The point is to get as close as you can to "doing nothing" while remaining totally alert.

It's not as easy as you might think. Most of us have developed a strong habitual resistance to being in the present. What usually happens is that by the time you've got to "three" or "four," you've become caught up in memories, daydreams, desires, worries, fears, regrets. This repetitive cacophony is going on in our minds most of the time, but in zazen you become more acutely aware of it.

It may come as quite a shock to realize how petty and compulsive your usual thoughts and feelings are. It did to me, anyway. I could see how Christian believers going through similar experiences saw them as a confirmation of humanity's inherent sinfulness, leaving them no way out but faith in some supernatural redemption. Buddhism addresses these matters more calmly, tolerantly, objectively, without getting so caught up in futile breastbeating. Trying to repress the "monkey mind" only stirs up more emotional entanglement. But if you just sit still, without any value judgments, and keep coming back to your breath, the disturbances, deprived of reinforcement, will tend to settle out, become less emotive, less subject to compulsive habits and associations. It's not a matter of eliminating thoughts or emotions, but of ceasing to *cling* to them—ceasing to cling even to your sense of progress in not clinging. The moment you start thinking: "Ah! Now I'm finally getting somewhere! Won't so-and-so be impressed!" you've drifted away from present awareness. Just calmly note the fact, and start again: "O-n-n-n-e . . ., t-w-o-o-o . . ."

After a couple months of daily sitting I started taking part in the monthly *sesshins:* one or more days of intensive Zen practice, primarily zazen, but with other activities carried out with a similar effort to focus mindfully on just what you are doing. A sesshin typically runs from 5:00 in the morning to 9:00 in the evening. Zazen is in 40-minute periods, alternating with 10-minute periods of *kinhin* (ultraslow walking meditation to stretch the legs). Beginning and end of periods are signaled by bells or wooden clappers. No talking except for minimal necessary communication during work. The procedure of serving and eating, which also takes place in the *zendo* (meditation hall), is elaborately ritualistic. Servers bring a dish, you bow to each other, they serve you, you make a palm-up gesture to indicate "enough," you bow to each other again, then they proceed to the next person. . . .

I particularly liked the longer sesshins (five or seven days). The first day of a sesshin you may still be preoccupied with your other affairs, but after three or four days you can hardly help settling into the sesshin rhythm. They say there are two kinds of Zen experience. One is sudden and unmistakable, like getting a bucket of water dumped on your head. The other is more gradual and subtle, like walking through a mist and then noticing that your clothes have imperceptibly become soaking wet. That's sort of what you feel like in the later stages of a sesshin. It all starts coming together.

It can also be pretty grueling, with fatigue, stiff shoulders, aching back, sore knees. Though it becomes easier as the body gets used to the cross-legged position, most people continue to experience some knee pain during sesshins. The point isn't to see how much pain you can stand (if it's really too much, you can always shift to some easier position), but to learn to deal with whatever comes with equanimity; to stop yearning for the past or the future and settle right in the moment. After a while you discover that suffering is caused less by pain itself than by cringing apprehension of future pain. The first day of a sesshin can be horrifying if you're sitting there thinking that you have seven more days of this to endure. But if you take it just one breath at a time, it's not so bad.

(This is where one of the greatest advantages of practicing with a group comes in. When you're sitting alone it's too easy to rationalize stopping when you feel a little discomfort; but when several participants have committed themselves to a sesshin and are all sitting there together, each person's effort encourages everyone else.)

As soon as you begin to get accustomed to the zazen, other responsibilities are thrust upon you which require equal mindfulness. If you're a server your mind mustn't wander or you might spill soup on someone. If you head up a dishwashing team consisting of people who aren't familiar with the procedures, you need to make sure dishes are put away in the right places, yet you don't want to disturb people's efforts to concentrate by yacking away about every detail. Each situation presents new challenges to find the right balance between efficiency and presence, calculation and spontaneity, effort and ease.

Hopefully some of these habits gradually become integrated into your everyday life. I don't want to give the impression that zazen is a cure-all, but I do think that some sort of regular meditation helps one to develop a little more patience and sense of perspective; to recognize certain problems as unimportant or illusory, and to deal more calmly and objectively with those that still seem significant.

After a year and a half of intensive day-to-day involvement with the center I got a bit burned out, and reverted to doing my daily zazen at home. I continued, however, to take part in the longer sesshins. I also started going to sesshins at some of the other centers in northern California, including one that Gary Snyder and others (including an old friend of Sam Thomas's and mine from the sixties) had recently built on their land in the Sierra Nevada foothills. As might be expected, they have a strong back-to-nature orientation: some of their sesshins are combined with seven-day backpacking trips—an arduous but powerful combination!

In early 1988 I started thinking about taking part in an intensive three-month "practice period" at the Tassajara monastery. For years I had vaguely imagined that going to a Zen monastery would be one of the ultimate things to do; now I began to think I might actually do it. In the spring I went to Tassajara for a week just to see what it felt like, and liked it very much indeed. Back in the Bay Area I took part in a few more sesshins, arranged my affairs, and in late September packed up and drove back down.

The first Zen monastery in the Western hemisphere (founded in 1967 by Shunryu Suzuki), Tassajara is located in the coastal mountains about a hundred miles south of the Bay Area. It used to be a hot springs resort, and still functions as such in the summer; but during the rest of the year it's closed to the public.

Besides Mel, who led the practice period, there were 26 participants (14 men and 12 women) plus two staff people who took care of technical maintenance work and shopping trips to town. During the next three months none of us left Tassajara and no one else came there except a couple visiting Japanese monks and two or three Zen Center people briefly down from San Francisco.

Eleven of us were there for our first practice period and had to go through a five-day initiation: a superintensive sesshin with even less physical and mental relief from zazen (no kinhin, no lectures, no work). Except for a half-hour break after each meal and bathroom breaks as needed, we had to remain seated on our cushions from 4:20 a.m. to 9:00 p.m.

Even more than in a sesshin, everything levels out. Time slows. Attention is reduced to the simplest things. Nothing to do but stew in your own juices (literally as well as figuratively: it's sweltering) and learn to calmly ignore the relentless little mucous flies that delight in crawling around your eyes, ears and nostrils. (The only solution is to accept them: "Okay, you little rascals, do what you must! I'm not moving.") Just sit, perfectly still, breath after breath. . . . The bell rings. Slowly get up, keeping eyes lowered. Come together for a ritual. Then back to your cushion for a meal. Then a break. Slowly exit the zendo, striving to maintain complete concentration despite the sudden splendor of the natural world outside. Have a cup of tea. Massage your aching legs. A few precious minutes are left for sitting by the creek and letting the sound of the water pour through your head. Then back to the zendo. Settle into the right posture. Become perfectly still. Just this breath, breath after breath. . . .

After it was over, we reverted to a somewhat less intense schedule. Every morning at 4:00 we were awakened by someone running down the main path jangling a loud bell. Just time to wash my face, do a few yoga stretches, put on my meditation robe and go to the zendo. The morning was like a sesshin: mostly zazen, with breakfast and lunch served ritual-style in the zendo. In the afternoon we worked for three hours. I was part of the miscellaneous contingent and did all sorts of different jobs—carpentry, hauling, gardening, dishwashing, cleaning, taking care of the library. After work came the most luxurious part of the day: a leisurely hot bath followed by an hour of free time. Then back on with our robes and to the zendo for dinner. Then a study period, then more zazen. To bed at 9:30. There was never any trouble getting to sleep: the next thing I heard was that jangling wakeup bell. . . .

Every fifth day we got to sleep till the indulgently late hour of 5:00, and after one period of zazen and breakfast we had free time until evening. This was generally spent doing laundry, packing a sack lunch and taking a hike, or sitting around reading, writing letters or quietly socializing. In the evening we had a class on Dōgen's "Genjō Kōan": "To study Buddhism is to study the self. To study the self is to forget the self. To forget the self is to be actualized by the myriad things. When actualized by the myriad things, your body and mind as well as the bodies and minds of others drop away. No trace of realization remains, and this no-trace is continued endlessly. . . ."

Within a few weeks the weather turned frigid. Shaded by the surrounding mountains, Tassajara becomes cold and damp in fall and winter, at least until midday, and there was no heating or insulation. At least the cold helped us wake up. Though the routine was Spartan in some ways, it was refreshing to get down to basics and live in a community in which everyone was quietly working together. For me a sesshin or a practice period is a hint of how life could be. Upon meeting anyone on a path we both stopped, bowed to each other, then continued on our way without saying a word. Wonderful!

Back in Berkeley, I resumed what has been my ongoing Zen practice ever since (brief daily zazen at home plus long sesshins a few times a year) and got back to work on my Rexroth book. I had accumulated hundreds of pages of notes, but eventually I decided to leave most of them out and pare the text down to a brief and relatively accessible presentation of a few main themes. It was finally completed in 1990. Sales have been pretty modest, but (one of the advantages of self-publishing) I've also been able to give copies to hundreds of friends and acquaintances, sometimes even to total strangers. I'll continue to do so with the numerous copies I still have on hand, but I've also included it in this collection because it goes into a lot of matters that are important to me but that aren't dealt with in my other writings.

In January 1991 the Gulf war brought hundreds of thousands of people into the streets for the first time in years. I immediately started writing "The War and the Spectacle." Most of the points in that text were already being widely discussed or intuited, but I felt that the situationist concept of the spectacle would help tie them together. With a little help from some friends I distributed 15,000 copies over the next few months. Besides mailing them to individuals, groups and radical bookstores around the world, I saturated the local antiwar milieu, handing them out at marches, rallies, demonstrations, films, concert benefits, radical theater performances in the parks, forums on "the war and the media," and appearances of Ramsey Clark and Thich Nhat Hanh. It was the most well received text I've ever done. Nearly everyone who got it read it, no one complained that they couldn't understand it, many people later told me that they had photocopied it and sent it to friends or entered it onto computer networks, and it was widely reprinted and translated.

One of the few critics of the piece expressed surprise that I took over two months to write such a short article. I envy people who can work faster, but for me that's about par for the course. I do write a lot —noting anything that has any conceivable connection with whatever topic I'm working on, sometimes virtually free-associating—but I'm not usually satisfied till I've drastically condensed the material, going over every detail numerous times, eliminating redundancies and exaggerations, experimenting with different rearrangements, considering potential objections and misconceptions. I feel that one carefully considered text will have a sharper and ultimately more far-reaching impact than a dozen slipshod ones.

Since I only tackle subjects that I'm really interested in, the process is usually pretty engrossing. Sometimes I get into the ecstatic "negative rush" state described in *Double-Reflection*—so many ideas flood through my mind I hardly have time to write them all down; out walking, I may have to stop every few minutes to jot down some idea; I may even get up in the middle of the night to scribble notes to myself. Sometimes I get so involved that if I faced imminent death my first concern would be: Just let me finish this piece, then I'll go happily!

At other times I get burned out and depressed; everything I've written seems boring and trite. I may work all day on some passage, lie awake thinking about it that night, then throw the whole thing out in disgust the next morning. As I get closer to publication I agonize over possible consequences. A poorly expressed point might lead to a lot of time wasted in misunderstandings; a well-expressed one might trigger a turning point in someone's life.

We all have a natural tendency to repress things that contradict our own views. The best way I know to mitigate this tendency is the one Darwin used: "I had, during many years, followed a golden rule, namely, that whenever a published fact, a new observation or thought, came across me which was opposed to my general results, to make a memorandum of it without fail and at once; for I had found by experience that such facts and thoughts were far more apt to escape from the memory than favorable ones." I try to follow this rule, playing devil's advocate on every issue, carefully considering any critiques of myself and immediately noting anything that occurs to me in the way of possible objections to my ideas—answering them if I can, modifying or abandoning my position if I can't. Even the most delirious attacks usually contain some valid points, or at least reveal misconceptions that I need to clarify.

It's necessary to strike a psychological balance. Too much worry about possible objections makes you afraid to do anything. Orthodox situationists scorn my mysticism, New Ageists feel I'm too rationalistic, old leftists denounce me for downplaying class struggle, arbiters of political correctness imply that I should express more contrition for being a white American male, academics fault my lack of scholarly objectivity, hangloose types find me too meticulous, some complain that my writing is too difficult, others accuse me of oversimplifying. . . . If I took all these objections too seriously, I'd become a catatonic! Eventually you just have to go for it.

As far as possible I try to make each project a new venture, choosing a topic I haven't explored or a method I haven't tried before. This makes it more interesting for me at least, and hopefully for the reader as well. I also try to avoid taking on too many things at once. It's easy to get burned out if you constantly absorb all the bad news of the world or try to contribute to every good cause. I generally concentrate on one or two projects that interest me so deeply that I'm willing to devote to them whatever time and expense is necessary, while ignoring most other things that I have no real intention of doing anything about.

Back to France in fall 1991, once again staying with Christian (in a household with his girlfriend and his brother). There were three side trips: to Grenoble to visit Jean-François Labrugère, a friend who has translated several of my texts with an exemplary meticulousness; to Warsaw to meet some young anarchists who were just discovering the situationists; and to Barcelona, where I joined some of my German friends. On the way back to Paris I stopped in the Dordogne region to see Joël and Nadine. I had turned them on to Rexroth years before, and they had eventually become as enthusiastic Rexrothians as I and had recently completed a translation of the first of his books to appear in French, *Les Classiques revisités*.

I spent a lot of my time in Paris exploring my biggest musical enthusiasm of the last few years, vintage French popular songs—scouring the flea markets and used record stores for old albums, taping my friends' collections, and trying to decipher the more obscure, slangy lyrics. It's a rich, fascinating world, from nineteenth-century cabaret singers like Aristide Bruant (the guy with red scarf and black cape pictured on the well-known Toulouse-Lautrec poster, which was commissioned to advertise the café where Bruant performed his own songs), through the tragic-sordid *chansons réalistes* (Fréhel, Damia, early Piaf) and upbeat music hall artists (especially the delightfully zany Charles Trenet) of the 1930s, to the post–World War II renaissance of great poet-singers: Georges Brassens (the greatest, ranging from worldly-wise elegies to outrageous satirical humor), Anne Sylvestre (a lovely lyricist, somewhat reminiscent of early Leonard Cohen or Joni Mitchell), Léo Ferré, Jean-Roger Caussimon, Jacques Brel, Guy Béart, Félix Leclerc; along with many excellent interpreters of earlier material, of whom my favorite is Germaine Montero.

It's hard to find such music here in the States, but my friends and I occasionally get a little taste when the Baguette Quartette performs at the local Freight & Salvage folk music club, which has hosted so many wonderful musicians over the last three decades. Although I've gone through a number of musical enthusiasms over the years, from the elemental sounds of Japanese taiko drum ensembles to the hard-boiled rebetika songs of the Greek urban underworld, I've always retained a special fondness for old-time American folk music, probably because it's the only kind I can also play. I still enjoy doing so with small gatherings of friends (including a few who date from my old Shimer and Chicago days) and I rarely miss the monthly East Bay Fiddlin' & Pickin' Potlucks, where a hundred or so people bring food and play music all afternoon at some suitably large house. Interspersed with eating and socializing, people cluster into their own preferred genres—bluegrass, say, in the back yard, Irish music in the den, group singing upstairs, 1930s swing around the piano (if there happens to be one), old-time fiddle tunes on the front porch, blues, or perhaps cajun or klezmorim, in the driveway or overflowing onto the sidewalk. I'm usually to be found with one of the old-time bunches, singing and playing fiddle or guitar—nothing fancy, but enough to have a good time. Everybody participates at their own level: less-skilled players like myself tend to follow the more versatile ones as best we can, but any of us are always free to initiate one of the numbers we know. The

152

EBFPP has been smoothly functioning for nearly twenty years now on a purely self-organized and volunteer basis. I sometimes think of it, and of countless similar circles and networks that are going on all the time without ever seeking or receiving notice in the spectacle, as modest foreshadowings of how things would function in a sane society. Not that it's any big deal. That's the point.

I still agree with the situationists that the arts are limited forms of creativity, and that it's more interesting to try to bring our creativity into the project of transforming our lives, and ultimately our whole society. When I'm engaged in that great game I find I have less inclination for artistic activities. But there's a time for everything. The situationist critique of "the spectacle" (i.e. of the spectacle *system*) is a critique of an excessive social tendency; it does not mean that it's a sin to be a spectator, any more than the Marxian critique of the commodity system implies that people should do without goods.

I've always found it amusing that radicals feel they have to justify their cultural consumption by pretending to find some radical message in it. Personally, I would far rather read a lively human being with a twinkle in his eye, like Rexroth, Mencken, Henry Miller or Ford Madox Ford, than some inane politically correct priggery. For that matter, I'd rather read Homer or Bashō or Montaigne or Gibbon than virtually any modern writer. I can still appreciate certain great works of the past, recognizing that their limitations were understandable in the context of their time; but it's hard to take seriously post-1968 visionaries who haven't even noticed the new possibilities of life. When it comes to contemporary authors, I scarcely read anything but frankly escapist works that have no pretensions of profundity or radicality. Some of my favorites are Rex Stout's detective stories (not so much for the plots as for the amusing world of the Nero Wolfe household and Archie Goodwin's lively narration); Jack Vance's fantasy and science fiction (for his remarkable variety of bizarre societies and his drolly sardonic and ironic dialogues); and the nonfiction science essays of Isaac Asimov, who has the rare knack of making just about anything he writes about both informative and entertaining, whether he's explaining the latest discoveries in astronomy or particle physics or speculating about what sex would be like in a zero-gravity space station.

In 1992 I set out to translate my Rexroth book into French. Even if it was never published, I wanted at least to have an adequate version on hand to give to friends and contacts. It was also a good opportunity to refine my still rather limited French skills. I prepared a first draft on my dandy new computer, then over the next year mailed successive drafts to Jean-François Labrugère, who made numerous corrections and suggestions for more idiomatic style. We circulated a provisional version in 1993; a revised version will be published in early 1997.

During the same period I also began working with Joël Cornuault on a series of translations of Rexroth's own works, beginning with a bilingual edition of thirty of his poems (*L'automne en Californie*, 1994) and most recently including a selection from his journalism (*Le San Francisco de Kenneth Rexroth*, 1997).

It's been a pleasure to collaborate with these two translators because both of them have the patience to carefully verify the precise nuance of each phrase, even though this can be pretty time-consuming when done by correspondence.

1993 brought a lot of things together for me, ultimately leading to the book you have in your hands. Early in the year I finally got around to reading all of Proust's *À la recherche du temps perdu* (*Remembrance of Things Past*). Immersing myself in that immense, sometimes tedious but usually fascinating work got me in the mood to explore my own past. Primarily for my own interest (though with the idea that I might eventually show the text to a few close friends), I started writing down whatever I could remember from my early days. One thing reminded me of another, and before I knew it there were over a hundred pages.

It turned out to be a good way to come to terms with a number of past problems and mistakes. Recalling some of the good old times also inspired me to reestablish contact with several old friends, including Mike Beardsley, whom I hadn't seen in over twenty years. I managed to hunt him up, we had some long phone conversations, and in June I flew to Chicago to see him. He had ended up in the rather stressful occupation of inner-city school teacher, gone through several tempestuous marriages and divorces, and let himself get way overweight; but he still had a lot of his old wild, independent spirit. It was great to see him again. To add to the nostalgia, we drove out to the old Shimer campus for a reunion that happened to be taking place at the same time and saw several other old friends for the first time since the sixties.

Two months later I got the news of Mike's sudden death. In an effort to deal with my sorrow I free-associated a long elegy celebrating our old friendship. Then I reworked it into a short statement which I circulated to a few mutual friends and relatives:

MICHAEL BEARDSLEY
(1945–1993)

Mike died August 29 of heart failure while in the hospital being treated for pneumonia.

We were best friends for just two years, 1961–1963, but they were vital, intensely exciting ones for both of us—meeting as roommates at Shimer College when we were just 16, then heading out on our own for bohemian explorations in California, Texas (where he and his first wife Nancy had their baby) and Chicago. Just a few years later a counterculture embodying some of our aspirations would surface and spread among millions of people; but in the early sixties it was still just brewing underground here and there; we and our fellow questers were still relatively isolated, clumsily groping our own way for new visions, new lifestyles. In some ways this isolation made things more difficult for us, but it also gave a special savor to the adventures and even the misadventures the two of us shared— discovering Zen and peyote, Rimbaud and the Beats, Henry Miller and Hermann Hesse, Leadbelly and Ravi Shankar; living from day to day, constantly experimenting, sometimes to the point of foolhardiness; hitching through vast, oblivious Mid-America, maybe getting stranded overnight but not really minding all that much, just strolling on down the empty highway humming Coltrane and imagining the great world out there waiting to be explored. . . .

We eventually went our separate ways, with only very sporadic communication over the next thirty years. Then a nostalgic mood luckily inspired me to hunt him up again, and I flew back to Chicago to see him just a couple months ago. Despite all the water under the bridge there were lively moments of our old camaraderie. I looked forward to a renewed friendship in the years to come. Then suddenly he was gone.

As I cried over his death I realized I was really crying mainly for myself, because a precious part of my own life was now gone. I know that others who were close to him feel this same kind of personal loss. It's sad to think of all the things we shared with him, or might yet have shared with him. Yet ultimately I don't think there was very much of life that he missed out on. Mike had a very tumultuous life, there were a lot of passions and pains, but he lived it with wonder and intensity. One time he barged into my room while I was asleep and exclaimed: "Ken! Wake up! The world is magic!" "Wha—? Oh, yeah I know, Mike, but I didn't get to bed till pretty late last night . . ." "But Ken, I want you to really see that the world is magic. Right here! Just look!" There was no arguing with him—I had to get up and see. And he was right, of course.

So long, old buddy.

It was Mike's death more than anything else that made me decide to publish this autobiography. I had looked forward to showing it to him and having him remind me of things I'd forgotten. Now it's too late. I'm not personally expecting to kick off any time soon, but this sort of shock does remind you that you don't live forever and that if you want to do something you'd do well to get on with it.

Bringing together so many loose ends in my life in turn encouraged me to get some of my old notes in shape. Since the late seventies I had been accumulating observations on different types of radical tactics and situations, but without ever managing to get them coherently organized. Now the two projects began to complement each other. The casual format of the autobiography lent itself to brief remarks on miscellaneous topics that would not have merited whole articles (answers to questions I am often asked, clarifications of various misconceptions, attempts to convey what I have found interesting about this or that), in some cases serving to illustrate or elaborate on topics presented more objectively in "The Joy of Revolution." Material could be shifted from one text to the other as appropriate.

I had also been thinking about reissuing my previous publications in some sort of collected form. Apart from a few extravagant pronouncements and slips into kneejerk situ rhetoric, I still stand by most of what I said in them, though they will no doubt seem obscure to people who don't engage in the sort of ventures they deal with.

For a while I thought in terms of several separate publications: reserving the autobiography for close friends while issuing the other writings as pamphlets or small books; or perhaps reworking parts of the autobiography as a commentary to the reissued texts; or putting out a journal that would include "The Joy of Revolution" plus miscellaneous material. Eventually it occurred to me that a lot of things would be simplified if I just put it all together in one big book. Incongruous as such a collection might seem, it would have the advantage of revealing both the interrelations (which might not otherwise be evident to readers) and the contradictions (which might not otherwise be faced by myself).

Knowing that it would be read by a rather diverse range of people, most, but not all, of whom would be familiar with the situationists, presented a number of interesting challenges, both in relating different aspects to each other and in finding the right balance between too little and too much explanation. The rather mixed result (part political chronicle, part self-analysis, part simple nostalgia) will probably not fully satisfy anyone—some will wonder why I go into certain matters at all, others will wish I had gone into juicier detail.

Once I envisioned publishing the autobiography, I trimmed out a lot of the personal details in the original draft, either because they might embarrass those involved or because they would be of little interest to most readers. With a few exceptions I have not referred to people by name unless they have already committed themselves to some sort of public activity.

The whole thing is admittedly very self-indulgent. Although I've mentioned a few painful episodes that were too crucial to omit, for the most part I've made it easy on myself and dealt only with things I enjoyed recalling and felt might be of interest to my friends and perhaps a few other people. If some readers consider me an egomaniac for presuming to write about my relatively unspectacular life, I hope that others will be encouraged to reexamine their own experiences.

"I round and finish little, if anything; and could not, consistently with my scheme. The reader will always have his or her part to do, just as much as I have had mine. I seek less to state or display any theme or thought, and more to bring you, reader, into the atmosphere of the theme or thought—there to pursue your own flight."

(Whitman, "A Backward Glance O'er Travel'd Roads")

Previous
Publications

DO WE NEED SNYDER FOR POET-PRIEST ?

EVEN ONE WHOSE APPREHENSION OF THE WORLD IS TOTAL...

TURNS INTO A SHOW WHICH FITS INTO THE PREVAILING SOCIAL SPECTACLE...

AND HIS WORKS BECOME THINGS WE CAN LISTEN TO OR BUY IN STORES, ADDING TO OUR COLLECTION OF "SIGNIFICANT EXPERIENCES."

GARY SNYDER, PETER ORLOVSKY & ALLEN GINSBERG IN THE HIMALAYAS

"SOMETHING SPECIAL!"

DO IT FOR ME!

SOME-DAY MAYBE I'LL BE A POET, TOO!

AND IT'S FREE!

BAAA!

Tonight's performer has said elsewhere, refering to the monopolization of "religious" (Total) experience by the priestly class, "We really don't need these people to mediate for us. Each person should be his own shaman."

And yet the present situation is no different essentially than the remainder of our fragmented lives: we submit, and even rush to be able to submit ourselves to passive acceptance and consumption of separate items. Of course, we are pickier and more sophisticated than most, and insist on consuming only "beautiful trips." Some of us are so liberated as to kiss only enlightened ass.

POETRY MADE BY ALL
—OR NOT AT ALL

IN THIS THEATER . . .

where the image of life substitutes for its realization, the only choice appears to be from among the variety of roles available. Separation—whether between the various roles in an individual actor's repertoire (e.g. at work and at leisure) or in the "communication" between one performer and another—reigns everywhere.

As if by unspoken agreement, everyone consents to the inevitability of this farce. Discontent confines itself to demanding a new director and more equitable casting. Some, dissatisfied with this form of "change," improvise more palatable characters, more amusing lines: alternatives within the range of roles allowed to them. In this way they rejuvenate a stale plot, and the Show goes on.

The least credible parts of the drama are reinforced by ideological sideshows. Thus, the entire genre is never questioned, postponing the day when we'll really bring the house down.

In a game where each alternative is a form of self-denial, the only real choice is the refusal to play.

IN THE REVERSAL OF PERSPECTIVE, each individual element of the drama is viewed in relation to the entire real possibilities: projected into the Whole. Constraint, mediation, and role are resisted and transcended by their opposites, by these three inseparable projects: participation, founded on the passion of play; communication, founded on the passion of love; and realization, founded on the passion to create.

By its own lights, the Show seems to go on undisturbed; founded on separation, on the fragmentary, it cannot conceive of the *unity* of these projects as: a transparency of human relations favoring the real participation of everyone in the realization of each individual.

Thus, the Show confidently observes its performers continuing to speak their lines, unaware that certain "reversals" are being introduced which cannot be "dramatically" resolved—except through its own destruction.

By taking our dreams and desires as the base of our activity, and by playing this game totally and coherently, we make ourselves a contradiction to everything which contradicts our fundamental project: the free construction of daily life.

[August 1970]

ODE ON THE ABSENCE OF REAL POETRY HERE THIS AFTERNOON

— A Poem in Dialectical Prose —

Poetry, as poets are fond of relating, originated from religious or magical incantations. The respect for the bard was due to the fact that *his words mattered.* Supposedly, the precise phrases and refrains were necessary to keep the crops growing, etc.

Literary poetry has lost this significance, and its most advanced creators know it. Rimbaud is the archetypal example of the attempt to recover the magical. He failed. And this failure was and is inevitable. The poem form precludes the possibility of the realization of poetry, that is, of the effective realization of the imagination in the world. The institution of poetry is itself a *social relationship* inimical to that project. It inherits the specialization of creativity, of authentic utterance, from its origin with the priestly classes, and it returns there. Even such a one as Rimbaud, for all his passion for freedom and the marvelous, ends by developing the conception of the poet as a new priest or shaman, a new mediator of communication. But the realization of poetry entails the direct creative activity of everyone, and hence cannot tolerate such mediation. "The problem is to *effectively possess* the community of dialogue and the game with time which have been *represented* in poetico-artistic works" (Guy Debord, *The Society of the Spectacle*).

* * *

"Divide and rule" may be said to be the essential tact of the social system that dominates us, but only if it is understood that this applies not only to separation between individuals, but equally to the division between various aspects of daily life. This enforced separation has attained *its* realization in *the spectacle,* the incarnation of the seemingly lived. The spectacle takes the truth of this society, namely its falseness and separation, and presents it as real, as reality, life to be contemplated by passive spectators who have no real life of their own. "The spectacle is not a collection of images, but a social relation among people mediated by images" (Debord). But in spite of all the images of satisfaction it presents, modern capitalism cannot hide the fact that it does not allow the fulfillment of real human desires. As the poverty of passive consumership (of commodities or culture) becomes more obvious, the spectacle provides a whole range of cultural activities which offer the *illusion* of "participation": Happenings, encounter groups, open readings, the World Game, be-ins, mixed-media festivals —anything that will take the passionate radicality, the ever-more-widespread poetry of revolt, and channel it into "constructive solutions" or fragmentary opposition, both of which equally reinforce the system they think they are overcoming. "The last hope of the rulers is to make everyone the organizer of their own passivity" (Raoul Vaneigem, *Treatise on Living*).

As with the spectacle in general, the communication of a poem is unilateral. The passive spectator or reader is presented with an image of what was lived by the poet. An open reading only apparently overcomes this criticism; it democratizes the role of poet, it shares access to the top of a hierarchical relation. It does not overcome that relation.

Of course, a certain degree of communication does take place, but it is communication in isolation, it is not directly tied to the real daily activities of the men and women involved. Since our daily activities are, in general, constrained and alienated, it is natural that poetic creativity (if it is not conscious of the project that supersedes separation, and hence literary poetry) in its own defense tends to retreat from daily life. It accepts an isolated realm where its partial game can play itself with a consoling illusion of wholeness. "Poetry rarely becomes a poem. Most works of art betray poetry. . . . At best, the creativity of the artist imprisons itself, it cloisters itself, waiting its hour, in a work which has not said its last word; but however much the author expects of this last word—the word preceding perfect communication—it will never be spoken until the revolt of creativity has taken art to its realization" (Vaneigem).

Poetry that is conscious of its own fulfillment in its own supersession never leaves daily life, for it is itself the project of the uninterrupted transformation of daily life.

* * *

The necessity for the total destruction of hierarchical power and the commodity economy remains with us. The traditional revolutionary workers movement failed to bring about this transformation of the world. At its most advanced moments (Russia 1905, Kronstadt 1921, Spain 1936, and Hungary 1956), however, it did *outline* the form that the revolution to come will take: the absolute power of workers councils. This antihierarchical form of organization begins from the direct democracy of the popular assembly and federates internationally by means of strictly mandated, immediately revocable delegates. In this way it avoids the possibility of the emergence of a new ruling class of bureaucrats or specialists.

The Leninist-type "vanguard party," so widely acclaimed at present, was one of the major reasons for the *defeat* of the classical workers movement. Consciously or not, by setting itself up as a separate, independent force, it prepares the way for its own "revolutionary" power *over* the people, as in the state-capitalist regimes of Russia, China, Cuba, etc. Any organization aiming to bring about the destruction of class society must begin by refusing to emulate this example of revolutionary "success." A revolutionary organization must abolish commodity relations and hierarchy within itself. It must effect the direct fusion of critical theory and practical activity, precluding any possibility of petrification into *ideology*. Just as the councils will control and transform all aspects of liberated life, the revolutionary organization must embody a critique of all aspects of presently alienated life. At the revolutionary moment of the dissolution of social separation, it must dissolve itself as a separate power.

The last revolution in human prehistory will realize the unity of the rational and the passionate; the unity of work and play in the free construction of daily life; the game of the fulfillment of the desires of everyone: what Lautréamont called "poetry made by all, not just by one."

[October 1970]

BUREAUCRATIC COMIX

The uprising in Poland is only the most recent gesture in the developing struggle against modern capitalism. But like other revolutionary moments, from Hungary 1956 to France 1968, it exposes the ideological falsifications of those who claim to speak for that movement, from the pseudo-socialist East to the bureaucrats of the Spectacle of Opposition....

It often happens that the "excesses" of a revolt are precisely its most revealing moments—when everything becomes transparent, tangible, within everybody's grasp. But it is also precisely these theoretico-practical advances which are obscured by the ideo-logues of the "left."

THE PEOPLE WOULDN'T HAVE HAD TO GO SO FAR IF THE RULERS HADN'T BEEN SUCH PIGS. OTHERWISE, WE COULD HAVE CONTINUED OUR NICE MANIPULATIVE "OPPOSITION." (DON'T FORGET TO VOTE FOR "COMMUNITY CONTROL" FOR "COMMUNITY ALIENATION"!)

"Then things began to move rapidly. The windows of the Communist party building were smashed. A group of youngsters climbed up the walls and into the building and began to throw out furniture, paper and other things, while people down in the street clapped their hands. When a very expensive table in Jacaranda wood was thrown out the window, everybody shouted with joy."

M
E
A
N
W
H
I
L
E...

CHRIST! ANOTHER SPONTANEOUS STRUGGLE WHERE THE PEOPLE ARE ACTING ON THEIR OWN AND FOR THEMSELVES. WHERE DOES THAT LEAVE US MOVEMENT LEADERS?

YOU CAN SEE WHY WE HAVE TO PUSH SACRIFICIAL MILITANTISM: ARMIES OF ACTIVISTS READY TO SACRIFICE THEMSELVES TO OUR IDEOLOGY (=DOGMA). ANY IDEAS FOR A GOOD SLOGAN?

HOW ABOUT "REVOLUTIONARY SUICIDE"?

I LIKE "FORGET YOUR LIFE: SERVE THE PEOPLE!"?

What a pity. Precisely because the insurgents in Poland, as in Watts - temporarily avoided such false-consciousness, they manifested a critique in acts of the commodity itself, demystifying that famous fetishism described by Marx over a century ago.

The looting of furs and champagne by the Polish celebrants is no more an example of their "attraction to the Western way of life" or "bourgeois revisionist degeneracy" than the looting of TVs in Watts was proof of the essential [...] these action integration should be considered positive [...] blacks into the American [...] order now possible! system... In this case, still the false desires and "needs" produced by the commodity system.

PORTRAIT OF ALIENATION

Their lives are so squalid that the majority can only live as a caricature of the Master...To the sacrifice of the dispossessed, who through his work exchanges his real life for an apparent one, the proprietor replies by appearing to sacrifice his nature as proprietor and exploiter; he excludes himself mythically, he puts himself at the service of everyone and of myth...Renouncing common life, he is the poor man amidst illusory wealth, he who sacrifices himself for everyone while other people only sacrifice themselves for their own survival. The more powerful he is, the more spectacular his sacrifice. He becomes the living reference point of the whole of illusory life." (Raoul Vaneigem, The Totality for Kids)

"The alienation of the worker in his product means not only that his labor becomes an object, an external existence, but that it exists outside him, independantly, as something alien to him, and that it becomes a power on its own confronting him. It means that the life which he has conferred on the object confronts him as something hostile and alien.

A commodity is therefore a mysterious thing...because the relation of the producers to the sum total of their own labor is presented to them as a social relation existing not between themselves, but between the products of their labor." (MARX)

"On the game in Watts, see the pamphlet, "The Decline and Fall of the Spectacular Commodity-Economy," by the Situationist International.

A critique of the commodity in a state-capitalist society becomes directly a critique of bureaucratic class rule itself. The official truth of the bureaucracy—that it does not exist as a separate class—is exposed as a lie by the events themselves. The rulers and their movement counterparts attempt to divert the radical critique of ALL HIERARCHICAL POWER into false choices between "good" and "bad" bureaucrats...

POLAND IS A PIG STATE, UNLIKE N. KOREA, ETC, WHERE THE RULERS (WHOSE RANKS WE ASPIRE TO JOIN) ARE SO KIND AS TO SERVE THE (SURVIVAL) NEEDS OF THE PEOPLE THEY EXPLOIT.

LIKE BERNADINE SAYS,* THERE ARE GOOD LEADERS AND BAD ONES. GOOD ONES ARE DEFINED AS THOSE WHO ARE ABLE TO MANIPULATE PEOPLE INTO "FREELY" FOLLOWING THEM, FOR SHUCKS, I'M A "NON-LEADER"!

*See the Tribe, December 18-25.

"REVOLUTION CEASES TO BE AS SOON AS IT DEMANDS SELF-SACRIFICE" (France, May 68)

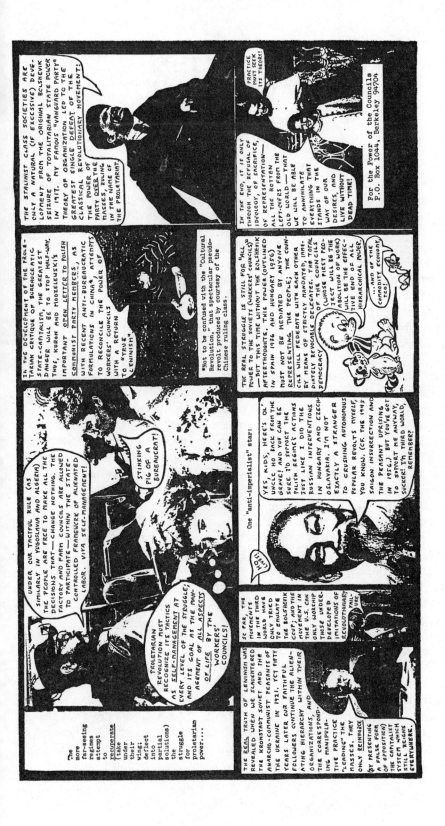

CRITIQUE OF THE
NEW LEFT MOVEMENT

(excerpts)

... With all too few exceptions the "democracy" of the New Left was a myth. ... As for a participatory democracy that would break down the separation between decision and execution, this was present only among a few small groups (for example, some of the earliest agitational experiments in the South) and, very briefly, in such massive actions as the spontaneous surrounding of the police car during the Berkeley Free Speech Movement. Usually whatever democracy there was lasted just long enough to elect a steering committee. ...

Such democracy as did exist in the New Left organizations cannot be separated from its lack of *subversive content*. The early SDS maintained a democratized marketplace of ideas which were only the ideas of a democratized marketplace. "This plethora of fragmentary issues finds its echo in the desire for decentralization and leaderlessness (which is less the absence of leaders than the creation of the conditions for leaders to take over) within SDS chapters. ... Many ... militants have seen in the relative autonomy of SDS chapters not the early forms of another hierarchical organization—which it is—but a healthy rejection of hierarchies, cell bosses, party chairmen, secretaries." (Robert Chasse, *The Power of Negative Thinking, or Robin Hood Rides Again*.) Chasse's critique, published April 1968, could hardly have been more definitively confirmed than by the subsequent history of SDS. That *the* New Left organization devolved into the control of three factions disputing the precise combination of Stalinist bureaucrats to worship has been liberally bemoaned by those who had proclaimed its essentially libertarian character; but they have never been capable of seeing the origins of this "degeneration" in the *incoherence* of the New Left. They have either maintained a discreet silence on this subject or impotently and tautologically referred to a "bureaucratization" that unaccountably grew out of this "healthy rejection of hierarchies." ...

With an ideology of "serving the people" the movement organizer justifies his reformist programs; for him they take on revolutionary significance. What is wrong with reformism is not the desire to ameliorate the immediate conditions of a number of people, but rather that these reforms are sought in order to transform these people into a constituency. ... When the organizer moves in, the totality is drowned in a sea of particulars; qualitative refusal is parcelized into particular defined needs. The organizers encourage the proliferation of a host of pseudoclasses: youth, blacks, women, gays, Chicanos. Separated according to their special interests, individuals are more easily manipulated.

Formerly the movement organizer (especially in the black and peace movements) relied heavily on guilt in order to motivate passive participation. Later he appealed to the "self-interest" of various groups —staying behind in order to coordinate their tactical alliance. As the movement decomposed, the old self-interest issues lost their recruiting power and new, more specific ones were improvised: gay vets for equal rights in the military, Asian women for separatist health care. Each hybrid made the frantic search for constituencies more absurd. . . .

Once the base had been "radicalized," divided up by the movement bureaucrats, it was reunited in a pseudototality of solidarity. . . . "It's all the same struggle." . . .

Antifascism and the Cybernetic Welfare State

The Movement adopted for itself an appropriate opponent in fascism. This convenient straw man enabled the Left to avoid defining itself positively; it provided a cover for the fact that the Movement failed to embody a radical critique of the system itself—of commodity production, wage labor, hierarchy. The daily misery produced everywhere by capitalism was made to seem normal—if not progressive—in the light of the barbaric excesses paraded before our eyes. . . .

The actual movement of modern capitalism is not towards fascism, but towards a qualitatively new mode of social domination: the Cybernetic Welfare State. In marked contrast to fascism, this new form, at the same time that it strengthens and extends the capitalist system, is also that system's natural development and rationalization. With the advance of the Cybernetic Welfare State, the various previous modes of domination become reduced to a consistent, smoothly running, all-pervading abstract control.

The Movement, since it does not make a radical critique of the *existing* system, is even more incapable of understanding the development of that system in the direction of greater subtlety. And so it happens that while it busies itself with things it *can* understand—superexploitation, the cop's club—it unknowingly enters into the service of the emerging cybernetic organization of life. Precisely because the Movement's is only a surface critique, its struggles for "participatory democracy," "quality of life," and "the end of alienation" remain within the old world as agitation for its humanized modification. . . . Bureaucratic capitalism does not always see the reforms necessary for its survival. In their search for constituencies, for issues to suck on, the Movement bureaucrats sniff out the incipient crises and, in their concern to appear as *practical* servants of the people, come up with reformist schemes with revolutionary ideology tacked on. . . .

169

Yippies and Weatherman

The rejection at its base of the Movement's degeneration into fragmentary opposition necessitated alternatives to Left politics which would recapture the feeling of unity embodied in the early New Left "total commitment." The most profound attempt was the Yippies, whose emergence expressed the widespread recognition that the Movement's neglect of the cultural revolt among its constituency was dangerous as well as artificial. The Yippies took their ideas on fun from bohemia, their communalism from the Diggers, and their moralism from the more romantic Third World bureaucrats. This fusion begat monsters: making a revolution for fun became doing it for the joy of surviving in the face of a capitalism made hostile by taunts. Reacting in images to the image of rightist reaction, Hoffman and Rubin tried to ride the wave of false consciousness in an effort to devalue it. Entering the spectacle as clowns to make it ridiculous, they created diversions which, far from promoting the refusal of the spectacle, merely made passivity more interesting by offering a spectacle of refusal. Actions such as the invasion of the Stock Exchange or the presidential candidacy of a pig were meant to advertise the decomposition of bourgeois values, while promoting (through, e.g., the "Festival of Life") their replacement with the less obviously recuperative aspects of the counterculture. The Yippies' practice was centered around creating chaos through good-natured terrorism, and creating myths to fill the void thus opened up. This myth-making made them conscious partners of the spectacle: foregoing the Movement's ambivalence toward the media, the Yippies' practical significance was seen by *themselves* as equal to the spectacle they could create through these media. . . .

Coming out of the student movement rather than the hip underground, Weatherman attacked the Yippies as not serious (sacrificial) enough, and appropriated only the signs but not the psychology of the hippies. Whereas the Yippies were an expression of what was nebulously there, the SDS bureaucrats who built the WeatherMachine forged a place for themselves at the vanguard of an increasingly passive and dwindling Left. Relating alternately to the images of the peasant guerrilla, the party bureaucrat, and the urban terrorist (in proportions varying with each militant's standing within the Weather hierarchy), Weatherman attempted to create a myth of powerful bravado which would force the hand of the entire "class" of white youth, the only group it deemed capable of assisting its project of flying kamikaze for the world war on America. Their strategy was based on the shock value of exemplary (suicidal) militancy. They succeeded in inheriting the mantle of the fading Panthers, who had held the Left spellbound for two years with the mere rhetoric of Acts. With Weatherman, this myth of concreteness was escalated to the concreteness of myth as Weatherman acted out the Panther slogans ("Take the initiative," "Off the pig," etc.). One of their songs says, "We used to talk but now we do it." The very concreteness of actually blowing a hole in the wall of a bank or courthouse placed Weatherman at the pinnacle of the spectacle of opposition. It was this "really doing something"—no matter how inane—that made them the focal point of all leftist discussions for over a year, against which each leftist measured his own inactivity. Particularly susceptible to such pressure were the students and intellectuals, dimly aware of their own impotence. In this religious division of labor, the leftist hero emerges from an ordeal of action to win the adherence of those who in their passivity are mystified by it. But interest in this kind of Passion Play, however intense, is always fleeting; by the time the cops closed down the show most of the audience had left. Weatherman first chose to return this spite by refusing to include anyone in their definition of the revolutionary motor. When even that failed to disturb America's conscience, they decided to include everyone, and dissolved into the hip underground.

The desire for total opposition was expressed in the attempts of both the Yippies and Weatherman for a revolution in daily life, attempts mediated and frustrated by ideology. While the Yippies created an illusory radical subjectivity based on romantic individualism and the thrill of watching themselves piss in public, Weatherman sought to smash all subjectivity in order to build a WeatherMachine in which all resistance to bureaucratic authority was deemed bourgeois. Thus the former built a politics based on its lifestyle and the latter tried to build a militarized lifestyle based on its politics. The recognition that the revolution must be made in living was dissimulated through the ritualization of living the revolution.

Communes and Collectives

The early urban communes . . . were to some degree (though not nearly so much as imagined) a free space in which the qualitative questions that bourgeois daily life represses were at least *posed*. But they were never answered—as the communes' rejection of the old world failed to take up the project of its supersession, the communes began to fall apart. While utopian communalists dreamed of a mass movement of changing heads, the communes failed even to survive, as their tolerance and passivity left them open to underworld and police harassment, internal manipulation, endless crashers, disease, mental breakdowns and rip-offs. . . .

Seeking to attract the counterculture as a constituency in order to revitalize the faltering Left, Movement bureaucrats endorsed the form of the commune as they rejected its content. The result of this enlargement of the scope of reformist activity was a widespread mechanistic synthesis of daily life and politics institutionalized in a commune form usually referred to as "collectives."

The commune movement's preoccupation with "lifestyle," though mystified and quite rigid, was at least a rudimentary critique of the capitalist daily life of augmented survival. In the collectives, on the other hand, there was a decided shift in emphasis from spontaneous social experimentation toward a total absorption in the politics of marginal survival. The collective, like the nuclear family it replaces, organizes the individual's personal subsistence in return for his allegiance to the collectivity. The communalization of economic poverty is accompanied by a communalization of intellectual poverty. Most collectives have a few informal hierarchs who get their power by synthesizing from amongst the garbage heap of leftist ideologies the particular form of eclecticism of that particular collective. Thus there are anarcho-nihilist collectives, Stalino-surrealist groups, Third World suicide terrorist cells, and social service units. The leaders establish their positions by mastering the mysteries of this melange and consolidate it through the management of political tactics (alliances, "actions," etc.) and of the reified experiments in daily life promoted by collectivist ideology. The struggle sessions against informal hierarchy are endless since there are neither rigorous criteria for membership in the collective nor exclusion of those who attempt to dominate or fail to participate autonomously. . . .

Women's Liberation

Women's Liberation, originating in opposition to the "male movement," never really escaped the latter's mystifications but only reproduced them in new forms. For the straw man of fascism it substituted male chauvinism. In attempting to overcome the overt hierarchy of the movement it created informal hierarchies. Criticizing the movement for defining itself only in terms of the oppression of others, it merely replaced the penitent militant purging himself before the image of Third World Revolution with the sister surrendering herself to abstract womanhood.

Within the movement the position of women has often been compared to that of blacks and other "super-oppressed" groups. But the "woman question" was essentially different in that it could never be considered as a question of "survival." The factors that constitute the particular alienation of women tend to be *central*, advanced: the family, sexual roles, the banality and boredom of housework, consumer ideology.

In the early discussion groups there was the beginning of a critique of daily life and especially of roles. But this critique underwent a closure and rigidified around the problems of women; it only considered women *qua* women. The individual found herself in a therapy session or encounter group where she was to "become sensitive to her oppression as a woman"—and wallow in it, going over each detail until her "sensitivity" became resentment and her critique a moral one. A politics of resentment toward the oppressor, men, and abstract solidarity with all women replaced any critical sense she may have had at the beginning of her "consciousness raising." Now the sister demanded not something so complex as a system to transform, but rather a living adversary to attack. Her rage to overcome her condition excited her aggression against men and her resentment materialized in the production of spectacles to haunt their guilty consciences. . . .

Sharing this melodrama was that lesser known antihero of female liberation—the sister's boyfriend. His dragged-out and slightly terrified look attested to his weary struggle to free himself from his oppression of his girlfriend. If he was at first hostile to her jeremiads, he soon recognized that his own alienation was insignificant compared to that of women. For this St. Anthony, besieged by the ghosts of his crimes against women, Women's Liberation came just in time to replace his impotent activity in the collapsing movement.

Women's Liberation rejected the hierarchy of the "male movement" but was never able to overcome hierarchy within its own groups. Since their organizational practice was based on an abstract democracy in which all women were admitted, the groups were forced to increasingly confine their internal practice to combatting informal hierarchy and specialization, using quantitative means: the small group, lots, automatic rotation of tasks, quantitative criteria for exclusion. But all these methods only concealed the maintenance of separations and inequalities absorbed initially. The contradiction between the antihierarchical position of the women's movement and its abstract solidarity with all women set the stage for the split of the antisexists and anti-imperialists at the Vancouver Conference (April 1971), where the antisexists of the *Fourth World Manifesto* exposed the anti-imperialists' manipulative appeal to sisterhood in order to preserve a Stalinist united front while in the same breath embracing a group of "sisters" sent to the conference as a public-relations corps by the North Vietnamese state.

The role of Women's Liberation has been to incite the dominant society to realize the abstract equality of total proletarianization. With demands for more jobs and a transference of housework into the public sector, the women's movement has worked, in effect, for the integration of women into a more rationalized system of alienation. The varieties of women's liberationists all have in common a reformist program, although some try to dissimulate this by claiming that women per se are a revolutionary class. They see not men and women in servitude to the commodity, but the commodity in the service of male chauvinism, which they facilely identify with power. . . .

CONTRADICTION
[unpublished drafts, April 1972]

ON THE POVERTY
OF HIP LIFE

(excerpts)

The values that formerly braced the organization of appearances have lost their power. . . . This disintegration of values opens up a positive void in which free experimentation is possible. But if experimentation does not consciously oppose itself to all the mechanisms of power, then at the critical moment, when all values are sucked into the vortex, new illusions fill the void; power abhors a vacuum.

The hippie's dissatisfaction, his dissociation from the old stereotypes, has resulted in his fabrication and adoption of new ones. Hip life creates and consumes new roles—guru, craftsman, rock star; new abstract values—universal love, naturalness, openness; and new mystifications for consolation—pacifism, Buddhism, astrology, the cultural debris of the past put back on the counter for consumption. The fragmentary innovations that the hippie did make—and lived as if they were total—have only given new life to the spectacle. . . .

Records, posters, bellbottoms: a few commodities make you hip. When "hip capitalism" is blamed for "ripping off our culture" it is forgotten that the early cultural heroes (Leary, Ginsberg, Watts, etc.) promoted the new lifestyle in the emporium of cultural consumption. These advertising men for a new style, by combining their own cultural fetishism with the false promise of an authentic life, engendered a quasi-messianic attachment to the cause. They "turned on" youth simultaneously to a new family of values and a corresponding family of goods. . . . The difference between the "real" and the "plastic" hippie is that the former has deeper illusions; he acquired his mystifications in their pure, organic form, while the latter buys them packaged: astrology in a poster, natural freedom in his bellbottoms, Taoism from the Beatles. While the real hippie may have read and helped develop hip ideology, the plastic hippie buys commodities that embody that ideology. . . .

People responded to the counterculture because its content was largely a partial critique of the old world and its values (notably, for example, early Ginsberg and Dylan). In late capitalism all art and poetry that isn't just junk on the highbrow cultural market or a sop to so-called popular taste must be critical, if incoherently or nihilistically, of spectacular nonlife. But as culture such a critique only serves to preserve its object. The counterculture, since it fails to negate culture

174

itself, can only substitute a new oppositional culture, a new content for the unchanging commodity-form. . . .

The project initiated by the Diggers in the Haight-Ashbury—the construction of a "free city" within the city, sustaining itself off the waste of its host and distributing its own survival freely—exposed the fact of material abundance and the possibility of a new world based on the principle of gift. But without directly challenging the social practice of capitalism, it remained merely a gesture, a militant avant-garde welfare program. Despite the Diggers' expectations, the state was not about to collapse around this self-management of garbage pickings.

Initially the Diggers' practice had been an appropriate response to the needs of the moment in the context of insurrectionary activity. They first organized to distribute food after the San Francisco ghetto riot (1966) and an ensuing curfew made it difficult to obtain. But they continued this project in a nonrevolutionary context, propped it up with an ideology of primitive communism, fetishized the idea of free distribution and became something of an antibureaucratic institution. In the end they were doing the welfare workers' job better than the welfare workers could, decompressing the radical critique of the family being lived by the runaways by advising them to go home "in the language of the street."

In the Haight there were attempts at directly challenging the urbanism of isolation and the authority which enforces it, and often with a strong sense of play (notably the early attempts to take over the street). But because pacifist and humanist ideology dominated its practice, the Haight became a morality play, a crusade more than a rebellion. Critical acts were lost in the utopian hope that society like a bad child would follow a good example. . . .

Like the sociologists who thought that the ghetto riots were an unfortunate consequence of the blacks' *attitude* toward existing conditions, the hippie thinks that alienation is merely a matter of *perception* ("it's all in your head"). . . . He "mellows out," pacifies himself so as to be "in tune" with the (capitalist-dominated) environment. All negative feelings are a head problem solved by turning on the "good vibes." Frustration and misery are attributed to "bad karma." "Bum trips" are a consequence of not "flowing with things." Psycho-moralizing about "ego trips" and "power trips," he holds them responsible for the present social poverty and harbors millenarian expectations based on the abstract determination of everybody to "love one another." Everything continues as it is factually while, by a dialectical deceit, he supplies a secret interpretation: that existing conditions will go away as soon as everyone acts *as if* they didn't exist. . . .

It was the promise of authentic community which attracted so many people to the hip milieu. For a while, in fact, in the Haight-Ashbury the boundaries between isolated individuals, living quarters and home and street began to give way. But what was to be a new life devolved into a glorified survival. The common desire to live outside the dominant society, since it could only be realized partially by living on the margins of that society, economically and otherwise, resulted in the reintroduction of survival as the basis for collective cohesion. . . .

In the rural communes, a false community of neoprimitives—who share only the mutuality of their retreat—assembles over the false crisis of a self-imposed natural alienation. This natural reserve is for them the sacred space in which they will return to the erotic bond of primitive communism and mystical union with nature. But in fact these zones for communitarian experimentation, which serve as shock-absorbers for the society at large, only reproduce the hierarchical patterns of former societies, from a rediscovered natural division of labor and shamanism to modified forms of frontier patriarchy. . . .

Like the bored retiree who takes up hobbies, the hippie deals with his malaise by "getting his head into something." He rejects both the work and the leisure of his parents, but only to return to both in his own way. He works in "meaningful" jobs, for "hip companies" in which the employees constitute a "family," and does subsistence farming and temporary work. Imagining himself a primitive craftsman, he develops this role, idealizing the Craft. The ideology he attaches to his pseudo-primitive (or pseudofeudal) occupation dissimulates its petit-bourgeois character. His interests, such as organic food, spawn thriving businesses. But the owners don't think of themselves as ordinary business-men because they "believe in their product." It's good vibes all the way to the bank.

The hippie's domestic leisure is just as pedestrian. Imagining he is rejecting the student role, he becomes a lifelong student. The free universities are smorgasbords where the most metaphysical as well as the most banal dishes are served up. Within its ideological boundaries the hippie's appetite is limitless. He reads the *I Ching*. He learns to meditate. He gardens. He picks up a new instrument. He paints, makes candles, bakes. His energy is insatiable, but it is all dissipated. Each thing he does is in itself irreproachable because trivial; what is ludicrous is the illusions he builds up around his activities. . . .

Abstractly rupturing with his past, the hippie lives a shallow version of an eternal present. Dissociated from both past and future, the succession of moments in his life is a disconnected series of diversions ("trips"). Travel is his mode of change, a drifting consumption of false adventures. He crosses the country continually in search of that "beautiful scene" which always evades him. His is a boredom always on the move. He hungrily devours every experience on sale in order to keep his head in the same good place. Wherever the hippie gathers with his fellows it is a space of unresolved tensions, of uncharged particles meandering around some spectacular nucleus or other. Hip urbanism—always trying to carve out a homey space where its false community could flourish—never failed to create for itself one more reservation where the natives stare blankly at each other because they're also the tourists. The Haight-Ashbury, the rock festival, the hip pad were supposed to be free spaces where separations broke down; but hip space became the space of passivity, of leisure consumption—of separations at another level. The rock concert in Oregon organized by the state to divert people from a demonstration—where the state gave out free grass and inspected the psychedelics before they were dispensed—is only the limiting case of the general tendency: space organized benevolently for tourists of dead time.

Hip life did have a more active content at its origins. The spectacular term "hippie" denotes far from homogenous phenomena and the subculture, and the individuals involved, passed through various stages. Some of the earliest of the subculture did have a conception of the new world as something to be built consciously, not as something that would just happen by turning on and coming together. . . . The hip movement was the sign of growing discontent with a daily life colonized more and more by the spectacle. But in failing to oppose itself radically to the dominant system, it constructed merely a counterspectacle.

Not that such opposition should have been political in the ordinary sense. If the hippie knew anything he knew that the revolutionary vision of the politicos didn't go far enough. Although the hip lifestyle was really only a reform movement of daily life, from his own vantage point the hippie could see that the politico had no practical critique of daily life (that he was "straight"). If the early hippie rejected "political" activity partly for the wrong reasons (his positivity, utopianism, etc.), he also had a partial critique of it, of its boredom, its ideological nature and its rigidity. Ken Kesey was correct in perceiving that the politicos were only engaging the old world on its own terms. But by failing to offer anything besides this, except LSD, he and others like him abdicated, in effect, to the politicos. Their pure and simple apoliticality left them open in the end, first to partial support for, and then to absorption into the political movement. . . .

If the pre-political hippies fell for all the illusions and utopian "solutions," if their critique of everyday life never recognized its historical basis and the material forces which could make it socially effective, still the emergence of the hippie revealed the extent of dissatisfaction, the impossibility for so many of continuing along the straight and narrow paths of social integration. Yet at the same time that the counterculture announced, if incoherently, the possibility of a new world, it constructed some of the most advanced paths of reintegration into the old one. . . .

CONTRACTION
[unpublished draft, April 1972]

REMARKS ON CONTRADICTION
AND ITS FAILURE

"Now . . . the story . . . does not disperse indefinitely like the banal actuality; rather it organizes itself. The principle of organization is the something that was secret in the actuality. Previously the actuality was indefinite and wandering because the organizing figure was unnoticed; now that it is allowed to claim attention, the rest falls into place. . . . By telling the story, the author frees himself from a certain phase of his life. . . . Obviously the malfunction of the flexible interplay of imagination and actuality has a general importance far beyond cases of a specific inhibition of writing."

—Paul Goodman, "On a writer's block"

" 'What are you working on?' Herr Keuner was asked. 'I'm having a lot trouble,' answered Herr Keuner. 'I'm preparing my next mistake.' "

—Bertolt Brecht, "Anecdotes of Herr Keuner"

In September 1972 the group "Contradiction," of which I was a member, dissolved itself. Judged by the goals this group had set for itself, it had *failed*.

* * *

"The author is embarked on telling the actual story, when suddenly he says to himself, 'Oh, but—I see, I remember—if I tell this and try to unify it dramatically, I shall have to mention—that. But I didn't foresee that!'"

—Goodman, *op. cit.*

The history of Contradiction cannot be separated from the history of what it undertook to criticize: the "movement" and the "counterculture" in the United States. The ambiguities in those at once real and spectacular entities were reflected in the quandaries we found ourselves in in our year-long wrestling with this project. Our effective acceptance of these notions, even if to criticize them, measured our own incomprehension of modern society and of our own position in it.

We sometimes actually recuperated where we were aiming at exposing recuperation. For example, very diverse and often admirably spontaneous acts, such as small discussion groups or practical rejection of sexual roles, might, in our drafts, find themselves joined together with the most cynical Stalinist manipulations under the category "women's liberation"; which category in turn was treated in the rather inappropriate context of the internal dynamic of the movement, as, e.g., a vaguely radical offshoot of or out of it. This, even if by inversion, was giving the little leftist organizations credit for an influence they only wish they had! The organization of our critique can be seen in retrospect as a continual attempt to unravel what we had raveled in the first place. In the process we got very entangled! Each problem that we ran up against (and we were at least lucid enough to recognize the multitude of them) found itself superficially solved by the re-arrangement or expansion of the original project *whose very form* was in fact the major source of our difficulties. We became a victim of our own project, the conclusion of which, by indefinitely receding into the future, pushed aside our engagement with matters of far greater importance and interest to us. We came to fetishize the fetishes we had wanted to demystify. It was left for reality itself to finally force our supersession of the project: When this very "movement" itself knew that it was dead (see the glut of analyses of "what went wrong" and attempts at artificial respiration by its old partisans in the period 1971–72), all that remained was to make a more accurate autopsy. This was too much. We prepared a selection of the most substantial of our "political and cultural manuscripts of 1971" for distribution to close comrades, and abandoned the project (and our journal) early in 1972.

(A few copies of these drafts found their way into the hands of less discriminating readers, who distributed them and even went so far as to express an interest in reprinting them. No such publication of the articles in this unfinished form was ever intended by Contradiction.)

Our drafts were good at tracing the internal contradictions and development of Yippies, Weathermen, political collectives, at examining the specific forms of the poverty of hip life, etc. But our attempts to place these developments within the context of the society as a whole— that is, of the opposition to that society—were crude, artificial, un-historical, or nonexistent. In fact, we did not fully comprehend the position of the hippie or the student leftist because we were too close to that position ourselves. We could analyze the absurdity of various ideas and manners, but we didn't know why they appeared in the first place.

Many attitudes, illusions, and behavior which we analyzed as hippie in fact pertain to a wider and yet nonetheless delimited social stratum. So that where we sometimes accepted the spectacular notion of the hippies as a cultural vanguard (while drawing different conclu-sions as to the merit of their "innovations") which was later followed and imitated in a diluted form by the society as a whole, it was more the case that a certain stratum produced certain ideas and manners, and that a part of that stratum—the hippie—merely expressed those *ideas and manners of uncertainty* in the most extreme and *visible* way.

179

To "accept" oneself, to passively "dig reality," to "flow with things" is nothing other than the *consumer ideology* of this stratum of society. So that if a minor functionary or mercenary of the spectacle takes up hippie manners and ideas, those manners and ideas are not being watered down; they are *returning to their origin.* This rather amorphous stratum includes notably the direct *producers and agents of social falsification*—ad designers, teachers, counselors, artists, psychologists—and so it is quite natural that it is so sensitive to the "failure of communication." (Whereas, in contrast, the direct producer of commodities has to be *forced* into the encounter groups which quite unsuccessfully try to instill a "sense of community" into his less compromising labor. He prefers watching sports and adventures to humbly imbibing cultural rehashes. He takes his alienation straight.) It is this stratum that worries about consuming only "quality" products. In this sense the hippie *is* a vanguard scout in that he helps to discover and unearth the products that embody such quality, from organic foods to organic illusions. When he attempts himself to produce and market these commodities in a way which avoids the hassles of "straight" society, he only rediscovers the logic of the craft guild, with the difference that the superabundance of his variety of pseudo-creativity rapidly forces its price to a pitiful level, leaving him more insecure than his medieval forbears. All that remains are the illusions, 700 years late. "Thus there is found with medieval craftsmen an interest in their special work and in proficiency in it, which was capable of rising to a narrow artistic sense. For this very reason, however, every medieval craftsman was completely absorbed in his work, to which he had a contented slavish relationship, and to which he was subjected to a far greater extent than the modern worker, whose work is a matter of indifference to him." (*The German Ideology.*)

To return to our "stratum." (I must note here the imprecision of my analysis, which is only partially attributable to the imprecise nature of this stratum. The sector or sectors of society to which I am referring are clearly neither of the classical proletariat nor of the ruling class—bourgeoisie, upper bureaucrats, technocrats, etc. But in between these two lie a number of strata which can be differentiated not only by their positions within the production system but also by their varying illusions and social aspirations. My "stratum" clearly does not embrace all of these.) The struggle against "dehumanization" or for "control over the decisions that affect one's life" is the confused reaction of this same stratum, which feels its alienation and impotence intensely but which, because of its ambiguous position, is led to express itself in continually oscillating and self-contradictory ways. The student "radical," who is generally destined for a place in this stratum but who can temporarily give vent to his self-indulgent confusions, simply expresses these longings in a more exaggerated, ideological form as, e.g., "community control" of some alienation or other, perhaps garnished with scraps of some long outmoded leftism. But this leftism is largely a *reflex*, an unimaginative response to contradictions that have become unavoidable. (Just as the hippie, in addition to embodying all the modern mystifications, digs up all the old ones—astrology, Buddhism, etc.—in his never-ending search for something that could really fulfill the promise that was disappointed in each "trip" before.)

The superficial nature of all these fantasies is revealed when one notes the ease with which the Weathermen become absorbed into the pastoral hippie idyll or the Yippies turn enthusiastic voters. What the "movement" thought it wanted was less important than *who it was composed of.* It didn't collapse because the junior Guevarists found out about Kronstadt, any more than "hip culture" was ripped off. All these apocalyptic visions found their *authentic* realization in *stores* and *religions*—and often in a combination of the two! In places like the San Francisco Bay Area, where the more archaic pseudoconflicts have been superseded, one can see the coming together of what was never essentially separate: an ad designer grows long hair, joins an encounter group, and dreams about chucking it all and going to the country; while a jaded youth, wiped out from smashing his "bourgeois hangups" (i.e. his subjectivity) in a Maoist collective or from the poverty of a rural commune, returns to set up a serve-the-people store or go into *dealing* "awareness" of one or another reified banality by joining up with an "alternative" media or perhaps leading an encounter group. Neither the be-ins of passive masses nor all the "happenings," neither the militants' ritualized "trashing" for every cause but their own nor the spectacular sabotage of a few suicidal guerrillas were able to turn a city upside-down like the workers of Pittsburgh did for a day in October 1971 out of mere joy in winning the World Series.

By no means do I wish to say that all of those struggles which found themselves included in "the movement"—or even all of those that thought they belonged under that spectacular label—were pure figments, purely passing fantasies. While most "opposition" to the Vietnam war, to take just one example, was simply a stale spectacle of humanist outrage and impotent "bearing witness," or was in the interest of political recruitment, many individuals accomplished admirable concrete tasks, whether by publicizing suppressed information or ways to fuck up the draft, or by desertion, "fragging," etc., within the army itself. And on the other hand, a few of the little leftist groups also had a small but nonetheless concrete effect on modern society; they were real "vanguards," but in a different sense than they thought. They served as a feedback warning mechanism and as unwitting idea men for a bureaucratic capitalism not always capable of seeing the reforms necessary for its survival. Many of these reforms (minus the ideological exaggerations) are already firmly established (e.g. Black Studies programs); others are no doubt on the way to being so, once a few snags get worked out (e.g. "community control" of police). Some of the unconscious trouble-shooters received bullets for their services. Others found their natural level and went into business as brokers of "people's survival."

In the same way, not *quite* all "hip" phenomena are contemptible. That label, usually denoting a heavy illusion of community and a community of heavy illusions, takes under its wing a few real breaks with the dominant mode of "life" and a few real experiments in the direction of community without illusions. These latter individuals will stand out from the slough of hippiedom precisely by their *ability* to stand *out* of it, i.e. to openly junk the entire religio-ideological superstructure; and by the fact that the very authenticity of their experiences, in combination with the intelligence that is able to distinguish between what is living and what is dead in those experiences, pushes them ineluctably toward a more and more rigorous radicality.

* * *

"I have mentioned our prompt critique of the mistakes of the pro-situs, not in order to imply that it is not in itself justified, but in order to note that the pro-situs are not our principal reference point (any more than ICO or the leftist bureaucrats). Our principal reference point is ourselves, our own operation. *The underdevelopment of internal criticism in the SI both reflects and contributes toward the underdevelopment of our (theoretico-practical) action."*

—Guy Debord, "Remarks on the SI Today"
(internal document of the SI, July 1970)

Contradiction's inability to confront its own history was in part a carryover from its failure to *coherently* confront its own prehistory around the time of its formation. Most of the future members of Contradiction came together, in the fall of 1970, largely around a critical consensus on their respective past activities, principally within the recently disbanded quasi-"situationist" groups the Council for the Eruption of the Marvelous and "1044." But the fact that we were able to express these critiques among ourselves and to individuals we happened to encounter is just as academic as the fact that some of the stronger members of Contradiction wrote pieces that were publishable but which, by being subsumed into the journal, got postponed beyond the point of timeliness or interest. We failed to make a *collective* and *public* accounting of ourselves, of our previous collective, public activity. (The one significant exception was our distribution of a barely adequate "Critique of 'On Wielding the Subversive Scalpel' by One of Its Authors"—with an appended "What Subversion Really Is" by one "Frederick Engels" of 1044—to those who had read that CEM pamphlet.) And so we remained somewhat entangled in leftovers from our past by having to diffusedly correct, over and over, the assorted fantasies (irrationalist or confusionist conception of détournement, manichean split between "coherent" and "incoherent" organization and activity, fetishism of not working, fetishism of communalism, etc.) which we had so actively disseminated during the year 1970, and which remained understandably linked, in the minds of many people, with our more recent and intelligent positions and projects.

The CEM's edition of *On the Poverty of Student Life* contained extensive additions (which, moreover, ranged from the inadequate to the mystical) and omissions, without the presence of these alterations in the original Strasbourg pamphlet being mentioned. And 1044's "Riot and Representation: The Significance of the Chicano Riot" (which, among other things, too facilely reproduced the SI's observations on Watts: looting or antipolice violence did not have quite the same significance for the Chicanos, because they took place in the context of very thick spectacular ideologies of violence and Third-Worldism which had arisen in the intervening five years) was signed "by Herbert Marcuse." If this perhaps enlarged—while reducing the quality of—its readership (e.g. it was reprinted in the *San Diego Street Journal*), it was at the expense of clarity: If Marcuse was forced to publicly deny the pamphlet (in the UC San Diego student newspaper), it was equally true that many people did not know this, and actually accepted it as being by him—which was giving this dialectically illiterate professor far too much undeserved credit.

Contradiction might have resolved many of its difficulties more quickly and more clearly if its members had been more rigorous in their relations with each other, and first of all on the question of their being *members of Contradiction in the first place*. The movement/counterculture critique had the merit of beginning (around October 1970) as a frank *testing* of our mutual practical accord, over and beyond the consensus regarding mistakes in our pasts. But the formation of Contradiction in December 1970, while being a correct recognition of the *manner* in which a delimited project was being carried out, simultaneously bypassed the tentative, experimental nature of that project; as if we had already found a satisfactory "general equality of capacities" among ourselves. The adoption of a wider range of activities (publication of a journal, enlarging of the movement critique, etc.) in fact allowed for a pseudoresolution of the differences in participation, quantitative and qualitative, which had shown up in the earlier delimited project, and which would undoubtedly have shown up even more clearly had we continued to collaborate on this sound basis. The more grandiose the projects, the easier for someone to be "working on" one for months; the more projects, the easier for someone to hide behind a flurry of apparent activity. In this way the weaker members bypassed the necessary development of their own autonomous practice, while the stronger members got bogged down in making up for the

183

weaker. The abstract desire to "cover" everything (arising out of our abstract aim of being a group "like the SI") contributed to the abstract need of these stronger members to try to salvage poorly prepared drafts, instead of simply rejecting them and perhaps also their authors.

That Contradiction was not a true *federation* of autonomous individuals contributed towards its not being a truly *autonomous* federation. If we were mystified about ourselves we could hardly avoid being mystified about others. Our premature group formation and the insufficiently shared participation in common projects within the group found its external corollary in the incredible amount of time and energy we wasted—going up to the point of fantasizing imminent collaboration or "federation"—with individuals with whom we shared no common projects, but only common ideas, "perspectives," or, in the final analysis, *pretensions*. (Sydney Lewis *had* participated in the beginnings of our movement critique, but had left town just before the formation of Contradiction. A series of progressively more confused letters, culminating in pathetic defenses of the most retarded leftist and hippie illusions, caused us to break with him in June 1971.) In particular, we too readily accepted membership or ex-membership in the Situationist International as implying a superior practical comprehension of matters on which we were unclear—an illusion that was reinforced when they perhaps proved to be right in other instances.

This was nowhere more strikingly revealed than in the history of our relations with Create Situations. We allowed their formulation of basically correct critiques of our lacks of organizational rigor and coherence to divert, obscure, or postpone for months our own demands and positions (most notably against their attempted "use" of the underground press by *soliciting* the publication there of their and our comics, their patronizing of "promising individuals" on their mailing list, and their otherwise sloppily and spectacularly "getting the critique around" so as to drum up, in short order, a "1000 situationists"). It was, in fact, precisely in our criticisms of them where this organizational incoherence was most evident. It sometimes happened that one or another of us would venture an opinion which was erroneously taken to express a group position; in other cases, such positions were, with insufficient reflection, accepted by the group, which then found itself obliged, perhaps the very next day, to retract what had shown itself as mistaken—and perhaps to do this with a similar lack of reflection; or finally, on those points where we did arrive at considered, collective positions, those positions were rendered meaningless by our failure to execute them, to pose them in practical terms (e.g., by simply refusing to have anything to do with them until they had definitively superseded the underground press strategy). We also "pragmatically" rushed into collaboration with them while important differences remained unresolved, as in my extensive correction of their translations of the SI pamphlets "Beginning of an Epoch" and "The Poor and the

Super-Poor." (Unfortunately, their bungling in the final layout and printing managed to reintroduce numerous—though usually not fundamental—errors in most of the articles. These pamphlets are presumably still available from C.S., P.O. Box 491, Cooper Station, NYC 10003.) Other divergences included our confused temporizing over our relations with individuals whom they had broken with; which hesitation was reinforced by Tony Verlaan's inability to adequately answer criticisms made of him in the Chasse-Elwell pamphlet "A Field Study." As was too often the case in our relations with groups and individuals, we had to be knocked over the head before we could draw the most elementary practical conclusions. Even when the crucial nature of our divergences could no longer be ignored and our communication had effectively collapsed, it still took Create Situations's manifestly *intolerable* proposal (to work with us as individuals while we remained members of a group under which "appearance" they would not deal with us) to finally force us to break with them, in July 1971. Truly, when they noted our failure "to recognize the moments that matter and what matters on a given moment" they were most correct precisely in regards to the long retardation of our relation with them.

Copies of correspondence and other documents relating to any of Contradiction's breaks can be obtained from me by anyone who can explain what good use he has to make of them.

* * *

"There were also people who were already beginning to spread this doctrine in a popularized form . . . using all the arts of advertisement and intrigue. . . . Nevertheless it was a year before I could make up my mind to neglect other work and get my teeth into this sour apple. . . . Although this work cannot in any way aim at presenting another system as an alternative to Herr Dühring's 'system,' yet it is to be hoped that the reader will not fail to observe the internal coherence underlying the views which I have advanced. . . . This is an infantile disorder which marks the first phase of, and is inseparable from, the conversion of the German student to social-democracy, but which will rapidly be thrown off in view of the remarkably healthy instincts of our working class."

—Engels, preface to *Anti-Dühring*

"When I hear the word 'situationist' I reach for my revolver."

—old proletarian saying

We broke with Point-Blank in December 1971 over their defensiveness in response to criticism. Around the time when we were coming to recognize some degree of our failure and to act accordingly (by making original, consequential contributions to the new revolutionary movement or nothing), the members of Point-Blank had come to prefer the *image of their success.* These little militants have since more than confirmed the diagnoses we made of them at that time. Their principal activity over the last year—which has even assumed the proportions of an avowed *strategy*—has been to broadcast the spectacle of their coherent radicality. Their reinvention of the history of others reveals—in good old psychoanalytic fashion—their own failings and defenses. They are compelled to utterly redefine "pro-situ" (as referring only to those who are *purely* passive and admiring) so that it won't include them. Again, they note approvingly that by 1966 "the SI's theory had gone beyond the experimental stage" *(Point-Blank! #1,* p. 57, exclamation mark theirs). It is, of course, *Point-Blank* that has gone beyond the experimental stage. They go "beyond the SI" by "revising" away whatever they don't comprehend there, that is to say, almost everything fundamental. They think they have discovered something when they find that Debord and Sanguinetti don't salivate, as they do, to the stimulus of every "partial opposition" with illuminating declarations that they're not "total." The barrage of exposés and simplistic "analyses" they serve up to the masses only says (with a few exceptions) the same things over and over; but then their principal effort has long revolved around how to package their reified rehashes in different "scandalous" ways. It is with good reason that they court those who are used to "learning" by the repetition method (see, on p. 92, the laughable attempt of these poor students of student poverty to justify their inability to be anything other than subversive campus mascots). To return to their disguised self-revelations, we find that the "obstacles" confronting the SI (around May '68 yet!) "centered around extending the radicalism of the SI beyond its immediate membership" (p. 60). It is in fact these little neo-Leninists who conceive of their task as "extending" the "radicalism" (i.e. the *explicit situationism*) of Point-Blank beyond its immediate membership. What "obstacles" they must run into!

It is one invariable sign of this sort of spectacular situationism that it scrupulously avoids making any practical decisions because it hopes that, in exchange, no one will make any practical decisions about *it.* It would like to present an image of an international community of situationists joined together around certain intriguing *ideas*—by the dissemination of which image and ideas any unimaginative impotence can hope to convince himself that he is alive. Thus, Point-Blank tells "who they are," with that "rigor" for which they have tried to make themselves famous, by omitting any mention of the annoying fact that they collaborated closely with Contradiction for nearly a year, or that we broke with them, and why. Or one Paul Sieveking, founder-member of English pro-situ clearing house "B.M. Ducasse" (= "The Friends of Lautréamont"), will try to simultaneously and publicly keep up connections with Create Situations and us by "agreeing" with the positions of whomever he happens to be talking to at the moment (which sidestepping we put a stop to by breaking with him in December 1971). Or an underground paper trying to fill up the current ideological void will put out a special issue on situationism which simply lumps together everyone who is able to babble a few slogans about the spectacle, sacrifice, Leninism, etc., and publishes a "Dictionary of Situationese" for the edification of those who aren't yet even capable of that.

The widespread and serious interest in situationist theories and methods in various sectors of society—even if through the absurd mediation of pro-situ propaganda—is one *sign* of the advance of modern prehistory and its critique. Of this advancing critique, however, the pro-situs themselves are only a confused and confusing *rear-guard*. That such backward infantile elements can capitalize on an apparent association with an apparently prestigious label in front of those who are often far more radical and original than them is an inevitably temporary phenomenon. The impotence of those who debate with voters, Jesus freaks, and a movement they admit is a dead horse, because anyone else would be more than a match for them; or of those who "publicize their existence" and are compelled to come back the next day to *announce* how scandalized everyone was, in case nobody noticed the first time around—this impotence is obvious to everybody but themselves, who are caught up in the brief exhilaration of that "certain notoriety" of theirs which they report with such poorly feigned indifference. It takes a pro-situ not to know one.

* * *

"However, that neither the World nor our selves may any longer suffer by such misunderstandings, I have been prevailed on, after much importunity from my Friends, to travel in a compleat and laborious Dissertation upon the prime Productions of our Society; which, besides their beautiful Externals for the Gratification of superficial Readers, have darkly and deeply couched under them the most finished and refined Systems of all Sciences and Arts."
—Jonathan Swift, *A Tale of a Tub*

In January 1971 Contradiction published the wall poster "Bureaucratic Comix," which noted the role of the various movement heroes, local and imported, vis-à-vis the recent workers' uprising in Poland. Our poster was reprinted in April by Create Situations; whose distribution of which, however, left something to be desired in the way of rigor, as noted above.

In April we distributed an "Open Letter to John Zerzan, Anti-Bureaucrat of the S.F. Social Service Employees' Union" at a meeting of that vaguely "participatory" but tame organization.

In June we published "Wildcat Comics," which was distributed principally to the San Francisco cable-car drivers whose wildcat strike some months earlier was discussed therein.

In July we published—in collaboration with Point-Blank—the comic-leaflet "Still Out of Order," which was distributed to telephone workers during their brief national wildcat.

In August we published a critique of the Anti-Mass pamphlet "Methods of Organization for Collectives," that attempt to revive the movement by incorporating into it, among other things, fragments of ill-digested situationism.

I consider that "Anti-Anti-Mass" was a decent if somewhat stodgy analysis; that in its time and place "Bureaucratic Comix" was an appropriate agitation, as evidenced, for example, by the speed and vehemence with which local militants ripped the poster from the walls of Berkeley, ordinarily noted for the peaceful coexistence of all cultural and political fragments ("It is good to be attacked; it proves that you have drawn a clear line between yourselves and the enemy," as one of their stars has said); and that, slightly excepting "Wildcat Comics," the worker agitations were pitiful, the product of an abstract desire to say something to workers when in fact we had hardly anything to say to them but abstractions.

Contradiction, which from its inception had declared its accord with the principal theses of the Situationist International, issued in May 1971 a statement which sketched some of those theses, along with the SI's "Minimum Definition of Revolutionary Organizations."

Contradiction reprinted English translations from the following SI texts: the first six chapters of Raoul Vaneigem's *Treatise on Living for the Use of the Young Generation* (January 1971, 2500 copies); *On the Poverty of Student Life* (May 1972, 2000 copies); and continued the distribution of 1044's editions of *The Decline and Fall of the 'Spectacular' Commodity Economy,* Vaneigem's *The Totality for Kids,* and "Desolation Row" (chapter on nihilism from the *Treatise*).

In our editions of the *Treatise* and *Decline and Fall* we made the mistake of leaving out our address, giving the impression that they had been published by the American section of the SI (which no longer exists).

Copies of "Territorial Management" (chapter from Guy Debord's *Society of the Spectacle*), along with a Contradiction comic, were handed out at the appearance in Berkeley of urbanist numbhead Palo Soleri in March 1971. That same month we also distributed copies of the SI's "Theses on the Commune," published as a wall poster by Create Situations.

I have published 750 copies of these "Remarks on Contradiction and Its Failure."

* * *

> *"My chief objection was not the vanity there is in writing one's life. . . . I was afraid of deflowering the happy moments I have known by describing and dissecting them. Well, that I refuse to do; I shall skip the happiness. . . . Shall I have the courage to relate humiliating events without saving them with endless prefaces? I hope so. . . . But I must begin with so sad and difficult a subject that laziness overtakes me already; I am almost inclined to throw down my pen. But at the first moment of loneliness I would regret it."*
>
> —Stendhal, *Memoirs of an Egotist*

That six months elapsed since the dissolution of Contradiction before any of its ex-members were capable of so much as a simple public statement of that dissolution shows that one does not embark on such enterprises with impunity. The incompleted, the unclarified, the unresolved, the falsified accumulate with painful results. The repressed returns. That long collective *coitus interruptus* that was the history of Contradiction, or rather of the radical projects initiated there and so little fulfilled, left us not only frustrated but chronically *blocked*. We are not the first nor will we be the last revolutionaries to mysteriously lapse into more or less cynical dabblings with culture, preoccupation with schemes for survival, or the most trivialized or false personal relations: you have to keep running to keep ahead of the clutches of the old world. Our inability to publicly resolve the collective stasis of our public practice was not unrelated to our failure to adequately pose the questions of the specific impoverishments of our individual lives. While rejecting the stupidities and illusions of our daily-lifist prehistory, we also, to a large extent, lost the playfulness and outrageousness of those beautiful days. If we forgot the most elementary lessons it was because we had ceased to live them; our theories had ceased to be the theories of our real lives. All that was left was, on the one hand, an articulate ideology of passion and pleasure which mediated our personal relations within and outside the group; and on the other, a tendency which reacted to the laughable results of that ideology by simply writing off our "personal" lives as a matter of coherent, collective concern.

No one was more a victim of all the contradictions of Contradiction than I. It was I who most pushed forward the premature extension of our activity to becoming a group "like the SI." I more than anyone identified with Contradiction as spectacular family. As one old comrade put it, "Knabb realized himself in situationist politics," which, if it expresses that the group was less alien to me than to the others—that I expressed myself most fully within it—also measures the degree of my more fundamental alienation. If I initiated and participated consequentially in more projects, I was often less radical in recognizing their failures and drawing appropriate conclusions. It was I who more than any of the others clung to illusions about possibilities for

Contradiction months after that form had become obviously obsolete and oppressive. In the interest of brevity I can say that if I could write a veritable *Anti-Dühring* about Point-Blank (a doleful undertaking to even imagine!) it is because I know whereof I speak; I have myself passed through the outskirts of that bizarre little ideological sub-world. There is hardly a thesis in the Debord-Sanguinetti portrait of the pro-situ (in *Theses on the SI and Its Time*) where I do not recognize myself—in the past and far too much right now!

As for the other members. They have all been content to passively recognize the errors of their past. And some of them seem to have included living with passion, rigor, and originality among those errors. So much have they "matured." They have risen as one in incomprehension and hurt defensiveness against the most elementary public criticisms of the fakery of one or another of their associates. Have they forgotten everything? Then they themselves will have to suffer that same criticism become even more public! Most of them have yet to really speak for themselves. And the ones who were best able to are now no longer able to at all. They are behind the times. And these times will leave them even further behind if they don't do something desperate.

* * *

"The time for writing is ripe, for I must spare nothing of what I have spoiled. The field has not yet been plowed. . . . The time of artistry is ended, the time of philosophy is ended, the snow of my misery is gone. . . . The time of summer is here; whence it comes I know not, whither it goes I know not: it is here!"

—Paracelsus

The members of Contradiction might well have confronted their dilemma by enlisting that fundamental tactic of breaking the impasse by concentrating precisely on the *resistance to the analysis*. This would have pointed not only to the basic collective organizational errors I have outlined in these "Remarks," but also to our individual resistances, that is to say, to our *characters*. These resistances were strikingly evident, around the final collapse of the group, in our sudden pathological indifference to our often very exciting past activity; to the reasons for that activity's devolution into boring routine; to the practical possibilities for superseding this state of affairs; and to each other. This phenomenon raises questions (sketched out in Jean-Pierre Voyer's beautiful "Reich: How To Use") which are obviously of crucial importance and which I have hardly dealt with here at all. Suffice it to say, for now, that if it is indisputable that the practice of theory is individually *therapeutic*, it seems to me equally true that an assault on one's own character is socially *strategic*, a practical contribution to the international revolutionary movement. The character of the pro-situ is objectively reinforced by the spectacle of his opposition to the spectacle (which character, of course, is most evidenced by his inability to recognize its existence, other than as a "banality," until excessive *symptoms*, perhaps visibly inhibiting his social practice, force his attention there). At the opposite pole, all the lucidity of an Artaud, who attacks his character in isolation, does not prevent the "external" commodity-spectacle he disdainfully brushes aside from reappearing in his internal world as the fantasy of being possessed by alien, malignant beings. Like a revolution in a small country, the person who breaks a block, a routine, or a fetish must advance aggressively to discover or incite radical allies outside, or lose what he has gained and fall victim to his own internal Thermidor. The dissolution of character and the dissolution of the spectacle are two movements that imply and require each other.

These formulations will have to be made more precise.

(January–March 1973)

<< REICH · HOW · TO · USE >>

by Jean-Pierre Voyer of the

Institute of Contemporary Prehistory

translated and published by the

Bureau of Public Secrets

p.o. box 1044, berkeley, california 94704

REICH
How To Use

"The thing contains in its second part, in a very condensed but relatively popular form, quite a few novelties that anticipate my book,[1] while at the same time necessarily barely touching on quite a few other aspects. Do you think it's a good idea to preview such subjects in this way?"

—Marx to Engels, 24 June 1865

1. The Notion of Character According to Reich

"To find love in Paris, one has to descend to the classes where the struggle with real needs and the absence of education and vanity have left more energy. To reveal a great unsatisfied desire is to reveal one's inferiority, an impossibility in France, except for those beneath everything. . . . Hence, the exaggerated praises of young women in the mouths of young men afraid of their hearts."

—Stendhal, *On Love*

As a result of his practical and theoretical struggle against resistances in analysis, Reich came to conceive of character (character neurosis) as the very form of those resistances.[2]

In contrast to a symptom—which must be considered as a production and concentration of character and which is felt as a foreign body, giving rise to an awareness of illness—a character trait is organically embedded in the personality. Unawareness of the illness is a fundamental symptom of character neurosis. An explanation of this degradation of individuality cannot appear except within an attempt to communicate, in this case within the analytic technique itself. However unilateral this technique may be, it rapidly revealed character for what it is: a defense against communication, a failure of the faculty of encounter. This is the price paid for the primary function of

---

1. The Institute of Contemporary Prehistory is presently preparing an *Encyclopedia of Appearances: A Phenomenology of the Absence of Spirit.*

2. *Character Analysis,* 1927–33 (Noonday, 1972).

character, the defense against anxiety.[3] There's no need to dwell on the origin of anxiety, on its causes and their permanence. Let us simply note the obvious fact that the particular form of one's character is a pattern that takes shape before the tenth year.

The discretion of this arrangement explains why it is not recognized as a social plague, and thus why it is lastingly effective. This setup produces damaged individuals, as stripped as possible of intelligence, sociability and sexuality, and consequently truly isolated from one another; which is ideal for the optimum functioning of the automatic system of commodity circulation. The energy which the individual could use to recognize and be recognized is *harnessed* to his character, i.e. employed to neutralize itself.

In all societies in which modern conditions of production prevail the impossibility of living takes individually the form of death, madness or character. With the intrepid Dr. Reich, and against his horrified recuperators and vilifiers, we postulate the pathological nature of *all* character traits, i.e. of all chronicity in human behavior. What is important to us is neither the individual structure of our character nor the explanation of its formation, but *the impossibility of applying it toward the creation of situations.* Character is thus not simply an unhealthy excrescence which could be treated separately, but at the same time an individual remedy in a globally ill society, a remedy that enables us to bear the illness while aggravating it. People are to a great extent accomplices in the reigning spectacle. *Character is the form of this complicity.*

We maintain that people can dissolve their character only by contesting the entire society (this is in opposition to Reich insofar as he envisages character analysis from a specialized point of view). On the other hand, since the function of character is to accommodate us to the state of things, its dissolution is a prerequisite to the total critique of society. We must destroy this vicious circle.

Total contestation begins with the critique in acts of wage labor,[4] in accordance with a first principle beyond discussion: "Never work." The qualities of adventure absolutely essential for such an enterprise lie exclusively outside character. Character destroys those qualities. The problem of opposing the entire society is thus also the problem of dissolving character.

---

3. The critical situation in which the magnitude of this price is fully revealed is love. It remains Reich's merit to have shown that character defense against anxiety is paid for in this situation by an incapacity for tenderness, which he labels, unfortunately, "orgastic impotence." At this level character is itself a symptom.

4. While Reich concluded in a very ambiguous manner that character is an obstacle to work, we contend that character is an obstacle to the *critique* of work.

2. Its Application to the Spectacle Effect

> *"The truest and most important concepts of the era . . . are precisely marked by the organization around them of the greatest confusions and the worst misrepresentations. Vital concepts are simultaneously subject to the truest and the most false uses . . . because the struggle between critical reality and the apologetic spectacle leads to a struggle over words. . . . The truth of a concept is revealed not by an authoritarian purge, but by the coherence of its use in theory and in practical life."*
>
> —*Internationale Situationniste* #10

> **Public:** *pertaining to all the people.*
> **Publicité:** *public notoriety; that which is done in the presence of the public; that which belongs to the public.*[5]
>
> —*Dictionnaire Larousse*

The publicity of misery is inseparable from the *idea* of its suppression.[6] This is how *spirit* comes to men and women. Misery is always misery of publicity. It is thus necessary to seek the reason for the persistence of misery in that which causes the misery of publicity.

Fetishism is the misery of publicity. It is the very form of social separation. Wherever there is opposition between individuals and the totality of their interrelations, this opposition takes the form of fetishism of the totality. Opposition between the whole and individuals takes place by *means* of parts of the whole which appear to be isolated, or which maintain illusory relations with the whole and with each other.[7] Deceived consciousness is the fundamental moment of fetishism. With it, things become what they seem. The absence of consciousness takes the form of consciousness.

---

5. Note that this last meaning, which makes for some fundamental plays on words in the original French text, is not present in the English word "publicity." Extracts of a letter from the author to the translator, in which he excellently elucidates this and some other aspects of his text, are available from our Bureau on request. (K.K.)

6. The reader will have recognized class consciousness here, and will therefore not confuse it with the spectacle of misery, which is the *advertising* version of the publicity of misery.

7. Alas! the opposition of the whole to individuals takes place only by *means* of parts of the whole. When the opposition of individuals to the totality becomes "total," things become totally clear.

The fetishism of the commodity is concentrated in its value. It took Marx thousands of pages of *Capital* to get to the bottom of this fetish. It is the yoke of value that weighs down human brows, be they bourgeois, bureaucratic or proletarian. Value is the relation between two quantities. What is more bizarre than the fact that x pounds of carrots are worth y quarts of wine or even z minutes of hairdressing? Value is the exorbitant autonomy of the commodity. It is dangerous to steal, loot or burn. It's even more dangerous to never work! Value exerts itself implacably,[8] while the deceived gaze only meets things and their prices.

In the nineteenth century, with the complete opposition between individual life and species life (everyday life versus automatic commodity circulation), all hopes were allowed (those of Hegel, those of Marx). At that stage things were clear: everyday life was *nothing*, circulation was *everything*. The nothingness of everyday life was a *visible* moment of the all-encompassing circulation. Fetishism scarcely deceived anyone but the ruling class and its toadies. Several times the proletariat launched an assault on the totality, and the publicity of misery came very close to triumphing over the misery of publicity.

Today things have changed considerably. The modernization of the struggles of the oppressed, and above all their incompletion, have brought about the rapid modernization of fetishism by the ruling class and its state since 1930. The rise of *scientific fetishism* was striking: Bolshevism, National Socialism and the New Deal appeared almost simultaneously. This modernization consisted essentially of *depriving* everyday life of what was left to it: its negativity, i.e. the publicity of its misery, the publicity of its nullity. The secret of the misery of everyday life is the real state secret. It is the keystone completing the edifice of separation, which is also the edifice of the state.

The spectacle—the scientific development of fetishism—is simply the private property of the means of publicity, the state monopoly of appearances. With it, only the circulation of commodities remains public. The spectacle is nothing but commodity circulation absorbing all available means of publicity, thus condemning misery to invisibility. The spectacle is the secret form of public misery, where value operates implacably while the deceived gaze only meets things and their use.

In the imperialist publicity of commodity circulation, value never appears. This is the spectacle of the invisibility of value. This "natural" invisibility constitutes the fundamentally spectaclist tendency of circulation which the bourgeoisie has exploited in the scientific development of fetishism. As long as value does not become public in a

---

8. The worker has the same advantage over the rich as the slave over the master. The slave knows fear; the worker, a living commodity, knows value.

different way, circulation is able to appear as a carnival of use (principally the use of money, needless to say). It is thus easy to understand the entrancement of the spectator confronted daily by value. This is the spectacle effect. It forestalls all ideas; everything seems accomplished. It forbids all recognition; the miserable being sees himself as alone in his misery. Money itself appears as the instrument of the abolition of value—the peak of inversion. As a result of all this, spirit does not come to men nor (what is even more regrettable) to women.

From his front row seat, Wilhelm Reich couldn't help being struck by the role played by character as anti-individual structure in the magnificent Nazi spectacle.[9] He leaves the farcical question "Why do workers revolt?" to the psychoanalysts, psychiatrists, sociologists and other servants of the spectacle, in order to pose the fundamental question: "Why don't they revolt?"[10] He attributes their submission to the crushing of the individual by character. This is hardly contestable. Necessary but insufficient. To say that this society hasn't got an intrinsically spectaclist tendency would amount to saying that the spectacle is the creation of the ruling class alone. That would be giving them too much credit! We know that the ruling class is the chief victim of its own illusions. It follows the trend.

We have already demonstrated the rationale of this tendency. Character is nevertheless undeniably real. It can be clinically detected. We now have to determine exactly what is analyzed in character analysis, once its insufficiency as a separate notion is recognized. As a separate notion it is nothing but one more fetish.

Our thesis is as follows. The quantitative reigns. All human relations are governed by the relation of quantity to quantity, though they appear as purely human relations—the deceived gaze only meets things and their prices. We have briefly reviewed the spontaneously spectaclist effect of the "natural" invisibility of value. For all that, value never ceases to be lived by each person as the inescapable necessity of his daily life. We have seen that this *lived secret* fulfilled the spectaclist tendency of commodity circulation. What is it that Reich clinically detects which he labels "character"? We contend that it is *value,* as inhuman necessity and otherwise invisible, that is grasped by this approach. It is even, up till now, the only concrete way of

---

9. See *The Mass Psychology of Fascism,* 1933–34 (Noonday, 1971) and *What Is Class Consciousness?* 1934 (in *Sex-Pol,* Vintage, 1972). In this latter small work Reich attains the height of Leninist naïveté. Despite his denials, he extols specialized historical knowledge to the extreme. There is even a curious foreshadowing of the Maoist conception of education as a spectacle of misery.

10. *Dialectical Materialism and Psychoanalysis,* 1929 (in *Sex-Pol*). *Mass Psychology* and *Dialectical Materialism* are both indelibly marred by a mechanistic conception of instincts.

approaching value as secret misery of individuality. Under this form Reich tracked down *the unconscious,* its misery and its miserable repressive maneuvers, which only draw their force and their magical pomp from the dominion of value over everyday life. Because human relations have been globally socialized *exclusively* in terms of value, which is their *negation,* authentic human relations, validated by pleasure, are preserved[11] within this socialization as *natural relations* (and thus illicit and clandestine ones), since all sociality, all humanity, is occupied (in the colonialist sense) by value, the only officially validated socialization. Whatever tends to escape the law of value thus takes the form of the *natural,* i.e. that which *by definition* escapes the mastery of humanity.

In his third Philosophical Manuscript, Marx measures the humanity of man, his socialization, by the degree of socialization of that "immediate, natural and necessary" human relationship: the relationship between man and woman. Value as universal socialization, as sole and inverted form of humanity, is also in fact the impossibility of socializing this relationship; which relationship *remains,* therefore, "the most natural," that is to say the most frustrated by the reigning social organization. Within a world of universal socialization by value, this naturalness becomes increasingly equivalent to its degree of decay,[11] just as the degree of naturalness of the Nambikwara Indians within our civilization tends to equal the degree of their extermination. This degree of decay—psychosis, neurosis, character—as index of the nonsocialization and nonhumanity of man, is the *real* object of psychoanalysis. That old swine Freud went so far as to identify naturalness with "savagery," and value-inverted socialization with "civilization." Psychoanalysis was and will remain the paleontology of this prehistory.

We support out thesis, still purely theoretical, with the following clinical observation: If, for one reason or another, an individual's character is dissolved, the phenomenal spectacular form of the totality is dissolved in its pretension to pass for the absence of value. Thus we have established, negatively for the moment, an identity between character and the spectacle effect. Whether the subject sinks into madness, practices theory or participates in an uprising,[12] we have ascertained that the two poles of daily life—contact with a narrow and separate reality on one hand and spectacular contact with the totality on the other—are simultaneously abolished, opening the way for that unity of individual life which Reich unfortunately labels "genitality." (We prefer *individuality.*)

---

11. According to the principle: "That which is not superseded rots; that which rots incites to supersession" (Vaneigem).

12. 1968 has provided us with abundant and most diverse data.

The works of Reich are the first since Marx that concretely shed light on alienation. The theory of the spectacle is the first theory since Marx that aims explicitly at being a theory of alienation. The synthesis of these two methods leads to some immediate consequences which we will develop in our forthcoming work.

First of all, we maintain that the practice of theory is inseparable from what Reich referred to as "genitality." Theory becomes continuous knowledge of secret misery, of the secret of misery. It is thus also in itself the end of the spectacle effect. Since the spectacle is the secret form of public misery, its effect ceases when the secrecy ceases. Its effect lies in its secrecy. Thus theory becomes increasingly identical to lived possibility (as opposed to probability, which is lived as doubt or indifference). Theory is *life* when everything is possible. It ceases to exist the moment it makes a mistake, and finds itself thrown back into boredom, into the spectacle effect. Real theory thus can't go wrong. It is a subject devoid of error. Nothing deceives it. The totality is its sole object. Theory knows misery as secretly public. It knows the secret publicity of misery. All hopes are permitted to it. Class struggle exists.

The spectacle is the absence of spirit. Character is the absence of theory.

The proletariat will be visible or it will be nothing. The proletariat *lives* in its own visibility. The organization of the proletariat is the organization of its visibility. The global practice of the proletariat will be its *permanent publicity* or nothing. Hitler, the Leninists and the Maoists understood this so well that they organized the visibility of the proletariat *by force*. A more ambitious capitalism wishes to realize the visibility of the *abolished* proletariat.

By itself, the visibility of misery is not the proletariat. Necessary but insufficient. The proletariat requires that the visibility of misery be public. The critique must be at once theory of publicity (of visibility) and publicity (visibility) of theory. Its aim must be *to ensure its own publicity*. It is when it's public that it doesn't go wrong. It is *not* the theory of publicity if it doesn't ensure its own publicity. Indeed, it is the height of absurdity for a theorist of publicity not to be able to ensure the publicity of his theory.

The proletariat is the finally realized unity of the theory of publicity and the publicity of theory.

We think these insights are superior to everything that a Lukács was able to say about class consciousness. They certainly have the advantage of brevity. As the ad men know, brevity is essential in publicity. ("Are you man enough for Granny Goose Potato Chips?"—one could not be briefer in contempt.) What they cannot imagine is that publicity will be even briefer at the moment of a Strasbourg of the factories. Visibility will flash like lightning, fire like a gun and rise like the sun, or it will not be.

For the moment our formulas may have only brevity in their favor. It may perhaps be necessary to introduce into them the concepts "Granny Goose" or "Potato Chips" in order for them to know their total clarity. A day will soon come when all the potato chips of the earth will no longer be able to smother the meeting of the theory of publicity and the publicity of theory.

JEAN-PIERRE VOYER
Paris, November 1971

DISCRETION IS THE
BETTER PART OF VALUE

(Addendum to "Reich: How To Use")

Here are some specifics on my Reich article. . . .

The 18th-century French author Marivaux wrote a play entitled "How Spirit Comes to Women." (You can easily imagine how!) . . .

I want to draw your attention to a difficulty in translating this text into English. In French, *publicité* refers both to "advertising" and to "public welfare," *res publica*, what belongs to the public. These two quite contrary senses make for a striking play on words, which I am developing in depth in my *Encyclopédie des Apparences*, but I don't see how it can be rendered in English. . . .

Misery is in fact the sole real property of the unhappy public. In this sense misery is common, communal—but only secretly so, not publicly.

In contrast, commercial publicity speaks of something that does not belong to the public, but it speaks of it in a public manner.

Thus, *publicité* includes three moments:

a) It is the character of that which belongs to the public, of that which the public possesses, of public property. *But,* this public property may very well be nonpublic, secret, not revealed. This is the case with misery.

b) It is that which is known by the public, that which is done in its presence. *But,* this knowledge may very well concern something which does not belong to the public. This is precisely the case with commercial publicity (advertising) in particular and with the spectacle in general.

Thus, in the spectacle, that which is public in the sense of "done in the presence of the public" is the totality of individuals and their relations. But this totality, even though it is composed of nothing other than themselves, does not belong to them. They are stripped of their own substance.

c) Finally, the third moment is the unity of the first two; the unity of that which belongs to the public and that which is known by the public. In a word, real *publicité* in the sense of 1789–1793. It is communism, community; the workers councils were a timid experience of this type of *publicité*. It is "practice which sees its own action."

In a very Hegelian language, this third moment is the totality of individuals suppressing itself in favor of the immediateness of the individual. The totality then becomes the concrete substance of the individual and the individual becomes the substantial power of the totality which exists for itself, as person. (Heil Hegel!)

The French term *publicité* renders all that, including that grotesque perversion of *publicité,* advertising.

I also want to clarify what I mean by "idea" in the phrase "the idea of its suppression." I have a very materialist conception of this term. What I mean, for example, is the taking of the Bastille by the people of Paris on 14 July 1789. That's what I mean by *idea.* This very material "idea" comes to people the same way "spirit" does.

In short, what I mean by idea is the third moment of publicité. And that's also what I mean by spirit.

It's both a material fact (the taking and destruction of the Bastille, material fact *par excellence*) and the contrary of a material fact, the *suppression* of this collective fact in favor of the immediateness of the individual. In a word, consciousness, the consciousness of that which makes itself. Etc.

Finally, I want to clarify the role that character plays for me, so that a too great importance is not given it through the reading of this article.

I take character in Reich's sense for *a mere symptom,* for the symptom of an effect which is still hidden, which still operates in the dark, *and which can only operate in the dark, since awareness of it is inseparable from its destruction* by the "people in arms." In my view, character is nothing but a symptom of the spectacle effect (which is itself only a particular form of the value effect).

On the other hand, inasmuch as it is a symptom, character can be an effective means of publicizing a secret misery, a misery still hidden. For the symptom, even if it is a symptom of an as yet unknown malady, cancer for example, *is* no less certainly a symptom of it, which at least lets the sick person know that he is sick and not in good health, which he might believe in the absence of the symptom.

But I think that to make character an independent entity, with its own history and its own rationale, is a misuse of the notion.

In any case I am developing all this in the *Encyclopédie des Apparences,* which should appear here at the end of the year. . . .

(Jean-Pierre Voyer to Ken Knabb, 20 April 1973)

DOUBLE-REFLECTION

Preface to a Phenomenology of the Subjective Aspect of Practical-Critical Activity

> *"When the thought has found its suitable expression, . . . which is realized by means of a first reflection, there follows a second reflection, concerned with the relation between the communication and the author of it."*
>
> —Kierkegaard, *Concluding Unscientific Postscript*

Overture

> *"Sooner or later the SI must define itself as a therapeutic."*
> —*Internationale Situationniste* #8 (1963)

Each time an individual *rediscovers* revolt he *remembers* his previous experiences of it, which all come back to him like a sudden memory of childhood.

We know that "whether the subject sinks into madness, practices theory, or participates in an uprising . . . the two poles of daily life—contact with a narrow and separate reality on one hand and spectacular contact with the totality on the other—are simultaneously abolished, opening the way for the unity of individual life" (Voyer).

Now, madness has its drawbacks* and an uprising is not available every day; but the practice of theory is constantly possible. Why, then, is theory so little practiced?

Of course, a few ill-informed people here and there don't know about it yet. But what about those who do? What about those who have found practical-critical activity, all its undeniable difficulties notwithstanding, to be so often fun, absorbing, meaningful, exhilarating, funny —something after all not so easy to come by—: How does it happen that they *forget*, that they come to imperceptibly drift away from the revolutionary project, going to the point of utter repression of the moments of realization they had found there?

The inexperienced will wonder why we engage in this strange activity in the first place. But to those who know why, what is strange

---

* The insane person makes this breakthrough at the cost of nonintervention. The individual places himself outside of history, beyond the possibility of collaboration. There must be method in our madness.

is that we do it so little and so erratically. The moments of real excitement and consequence come to us almost exclusively by accident. We lack the consciousness of why we haven't done what we haven't. Why is it that we don't revolt *more?*

Marx understands practical-critical activity as "sensuous human activity," but he doesn't examine it *as such,* as *subjective* activity.

The situationists understood the subjective aspect of practice as a *tactical* matter. ("Boredom is counterrevolutionary.") They posed the right question.

It's about time we looked into this activity itself. What does it consist of? What does it do to us who do it? Whereas the sociologists study man as he is "normally"—that is, reduced to survival, a sum of roles, a sum of banalities—we are going to study him when he acts to suppress all that: *Homo negans.* "By acting on external nature to change it, he at the same time changes his own nature" (*Capital*).

The workers are becoming theoretical and the practice of theory is becoming a mass phenomenon. Why take up this investigation now? *Why, comrades, has it not been taken up till now?*

The Theorist as Subject and as Role

> HOLMES: *"My mind rebels at stagnation. Give me problems, give me work, give me the most abstruse cryptogram, or the most intricate analysis, and I am in my own proper atmosphere. I can dispense then with artificial stimulants. But I abhor the dull routine of existence. That is why I have chosen my own particular profession, or rather created it, for I am the only one in the world. . . . I claim no credit in such cases. My name figures in no newspaper. The work itself, the pleasure of finding a field for my peculiar powers, is my highest reward. But you yourself had some experience of my methods of work . . ."*
>
> WATSON: *"Yes, indeed. I was never so struck by anything in my life. I even embodied it in a small brochure."*
>
> —Arthur Conan Doyle, *The Sign of the Four*

The alienation of the proletarian consists in this: his work has substance but no freedom; his leisure has freedom but no substance. What he does of consequence is not his, and what he does that is his has no consequences; nothing is at stake in his play. (Hence the appeal of all those "dangerous games"—gambling, mountain climbing, the foreign legion, etc.)

It is this social schizophrenia, this desperately felt need to see their own action, to do something that is *really theirs*, which causes masses of people to take up crafts or vandalism; and still others to try and suppress the split by attacking the separation in a unified way, by taking up *coherent vandalism: the craft of the negative.*

What does it feel like? You already know, reader—or at least you once did. It's like when you share a secret or pull off a beautiful prank. Only this feeling is shoved to the margin of life so that its image can take center stage. It ends up being forgotten.

Well, we don't want to forget. A revolution is the most practical joke on a society that's a bad joke.

For the purposes of my investigation I artificially distinguish aspects of revolutionary activity which are inseparable. For simplicity of expression I speak of "the theorist"—the practicer of theory—in order to examine a genre of activity whose modalities are in some respects quite different from that of a crowd of people who riot on one day without having given the subject much thought the day before. While certain phenomena examined here are common to all moments of radical negating activity, others are obviously superseded at the moment of a mass uprising. This Preface is principally concerned with the situation of the revolutionary in a nonrevolutionary situation.

The practice of theory has its own peculiar satisfactions, but also its own peculiar pitfalls, arising from its own unevenness of development, from the unevenness of its relation to the revolutionary movement as a whole, and from the fact that the theorist is a repressed individual like everyone else. The movement of history is an awe-ful force to be linked up with: you become drunk with clarity, or just as quickly drunk with delusion.

Thus, our* *Phenomenology* will at the same time be a *Pathology*.

* * *

The *negative rush* is concentrated sequential critical activity engendering a more or less continuous orgastic rupture of the spectacle effect. In the negative rush ("rush" being understood in the drug sense, as an almost unstoppable exhilaration) a sort of "domino effect" of ideological unblocking occurs: the destruction of one illusion leads one to examine others more closely; the undertaking of a practical project suggests others which correct, reinforce or expand it; idea follows idea in such rapid succession that the theorist is taken over, possessed, like a *medium* transmitting the historical movement's own oracle back to itself; the complexity of the world becomes *tangible*, transparent; he sees the points of historical choice. As he breaks out of the ordinary passivity and begins to move theoretically at the dizzying pace of events, he is swept off his feet like the masses are at the insurrectional moment. (An insurrection is a *public* negative rush.) But if those

---

* *our:* The "Phenomenology" is not a forthcoming book by me. Its development is one of the global proletarian tasks of the coming decade. Right now we are, so to speak, at the stage of trying to figure out the table of contents. Its next installments (in-depth studies, case studies, other prefaces, critiques of this one) are going to come from . . . *who?*

masses are unprepared for the explosion which violently threatens the old reality and the "sanity" that goes with it, they have *company* in their crisis, which they can thus see is general and not merely personal. The radical theorist, on the other hand, must be prepared for the personal crises which the radical comprehension and elucidation of the general crises in the society may entail. Alienations against which we have evolved partial, religio-characterial defenses are *discovered afresh* on terrains where the theorist is as yet defenseless. The commodity *form* reappears at each new level; the theory of value is seen as a *valuable theory*, and the theorist as its prophet. A revolutionary concept becomes his muse. He is love-struck. He is the opposite of the militant for he serves his goddess rapturously. The situation is ambiguous. The theory may correct its mystified excesses; or the theorist, in his infatuation, may simply flip out and sink into a theoretical narcissism.

There are also collective negative rushes. The meeting of congruent, parallelly developed projects cuts away the respective petrifications, hesitations and dead ends, putting each person's efforts into a broader and more precise perspective. A single decisive encounter can touch off a veritable fireworks of exciting subversive activity for days at a time, a person or a text acting as a catalyst for a whole little milieu. Historical relations become personal relations. ("If you are profoundly occupied you are beyond all embarrassment.") The disparate survival tastes recede into the background; everyone discovers a common sense of humor (for where there is contradiction, there the comical is also present). The whirl is often very contagious, infecting the ordinarily nonparticipating with a desire to go beyond a mere contact high.

It doesn't last. Leaving aside the innumerable objective impediments that weigh on this sort of effort, we may note that what engenders the chain reaction is less a "critical mass" than a mass of critiques, a clash of challenges. The sparks come from independent poles striking against each other. When the poles come together, the charges are neutralized in a community of mutual congratulation, contradiction is put on a pedestal and forgotten, and the grouping stagnates; all they have in common are illusions of collective participation and memories of the time when it wasn't illusory.

* * *

In contrast to the pure revolutionary pretension, the *revolutionary role* is *well-founded illusion*. It is not just a stupidity that can be neatly avoided by being sincere or humble, but a constantly engendered objective product of revolutionary activity, the shadow that accompanies the radical accomplishment, the *reactionary* possibility, the internal or external backlash of the positive.

The positive is the inertia of the negative. Thus, we see an incisive negating action devolve into militantism (imitation of the negative, the practice of repetition); or a demystified judgment of one's possibilities lead to a successful action which leads to a remystification of one's capacities (revolutionary megalomania). The spectacle, shaken up by the negative, reacts by seeking a new equilibrium point, incorporating the negative as a moment of the positive. The revolutionary role is the form taken by this restored equilibrium in the individual. The character of the revolutionary is objectively reinforced by the spectacle of his opposition to the spectacle. The rupture of the veils of false-consciousness (ideology, the spectacle effect) places the negating subject in open contradiction with the very organization of unconsciousness (character, capital) and its strong-arm defense (character-armor, the State). The organization of unconsciousness defends itself like a puncture-proof tire: it uses the very negating activity to plug up and seal the puncture. Just as a ruling class in a tight position will offer some revolutionaries a place in the government, character gives the subject a "better position" where he acquires a vested psychological interest in the maintenance of the spectacular-revolutionary status quo. Dissatisfaction striking transforms itself into self-satisfaction at having struck so well. What was an effort at personal liberation returns as a feather in the cap of one's "personality." Politics builds character.

(But no excuses for fakery. There will be nothing more vulgar than future "theorists" lamenting, in a self-indulgent neo-Dostoyevskian manner, the role-traps their difficult position as theorist sets for them. It is simply a matter of grasping the objective bases that engender the role or support the pretension—the better to catch the role and the quicker to eject the pretender.)

It is sometimes difficult to chart a path between the use of the revolutionary role to resolve one's individual problems and the use of the role of being nonrevolutionary as a defense against dialectics in one's everyday life. A worker understandably wants to leave his work as separate as possible from his efforts at life. But the quandary of the revolutionary is brought out every time someone asks him "What do you do?" Precisely to the extent that he is not a militant, his "business" is not something he can neatly hang up in the hall before getting down to his pleasure. Every time he suppresses his revolutionariness something goes out of him. He's suppressed part of himself. It's a lie, a self-abasement, a betrayal. But if he identifies himself as "a revolutionary" a whole new series of problems emerges, even leaving aside the crude misconceptions this gives rise to in a stranger (immediate pigeonholing as a militant). Hence the *particular* miseries in the love relations in the situationist milieu (in addition to about all the ones shared with everyone else): pathetic attempts to crudely engender love out of comradeship or comradeship out of love; spectacular isolation as a special, weird type of person (e.g. the groupie phenomenon); the

Pygmalion effect (the revolutionary finds he has a lover who is the very image—and only the image—of his practice; whose automatic affirmation of all his actions is the very epitome of all the weakness and self-abasement he detests); etc. In fact, in their efforts to unite substance and passion they are living out in miniature the clash between the crises of the old order and the signs of the new, signs which will of necessity remain almost exclusively inscribed in negative for a long time still. The old marginal forms of separate, isolated play —art, bohemian experimentation, storybook love—are more and more squeezed out in the global planification, simplifying the problem as it creates new complications on another level: Dialogue finds itself up against the fact that it must concern itself with the *suppression of the conditions that everywhere suppress dialogue.* Dialogue is revolutionary or it doesn't last, and begins to know it.

Behindism, or Theory Colonization

> *"Yet he dismisses without notice his thought, because it is his. In every work of genius we recognize our own rejected thoughts: they come back to us with a certain alienated majesty. . . . Tomorrow a stranger will say with masterly good sense precisely what we have thought and felt all the time, and we shall be forced to take with shame our own opinion from another."*
>
> —Emerson, "Self-Reliance"

In certain kinds of races (e.g. bicycling), if you can get close enough behind the front racer you can get a free ride—the person in front breaks the wind and creates a vacuum that sucks you along behind. The *behindist* is a person who has such a relation to revolutionary theory or theorists: no matter how much he "advances," he is always following in the wake of others.

The behindist relation acquires sense only in the context of creativity, of qualitative content. (In this regard, the linearity of the "race" analogy may be misleading.) Thus, the phenomenon is known among writers who try to break out of the overpowering influence of a master and find "their own voice"; and it is also involved in the rapid turnover in music groups, where each member goes off to form his own group, whose members in turn go off a few years later to form *their* own groups. And thus there is no behindism in the leftist milieu, where the qualitative is absent and the leader-follower relation, far from being considered a problem, is rather aimed at; or if it is vaguely felt as a problem, is easy for those on the bottom to break out of. (It doesn't take much self-respect to resent patent manipulation, much initiative to reject it, or much imagination to bypass a milieu of artificially enforced scarcity of intelligence.) Behindism is the "progress disease" of the most advanced sector of the revolutionary movement.

The more objectively correct the theory, the stronger its imperialist grip on the behindist.

Consciousness of human practice is itself a type of human production, in which masses of people participate in various ways and with varying degrees of consciousness. *Expressed* theory is only a moment in this process, a *refined* product of practical struggles, consciousness momentarily *crystalized* in a form on the way to becoming broken down again into raw material for other struggles. Only in the upside-down world of the revolutionary spectacle does this *visible moment* of theory seem to be *theory itself,* and its *immediate* articulator its *creator.*

The alienation of the behindist to the profit of the myth of revolution (which is the result of his own semiconscious activity) expresses itself in the following way: the more he appropriates, the less autonomous he becomes; the more he participates partially, the less he comprehends his own possibilities to participate totally. The behindist stands in an alien relation to the products of his activity because he alienates himself *in* the act of production (the activity is not passionate but imposed, it is not the satisfaction of a desire to revolt but only a means for satisfying other desires, e.g. recognition by his peers) or *from* the act of production (his participation tends heavily toward the *distributive* aspect* of the process).

Fundamentally, coherence is less the development of one's theory or one's practice than the development of their *relation with each other.* Thus, we see the behindist as suffering from a theoretico-practical *imbalance,* taking in theory all out of proportion to his use of it, or engaging in a practice that has always been *initiated* by others. His is the appropriation that always comes too late. He is protected from risks. He doesn't *discover,* he is *informed*—which books are essential, which rebellions were the most radical, which people are ideologues, what the proper reasons for a break are. . . . Everywhere he turns, someone's been there before him. The general theory is his *personal spectacle.* Yet so much is he in the thrall of the theory that the more he is incapacitated by it, the more he feels the need to pursue it further, always supposing that that magical insight which will finally let him "understand" what to do and how to do it is just around the corner. So much is he on this treadmill that when he comes upon a terrain where he has not been preceded he supposes that this can only

---

* "Before distribution becomes distribution of products, it is (1) distribution of the means of production, and (2) (which is another aspect of the same situation) distribution of the members of society among the various types of production (the subsuming of the individual under definite relations of production). It is evident that the distribution of products is merely the result of this distribution, which is comprised in the production process and determines the structure of production." (Marx, *A Contribution to the Critique of Political Economy.*)

have been because it wasn't "important enough"—as if there weren't millions of subversive projects worth doing, most of which haven't even been conceived of yet. The radiance of past subversion engenders a narrow de facto orthodoxy as to what constitutes "coherent practice."

Behindism is a permanent organizational problem of our epoch. One who is locally autonomous may very well be behindist in relation to the global movement as a whole, or to its most comprehensive theorists. (In the final analysis, the proletariat is collectively behindist as it struggles for the *self-management of its own theory*.) Generally speaking, the *practical* reading of a radical text is characterized by a critical, seemingly almost callous attitude, which constantly has an eye out for what can be ripped off from it, and which cares little for the intrinsic merit of what can't. Whereas the feeling "This is absolutely fantastic! There's so much I don't know! I'm going to have to read a lot more of this!" announces the nascent theory colonization.

Each revolutionary has to make his own mistakes, but it is pointless to repeat ones that have already been made and overcome by others. The problem is to continually discover a balance between appropriation of certainties and exploration of new terrains. It seems to me that *conception* is the aspect that can least be dispensed with, as the behindist attempts to break out of his vicious circle. Once a project is chosen and begun, the consultation of a text or a person is less mystifying because the point of contact is narrower and more precise.

It is important to distinguish the behindist, who is in a difficult position because of his relation to other revolutionaries, from that vast mass of hangers-on who merely find it passionate to associate with revolutionaries, or at least to let other people know that they do. The hanger-on imagines that he is more advanced than the masses because his more or less accidental proximity to revolutionaries lets him know which way the wind is turning. He wants to appreciate the radical acts of others *aesthetically,* as *better spectacles* than are ordinarily available. Thus, even as a spectator of revolution he doesn't see its entire uneven and contradictory process, but solely its latest *visible results.* In this sense, he is not even the spectator of the revolution, but only of its *recuperation.* He can see a thousand people in the streets, but he can't hear the subjects of a million conversations: if the revolution doesn't proceed in a neat, cumulative, linear fashion, he announces that it's no longer there* (and the worst of the hangers-on in this regard are the retired revolutionaries). He seeks not to subvert this

---

* "Indeed, how ridiculous! And yet how rich with such ridiculous things is history! They repeat themselves in all critical periods. And no wonder! For, with regard to the past, all is looked on favorably, and the necessity of the changes and revolutions that occurred is acknowledged; its application, however, to the present situation is opposed with every means available. The present is made the exception to the rule because of shortsightedness and complacency." (Feuerbach, *Principles of the Philosophy of the Future.*)

world but to arrive at *an accommodation with its subverters*. If his *complacency* is disturbed he *complains* about the revolutionary movement in exactly the same way he would complain about a defective commodity or a politician who sold him out, and supposes that he is demonstrating his autonomy when he threatens to withdraw his priceless *vote of confidence*. The serious behindist will not hesitate to separate himself from his best comrades if he sees no better way to develop his autonomy; whereas it suffices for the hanger-on to find himself in a milieu where revolutionary pretensions are not fashionable to drop his without a second thought.

How To Win Friends and Influence History

> " 'How?' you ask. Rather a large order, I admit. And in attempting to harvest the material to fill it, we must tread our way down devious and dubious paths, for so much depends upon you, upon your audience, your subject, your material, your occasion, and so on. However, we hope that the tentative suggestions discussed and illustrated in the remainder of this chapter will yield something useful and of value."
>
> —Dale Carnegie, *How To Develop Self-Confidence and Influence People by Public Speaking*

A hero in a renaissance fantasy discovers (on the moon, I believe) the abode of all the *lost things* of history, all the things that were lost and never again found. Imagine if we were to see gathered in one enormous pile all the *lost situationist schemes*! However, we too would probably have to ascend to the moon to find them, for, as Swift observes, "the whining Passions and little starved Conceits are gently wafted up by their own extreme Levity . . . and . . . Bombast and Buffoonery, by Nature lofty and light, soar highest of all."

How often have we seen a promising project start out with enthusiasm, become boring and then get dropped? How often have we seen a project expand itself (and a good project almost always tends to expand itself) to the point where it dominates its initiator, to the point where he gets so bogged down in the immensity of his self-imposed tasks that he ends up repressing the whole experience like a wiped-out C.P. militant after the thirties? How many will never return? Alas!

Of course, it's true that in most of these cases we're probably not missing much: how could a theorist elucidate the organizational tasks of the masses if he can't organize his own ongoing tasks? Do we suppose someone will be able to criticize the economy if he hasn't worked out the *economy of his critique*?

We need to elaborate the morphology of the *single project*. For example: conception → commencement → expansion → reorientation → paring down → final attack → realization → aftereffects; or even perhaps: foreplay → orgasm → relaxation. And we certainly need to cultivate the *art of the interrelation of projects.* In spite of occasional lip service to Fourier, how often do we see a revolutionary consciously varying his activities, selecting two or three different types of projects among which he can skip according to mood? Or choosing a project for its educative value so that, like certain musicians, he discovers as he communicates? Or carefully seeking the optimal collaboration/rivalry ratio with his comrades?

We can't intervene among the workers if we don't know how to intervene in our own work. The agitators must be agitated. "Prepare new successes, however small, but daily."

(Yes, we can foresee a *competentism* which will arise out of the popularization of critical techniques (e.g. the widespread ability to turn out a crudely "correct" leaflet for any occasion). But this proliferated misuse, by undermining the flimsy basis of a tiny minority's monopolization of a situationist image, will in turn dialectically force its own qualitative supersession.)

* * *

"It is hard to decide whether irresolution makes men more wretched or more contemptible; and whether it is always worse to take the wrong decision than to take none."

—La Bruyère, Characters

The alpha and omega of revolutionary tactics is *decision.* Decision is the great clarifier: it brings everything back into focus. Like a ray of sunshine finally breaking through an overcast sky, the concrete proposal disperses the clouds, dissolves away the fog of speculation. The simplest method of *bullshit detecting* consists in noting whether an individual's decisions lead to acts and his activity to decisions: "Oh, I see, you think x: then that means that you are going to do y?" *Panic!* "Er . . . no . . . ah, I was just saying . . ."

Consider the exhilaration of *conversion* to a religion or a fad: it is the brief moment of conscious choice among the various modes of submission to the given. One makes the big step and *decides* to serve Christ or to join a fan club or a political group. The rush, however, is attributed to the content of the choice.

Commodity society contains this contradiction: it must arouse these eagerly entertained enthusiasms, both to keep the ideological market going and to maintain the psychological survival of its consumers; and yet in so doing it is playing with fire: one decision may lead to another. Most consequential revolutionaries can trace their development back to a decisive moment when they determined upon—or, more often, *stumbled* upon—a small but concrete act. Often enough they hesitated, doubted themselves, thought that what they were doing was maybe stupid and in any case insignificant. But in retrospect it can often be seen that that conversation, letter, leaflet, or whatever, marked a starting point—nothing was quite the same afterwards. In fact the embarrassment, the awkwardness, is almost the mark of this type of moment: the blush of the revolutionary virgin ceasing to be one. In subversion, one can start anywhere. But the subjective power of the act is proportional to the degree to which the person subverts not only a situation but also himself as a part of it. Long experience has shown that to critique the branch you are sitting on is the most exciting and often even the essential beginning. The practice of theory begins at home.

* * *

"When in doubt have a man come through a door with a gun in his hand."
—Raymond Chandler

Decision is intervention, disruption, drawing the line. It has an arbitrary character, aristocratic, dominating. It is necessary mediation, the subject imposing himself by imposing on himself. Decision is *aggressive limitation:* an act is made possible by the elimination of other possible acts. It is the interposing of an arbitrary *limiting element.* (The words "decide" and "concise" both trace back to a Latin root *to cut.*)

The limiting element may even be random. It is only necessary that the element of randomness be calculated. The experiments of the surrealists were generally marked by an avowed surrender to the irrational or the unpredictable—which is tantamount to worshiping one's own helplessness. Of itself, the action of chance is naturally conservative and tends to reduce everything to an alternation between a limited number of variants, or to habit. We invoke randomness not for its own sake but as a counter-conditioning agent. The systematic use of chance is the "reasoned disordering" of behavior, on the principle that the end of conditioning is reached by the straight and narrow path of conditioning itself. In general, a dominated conditioning exposes the hidden dominating conditioning.

Existing in a haze so omnipresent we can scarcely discern it—like a fish trying to comprehend "water"—we introduce *one more* routine, arbitrary enough that we can see it and therefore alter it, just as a person trying to quit smoking will temporarily shift to gnawing candy. Discovering a fetish, we turn it against itself. To burn or detourn commodities would mean nothing to people who were not dominated by them. But since we *really are entranced* by the commodity-spectacle, we can turn the charm into a countercharm, the fetish into a talisman. The antimanipulative antiaesthetics of détournement has no other basis: The less magic possessed by an image, the less *authority* is there to manipulate the observer (in the limiting case, the communication

214

draws its power *exclusively* from its own truth); the more magic it possesses, the more the *already existing* authority is drawn on to denounce the conditions that could make such a manipulation possible. It only remains to add that détournement is not only for demystifying others.

* * *

"Nothing clears up a case so much as stating it to another person."
—Sherlock Holmes

"To judge that which has contents and workmanship is the easiest thing; to grasp it is more difficult; and what is most difficult is to combine both by producing an account of it," as George Hegel said a while back, in another preface to another Phenomenology. It is commonly known how merely writing down a question and trying to answer it can often cut through a welter of confusions. (For example: "What are my current obstacles in this project?" "Where do I stand in relation to this theory? to that person?" "What is the role of such and such an ideology in the society as a whole?" "What are the present options?") The secret resides partly in the intrinsic clarification arising from a forced centering on one issue,* and partly in a subjective demystification that comes from the objectivization of the problem: by "expressing" (objectifying) the data, you achieve a "distanciation" that allows you to better come to grips with the problem (assuming it is something that can be come to grips with at all). This process of objectification is the essential element in the real subjective efficacy of all the religions, therapies and "self-improvement" programs (confessing to a priest or a psychoanalyst, for example).

The practice of theory is less concerned with victories—victories take care of themselves—than with problems. It is less a matter of finding solutions than of discovering the right questions and posing them in the right way. It looks for the nexuses, the crossroads, the choices that "make a difference." Subversion does not aim to confuse, but to make things *clear*—which is precisely what throws the ruling spectacle into such a confusion. Subversion only seems to come out of nowhere because this world is nowhere. In contrast to advertising, the "art that conceals its art," détournement is the art that reveals its own art; it explains how it got here and why it can't stay.

---

* "The discussion of these perspectives leads to posing the question: To what extent is the SI a political movement? . . . The discussion becomes somewhat confused. Debord proposes, in order to bring out clearly the opinion of the Conference, that each person respond in writing to a questionnaire asking if he considers that there are 'forces in the society that the SI can count on? What forces? In what conditions?' . . ." (Report on the Fourth Conference of the SI, September 1960, in *I.S.* #5.)

By defining the real issues, we force the most radical polarizations and thus push the dialogue to a higher level. That's what makes for our "disproportionate influence" that drives our enemies wild. Our strategy is a sort of "revolutionary defeatism"—we incite rigor and publicity even if they are applied first of all against us. Our method is to expose our own methods; our force comes from knowing how to make our mistakes count.

If the theorist possesses an influence, he wields it precisely to set in motion the withering away of this state of affairs. In this sense, he detourns himself, his own de facto position. He *democratizes* whatever really separates him from other proletarians (methods, specialized knowledge) and *demystifies* the apparent separations (his accomplishments are proof not of his amazing capacities, but of the amazing capacities of the revolutionary movement of his era). He would like his theories to grip the masses, to become part of the masses' own theory. But even more importantly, he tries to make it so that even the defeat of his theories is nevertheless conducive to the advance of the movement which has tried them and found them wanting. Even if his theory of social practice falls short, he wants the *way* he practices theory socially to be both exemplary in itself and instructive in the way it lays open to the light of day the stages on that theory's way.

To supersede is sweet; but sweeter still to incite one's own supersession!

The practice of theory being the *practice of clarity,* anyone who claims to be a revolutionary should be able to define what his activity consists of: what he has done, what he is doing, what he proposes to do. This is an absolute minimum base, without which all discussion of theory, tactics, etc., is just so much idle running at the mouth. Anything less is an insult—we should never have to *guess* whether someone is bullshitting, what the odds are that they'll accomplish what they vaguely suggest that they will.

Theory is the proletariat's continuous "true confession" to itself, the incantation that exorcises the false problems in order to pose the real ones. But the proletariat can only "express itself" through the struggle for the means of expression. Whatever the subjective diversity of a million distinct and contradictory miseries, the solution is unitary and objective because the diversity of misery is maintained by unitary and objective means. For the proletariat, "producing an account" of its own conditions is inseparable from *settling its account* with whatever and whoever maintains them.

Affective Détournement: Alternative to Sublimation

"I played sly tricks on madness."
—Rimbaud, *A Season in Hell*

The chief defect of all psychoanalysis—Reich's included—is that it considers neurosis or character as a separate phenomenon, and thus by implication has the notion (even if only as an unrealizable ideal) of a possible "healthy individual" within the present society. But to attack character in isolation is doomed to defeat because it doesn't function in isolation. For the most part, character formations, if broken up, will simply re-form in a slightly different way; the only alternative is madness or death. Character is the miserable defense of the world against its own misery. The call to break up character defenses is a call to break up the conditions against which we require defenses. There is no revolutionary psychoanalysis, but only a revolutionary use of it.

It has for a long time been commonly recognized that political activity is often merely a poor compensation for personal failure. But it is equally true that as a whole our "personal" activity is merely a poor compensation for revolutionary failure. One repression reinforces another. Characterological fixation tends to reproduce itself as ideological fixation, and vice versa. A personal block reinforces a theoretical block. Ideology is a defense against subjectivity, and character is a defense against the practice of theory.

A person attempting to criticize someone or something he previously respected, for example, will often feel the classical oedipal resistances, as if he were about to kill his father: self-doubt, guilt, hesitation, chickening out at the last minute. Note how often someone who has made a perfectly good critique feels obliged to tack on an apologetic coda: "I'm sorry, I only did this because I had to; now I'll try to make up for it with a positive contribution."

affective détournement: *Subjectively double-reflected critical activity, i.e. conscious interplay between critical activity and affective behavior; orientation of a feeling, passion, etc., toward its proper object, toward its optimal realizable expression.*

The notion of affective détournement is indissolubly linked to the recognition of the subjective effects of the work of the negative and to the affirmation of a playful-destructive behavior; which places it in complete opposition to the classic positions of psychoanalysis or mysticism.

217

At its simplest, affective behavior and critical activity can be played off against each other, the one manipulated in support of the other, without there being any particular, direct connection between them (or at least not a conscious one). Because of the interconnectedness of repressions, when the subject breaks a constraint, a fixation or a fetish, the two poles of political mystification—empiricism and utopianism—are simultaneously weakened, opening the way for a practical grasp of events. The spectacle effect is broken, dissolving the appearance of necessary impotence, or, what amounts to the same thing, the haze of a myriad of "possible" projects which will never be realized.

Reich noted that when his analysis was getting to a sensitive point, the patient might come up with a flood of hitherto repressed material as a decoy, a superficial distraction, a sort of "bribe" to the analyst. I have found that one can arrange one's "self-analysis" so that the "bribe" is paid to oneself in the form of temporarily increased energy and historical lucidity. Character will win out; but you can blackmail it, make it *pay* by making it squirm.

Inversely, certain types of brief subversive interventions can be undertaken somewhat arbitrarily or voluntaristically with the simple aim of jostling oneself out of a rut.

More directly, and thus more complexly, the content of an affect may be related to the content of critical activity, the "overlapping" being transformed from an unconscious hindrance to a conscious alliance.

Affective détournement does not claim to realize passions, to definitively destroy frustrations. Whereas sublimation substitutes a realization on one plane in exchange for a nonrealization on another, a substitution characterized by the repression of the original desire, affective détournement openly proclaims its origin as frustrated desire. Although it aims to strike back at the origin of the frustration, it is distinguished, on the other hand, from the whole revenge syndrome (fixation on the hated object, which thus also pushes the original desire out of the picture) by the fact that the subject dominates: the particular object of aggression (if there is one) is treated as a mere means.

That lost love, the dream that ended too soon—every missed possibility is another fact that demands to be *corrected historically*. In the words of a definition of poetic cubism, affective détournement is a "conscious, deliberate dissociation and recombination of elements," the *juxtaposition* of an affect and a revolutionary project, going up to the point of the supersession of one or both of the original elements. The supersession may be simple negation—an exorcism of the defeatist aspects of the affect or the project—or it may be a more positive matter of mutual augmentation. It is only through a spectacular perversion that desire is seen as something that simply "happens" to a person, the unilateral presentation of a fixed object to a person who need only "have" a desire for it. The expression "to conceive a desire" retains the comprehension that one participates in the development of one's desires. Every realized possibility demands to be realized more. Affective détournement fathers a new desire on the old one by introducing it into historical company.

Nothing is more predictable than the recuperation of our techniques, in the form, for example, of encounter or happening type sessions devoted to "anticharacter" therapy in a "radical perspective." (This would be a purer form of the ideology which is now being sought in the more diffuse forms of "radical therapy" or "alternative culture," and which accounts for the enormous currency of Reich, whose works are seen more or less consciously as providing a missing link in the search for a viable psychosocial reformism.) Suffice it to say that it is not by changing ourselves that we will change the world—a fantasy which meets its truth in the Stalinist "construction of socialism" by the construction of "socialist man" (on the procrustean model). Anyone who announces his being able to function better as a revolutionary victory is just advertising the system. Affective détournement breaks with the notion of permanent cure. Either repression returns—as modified exploitation or symptom—or it never left: to claim any *fundamental* liberation within commodity society is to proclaim one's own *fundamental* compatibility with reification. Illusion of permanence or permanent illusion.

All techniques are allowed, not only psychoanalysis: they need only begin with a demystified comprehension of the totality and contain their own critique. Affective détournement is an ongoing and disabused skirmishing in the conditions of continuous *dual power within the individual.*

Sleepers Awake

The forces that want to suppress us must first understand us—and that is their downfall. The unconsciousness of the spectacle already puts it at our disposal to a certain extent: as if we suddenly had the cities all to ourselves, like a child running through the silent ruins in a Chirico painting. When you detourn a film, an ad, a building, a subway, you demystify its apparent impregnability; just for a moment, *you* dominated *it;* it is just an object, just technology. Or is it? Didn't you notice how you felt a little bit *at home* with it?

The image of class struggle that separates us from the spectacle cedes too much to the enemy without a fight because it separates us from our essence. The spectacle is not just the image of our alienation, it is also the alienated form of our real aspirations. Hence its grip on us. The compensatory fantasies draw their power from our real fantasies. Therefore, no puritanism towards the spectacle. It is not "just" a fetish; it is also a *real fetish,* i.e. it really is *magical,* it really is a "dream factory," it really does expropriate human adventure. The Maldororean passion perfectly captures the ambivalent attitude appropriate toward the spectacle: to tenderly and sincerely embrace it as, with a loving and delicate caress, we slit its throat.

We are still experimenting in the dark. The most powerful weapon the society possesses is its ability to prevent us from discovering the weapons we already have—how to use them. We have to practice a global "resistance analysis" on the society itself, interpreting not primarily its content but its resistances to the "interpretation." Each subversive action is experimental like a move in the children's game: "You're getting warmer." It is by making history that you learn to comprehend it; by playing against the system that you discover its weaknesses, where it lashes back. In the final analysis that's really what the "dérives" were all about: Is it entirely coincidental that the modern critique of urbanism and the spectacle issued from the "psychogeographical" researches of the fifties? One learns most precisely how the system operates by observing how it operates on its most precise enemies.

The revolutionary movement is its own laboratory and provides its own data. All the alienations reappear there in concentrated form. Its own failures are the lodes that contain the richest ore. Its first task is always to expose its own poverties, which will be continually present, whether in the form of simple lapses into the dominant poverties of the world it combats or the new poverties that its very successes create for itself. This will always be the "precondition of all critique." When dialogue has armed itself, we can try our luck on the terrain of the positive. But till then, the success of a revolutionary group is either trivial or dangerous. Taking our cue from commodity production, we have to learn how to manufacture organizations with their own "built-in obsolescence." In revolution we lose every battle but the last one. What we must aim at is to *fail clearly,* each time, over and over. Everything fragmentary has its resting place, its place in the spectacle. But the critique that wants to end the Big Sleep can have "nowhere to lay its head."

Be cruel with your past and those who would keep you there.

[May 1974]

THEORY OF MISERY,
MISERY OF THEORY

A Report on the New Conditions
of Revolutionary Theory

"Better be a debtor than pay with coin that does not bear our image!"

—Nietzsche, *The Gay Science*

1

The organized theoretical effort (the most advanced since Marx) carried out by the members of the Situationist International has not only burned itself out, it seems content to accept a place among the curiosities in the museum of revolutionary history. Rather than trying to get back on its feet, this fallen theoretical dragon prefers to pride itself on the still-impressive reverberations from its past exploits— exploits that are becoming distant enough to take on a comfortingly legendary character.

The misadventures of the situationists' theory and those to which comparable movements of revolutionary intellectuals in the past succumbed are finally reunited in the very nature of their failures. Just as with Marxist thought and other later efforts to develop a revolutionary critique, all the achievements of the real situationist theoretico-practical effort ended up undergoing a total *inversion* of their meaning. They now constitute nothing more than one particular form of cultural verbiage within the general pseudocommunication imposed by existing conditions, a pseudocommunication that is as prevalent among those who revolt against those conditions as among those who accept them.

The real situationist spirit, the spirit that (to those capable of grasping undertakings of this order) was so clearly at the origin of the situationist adventure, no longer has any choice but to turn without mercy against the edifice of its own *petrified* theory, against its entire past and its former values, or else be swept from the revolutionary battlefield as a source of useless and antiquated verbosity.

From now on no new development of revolutionary thought will be possible unless the situationist *critical power* is applied not only to the old SI organization but to situationist theory itself. The project of developing a theory of combat that contains its own critique must be taken up again from scratch.

To accomplish this, the situationists' theory must no longer be judged on the terrain where it *wants* to be judged, namely on its theoretical *intentions,* its scientific validity, its program, etc. To hesitate to go beyond this terrain and make a more vital critique— whether out of some unwarranted concern for intellectual objectivity or out of respect, because so far no one else has done any better (1917 Russia didn't come up with any theory better than Lenin's)—would *at best* amount to assuming the drawbacks of a disembodied orthodoxy à la Korsch or the sort of illusion characteristic of Lukács. If the situationists' theory still *directly* interests the revolutionary movement, it is as an object lesson of what such a theory could *become:* one more ideology of revolution, one more system of representation expressing something other than what it intends and serving ends other than its explicit ends.

2

The situationists' theory made itself known as the *revolutionary theory of dissatisfaction.* It found itself at the converging point of all the lines of force that are transforming the conditions of existence—and consequently of *struggle*—in contemporary society, both because it was made possible by those conditions and because it was capable of expressing them. As a critique of a particular *stage* of a commodity society that was far from having *concretely* developed all its material consequences (including the revolutionary opposition to itself), the situationists' theory ran the risk of becoming the expression of *all* the dissatisfaction released in this process; that is, not only of the *profound* dissatisfaction linked to the proletarianization of all sectors of social existence— dissatisfaction that has become really *revolutionary*—but also of that far more widespread *superficial dissatisfaction* stemming from particular features of the present stage as well as from the ever-increasing frustrations of old habits and tastes. The situationists' theory was not in a position to see well enough the danger contained precisely in the *spectacular logic* of the conditions it combatted, which led it to be understood, and ultimately to understand itself, according to the logic of *illusion,* and thus to be assimilated by the existing order as a *cultural code of integrated dissatisfaction.*

The hierarchized consumption of economic goods, of phony relations among individuals, and of phony objects of struggle which the spectacle of modern dissatisfaction now provides in superabundance has as its immediate subjective counterpart this form of superficial dissatisfaction, which in fact constitutes the only real *subjective basis* upon which the present social system can function.

When this superficial dissatisfaction feels obliged to express itself in "situationist language," the optical illusions and confusions it creates stem from the very nature of existing conflicts. The revolutionary goal of establishing the sociohistoric conditions of "enjoyment without restraint" intersects with the ordinary publicity of enjoyment within the economy (ranging from glorification of current conditions to fantasies of bureaucratic-ecological reforms), sometimes to the point that the expressions of the two are confused with each other. This apparent resemblance comes from the fact that they reflect the same historical conflict, though seen from opposite sides of the barricade. But even though they sometimes appear very close, superficial dissatisfaction is qualitatively as far removed from revolutionary dissatisfaction as are the resigned victims of existing conditions. The spread of superficial dissatisfaction—the generally assumed standpoint that henceforth dominates the perception and all the representations of contemporary social life—simply expresses the fact that things have become so unsatisfactory that no one can be *quietly resigned* anymore; even resignation has had to adopt the pose and language of dissatisfaction.

It is not surprising that the revolutionary theory that reintroduced the *dialectical method of the totality* into the struggle (in order to put the comprehension of the social question on better bases) was able, even while remaining fundamentally uncomprehended, to strike such a sympathetic chord in these social conditions where the economy dominates human life in a *totalitarian* manner. This modern aspect of the notion of totality has become familiar to everyone, if only because everyone has been conditioned to it through the rules of hierarchized consumption: if each level of hierarchized consumption and power can do nothing but covet the next higher level, this is because hierarchical organization presents the *totality* of economic benefits and social powers to people's covetous desires.

The *totality* effectively serves as the new universal standard of reference of social needs, but only considered passively, as the external totality of economic goods. Consequently, whether superficial dissatisfaction respects all the economic rules or ends up infringing some of them in the name of what it believes to be a revolutionary program, the objects it covets will always bring it back to where it started, subjected to the same principle of an economy of social life and consequently to an *economy of its consciousness and practice.*

Even if a *constituted* situationist theory had never existed as a possible source of inspiration, the system of commodity consumption implicitly contains its *own situationism* in the form of a utopian fantasy of defectless and limitlessly consumable economic pleasures. Because the sphere of consumption (which amounts to all the social life nominally left to the initiative of individuals) is only one aspect of the economic process, is unable to free itself from its limits, and is absolutely dependent on its economic complement, its natural situationism tends to become *genuinely situationist*. But before this can take place the concept of pleasure inherited from the economic era must be fundamentally *transformed*.

Modern commodity production and consumption have eliminated many human capacities that people in previous eras possessed to at least some degree and that in some cases were necessary simply to ensure their survival. What is now actually taught, desired and practiced in the sphere of social consumption is simply the perfected *economy* of pleasure and of the capacity for living; what are being imposed everywhere, without encountering any real revolutionary resistance, are the petty culture, enjoyments, tastes and manias of *antihistorical humanity*. These are the same traits of general mediocrity that end up poisoning and rendering impossible every attempt at serious revolutionary struggle. Because it comes to him from *outside*, the habit of economic pleasure keeps the individual in his place, separate from the rest of the world; and this externality of economic pleasure, which excludes all fundamental initiative in decision and action, is precisely what is desired and consumed.

3

Some people still believe, for example, that the stupefying power of advertising lies in the fact that it makes people buy more useless goods. Actually, when advertising vaunts the merits of this or that particular commodity or of this or that pseudoneed that absolutely must be satisfied, it inevitably runs up against the contradiction of a competing product, of a consumers union, or of people's ordinary common sense. But beyond the commercial terrain, what advertising really imposes without meeting any resistance (by deflecting the spectator's attention from the fact that the language of advertising already implies and presents the happy spectacle of the *total approval of the existing system*) are all the socioeconomic presuppositions of which advertising is only one of the least serious consequences; along with the mode of subjection that is linked to those presuppositions, the poverty of the needs that result from them, and the absurd pretense that the latter can be satisfied within the rules of consumption. The fact that advertising has proved capable of turning itself into an object of spectacular debate, provoking people into declaring themselves for or against it, is an extreme example of its present stupefying power.

But if we judge it on the basis of its power of stupefaction, commercial advertising is far less dangerous than other, less obvious forms of publicity, whether in the political or the "cultural" sphere (including even the purely scientific sector). In reality, all colonized daily life contains all the stupefying power of the publicity of the present world: In a certain sense the Lip workers have recently produced much more formidable advertisements for the existing way of life than has Madison Avenue, if we take into account all their respective potential mystifying effects.

<h1 style="text-align:center">4</h1>

As *critique of alienated labor* and *project of its revolutionary abolition,* the situationists' theory meets, as a favorable objective terrain, the phenomenon of an increasing declassment of a sector of the population that was previously integrated and subdued but that is now more inclined to turn against the institution of work. A *structural crisis of the modern economy,* however, tends to throw individuals into revolutionary ideology well before they are in a position to grasp revolution as the only historical solution capable of practically dissolving the alienation of human activity. Those who treat work as the heaviest fetter on the new forms of struggle and consciousness remain dominated by the work-world, which casts those it declasses into solutions of peripheral survival, hustles, petty criminality and dubious revolutionary fantasies.

Modern economic transformation modifies the conditions of alienated labor, changes the composition of social classes, destroys their traditionally established representations, reconstructs the environment from top to bottom, and alters all the rules of the global politico-economic game, but ultimately leaves the declassed individuals in the *same antihistorical destitution* as the others whom it still employs. The aspects of alienated labor which are now more or less confusedly resisted everywhere, and which are explicitly denounced as archaic by the new mentality that is developing into the *subjective corollary* of the modern forms of commodity production, are for the most part the same aspects that the work-world itself is attempting to phase out.

The fact that the remnants of know-how that were formerly linked to certain sectors of material and intellectual production, along with virtually all traces of *practical sense,* are tending to disappear from the social terrain is a direct consequence of the extreme fragmentation and absurdity of tasks in commodity production. (The *total* colonization of workers' gestures and decisions within their direct economic alienation is only one aspect of the colonization of all social life.) All capacities and desires for autonomous, *non-externally-dictated* activity are being utterly destroyed among the present population. *Powerless laziness,* which goes so far as to reject the pseudoactivities offered within production without being able to *reinvent* human activity on other bases, is emerging everywhere as the normal subjective attitude in the face of the new state of social reality.

A parallel conflict related to modern conditions of alienated labor arises from the model of *maximum economic enjoyment* embodied in the *cadre* social stratum, a model which is presented as the ultimate meaning of existence nor only for the cadres but for all subservient social strata. Modern proletarians are molded into the average cadre mentality. Peasants, blue-collar workers, intellectuals, etc., are tending to lose the particular representations they once had, which are being replaced with the typical representations, tastes and desires of the cadres. This homogenization of subjective alienation manifests itself for example in the work-world by the fact that the demand for individual participation in economic decisions (or, outside of work, in political decisions), which was previously limited to the cadre socioeconomic level, is now becoming the natural demand of all types of workers, at the same time as it is becoming the official critique that the organization of labor makes of itself.

We can judge the extent of the problems that will present themselves to the revolutionary movement in the years to come by considering that the global cultivation of proletarian talents and the long apprenticeship of a new form of *all-encompassing practical sense* will have to start out from a near-total loss of all the old talents and from a current state of spirit that has neither the taste nor the preparation for any free practical enterprise whatsoever.

5

As a *theory of individual autonomy,* the situationists' theory, once deprived of its *negative spirit,* becomes virtually indistinguishable from the bourgeois ethical vision of abstract individual freedom. But the real poverty that can delude itself in this way about its own lot is no longer so much the nominal freedom of labor in the face of capital as it is that *freedom of pure appearance* bred to the rules of consumable pleasure; that freedom of irresponsibility which continually resorts to external means of valorization and which gets "into" this or that while remaining separate from everything.

The nature of the freedom demanded by those who identify their own superficial dissatisfaction with the situationist project can, like all ideologies of refusal, be understood as a banal daydream of social advancement. The individual molded by present-day conditions, who has in fact lost all individual qualities, dreams of reaching a classless society *just as he is.* Scarcely concerning himself with accomplishing anything *despite* present conditions, he can hardly pursue revolution as the sociohistoric means of *extending* such accomplishments; he merely dreams that his wretchedness will be less difficult to take than in the old world. He still hasn't felt the need to make himself a master of social life, and as a consequence of the narrowness of his actual needs he is still very poor at identifying the real obstacles to a revolution; he simply wishes that his present masters would stand aside in the face of a *proletarian miracle.* Thus, even when he sincerely believes himself capable of doing without authority, he is already setting himself up for the new power that will subdue him.

When a revolutionary theory is no longer in a position to effect its practical task of *transforming existing conditions of consciousness,* the poverty and lack of originality of those who carry on within its ruins rapidly attain caricatural proportions. The average revolutionary in such conditions tends to be subject to the *average alienations of his era.*

Even if, for example, he scorns the crude boss stereotype, the contemporary revolutionary has in no way rid himself of *hierarchical needs.* The motives that make him identify with the "revolutionary camp" suffice to demonstrate this. Unable to count for much in the existing social hierarchy, he tries to console himself by dreaming of a future society; not necessarily because he intrigues for a dominant role in it (usually nothing in him leads him to such an illusion), but because this assures him a share of the hierarchical status that membership in the revolutionary community provides within the *present* society. Among diverse other obligations that such a position brings with it, the contemporary revolutionary feels obliged to despise the old world and its most *conspicuous* servants, just as some poorly paid European workers still despise the immigrant laborer: because he reflects their own slavish image *too crudely.*

But through the vicissitudes of his theatrical subadventure the average revolutionary ends up demonstrating much more directly his profound need for a hierarchical environment: the solidity of his ideology, the degree of conviction he can give to it, depends directly on the *absolute ideological assurance* embodied in the personality of the leader. Conversely, if he himself happens to be in a leadership position, he feels an absolute need to be followed, since it is only the blind conviction of his followers that can support him in his role (objectively and, above all, subjectively). Whether he follows others or others follow him, the same need for illusion and show underlies his mentality.

Experimental egalitarian associations that develop in the coming struggles must no longer accept within themselves—and must combat externally—any *theoretical followerism* that does not simultaneously assign itself the humility and discretion that was characteristic of the *serious student* of classical education.

Revolutionary ideology is not merely a state of social false consciousness; it constantly manifests itself as a direct practical refusal of truth and of its concrete consequences. As an aspect of revolutionary ideology, the sole function of egalitarian voluntarism is to furnish an honorable decor for the flight from practical tasks.

It is notorious that anarcho-situationist egalitarianism has always refused to recognize the hierarchical aspects of its actual organizational functioning. This major practical evasion finally reduced the situationists' theory regarding revolutionary organization to a mere *counterideology* opposed to the dominant hierarchical organization, enabling the participants to share the illusion and the official lie of equality rather than to bear the shame of admitting their failure to achieve it. Yet the possibility of effectively anticipating all the new problems while there was still time to do so (notably for the old SI) hinged upon the admission of this failure and upon the recognition of the theoretico-practical conclusions resulting from it.

7

The *ideological need* which persists in individuals molded to the rules of commodity society's social relations, and which consistently regenerates itself even within their revolt, is totally contrary to the real theoretical sense and intuition on which will depend the course and ultimate outcome of all real theoretico-practical rebellion from now on.

Ideology, regardless of whatever element of scientific truth it may contain (Marxist-situationist theory, for example, still contains a substantial scientific foundation long after its inversion into ideology), is a veil placed between the individual and reality, and it reflects a system of interests that want to *preserve* this veil. Within the revolutionary counterideology opposed to existing conditions—which functions in a manner analogous to the *social spectacle* it depends on—the interests of the separate and the real need for separation that dominates it are dolled up in a hollow affirmation of the totally opposite state of affairs. Nevertheless, the ideological foundations of all modern revolutionary pseudothought, whether semiofficial or antiofficial, can be directly detected by its theoretical and practical *sterility*.

Ideological consciousness—which only rarely takes the form of gross ignorance—is essentially consciousness of *content,* i.e. the direct, positivistic assimilation of some *external* reality, whether that reality is a theoretical master or an individual or sociohistorical situation. Ideological consciousness functions by identifying with things, and is in fact based on the *need* for such identification. Dialectical consciousness, in contrast, derives its *anti-ideological force* from its capacity to discern the *form,* to grasp the processes concealed behind the immediate perception of content. Awareness of form, of the *nonvisible* part of reality (an awareness that is always lacking in ideological consciousness) is the indispensable condition for determining the ultimate meaning found in the *relation* of form and content.

Behind the screen on which the drama of contents is projected (the spectacular character of modern society can be understood as the systematic social organization of this screen) the *work of negation* proceeds mainly at the level of forms before itself becoming a visible content. (Human activity can be seen as the higher form that has this privilege of creating its own contents, of transforming them, or of withdrawing from them, at will.)

While dialectical consciousness depends on the faculty of *distancia-*

tion vis-à-vis content, ideological escapism reflects the *impairment* of that faculty. Unable to theoretically and practically master existing forms, ideological thought is instead totally subjected to them.

The negating faculty of distanciation can be understood as the faculty of turning in on oneself, of breaking one's own immediate relations with existing conditions; and ultimately, as the individual's capacity to take part in the internal conflicts that result from those relations.

The individual capable of distanciation is an individual reconciled with his true individuality, i.e. capable of looking at himself from the standpoint of his *development* and of the fundamental historical conflict upon which his development depends. It is through the faculty of distanciation that the individual preserves his capacity for freedom and is able to carry out and verify the practical development of that freedom in struggle.

The individual who lacks the faculty of distanciation is an individual continually clinging to externally determined values. Separated from himself, he ends up *interiorizing* the external social separation of the proletarian condition. He remains a stranger to himself just as he remains a stranger to the perspective of revolutionary theory even if circumstances have led him to superficially devote his existence to it.

In the same way, the historical movement by which the proletarian class progressively frees itself from the total externality of its original sociohistorical condition is nothing other than an act of *historical distanciation* upon which hinges, among other possibilities, the possibility of a *class consciousness*.

8

Because he remains above all an external being, the unoriginal individual produced by existing conditions feels the need, once present social conflicts touch him directly, for his gestures of revolt to be embodied in *mythological heroes*.

Christ is essential to the Christian mentality because he is the subjective incarnation connecting earth with heaven; he is the external subjective being who makes the Christian mentality possible because it is the earth, and the role that this mentality plays on it, that constitute for Christianity the actual inaccessible heaven. In the ordinary revolutionary mentality—within which the situationist mentality distinguishes itself only by a more marked and often more blind voluntarism—revolutionary heroes literally perform the function of Christ. The romantic vision of supertheorists and of a select few historical uprisings carries out, through the sacred person of the heroes, the union of terrestrial triviality with the heaven of universal history. The Bolsheviks were great pioneers in this type of cultifying: Lenin declared that to really be a Marxist one should always ask oneself, "What would Marx have thought and done in this situation?" The personal spectacular talents of the former SI (which at the same time constituted some of its real practical talents) attempted the highest stage of this classic heroic drama, decisively augmenting the concretization of myth: with the SI, a community of demigods found itself invested with the power of announcing the new conditions of paradise.

In opposition to the most elementary common sense, the contemporary revolutionary begins his task by no longer looking himself in the face. Instead, he successively identifies (in decreasing order of abstraction) with "the movement of history," the epic of a *disembodied* "proletariat," the romantic personalities of his intellectual masters, and finally and most directly, with the petty leaders that daily life puts in his path. Like all religious devotees, he arranges his own *biblical universe* wherein are gathered all the fantastic episodes that define the meaning of his rites. He learns, for example, that "the Paris Commune was the dictatorship of the proletariat" and that the blacks of Watts embodied "the critique in acts of everyday life," while being warned against "sociology" and "structuralism," which he is taught to see as evil offshoots of "the commodity" and "the spectacle."

Just as he ends up making a pitiful farce out of his whole concrete life (in this regard the average revolutionary is a worthy child of the present era), so his thought is nothing but a pale imitation of what others, because they have lived the necessary degree of adventure, have thought for him and before him. Depending on which sect he belongs to, he salivates at the most *miserable clichés,* which serve as collective bonds and representations among him and his companions; he prides himself on understanding the ideological in-references; he never jokes about anything except the scapegoats that his ideology designates because he knows that, like himself, his companions would be incapable of laughing at anything else. His self-expression within the group, and ultimately his only truly personal fulfillment, is reduced to demonstrating as often as possible that he is a servile student of the sect and the sectarianism that contain him.

9

Certain practical tasks induce revolutionaries to collaborate with each other; but more often than not they fail to achieve the slightest objective they have set for themselves because they have begun by carrying out this collaboration in an inappropriate manner. The qualitative weakness of the modern revolutionary movement continues to demonstrate that in the *manner of associating,* more than in anything else, everything remains to be learned. The depth of the objectives that revolutionaries are capable of setting for themselves in the course of their struggles, and their chances of achieving those objectives, depend dialectically on their competence in dealing with organizational questions.

Nevertheless, when things come to the point where association becomes a practical necessity, it is always possible to judge the worth of an individual—that is, the nature of the relations he maintains with himself, with others, and with reality as a whole—by noting that ideological escapism, which is not always immediately detectable on the level of ideas alone, will invariably leave the individual in a constant state of poverty and impotence.

Ideology, which must always be understood as not only a particular state of false consciousness but also as a set of material and subjective conditions that require such false consciousness, prevents *any* progress in the capacity for living or struggling. It is the worst school for such capacities, and is always promoted by people who basically do not want anything to change and who, above all, do not want to change *themselves*. The modern slave, whether he is a revolutionary or someone who is quite satisfied with present conditions, or something in between, is a supremely *antidialectical* being, the creature of an era where all progress, all taste for progress, and all understanding of progress have been repressed. Whenever urgent external circumstances disturb his complacency and force him to recognize his slavish position, he strives only to regain his illusion of freedom as soon as possible. Knowing nothing of time nor of "the organic progression of activity," he is the man of simulation and show, because that is the only mode of self-affirmation that can indefinitely ignore time.

10

Any revolutionary theoretical counterattack, whether it amounts to a new style of situationist struggle or to the emergence of some qualitatively different form, must render impossible the element of *superficial approval* that has prevailed over the last few years without encountering any effective opposition.

We have to begin by recognizing that the current vanguard of revolutionary theory has not only ceased keeping abreast of reality, it is dragging along a hundred leagues behind it. We might sum up the present crisis of revolutionary theory by saying that it found itself sooner than it expected having to *theoretically* overcome not only the society it is fighting but its own internal problems *arising out of the struggle itself*. At the center of these problems must be counted the rapid obsolescence of its previous ideas: their glaring inadequacy when it comes to trying to understand the stage now reached by the real revolutionary movement and to *acting in it* rather than merely enthusiastically announcing its existence.

The mass of new questions to which revolutionaries have so far been unable to find responses risks becoming time and terrain lost for the revolution itself. The contrast between the richness of this historical period and the scandalous silliness of its revolutionary critique has become glaring enough to rouse a new generation of revolutionaries to do something about it.

The coming struggles for practical theory will have to detect and combat not only the classic and generally known forms of alienation, but also the new forms of alienation stemming from the return of class struggles—notably, the forms of alienation that reconstitute themselves within the very heart of theoretical and practical struggles.

Knowledge, even very sophisticated knowledge, of the old revolutionary movement and the obstacles it ran up against proves quite inadequate when it comes to mastering the problems and tasks of the modern revolutionary movement. The revolution that is coming back into play can in scarcely any regard be equated with its past experiences. Taking the valid findings of classic Marxist-situationist theory as a point of departure, revolutionaries must henceforth learn to understand their revolution *as it happens*, by reinventing for it the theory that it requires *now*. It is no longer so much a matter of demonstrating that the old world should be and is going to be destroyed as of understanding the *development* of this destruction. The critical power of theory must first of all be brought to bear on the revolutionary movement itself; for in this movement, despite all its weaknesses and confusions, the construction of the new world has already begun. In its next stage, revolutionary theory will take on the character of a *theory of social war*. Losing the taste for skirmishes and games without consequences, it will know that in each fight the total stakes of this war are put in question.

Contrary to prevalent assumptions, the present revolutionary movement is far from having the victory of a situationist revolution within reach. A new class of rulers—whose members could be recruited, under the cover of the next revolutionary assault, from all the present spheres of social life (from among the most extremist revolutionaries as well as from the current ruling classes)—would certainly have better reasons for optimism than the amorphous minority of revolutionaries scattered around the world who intend the live the Marxist-situationist program *all the way*. There exists no *serious opposition* to the semirevolution which is being confusedly carried out before our eyes and which aims, whether peacefully or violently, at nothing more than reforming a few social irrationalities that have become *too glaring*. As for a genuinely situationist revolution, it is only on the *horizon* of present conflicts. For the moment the situationist program actually serves only as a *source of inspiration for a new status quo of the existing order*—just as, in another era, the communist program served to justify the kindred regimes of the Bolsheviks and the social democrats.

DANIEL DENEVERT
Paris, November 1973

TO CLARIFY SOME ASPECTS
OF THE MOMENT

(excerpt)

. . . In the period following the May 1968 occupations movement, reality has not ceased extensively confirming radical historical thought, but the individuals who strove to be the most conscious bearers of that thought have not proved capable of being so effectively. The most revealing example of this *apparent* failure is obviously the crisis of the Situationist International, but it is also reflected in the "pro-situ" phenomenon and the general inversion of situationist activity and thought into an ideology, *situationism.*

Situationist-inspired revolutionaries have not escaped the process of ideologization. What we said above about the most modern expressions of revolt applies equally to this "councilist" current; it, too, has played its part in the dramatic death throes of leftism. Rather than detailing everyone's particular mistakes, we intend to deal with what is essential.

If situationism has been despised and criticized, it has always been for *false* reasons, from a perspective that has itself remained pro-situationist. The pro-situ regression was considered as an aberration, as the dregs of a movement, as a trendy fad, and never for what it really was: the qualitative weakness of *the whole,* a necessary moment in the global progress of the revolutionary project. Situationism is the adolescent crisis of a situationist practice that has attained the *decisive* moment of a first important extensive development, the moment where it must practically dominate the spectacle that is taking hold of it.

If we ourselves can pitilessly deride these hesitations, weaknesses and poverties, it is not because we are geniuses who have descended from the heavens, but because we ourselves have experienced them in our own past activities. You can recognize a pro-situ by the way he generously distances himself from the confusions of the moment, which he can sometimes partially understand and denounce. The pro-situ levels his critique on the perverted world "by placing himself, like a classic novelist, at the omniscient point of view of God." Failing to comprehend real social or personal development, he is characterized by a total lack of lucidity regarding his own historical engagement.

The "situ milieu" has become a whorehouse worthy of the old artist milieus, full of shabby little roles, self-seeking hypocrisy in relationships, false consciousness, pseudocritiques of bad faith, scapegoats on whom are concentrated all spite and idols on whom are concentrated all jealousies.

What revolutionaries have lacked most up to now is dialectics, the *sense* of necessary mediations, the calculation of the relation between revolutionary practice and the totality it wants to transform, the practical appropriation of their own theory.

We have to resume "the dialectical process of the meeting of the real movement and its unknown theory" while recognizing that this dialectical process is equally present within the *development* of the individuals who are the most conscious bearers of this theory. Theory must still meet its own producers.

All the essential requirements formulated by the situationists regarding organized revolutionary practice were right, and it is first of all because they were right that they were taken up by others, above all among the generations who *lived* the occupations movement in France. But truth is itself a historical process, a process that dialectically gains truth. All utilized concepts, including basic minimum requirements, are of value only insofar as they elucidate the *development* of conscious practice within the global reality, a practice that creates and transforms itself in a nonlinear manner.

In this movement the minimum requirements cannot be simply applied as so many recognized and invariable truths; they must *essentially* traverse in practice the paths toward their own effective encounter, toward their *practical truth.*

The nondialectical application of these requirements, which reflected the poverty of the pro-situationist current in regard to its own project, was the necessary first step towards the effective realization of that project.

The authentic may be hidden behind a certain margin of error before being able to sweep it away for good. The course of history leaves behind a lot of debris. The false is a moment of the true. You don't decide to be a situationist, you have to *become* one. Revolutionary practice must discover, within the confusions of struggles, all the complexities and interlinkings of its different moments. Revolutionaries do not themselves escape from the complex and contradictory process of the conditions of production of class consciousness.

The SI itself contributed toward its subjugation to spectacular processes, notably in the *preeminence* of what was positively realized and in a certain margin of theoretical certainty that was derived from the *objectively experimented* portion of the situationists' activity. It is this comfortable settling down within the positive that characterizes the *situ role.* The more effective the objective position of the SI in present history became (and the same will apply for all future revolutionary organizations), the more perilous its heritage became for each of its members to assume.

This aspect of itself which the SI too unselfcritically exhibited found its extension, at a more extreme degree of reification, in the overall *weakness* of the current to which it gave birth.

The degree of general false consciousness was still sufficient to ensure that the influence radiating from the SI was that of its weakness rather than of its strength. (This weakness is what appears as its strength in the perspective of the spectacle, e.g. the "merits" of the SI that the press has recently begun to acknowledge, after having scarcely so much as mentioned its existence during the previous decade.) But this radiance was itself possible only due to the *quality* of the project in acts from which it drew its radiant power.

The occupations movement was the fulfillment of the Situationist International, and this fulfillment was its end. May 1968 was the realization of modern revolutionary theory, its overwhelming confirmation, just as it was to a certain extent the realization of the individuals who participated in the SI, notably in the revolutionary lucidity they manifested within the movement itself.

But for the SI the occupations movement remained the *conclusion* of its long practical research without being its supersession. The situationists did not prove capable of laying the practical foundations for a more advanced stage of their existence. This retrospective judgment is only apparently trivial. Because of what they must know about themselves and about the limits they ran into in their internal relations, the situationists are in fact the only ones who can really grasp and reveal their real significance.

What is at issue in the crisis of situationist-inspired practice, whether in the mass of idiotic little roles it has given rise to or in others' honest requestionings, is the *whole fundamental question of organizational method*. We have to critically reconsider organizational methods, to take up once again the notions of radical practice, of exemplariness, of communication of theory, in a disabused manner; remaining disabused first of all regarding the diverse political and pseudotheoretical heirs of those notions that have proliferated in the wake of May 1968. We have to confront once again the complex and contradictory conditions of production of class consciousness in an era that continues to demonstrate its capacity to maintain the conditions of unconsciousness. The mechanisms of false consciousness are becoming more sophisticated, gaining in subtlety what they lose in strength; it is this new fragility that must be comprehended and attacked. We have to attack the *reality* of this era and no longer merely its superficially understood abstract qualities; to attack its hesitations, its weaknesses and its poverties; to make shame yet more shameful.

While the situationists were putting themselves in question, engaging in an "orientation debate" in an effort to determine the appropriate next stages in their venture, the satellite groups they had given rise to followed a hundred steps behind, taking the SI as an uncriticized model and constituting themselves on the inadequate basis of a limited implementation of a few certitudes derived from the SI's previous experience.

The *dynamic* human richness that would normally be expected in historic encounters has not been evident in recent relations among revolutionaries. The would-be most advanced nucleus of consciousness was in no way separate from the world of separation, though it remained trivially separated from itself. The necessity for each group to prove itself, to discover the bases for its own practice—a necessity that is inseparable from striving for practical truth—was understood as the absurd requirement to *give proofs* to other organizations that were playing the same sordid game. The "councilist" supermen devoted themselves to contemplating the illusions they were barely able to generate within their petty functionary relations.

The lives of revolutionaries during these last three years would by themselves provide all the necessary data for a critique of the prevalent absence of communication.

The initial attempts to form autonomous groups, which now can easily be seen as having been far too tainted or compromised with the poverty of a certain period, were nevertheless not the result of a mere passing fad. This *minimum condition* of organized practice was inscribed in the needs and possibilities of the individuals of that period, and their failure has also revealed the limits of that period. This failure is not susceptible to any simple or simplistic explanation (political reification, theoretical underdevelopment, practicism, etc.). Although such explanations obviously contain a certain element of truth, they are only particular effects of a complex entanglement of factors whose *concrete unity* remains to be grasped. We could already enumerate many aspects of this unity, aspects that are not unrelated to the general poverties and possibilities of this period.

Revolutionary thought is completely contrary to a system of ideas (whereas *situationism* is nothing other than such a system) magically claiming correctness or truth in the style of all the presently decaying forms of separate thought, whether scientific, philosophical or political. Our knowledge does not obey the logic of separate knowledge, but the antilogic of *historical existence,* of the movement to realize the individual in history. Our superior understanding of the world stems from our participation in its conscious transformation. Revolutionaries of our era have to be in their acts the closest and surest companions of the work of the negative; their consciousness must cleave to the totality of the work of the negative in the ongoing historical process.

If we have had to reiterate some elementary points about the nature of theory, this is because the use of theory has been *forgotten* in the aftermath of May. It is no longer a matter of abstractly denouncing the abstractness of a few critical terms or concepts that bore the whole subversive weight of reality during a moment whose condi-

236

tions have now elapsed. We have to apply ourselves to resharpening those terms and concepts, giving them back their deadly cutting edge, so as to refine, for ourselves and for all those with good reasons to take after us, their *use* in the service of historical lucidity.

All the weapons that will vanquish the commodity system—including notably that central weapon: consciousness—are already being forged. The more this craft requires extreme capacities because of the conditions that have produced it, the more easily will the heavy artillery of converging pleasures storm all the walls that still separate us from our realization in history.

Without prejudging the precise forms that modern revolutionary organization must take in the new era, it seems to us that from now on *each of its aspects* must explicitly contain *its own critique* as being a mere aspect—so as to leave no opening for that *positivism* that generally attacks everything that threatens to overthrow existing conditions.

The forces of negation that are beginning to see the light of day must find themselves in the same relation to revolutionary organization as a luminous source in front of a point of refraction: an organization has no reason to exist other than as a *link with history,* both for its participants and for those outside it. Irresistibly rebellious forces must be able to recognize themselves in it without losing themselves in it; to recognize in it their own historicity, to be placed before it as before the immensity of their own tasks, the immensity of what remains to be done. A means is not something admirable in itself; as soon as it is seen as such, its essential purpose has been lost. Its element of positive realization acts like dead labor on living process: it petrifies everything.

Organizational methods must return dialectically to their own foundations, explicitly including themselves in the fluid movement of historical maturation, emerging from it only the better to reimmerse themselves in it. The miserable contemplative manias of the reign of mass passivity must not be able to find any organizational petrification to get their grips on. Going beyond its elements of positive realization, modern revolutionary organization will have to be a dictatorship of the negative: a practice that bears within itself the critique of the spectacle.

The totally inhuman reality of the commodity as a *social relation* constantly gains in cohesion, *tending* toward total reification of the world. The spectacle, which is the expression of this movement, tends to degenerate into a mere tautological representation of the *economic,* an image of the ensemble of socially accessible enjoyments. But in this unifying process this coherence of the commodity-as-subject-of-the-world at the same time brings out into the open the *fundamental incoherence of its alien coherence.*

The system's processes of internal wear and tear, along with the diverse movements that are tending toward its radical negation, only accelerate this global process of unification, dialectically forcing the whole system to put all its cards on the table, thereby exposing the *coercive solidarity* of all its spectacularly separate aspects. The potential practice of revolutionary organization and the movement for more class consciousness which is the bearer of the historical negation of the commodity are inseparable from this global movement. "We are necessarily on the same path as our enemies—usually preceding them —but we must be there without any confusion, *as enemies.*"

The moment when the commodity appears as the homogenous and total fulfillment of universal history is at the same time the moment of its radical historical negation, the moment of the *conscious struggle for the totality.*

What above all characterizes our era is the *intensification of this process in time,* an intensification linked to the return of the proletariat as an acting historical force. But this process is not itself uniform, it has neither a constant intensity nor a linear growth. It develops erratically in time and in space, oscillating from wonderful moments of breakthrough where everything seems possible to low points where nothing does, but where, nevertheless, everything continues.

DANIEL DENEVERT
Paris, January 1972

238

DECLARATION
Concerning the
Center for Research on the Social Question

PARIS, MARCH 1974

Declaring our solidarity with the struggles for a *practical theory* of the proletariat, through which that social class is today rediscovering the true nature of its existence and the fullness of its perspectives, which had been repressed, falsified or forgotten with the global crushing of the old worker movement;

Considering,

that as revolutionary proletarians our individual liberation is contingent on the worldwide liberation of the proletariat;

that this liberation must consist notably in the *abolition of the global economy,* whose management is shared by the different states and dominant national classes, a management from which they derive the *power* that presently enchains humanity;

that the subjection of the masses to the economy consists not only in the subjection of the workers to the class and state owners of the means of production, but also in the enslavement of the individual to the rules of life, thought and action that follow directly from the *commodity form* of global production;

that the proletariat has been enchained up till now at least as much by its own servile acceptance of a servile life as by its forced submission to the laws of the economy, and that this subservience *is now in the process of changing;*

Considering,

that the necessary conditions of its emancipation and of the subsequent free blossoming of a revolutionary social life remain the abolition of the economy and of the state, and in general of all forms of power or authority *external to individuals;*

that the weapon and the principal condition for bringing the present social war to a *decisive victory* is the appropriation and development by each proletarian of a form of thought bound up with his struggle

239

and superior to the partial theories and scientific knowledge known up till now: *revolutionary theory,* born out of the struggles of the old worker movement and reemerging today in the war against the socio-historical conditions of modern capitalism;

that in striving toward the goals it sets itself, this new revolutionary consciousness must develop *against* all the rules of dominant thought and consciousness;

that this is ultimately nothing other than each individual's mastery of the free theory of his own social existence—something that has so far not known any lasting and decisive development;

that as a *situationist* has put it, what is above all important is that "the workers become dialecticians" and manage their own lives themselves, without any delegation of power;

that our era is seeing the appearance and action of the first worker dialecticians;

Considering,

that our era now calls for the formation of international organizations of revolutionary proletarians which, with the support of their class comrades in every region of the world, will be able to hold their own against any other current power;

that it will require nothing less than this to counteract the lies, falsifications and daily humiliations by means of which our present masters maintain us in an *organized ignorance* of everything concerning the reality of life, and to finally give some solid bases to our struggle and make possible a decisive breakthrough;

Considering,

our contempt for revolutionary pseudo-organizations that seek to constitute themselves on bases more limited than those described above;

that the rampant organization-mania of revolutionaries (which gives rise, as a natural reaction, to various honestly or tactically spontaneist tendencies) is a reflex left over from the worst traditions of the worker movement and from the long period of mass powerlessness that we have just gotten through;

that we consider the gesticulations, pretensions and daydreams of little "radical" groups to be as meaningless as a mundane petition;

that henceforth any *revolutionary organization* that presumes to present itself with an underdeveloped theory or practice should be considered a mockery and an *insult* to the other workers who are everywhere entering the struggle;

that a revolutionary organization should be judged by the fullness and radicality of its objectives and *how* it acts to attain them;

that it is now up to the workers themselves to create organizations in accordance with their objectives; and that what defines a revolutionary worker is not the practice of, or qualification for, this or that occupation, but his *irreducible hostility* to the institution of work;

Considering,

our contempt for revolutionary sects and for "autonomous" groups that have no autonomy except within their little self-managed ghettos;

we founded, on 28 September 1973, the *Center for Research on the Social Question* (CRQS), an intentionally limited semiorganizational complement to our respective and *distinct* activities as revolutionary theorists; and which has since functioned according to the following rules:

1. The members of the CRQS are chosen from among the revolutionaries who have personally demonstrated their loyalty, their talents and their obstinacy in the struggle for *practical theory,* and who choose to associate within this semiorganizational framework while continuing to address the revolutionary movement *in their name only.* While a member of the CRQS, each comrade agrees to all the present rules, attends to their application, and fulfills all the practical duties that follow from them.

2. The organizational function of the CRQS is strictly limited to the *material support* it can provide to distinct activities conducted *exclusively* under individual responsibility. The CRQS does not seek to set forth or defend *coherent collective positions,* although the general bases of modern revolutionary theory are naturally recognized by its members. No enterprise can be conducted in the name of the CRQS apart from a few precisely delimited *administrative* tasks. In particular, neither public declarations nor practical interventions can be atrributed to the CRQS; they remain solely the responsibility of their authors or signatories.

3. The managerial tasks on which depends the successful functioning of the present *accord* are equitably carried out by all the members in accordance with the rules of total democracy. The general assembly of the members has all power of decision; its majority decisions are executory.

4. Each member of the CRQS has the duty to resign, and if necessary to make public his reasons, (1) if he comes to consider that the *minimum solidarity* that he owes the other members is no longer justified by the nature of their theoretical or practical orientations;

(2) if he considers that the limited formula of the CRQS is being maintained after it has outlived its usefulness; or (3) if he joins any other organization whatsoever.

5. Any member whose attitude or expressed positions contradict the present rules will be immediately excluded. A member will also be excluded if he has seriously failed in the implementation of a decision of the general assembly or if he has in any way fallen short of the principles of revolutionary honesty.

6. Each member of the CRQS is free, in accordance with his affinities and the needs of his practice, to establish alliances outside the association, on the sole condition that the other members are straightforwardly informed of them.

7. In accordance with the lessons it will draw from its functioning, the CRQS must fix a number of members beyond which it will divide itself into two groups, one of which will form a new and distinct association.

8. Openly declaring its aims, the CRQS shall each year elect a person legally responsible for the association [*legally required in France for registering publications, etc.*]. This person shall have no prerogatives over the other members.

9. The CRQS will be automatically dissolved (1) whenever the member solidarity that presently makes this framework possible is no longer sufficiently assured; or (2) whenever the reality of the revolutionary movement has made possible and defined better forms of organization.

FRANÇOISE BLOCH, JEANNE CHARLES,
JOËL CORNUAULT, DANIEL DENEVERT

YOUNG MEN, YOUNG WOMEN

whatever your age,
if you are intelligent or beautiful
or have some other talent,
please don't tell us about it.

Avoid addressing to P.O. Box 42-10, 75462 Paris
useless and tedious letters
or ill-considered requests to meet us.

You will move all the better in the direction of history.

NOTICE
Concerning the Reigning Society
and Those Who Contest It

BERKELEY–SAN FRANCISCO, NOVEMBER 1974

Considering,

that "the critique which goes beyond the spectacle must *know how to wait*";

Considering,

that spectacular society maintains us in an organized *social schizophrenia,* offering up utopian or nostalgic fantasies without practical consequences or empirical engagement in the here-and-now without consciousness of the totality;

that this dominant organization of confusion finds its natural expression, and reinforcement, within the very movement that wants to oppose it—in the abstract organizational form that precedes its content or the concrete association that remains unconscious of its form;

Considering,

that the unceasing criticism of the revolutionary milieu, far from being a narrow or "sectarian" matter, is a central tactic, in that that milieu tends to reproduce within itself in concentrated form the principal contradictions and miseries of the dominant society it combats;

our contempt for almost all existing radical organizations, which, whether presenting themselves as a leadership to be followed or as an example of an ameliorated style of life to be imitated, give rise to illusions of the possibility of fundamental change without the *complete overthrow of all existing conditions,* the negation of the commodity economy and of the state;

Considering,

that the *next revolution* requires that, for the first time in history, the masses of proletarianized individuals develop the *practical consciousness* of their own struggle, unmediated by leaders or specialists;

that a *second international assault* on class society, beginning diffusedly in the fifties and obtaining its first decisive victory in the open struggles of the late sixties, is already entering a new phase—junking the illusions and reruns of half a century ago and beginning to confront its real problems;

that in the United States, after a decade of widespread struggles questioning all aspects of modern society but for the most part from naïve or separatist perspectives, it is now the workers themselves who are beginning to *struggle autonomously* against the reign of separation, against the institution of work and its flip side, alienated leisure consumed in passivity;

that while the new class struggle here has not lagged behind that of the other modern industrialized countries, *its consciousness of itself has* (the fact that the principal texts of the Situationist International are not yet available in the most advanced spectacular society is merely the most glaring expression of this theoretical underdevelopment);

that proletarians must be confronted with the immensity of their tasks —the tasks of a revolution which, this time around, they will have to run themselves;

that if we are "difficult to understand" it is not because our language is unnecessarily complex, but because the problems of the modern revolutionary movement are *necessarily complex;* and that it is the very progress of this struggle toward the moment of the *radical simplification* of the social question which is beginning to make us less difficult to understand;

Considering,

that a revolutionary organization can in no way be itself an alternative to the dominant society; that until the masses have created the *conditions* for the construction of a liberated social life—in seizing and transforming the material technology and overthrowing all authority external to themselves—all positive radical accomplishments tend to be recuperated into the system as real reforms or as spectacular revolution;

that the function of revolutionary organization—as of revolutionary theory and practice in general—is fundamentally *negative, critical,* attacking the *obstacles* to the realization of the conditions of positive social creativity;

that if they are to be realized in practice, theoretical tendencies or differences must be translated into organizational problems;

Considering,

that the practice of theory begins at home;

244

We declare,

that we do not constitute an ongoing revolutionary organization, formal or informal, even in cases where some of us share or have shared the same mailing addresses;

that each of us, in writing a text or in translating a text of another, is speaking to the revolutionary movement *in his name only,* although the general bases of modern revolutionary theory are recognized by all of us;

that if some of us have discussed and even collaborated on certain projects, we have just as often consciously avoided this, one or another among us preferring to *make his own mistakes* rather than rely on the protection of the good advice of his comrades;

that insofar as we do associate among ourselves or with others, we define the manner and delimit the scope of our collaboration; aiming always at inciting rigor and autonomy among the radical currents, we refuse contact with those with contrary aims or with those with whom the concrete bases for collaboration are lacking;

that the decision to pursue our respective activities independently is based on particular considerations and not on any spontaneist anti-organizationism;

that these considerations include: desirability for each of us to develop a maximum of theoretico-practical autonomy; desire to facilitate the development of distinct strategies in fruitful rivalry with each other; the state of the struggle for practical theory in this time and place;

that this decision is subject to change when the reality of our own situations or of the revolutionary movement has made possible and defined forms of association more appropriate to the tasks we set ourselves.

TITA CARRIÓN, ROBERT COOPERSTEIN, ISAAC CRONIN, DAN HAMMER, KEN KNABB, GINA ROSENBERG, CHRIS SHUTES

So. You think you have something in common with us (beyond the misery that everyone shares). . . . You see something of interest in what we say. . . . Things you've already thought yourself. . . . We took the words right out of your mouth. . . .

Don't bother to let us know about it.

Leave off sending us your useless praises, your idle opinions, your tedious questions, your pointless requests to meet us. We don't want to hear about your "agreement" with us unless it bears on some practical matter.

You think you have something in common with us? Prove it.

The Situationist International, with a handful of supporters in all the chief capitals of Europe, anarchists playing at revolution, talk of "seizing power," not so as to take it, but simply to destroy it, and with it even their own authority.

—*L'Aurore*, November 16, 1966

•••

The accused have never denied the charge of misusing the funds of the student union. Indeed, they openly admit to having made the union pay some $1000 for the printing and distribution of 10,000 pamphlets, not to mention the cost of other literature inspired by the "Situationist International." These publications express ideas and aspirations which, to put it mildly, have nothing to do with the aims of a student union. One has only to read what the accused have written for it to be obvious that these five students, scarcely more than adolescents, lacking all experience of real life, their minds confused by ill-digested philosophical, social, political and economic theories, and perplexed by the drab monotony of their everyday life, make the empty, arrogant and pathetic claim to pass definitive judgments, sinking to outright abuse, on their fellow students, their teachers, God, religion, the clergy and the governments and political systems of the entire world. Rejecting all morality and legal restraint, these cynics do not hesitate to commend theft, the destruction of scholarship, the abolition of work, total subversion and a world-wide proletarian revolution with "unlicensed pleasure" as its only goal.

—summing-up of Judge Llabador,
Strasbourg, December 13, 1966

•••

Then appeared for the first time the disquieting figures of the "Situationist International." How many are there? Where do they come from? No one knows.

—*Le Républicain Lorrain*, June 28, 1967

•••

Situationism is no more the specter that haunts industrial society than was communism the specter that haunted Europe in 1848.

—*Le Nouvel Observateur*, January 3, 1968

•••

It's the tune that makes the song: more cynical in Vaneigem and more icy in Debord, the negative and provocative violence of their phraseology leaves nothing standing among what previous ages have produced — except perhaps de Sade, Lautréamont and Dada. . . . A snarling rhetoric which is always excessive and always detached from the complexity of facts upon which we reason not only makes the reading disagreeable but also staggers thought. . . . At least we should be ready for it.

—*Le Monde*, February 14, 1968

•••

M. Debord and M. Vaneigem have brought out their long-awaited major texts: the *Capital* and *What Is to Be Done?*, as it were, of the new movement. This comparison is not meant mockingly. . . . Under the dense Hegelian wrappings with which they muffle their pages several interesting ideas are lurking. M. Debord and M. Vaneigem are attempting, for the first time, a comprehensive critique of alienated society. . . . Their austere philosophy, now authoritatively set forth, may not be without influence on future Committees of 100, Declarations of the 121, and similar libertarian manifestations.

—*Times Literary Supplement*, March 21, 1968

•••

The situationists . . . are more anarchist than the anarchists, whom they find too bureaucratic.

—*Carrefour*, May 8, 1968

•••

WARNING: Leaflets have been distributed in the Paris area calling for an insurrectionary general strike. It goes without saying that such appeals have not been issued by out democratic trade union organizations. They are the work of provocateurs seeking to provide the government with a pretext for intervention. . . . The workers must be vigilant to defeat all such maneuvers.

—*Humanité*, May 20, 1968

•••

This explosion was provoked by a few groups that revolt against modern society, against consumer society, against technological society, whether it be communist in the East or capitalist in the West; by groups which, moreover, do not know what they would put in its place, but which delight in negation, in destruction, in violence, in anarchy, brandishing the black flag.

—Charles de Gaulle,
televised speech, June 7, 1968

•••

Who is the authentic representative of the Left today: the Fourth International, the Situationist International or the Anarchist Federation? . . . The Strasbourg pamphlet . . . acted as a kind of detonator. . . . We did all that we could in helping to distribute the pamphlet.

—*Obsolete Communism: The Left-Wing Alternative*, Daniel and Gabriel Cohn-Bendit (1968)

•••

The notion of "spectacle" (drama, happening, mask) is crucial to the theories of what is probably the furthest out of the radical factions. . . . In our consumer-technologies, life is merely a bad play. Like Osborne's Entertainer, we strut about in a bankrupt side-show playing parts we loathe to audiences whose values are meaningless or contemptible. Culture itself has become frippery and grease-paint. Our very revolutions are melo-drama, performed under stale rules of make-believe; they alter nothing but the cast. . . . Compared to the Strasbourg absolutists, Monsieur Cohn-Bendit is a weather-beaten conservative.

—*The Sunday Times*, July 21, 1968

•••

. . . "situationists" (whose main contribution to the May Revolution were graffiti, joyful and non-sensical). . . . A group of "International Situationists" — a latterday incarnation of surrealism — seized the university loudspeaker system for a time and issued extravagant directives.

—*Red Flag, Black Flag*,
Patrick Seale and Maureen McConville (1968)

•••

. . . the Situationist International, which has its base in Copenhagen and which is run by the security and espionage police of East Germany.

—*Historama* 206, December 1968

•••

The situationists . . . make use of street theater and spontaneous spectacles to criticize society and denounce new forms of alienation. . . . Even though the small situationist group concentrated principally on the student situation and the commercialization of mass culture, the spring revolt was less a questioning of culture than a political criticism of society.

—*The May Movement: Revolt and Reform*,
Alain Touraine (1968)

•••

Diderot wrote the preface to a Revolution and so the surrealists and the situationists have written the preface to a new Revolution. . . . Claims grew into *contestation*; the games and the playful demonstrations of the anarchist-situationist minigroup gave way to more serious activity.

—*Reflections of the Revolution in France: 1968*,
ed. Posner (1970)

•••

The way out is beginning to become clear: it's there in the works of Wilhelm Reich and R.D. Laing, in the ideas in all of our heads in our maddest moments when we say to ourselves, "I can't say that, they'll think I'm nuttier than a fruit cake," very clearly in the ideas of the Situationist International.

—*Fusion*, Spring 1970

•••

Although the language and tone of the essay are markedly similar to those of the Situationist manifesto, there are important differences between Bookchin and the Situationists. He explains these (in a personal letter to the editor) as follows: "The Situationists have retained very traditional notions about the workers' movement, Pannekoek's 'council communism,' almost Stalinist forms of internal organization (they are completely monolithic and authoritarian in their internal organization), and are surprisingly academic."

—*"All We Are Saying . . ."*, ed. Lothstein (1970)

The Situationist International imposed as the thought of the breakdown of ¡ begun before our eyes.

The French Minister of the Interior ¡ respond to the S.I. with the same rage putting itself forward in an era which little time its hegemony in the struggle of class struggles. The theory, style ar adopted by thousands of revolutionaric but even more profoundly, it is the wh be convinced of the truth of the situal realize them or to combat them. The where translated and discussed. Its e; walls of Milan and the buildings of the nia to Calabria, from Scotland to Spa cipal theses infiltrate clandestinely or submissive intellectuals at the outset part, to disguise themselves as moder if only to demonstrate their capacity tc system that employs them. If the diffi where denounced, it is only because expression of a historical subversion v

What are known as "situationist ideas' of the period of the reappearance of What is new in those ideas corresponds society and to the development of its e¡ and its oppression. . . .

The S.I. not only saw the modern prol to meet it. We did not put our ideas influence, as only the bourgeois or bɩ capable of doing (and that without last which were necessarily there alread; articulating them we contributed to rer rendering the critique in acts more the the time its own. . . .

When one reads or rereads the issues of the S.I. it is quite striking to what degree and how often these *fanatics* have made judgments or put forward viewpoints which were later concretely verified.

—*Le Nouvel Observateur*, February 8, 1971

• • •

Internationale Situationniste 1958-69 . . . provides a fascinating record of this groupuscule which began in the French tradition of political-cultural sectarianism and ended by playing a prominent part first in the disturbances at Strasbourg University in 1966 and then in the more dramatic "events" of May 1968. Many of the slogans which achieved fame on the walls of Paris may be found here in some form, and the ideas which influenced the rebels so much were being worked out in these pages during the previous ten years. There is a certain irony in such a publication . . . here they are neatly packaged as a highly marketable commodity in a clearly spectacular way.

—*Times Literary Supplement*, February 19, 1971

• • •

The concept of the spectacle, which derives from the French Situationists . . . is a useful analytic device: it simplifies a world of phenomena that seem otherwise disparate. Surely the spectacle is conspicuous, once one learns to see it in its many dimensions.

—*Liberation*, May 1971

self in a moment of universal history
world, a breakdown which has now

d the federated anarchists of Italy
ever has such an extremist project,
emed so hostile to it, affirmed in so
ideas, itself a product of the history
example of the S.I. are today being
in the principal advanced countries;
e of modern society which seems to
onist perspectives, whether it be to
oks and texts of the S.I. are every-
gencies are plastered on the factory
University of Coimbra, from Califor-
from Belfast to Leningrad, its prin-
e proclaimed in open struggles. The
their careers feel obliged, for their
te situationists or semi-situationists,
understand the latest moment of the
e influence of the S.I. can be every-
e S.I. is itself only the concentrated
ich is everywhere.

are nothing other than the first ideas
he modern revolutionary movement.
precisely to the new character of class
emeral successes, its contradictions

arian subversion coming . . . it went
n everybody's mind" by an outside
eaucratic-totalitarian spectacles are
g success). We articulated the ideas
in those proletarian minds, and in
ering such ideas active, as well as to
retical and more determined to make

The situationists, although in many ways they are the heirs of surrealism, dadaism and some millenarian trends, rejoin the modern currents in post-Marxism and even go further in their quasi-Marcusian analyses of alienation in capitalist-bureaucratic society, which is the purely political aspect of their ideas. . . . The *enragés* and the situationists had the chance to put their ideas into practice in the first Committee of Occupation of the Sorbonne (14-17 May 1968) which, under their influence, set up total direct democracy in the Sorbonne. . . . The members of the Situationist International go so far as to deny that they have any ideology at all since any ideology is alienating.

—Richard Gombin
(National Center for Scientific Research, Paris)
in *Anarchism Today*, ed. Apter and Joll (1971)

• • •

At the beginning of 1968, a critic discussing situationist theory mockingly evoked a "glimmer wandering vaguely from Copenhagen to New York." Alas, the glimmer became, that same year, a holocaust which arose in all the citadels of the old world. . . . The situationists have uncovered the theory of the subterranean movement which torments the modern age. While the pseudo-inheritors of Marxism forgot the role of the negative in a world swollen with positivity, and simultaneously relegated dialectics to the museum, the situationists announced the resurgence of this same negative and discerned the reality of the same dialectics, whose language, the "insurrectional style" (Debord), they again found.

—*Les Temps Modernes* 299-300, June 1971

• • •

It was not in America but among the Western European student movements that the recent renaissance of interest in Reich first began. In France, where he was practically unknown, his theories were initially rediscovered by the Situationists.

—*Liberation*, October 1971

• • •

The Society of the Spectacle . . . has led the discussions of the entire ultra-left since its publication in 1967. This work, which predicted May 1968, is considered by many to be the *Capital* of the new generation.

—*Le Nouvel Observateur*, November 8, 1971

• • •

But the situationists never arrived at an adequate practice. Afraid to get their hands dirty in the confusion of radical activity (which they scorned as "militantism") they confined their interventions to the theoretical level.

—*Anarchy* 7, Winter 1972

• • •

The Situationists . . . constantly talk of "workers" (sic) councils . . . while demanding the abolition of work! Unfortunately they seem to confuse attacks on the *work ethic* and on alienated labor, both of which are justified and necessary, with attacks on work itself.

—*Workers' Councils and the Economics of a Self-Managed Society*, Solidarity (March 1972)

• • •

Miss Martin said the "situationists" were a political movement active in France in the 18th century, and that there had been "talk" on the campus of a revival under that name in Berkeley.

—*San Francisco Examiner*, May 18, 1972

• • •

Without some attempt at a coherent analysis of the general economic situation, why not accept, for example, the Situationists' explanation of May 68: everyone was all of a sudden fed-up and discovered alienation and hit the streets?

—*Internationalism Bulletin* 1, Summer 1973

• • •

In the confusion and tumult of the May Revolt the slogans and shouts of the students were considered expressions of mass spontaneity and individual ingenuity. Only afterward was it evident that these slogans were fragments of a coherent and seductive ideology and had virtually all previously appeared in situationist tracts and publications. . . . Mainly through their agency there welled up in the May Revolt an immense force of protest against the modern world and all its works, blending passion, mystery, and the primeval.

—*Protest in Paris: Anatomy of a Revolt*,
Bernard E. Brown (1974)

• • •

Brown . . . portrays (and unsympathetically so) the elements of the French intelligentsia who raised the banners of unreason, passion and primitivism. The anarchists and the "situationists" upon whom he concentrates most, represent in this interpretation a traditional force of romantic but destructive politics, determined to resist progress.

—*New Republic*, March 16, 1974

• • •

Other groups, like the Situationist International, are also important, though they lack an understanding of capital. . . . The communist revolution implies an action *from* the enterprise, to destroy it as such. The rebellions in the U.S. remained on the level of consumption and distribution. (This point was not fully understood in an interesting text by the Situationist International: *The Rise and Fall of the Spectacular Commodity Economy*.)

—*Eclipse and Re-emergence of the
Communist Movement*,
Jean Barrot and François Martin (1974)

• • •

Pillaging and detourning in a lively and unconstrained manner a rich material of news clips, sequences filmed in the street, ads with naked women, press photos, scenes from American westerns, war propaganda, Soviet and Polish films, flashes from fashion ads, mixing in quotations from Clausewitz, Marx, Machiavelli, etc., interrupting the flow to wickedly announce to the spectator that if the rhythm he has given the images continued it would be seductive, "but it won't continue," Debord pursues the aim of his book without limiting himself to "illustrating" it. . . . If war, according to Clausewitz, is a continuation of politics by other means, the cinema, according to Debord, is a continuation of theory with other weapons. . . . Debord's indignation (the word is too feeble) splashes out in superb images of contemporary subversion: from the Asturias to Gdansk and Gdynia, from Poznan to Budapest, from police actions all over the world to May 68. It is no longer a matter of filming the world, it is necessary to change it. . . . Debord says (in his own way) that it is not necessary to hope in order to demolish, nor to succeed in order to continue to want life really to be life. Brecht dreamt all his life of adapting *Capital* to the stage. Guy Debord has found a producer crazy enough and wise enough to permit him to *re-form* his *Society of the Spectacle* on the screen. See it.

—*Le Nouvel Observateur*, April 29, 1974

These commando actions undertaken by a group of anarchists and "situationists," with their slogan: *"Never work!"* . . . How has a handful of irresponsible elements been able to provoke such serious decisions, affecting 12,000 students in Letters and 4000 in Law?

—*Humanité* (newspaper of the French Communist Party), March 29, 1968

• • •

Those who want to understand the ideas lying behind the student revolts in the Old World ought to pay serious attention not only to the writings of Adorno and of the three M's — Marx, Mao and Marcuse — but above all to the literature of the Situationists. . . . Debord's book . . . rejects the idea of proletarian revolution in the same way as it repudiates Socialist democracy, Russian or Chinese Communism, and traditional "incoherent anarchism." . . . One has to destroy all authority, especially that of the state, to negate all moral restrictions, to expose fossilized knowledge and all "establishments," to bring truth into the world of semblance, and to achieve what Debord calls "the fulfillment of democracy in self-control and action." He fails to say how to achieve this program.

—*The New York Times*, April 21, 1968

BIBLIOGRAPHY

Internationale situationniste: 1958-69
Reprinting of the complete text of issues #1-12. (Van Gennup, 1970.)

Traité de savoir-vivre à l'usage des jeunes generations
By Raoul Vaneigem. (Gallimard, 1967.)

La société du spectacle
By Guy Debord. (Champ Libre, 1967.)

Enragés et situationnistes dans le mouvement des occupations
By René Viénet. Documented and illustrated. (Gallimard, 1968.)

La véritable scission dans l'Internationale
Theses on the S.I. and Its Time, by Guy Debord and Gianfranco Sanguinetti. (Champ Libre, 1972.)

La société du spectacle
Film by Guy Debord. 35mm. 80 minutes. B&W. (Simar Films, May 1974.)

L'Internationale situationniste
Chronology and bibliography (with an index of insulted names). By Jean-Jacques Raspaud and Jean-Pierre Voyer. (Champ Libre, 1972.)

A somewhat unreliable English translation of *Society of the Spectacle* is available from Black & Red (P.O. Box 9546, Detroit 48202), and another one is distributed by Compendium Bookstore (240 Camden High St., London NW1). A somewhat clumsily translated *Veritable Split in the International* is also available from Compendium, or direct from the publishers: B.M. Piranha, London WC1V 6xx.

• • •

Their manifesto is the now well-known book by Guy Debord, *The Society of the Spectacle.* In order to criticize the system radically, Debord, in an epigramatic and Adornian style, constructs a concept of "spectacle" derived from Marx's conceptions, and even more from Lukacs, of "commodity fetishism," alienation and "reification."

—*L'Espresso*, December 15, 1968

Their general headquarters is secret but I think that it is somewhere in London. They are not students, but are what are known as situationists; they travel everywhere and exploit the discontent of students.

—*News of the World*, February 16, 1969

• • •

You know, I more or less agree with the situationists; they say that it's all finally integrated; it gets integrated in spectacle, it's all spectacle.

—Jean-Luc Godard, interview, March 1969

• • •

The Situationists, however, have made their usual ambiguous contribution. In a very interesting and well-informed book, *Enragés et situationnistes dans le mouvement des occupations*, René Viénet attacks the anarchists – along with every single left-wing group other than the situationists themselves.

—*Anarchy* 99, May 1969

• • •

The occupation committee, which was re-elected every day, was not able to guarantee continuity, in addition to which situationist factions had gained a certain influence. On Thursday the 16th, the latter distributed a leaflet denouncing the "bureaucrats" who disagreed with their slogans and working methods. . . . The situationists set up a "council to maintain occupation" which, in their inimitable Hegelianistic-Marxist terminology, expiated on the same themes.

—*The French Student Uprising*, Alain Schnapp and Pierre Vidal-Naquet (1969)

• • •

Too extreme for those of the old left intelligent enough to understand it, and too incomprehensible for those of the new left extreme enough to live it.

- Grove Press position on Viénet's book, 1969

• • •

The Situationist pamphlet "Theses on the Commune" refers to the Commune as the greatest carnival of the nineteenth century, but to try to burn down the Louvre is merely symbolic.

—*The Death of the Family*, David Cooper (1970)

• • •

Because it came into being for the mos of the modern era, the S.I. openly pro thought it was a joke. The silence mai of social observation and the ideolog years (a very short period on the scal false consciousness of the submissive understand what exploded in France deepened and extended itself. . . . T specialists of power, this revolutiona and thoughtless negation. . . . It has occupations movement did have some ationist ideas: even those who are ur positions in relation to them. . . .

A generation, internationally, has beg

May we cease to be admired as if we the era know the terror of admiring it

— THE REAL SPLIT IN THE INTERN
Public Circular of the Situationist
April 1972

In those mystical days of May . . . the poets of Paris have attained a similar state of frenzied anti-doctrinal comic anarchism to the yippies, though suckled on Dada, not L.S.D.

—*Play Power*, Richard Neville (1970)

• • •

In the extreme case, the anarcho-situationist groups all but deny the persistence of traditionally recognized forms of oppression, and put forward a model of contemporary capitalism as dependent solely on psychological oppression, a strategy that sees class society defeated by the "return of the repressed," and an organization and tactics confined to the symbolically terrorist actions of small groups.

—*New Left Review* 64, November 1970

• • •

We are here concerned with only two small groups who alone set the scene for the May events and provided the insurrection with a dialectical backbone. These few outlaws, the *Enragés* and the *Situationists*, universally despised by political organizations and student bodies, have their base on the surrealistic fringes of the Left Wing. From there they have nurtured one of the most advanced, coherent revolutionary theories (though often plagued by academic arrogance and "in" references), which provoked a near-liquidation of the State.

—*BAMN (By Any Means Necessary)*, ed. Stansill and Mairowitz (1971)

BUREAU OF PU

part in the prerevolutionary moments
claimed its goals and almost everyone
tained on this count by the specialists
...es of working-class alienation for ten
... of such events) . . . had prepared the
intelligentsia neither to foresee nor to
... May 1968, and which has since only
... the benighted consciousness of the
... crisis first appeared only as a pure
...nfortunately been discovered that the
...ideas after all, and that they were situ-
...aware of those ideas seem to set their

...n to be situationist. . . .

...ould be superior to our time; and may
...elf **for what it is.**

...ATIONAL
...ternational

It is necessary to attribute this revolt to a coming
to consciousness on the real nature of "consumer" society — a coming to consciousness (and
its articulation) which has its source in the intellectual (and practical) activities of a small group
of insolent but lucid insurgents: the Situationist
International. Now, by a paradox to which history holds the secret, the S.I. remained practically unknown in this country for over ten years,
a phenomenon which verifies Hegel's reflection:
"Every important revolution which leaps into
view must be preceded in the spirit of an era by a
secret revolution which is not visible to everyone
and still less observable to contemporaries, a
revolution which is as difficult to express in words
as it is to comprehend."

—*Le Nouveau Planete* 22, May 1971

• • •

The resolution unanimously adopted by the
Anarchist Congress calls for some explanation.
The influence of the Situationist International,
particularly negative on numerous Scandinavian, North American and Japanese extra-parlia-
mentary groups, has been active in France and
Italy since 1967-68 with the aim of destroying the
federated anarchist movement of these two countries; this in the name of a theoretical discussion
which the situationists usually submerge in an
ocean of insolences and vague and tortuous
phraseology.

—Communiqué of the Italian Anarchist
Federation, *Umanita Nuova*, May 15, 1971

• • •

Debord and Sanguinetti . . . quote extensively
from the bourgeois press in order to demonstrate
the "importance" of the S.I. . . . They impute a
revolutionary consciousness to even openly reformist movements; when they say that "youth,
workers, homosexuals, women and children dare
to want everything that had been *forbidden*
them" (thesis No. 12) they fail to see how movements which only question isolated aspects of
bourgeois society are easily recuperated. . . . A
large part of "61 theses . ." is concerned with a
critique of the pro-situs and there is little to dispute about it. . . . In going beyond the S.I. . . . we
face the same difficulties that it confronted. . . .
We make no pretensions about ourselves.

—*Point-Blank!* 1, October 1972

• • •

In recent years the Situationists have produced
far-ranging analyses . . . using the concept of
the "spectacle," the idea that the media and
other mechanisms of advanced capitalist society
enable revolutionary attacks to be distorted and
coopted in ways that cast doubt on the efficacy of
traditional modes of revolutionary activity.

--*Counter Course*, ed. Pateman (1972)

• • •

The S.I., although it presented the "most developed, most comprehensive, most modern" revolutionary theory yet to be found anywhere, is still
not the end-all of revolutionary theory and practice. The sexual politics of the new women's
movement, coupled with the communal lifestyles and counter-institutions which have
emerged, are among the American contributions
which can aid in the development of a coherent
post-Situationist critique of our conditions.

—*New Morning*, February 1973

• • •

I could understand it, but it would be over the
heads of our readers. Besides, why would they be
interested in something that happened in *France*
in 1968?

—editor at Straight Arrow Books, April 1973

• • •

The notion of *recuperation*, first introduced by
the Situationists, refers to the manner in which
the repressive system seeks to neutralize or contain the attacks launched against it by *absorbing*
them into the "spectacle" or by *projecting* its
own meanings and goals onto these oppositional
activities. . . . More generally, as the Situationists
have pointed out, the destruction of the repressive order requires the simultaneous transcendence of the language which conceals and guarantees it.

—*Marx, Freud and the Critique of Everyday Life*,
Bruce Brown (1973)

—*Le Nouvel Observateur*, April 29, 1974

• • •

For those who newly discover it, S.I. theory has a
way of seeming like "the answer I've searched
for for years," the answer to the riddle of one's
dead life. But that's exactly then a new alertness
and self-repossession become necessary.

—*The Minimum Definition of Intelligence*,
For Ourselves (May 1974)

• • •

The Makhnist Situationist International pig
countergang created by the CIA from scratch in
1957 in France under the slogans "Kill the
Vanguards!," "Workers Councils Now!," and
"Create Situations!," is the paradigm example
of a CIA synthetic all-purpose formation. The
loose and programless anarchist "left cover"
countergang on the SI model is ideal for the CIA
for the recruitment of new agents, the launching
of psywar operations, the detonation of riots,
syndicalist workers' actions (e.g., LIP strike),
student power revolts, etc., the continual generation of new countergang formations, and infiltration, penetration and dissolution of socialist
and other workers' organizations. . . . During the
1968 French general strike the Situationists
united with Daniel Cohn-Bendit and his anarchist thugs in preventing any potential vanguard
from assuming leadership of the strike — thus
guaranteeing its defeat. In the U.S. Goldner and
his Situationist International offshoot group Contradiction have been assigned to play the same
kind of role: namely to stop the Labor Committees from developing into a mass-based working-
class party.

—*New Solidarity* (newspaper of the
National Caucus of Labor Committees),
August 28 and September 6, 1974

PROPOSAL

Ken Knabb will translate any or all of
the situationist books when he can find
a suitable publisher.

Conditions:

- Knabb must have final approval of the
translation.

- If there is to be any annotation or
commentary, he will provide it.

- In the case of an anthology of articles
from the S.I. journal, he will make the
selection. With this possible exception,
the American editions must be un-
abridged and follow the basic format of
the French originals.

- All matters of the form and content of
the texts must be subject to the final
approval of their authors, with whom,
if they so wish, Knabb is prepared to
collaborate.

BUREAU OF PUBLIC SECRETS
P.O. Box 1044
Berkeley, California 94704

January 1975

...JBLIC SECRETS

bureau of
public secrets

I tell you that which you yourselves do know. . . .
Now let it work. Mischief, thou art afoot,
Take thou what course thou wilt.

(Shakespeare)

January 1976

THE SOCIETY OF SITUATIONISM

"Even if a *constituted* situationist theory had never existed as a possible source of inspiration, the system of commodity consumption implicitly contains its *own situationism*."

—Daniel Denevert, *Theory of Misery, Misery of Theory*

1

The second proletarian assault on class society has entered its *second phase*.

2

The first phase — beginning diffusedly in the 1950s and culminating in the open struggles of the late sixties — found its most advanced theoretical expression in the Situationist International. *Situationism* is the direct or implicit ideologization of situationist theory, within the revolutionary movement and in the society as a whole.

3

The S.I. articulated the whole of the global movement at the same time that it participated as part of it in the sector where it found itself, taking up "the violence of the delinquents on the plane of ideas" and giving immediate practical follow-through to its theoretical positions. It thus presented a model to the revolutionary movement not only in the form of its conclusions but also in exemplifying the ongoing negating *method*; which method was the reason that its conclusions were almost always right.

4

In generating among many of its partisans the same exigencies that it practiced itself, and in forcing even the most unautonomous to become at least autonomous from it, the S.I. showed that it knew how to *educate revolutionarily*. In the space of a few years we have seen a *democratization of theoretical activity* that was not attained — if it was even sought — in the old movement in a century. Marx and Engels were not able to incite rivals; none of the strands of Marxism maintained Marx's unitary perspective. Lenin's observation in 1914 that "none of the Marxists for the past half century have understood Marx" is really a critique of Marx's theory, not because it was too difficult but because it did not recognize and calculate its own relation with the totality.

5

The very nature of the situationists' mistakes — exposed and criticized by them with pitiless thoroughness — is a *confirmation of their methods*. Their failures as well as their successes serve to focus, elucidate and polarize. No other radical current in history has known such a degree of intentional public theoretical debate. In the old proletarian movement consequential theoretical polarization was always the exception, the explosion that came out contrary to the intentions of the theorists themselves and only as a last resort when the very continuation of a factitious unity was visibly no longer possible. Marx and Engels failed to dissociate themselves publicly from the Gotha Program because "the asinine bourgeois papers took this program quite seriously, read into it what it does not contain and interpreted it communistically; and the workers seem to be doing the same" (Engels to Bebel, 12 October 1875). Thus, in defending by silence a program against its enemies, they defended it equally against its friends. When in the same letter Engels said that "if the bourgeois press possessed a single person of critical mind, he would have taken this program apart phrase by phrase, investigated the real content of each phrase, demonstrated its nonsense with the utmost clarity, revealed its contradictions and economic howlers . . . and made our whole Party look frightfully ridiculous," he described as a deficiency of the bourgeois press what rather was precisely a deficiency of the revolutionary movement of his time.

6

The concentrated expression of present historical subversion has itself become *decentralized*. The monolithic myth of the S.I. has exploded forever. During the first phase this myth had a certain objective basis: on the level on which it was operating, the S.I. had no serious rivals. Now we see a public and international confrontation of autonomous situationist theories and ideologies which no tendency comes close to monopolizing. Any situationist orthodoxy has lost its central referent. From this point on, every situationist or would-be situationist must follow his own path.

7

The first critiques of situationism remained fundamentally ahistorical. They measured the theoretical poverties of the pro-situ up against the theory of the first phase. They saw the subjective poverties and internal inconsistencies of this milieu, but not its position as related to the sum of theoretical and practical vectors at a certain moment; they failed to grasp this "first non-dialectical application" as the qualitative weakness of the *ensemble*, as a necessary "moment of the true." Even *Theses on the S.I. and Its Time* — in so many respects the summation of the first phase at its point of transition into the second — scarcely broaches the properly historical aspect of situationism.

8

At each stage of the struggle the partial realization of the critique generates its own new equilibrium point with the ruling society. As the theory escapes its formulaters, it tends through its autonomous ideological momentum to be run through all possible permutations and combinations, though principally those reflecting the new developments and illusions of the moment. Caught in the transition of the first phase to the second, the pro-situationists in the post-1968 "ebbing of May" period were the embodiments of the *inertia* of a confirmed theory. This ideological lag — in which the partisans of situationist theory failed to confront the new developments in their own practice, that of the proletariat and that of the society as a whole — measured the weakness of the situationist movement; while the unprecedented quickness with which it engendered its own internal negation — effectively *sabotaging itself* in order to affirm the explosion that had already escaped it and clear the ground for the new phase — marks its fundamental vindication.

9

The pro-situationists saw the issues of the second phase in terms of those of the first. In treating the new, widespread and relatively conscious worker struggles as if they were isolated nihilist acts of an earlier period, which therefore lacked first of all the proverbial "consciousness of what they had already done," the pro-situs only showed that they lacked the consciousness of what others were already doing and of all that was still lacking. In every single struggle they saw the same simple, total conclusion and identified the progress of the revolution with the appropriation of this conclusion by the proletariat. In thus *abstractly concentrating* the intelligence of human practice above the complex process of the development of class struggle, the activist pro-situs were the would-be bolsheviks of a fantasized *coup of class consciousness*, hoping by this shortcut to bring about their councilist program whose implications they overstepped out of incomprehension or impatience.

10

The S.I. did not apply its theory *to the very activity of the formulation of that theory*, although the very nature of that theory implied its eventual democratization and thus put this question on the order of the day. In the aftermath of May neither the S.I. nor the new generation of insurgents it had inspired had really examined the *process* of theoretical production, either in its methods or its subjective ramifications, beyond a few vague, empirical rules of the thumb. The backlash of the partial realization of situationist theory flung them unprepared from megalomaniac delirium, to incoherence, to chain-reactions of contentless breaks, to impotence and finally to the massive psychological repression of the whole experience, without their ever having asked themselves what was happening to them.

11

Even if the S.I. attracted many poorly prepared partisans, the very fact that such a mass of people with no *particular* experience in or aptitude or taste for revolutionary politics thought to find in situationist activity a terrain where they could engage themselves autonomously and consequentially confirms the radicality of both the theory and the epoch. If the situationist milieu has manifested so many pretensions and illusions, this was merely the natural side-effect of the first victory of a critique that burst so many pretensions of and illusions about the ruling society.

12

To the extent that the ideologies of the first phase suppressed anything to do with the situationists — including therefore the concepts most explicitly associated with them — the eventual discovery of the situationist critique had the contrary exaggerated effect of giving the situationists an apparent *monopoly* of radical comprehension of modern society and its opposition. Hence the adherence to

the situationist critique had the abrupt, fanatical character of a sudden religious *conversion* (often with a corresponding ulterior rejection of it *in toto*). In
contrast, the young revolutionary who now adheres to situationist positions
tends to be less subject to this fanatical excess precisely because diverse
nuances of situationist struggle and of its recuperation are a *familiar aspect of
his world*.

13

In the second phase, revolution has moved from being an apparently marginal
phenomenon to a visibly central one. The underdeveloped countries have lost
their apparent monopoly of contestation; but the revolutions there haven't
stopped, they have simply become *modern* and are resembling more and more
the struggles in the advanced countries. The society that proclaimed its well-
being is now *officially* in crisis. The formerly isolated gestures of revolt against
apparently only isolated misery now know themselves to be *general* and pro-
liferate and overwhelm all accounting. 1968 was the moment where the revolutionary movements began to see themselves in *international company*, and it
was this global visibility that definitively shattered the ideologies that saw revolution everywhere but in the proletariat. 1968 was also the last time major revolts
could seem to be *student* revolts.

14

The proletariat has begun to act *by itself* but as yet scarcely *for itself*. Revolts
continue to be, as they have been over the last century, largely defensive
reactions: the taking over of factories abandoned by their owners or of struggles
abandoned by their leaders (particularly in the aftermath of wars). If sectors of
the proletariat have begun to speak for themselves, they have yet to elaborate an
openly internationalist revolutionary program and effectively express their goals
and tendencies internationally. If they serve as examples for proletarians of
other countries, it is still through the *de facto* mediation of radical groups and
spectacular reportage.

15

The ideology of the first phase that stressed the concrete realization of radical
change without grasping the negative or the totality has found its realization in
the proliferation of the so-called *alternative institutions*. The alternative institution differs from classic reformism in being chiefly an immediate, *self-managed
reformism*, one that *does not wait for the State*. It recuperates the initiative and
energy of the mildly dissatisfied and is a sensitive indicator of defects in the
system and of their possible resolutions. Alternative production — whose development on the margins of the economy recapitulates the historical development of commodity production — functions as a *free-enterprise* corrective to the
bureaucratized economy. But the democratization and "autogestionization" of
social structures, though productive of illusions, is also a favorable factor for the
development of the revolutionary critique. It leaves behind the superficial focuses of struggle while providing a safer and easier terrain from and on which to
contest the *essentials*. The contradictions in participatory production and alternative distribution facilitate the detournement of their goods and facilities, going
up to the point of quasi-legal "Strasbourgs of the factories."

254

16

The hip notion *trip* expresses the fact that as commodities become more abundant, adaptable and disposable, the individual commodity is devalued in favor of the ensemble. The trip offers not a single commodity or idea but an organizing principle for selecting from among all commodities and ideas. In contrast with the block of time where "everything's included," which is still sold as a distinct commodity, the commodity character of the indefinitely extended trip (art, craft, pursuit, fad, lifestyle, subcult, social project, religion) — carrying with it a more flexible complex of commodities and stars — is obscured behind the quasi-autonomous activity whereby the subject seems to dominate. The trip is the moment where the spectacle has become so overdeveloped that it becomes *participatory*. It recovers the subjective activity lacking in the spectacle, but runs into the limits of the world the spectacle has made — limits absent in the spectacle precisely because it is separate from daily life.

17

The diminution of the exclusive sway of work and the fragmentation of the consequently expanded leisure give rise to the widespread *dilittantism* of modern society. The spectacle presents the super-agent who can tell to a degree the correct temperature at which saké should be served and initiates the masses into exotic techniques of living and to connoisseur enjoyments previously reserved for the upper classes. But the heralded "new Renaissance Man" is no closer to mastering his own life. When the spectacle becomes overdeveloped and wants to cast off the poverty and unilateralness at its origin, it reveals itself as simply a *poor relative of the revolutionary project*. It may multiply amusements and make them more participatory, but their commodity basis ineluctably forces them back into the matrix of consumption. Isolated individuals may, in a caricature of Fourier, come together around ever more precise nuances of common spectacular tastes, but these nexuses are all the more separated from each other and from the social totality and the sought-for passionate activity founders on its triviality. The new cosmopolitan remains *historically provincial*.

18

The spectacle responds to the increasing dissatisfaction with its tendency toward lowest-common-denominator uniformity by *diversifying* itself. Struggles are channeled into struggles over the spectacle, leading to the semi-autonomous development of separate spectacles tailor-made for specific social groupings. But the singular power of a spectacle comes from its having been placed for a moment at the center of social life. Thus the increase of spectacular choice at the same time reduces the spectacular power that depends on the very magnitude and undivided enthrallment of the pseudo-community the spectacle draws together. The spectacle must contradictorily be all things to all men individually while continually reasserting itself as their single, exclusive unifying principle.

19

The spectacle revives the dead, imports the foreign and *reinterprets* the existing. The time span required for things to acquire the proper quaint banality to become "camp" continually decreases; the original is marketed simultaneously with its spoof, from which it is often scarcely distinguishable; aesthetic discussions increasingly center around the simple question as to whether something is a parody or not. This expresses the increasing contempt felt for the cultural spectacle on the part of its producers and consumers. Society produces a more and more rapid turnover of styles and ideologies, going up to the point of a delirium that escapes no one. As all the permutations and combinations are run through, the individual poverties and contradictions make themselves known and the common *form* that lies behind the diverse contents begins to be discerned; "to change illusions at an accelerating pace gradually dissolves the illusion of change." With the global unification exerted by the spectacle, it becomes increasingly difficult to idealize a system because it is in a different part of the world, and the global circulation of commodities and therefore of people brings ever closer the historic *encounter of the Eastern and Western proletariats*. The recycling of culture sucks dry and breaks up all the old traditions, leaving only the spectacular "tradition of the new." But the new ceases to be novel and the impatience for novelty generated by the spectacle may transform itself into an impatience to realize and destroy the spectacle, the only idea that continually remains really "new and different."

20

Inasmuch as situationist theory is a critique of all aspects of alienated life, the diverse nuances of situationism reflect in concentrated form the general illusions of the society, and the ideological defenses generated by the situationists prefigure the ideological defenses of the system.

21

Situationist theory has come full circle when its critique of daily life is drawn on to provide the *sophisticated vocabulary* of a justification of the status quo. Individuals expressing dissatisfaction with self-satisfied pseudo-enjoyments in the situationist milieu, for example, have been characterized as lacking a "capacity for enjoyment," a "sense of play" or even "radical subjectivity," and accused of "voluntarism" or "militantism" for having concretely proposed radical projects or more experimental activities.

22

Vaneigemism is an extreme form of the modern *anti-puritanism* that has to pretend to enjoy what is supposed to be enjoyable. Like the city dweller who affirms his preference for "living in the country" although for some reason he never goes there or if he does soon gets bored and returns to the city, the vaneigemist has to feign pleasure because his activity is by definition "passionate," even when that activity is in fact tedious or nonexistent. In letting everyone know that he "refuses sacrifice" and "demands everything," he differs from the man in the ads who "insists on the best" only in the degree of his pretension and in the often scarcely more than token ideological avowal of the obstacles that remain in the way of his total realization. Dissatisfaction and boredom are forgotten in their boring, ritual denunciation, and at a time when even the most retrograde ideologies are becoming frankly pessimistic and self-critical in their decomposition, the vaneigemist presents an effective *image of present satisfaction*.

23

Vaneigemist *ideological egoism* holds up as the radical essence of humanity that *most alienated condition of humanity* for which the bourgeoisie was reproached, which "left remaining no other nexus between man and man than naked self-interest"; differing only accidentally from the bourgeois version in envisaging a different means of realization for this collection of isolated egos. This position is contradicted by the actual historical experience of revolutions and often even by the very actions of those who invoke it.

24

The situationists' criticality and often appropriate calculated "arrogance" and use of insults — once taken out of the context of active struggle to *change things* — find a natural place in a world where everyone is presented with a spectacle of inferiority and encouraged to think that he is "different"; where every tourist seeks to avoid "the tourists" and every consumer prides himself on not believing the ads (an illusion of superiority that is often intentionally programmed into ads in order to facilitate the simultaneous penetration of the essential subliminal message). The pseudo-critical individual affirms his *static superiority* through his contemptuous and consequenceless critiques of others who have cruder or at least different illusions. Situationist *humor* — product of the contradictions between the latent possibilities of the epoch and its absurd reality — once it ceases to be practical, approaches simply the median popular humor of a society where the good spectator has been largely supplanted by the *cynical spectator*.

25

As *reinvestors* of the cultural riches of the past, the situationists, once the use of those riches is lost, rejoin spectacular society as simple promoters of culture. The process of the modern revolution — communication containing its own critique, continuous domination of the present over the past — *meshes* with that of a society depending on the continuous turnover of commodities, where each new lie criticizes the previous ones. That a work has something to do with the critique of the spectacle — in manifesting an element of "authentic radicality" or in representing some theoretically articulated moment of the decomposition of the spectacle — is hardly disadvantageous for it from the standpoint of the spectacle. While the situationists are right in pointing out the detournable elements in their forebears, in so doing they simultaneously win for those forebears a place in the spectacle, which, because it is so sorely lacking in the qualitative, welcomes the affirmation that there is some to be found among the cultural goods it markets. The detourned fragment is rediscovered *as* a fragment; when the use goes, the consumption remains; the detourners are detourned.

26

Such a vital concept as *situationist* necessarily knows simultaneously the truest and the most false uses, with a multitude of intermediate confusions.

27

As with other pivotal theoretical concepts, one cannot suppress the interested confusionism engendered by the concept *situationist* by suppressing its label.

The ambiguities of the term "situationist" reflect the ambiguities of the situationist critique itself, at once separate from and part of the society it combats, at once separate party and its negation. The existence of a distinct "situationist milieu" — at once social concentration of advanced revolutionary consciousness and social embodiment of concentrated situationism — expresses the contradictions of the uneven development of conscious struggle in this period; since while to be explicitly situationist is hardly a guarantee of intelligent practice, not to be so is virtually a guarantee of aims of falsification or of an ignorance increasingly difficult to maintain involuntarily. The "spectacle" will be considered as a specifically situationist concept as long as it is considered as merely one more peripheral element of the society. But in simultaneously repressing its central aspects and the theory that has most radically articulated them and then thinking to kill two birds with one stone by lumping these uncategorizable entities together, the society confirms their real unity; as when for example a bibliography contains a section: "Daily Life, Consumer Society, and Situationist Themes."

28

For the S.I., the situationist label served to draw a line between the prevalent incoherence and a new exigency. The importance of the term withers away to the extent that the new exigences are widely known and practiced, to the extent that the proletarian movement becomes itself situationist. Such a label also facilitates a spectacular categorization of what it represents. But this very categorization at the same time exposes the society to the very *coherence* of the diverse situationist positions that makes possible a single label, the power of this exposure depending on the net total of significances carried by the term at a given moment. It is the *trenchancy* of the term which is at issue in the diverse struggles over whether someone or something is situationist, and it is a notable measure of this trenchancy that the term "pro-situationist" has been rendered universally recognized as pejorative. Although association with the label serves as no defense for acts, the actions of situationists do in a sense defend the word, in contributing toward rendering it as concentrated and dangerous a bomb as possible for the society to play with. The society that with little difficulty presents sectors of itself as "communist," "Marxist" or "libertarian" finds it as yet impossible or inadvisable to present any aspect of itself as "situationist," although it certainly would have done so by now if for example a "Nashist" (opportunistic neo-artistic) sense of the term had prevailed.

29

At its beginnings, as long as no one else is very close, the situationist critique seems so intrinsically anti-ideological that its proponents can scarcely imagine any situationism other than as a mere gross lie or misunderstanding. "There is no situationism," such a term is "meaningless," declares *I.S.* 1. A simple differentiation suffices to defend the term from misuse: the 5th Conference of the S.I. decides that all artistic works produced by its members must be explicitly labeled "anti-situationist." But the critique that opposes itself by definition to its ideologization cannot definitively or absolutely separate itself from it. The S.I. discovers a tendency "infinitely more dangerous than the old artistic conception we have fought so much. It is more modern and thus less clear. . . . Our project takes shape at the *same time* as the modern tendencies of integration. There is thus an air of resemblance as well as a direct opposition, in that we are really contemporary. . . . We are necessarily on the same path as our enemies — more often preceding them" (*I.S. 9*).

30

It is notorious that the modern intelligentsia has often utilized elements of situationist theory, formerly without acknowledgment, more recently — when such a plagiarization has become more difficult and when at the same time spectacular association with the situationists adds more to one's prestige than knowledge of dependence on them detracts from it — more often with acknowledgment. But even more significant are the numerous theoretical and ideological manifestations that, in spite of no direct influence or even knowledge of the situationists, are ineluctably drawn to the same issues and the same formulations because these are nothing other than the intrinsic pivotal points of modern society and its contradictions.

31

To the extent that the situationist critique extends and deepens itself, modern society — merely to minimally understand its own functioning and opposition, or to present the spectacle reflecting what is most generally desired — must recuperate more and more elements of that critique, or in repressing it become the victim of its own correspondingly increasing blind spots.

32

Everything the S.I. has said about art, the proletariat, urbanism, the spectacle, is broadcast everywhere — minus the essential. While in the anarchy of the ideological market individual ideologies incorporate elements of situationist theory separated from their concrete totality, as an ensemble they effectively reunite the fragments as an abstract totality. All of modernist ideology taken as a block is situationism.

33

Situationism is the stealing of the *initiative* from the revolutionary movement, the critique of daily life undertaken by power itself. The spectacle presents itself as the originator or at least the necessary forum of discussion of the ideas of its destruction. Revolutionary theses don't appear as the ideas of revolutionaries, that is as linked to a precise experience and project, but rather as an unexpected outburst of lucidity on the part of the rulers, stars and vendors of illusions. Revolution becomes a moment of situationism.

34

The society of situationism does not know that it is; that would be giving it too much credit. Only the proletariat can grasp its totality in the process of destroying it. It is principally the revolutionary camp that generates the diverse illusions and ideological nuances that can shore up the system and justify a restored status quo. The very successes of revolts having arrived at an ambiguous point of equilibrium with the system serve in part to advertise the greatness of a system that could generate and accommodate such radical successes.

259

35

By its very nature situationism cannot be immediately or fully realized. It is not supposed to be taken literally, but followed at just a few steps distance; if it were not for this albeit tiny distance, the mystification would become apparent.

36

In producing its situationism, the society shatters the cohesion of other ideologies, sweeps aside the archaic and accidental falsifications and draws the fragments capable of reinvestment to itself. But in thus *concentrating the social false consciousness*, society prepares the way for the expropriation of this expropriated consciousness. The sophistication of recuperation forcibly disabuses revolutionaries, its unity pushes the conflict to a higher level, and elements of situationism diffused globally provoke their own supercession in regions where they had not yet developed from an indigenous theoretical base.

37

The S.I. was exemplary not only for what it said, but above all for *all that it did not say*. Diffuseness dilutes critical power. Discussion of things that don't make any difference obscures the things that do. Entering onto the platform of ruling pseudo-dialogue turns truth into a moment of the lie. Revolutionaries must know how to be *silent*.

KEN KNABB

NOTES TOWARD A
SITUATIONIST MANIFESTO

A qualitative leap has been made in the period since the S.I. ceased its experimentation around 1968.

The assault of the proletariat, rediscovering little by little the necessity of a revolution and defining in its struggles the conditions and stakes of a "new epoch," has been qualitatively confirmed and precised. The nature of this assault now allows the elimination or modification of certain premature hypotheses and slogans of the old theory and also reveals certain *limits*, the overcoming of which would create the conditions of a qualitatively different epoch.

In obvious connection with the return of the social revolution, we are witnessing a development, *without precedent* in the modern epoch, of partial-reformist contestation drawing its inspiration from *modern* themes taken from revolutionary struggles as it progressively abandons its traditional themes. This phenomenon joins with the new orientation taken by the spheres that run the present society; faced with the assault of the *negative*, they have decided to obtain, at any cost, people's *active* participation in their own alienation; they are exploring and establishing the futuristic conditions of this participation, on a program of the modification of daily life, of mores, of the social utilization of space and time, of proletarians' role in production and of this production itself. Hence all the liberalizing experiments, questionings of the assumptions, the goals and the power of the economy itself, declarations, studies and programs promising the transformation of existence, which are accompanied, by an irony of the logic of statist power, by a sector-by-sector reinforcement of the *means of control* over social life. This is one of the contradictions which is going to dominate all social life in the next few years: the power of the economy and the State can't confront the present collapse and consider liberalizing the society without reinforcing its bureaucratic control, and it can't reinforce its bureaucratic control without substantially liberalizing the anachronistic social structures whose negative and negating consequences have become uncontrollable.

Power cannot know how far it will be swept along by this course. This is why it so willingly leaves it to the diverse shades of contemporary critical thought to explore its possible stages, including the worst envisageable ones; this is why it encourages experimentation with solutions aimed at transforming populations into credulous and cooperative actors of a renovated alienation. Its major concern, since it has already given up getting out of the present period in one piece, is to keep the damage to a minimum and avoid generating situations of irreversible disequilibrium. It is this process, taken up on a global political scale as well as internally in the various states and modified or postponed according to local necessities, in which is inscribed the considerable development — if one takes for comparison the pre-1968 epoch of the triumphant and euphoric economy — of a *spectacle of contestation and social transformation*.

To be sure, contestation has always had its place in the spectacular universe, but as a peripheral and negligible sector; now it shares the center of the stage, openly competing with satisfied submission's eulogy of existing conditions. In place of the capitalism-stalinism opposition which was at the base of the spectacle of the preceding period, is now substituted the familiar imagery of existing society grappling with the forces and processes announcing its *internal negation*.

In the spheres of high politics one now sees everywhere the still-groping rise of a *neo-reformism*, supported by the *foil* of a certain revival of rightist or semi-fascist manifestations.

The ensemble of the present tentatives from which Western capitalism is developing its own reexamination and preparing its necessary restructuring is indicative of the pivotal and even *profoundly historical* character of this epoch. As the signs and risks of a *total negation* develop, a terrain of experimentation constitutes itself in reaction, from which the *ideology* is being elaborated that will prop up the reorganization of the faltering system in the next few years. It is a matter here of a *stalinization* of Western capitalism, in the sense that the necessary restructuring conceived to safeguard state domination must be conducted in the most centralized and controllable manner possible, no longer in the name of the natural needs of the workings of the economy but to save the *economic order itself*, in the name of an ideology imposing a *global conception of existence* and preparing the favorable conditions for cybernetic society. But in order to conduct this operation, power finds itself constrained in the short run to descend to the favored terrain of revolutionaries, of which it has a horror: that of *adventure*. If its goals are clear, it nonetheless does not have the process it finds itself engaged in *under control*. This is a central point for the historical understanding of the present period and of the manner in which the alternative of revolutionary adventure articulates itself there. None of the rulers can say any longer what the consequences of the reformist measures that they are forced to take today will be; they all see their time running out and the last-ditch palliatives they urgently need to develop or generalize, but they hesitate before these correctives whose process and results are uncertain. This paralyzing uncertainty leads them rather to give a clumsy and inadequate priority to the only one of their instruments that remains without surprises and that they know well — *their police*.

Revolutionary theses are being taken up everywhere, inspiring the thinkers underwritten by the State and the future technicians of the control of populations; they are used with the greatest cynicism to praise modern merchandise as well as to justify the possible necessity of a bureaucratically planned privation of this merchandise. In a way, they have never been so known and popular; but only on rare occasions are they understood, used and developed on their own terrains. The spectacle effect obliterates their origin and their meaning. They don't appear as the ideas of revolutionaries, that is to say linked to a precise experience and project, but rather as an outburst of lucidity on the part of the rulers, stars and vendors of illusions.

This popularity of our anesthetized theses defines a primary difficulty for the realization of a situationist manifesto. It will have to be conceived so that the point of view which it develops cannot appear as the "extreme left" of the existing currents of contestation. It must convey as unambiguously as possible the critique and supercession of them. That is, it must shatter the "in" status that situationist theory holds today. It is this very rupture which principally defines the content of and need for a manifesto.

In presenting his film, for example, Guy Debord, renouncing the continuation of an offensive position, has actively contributed to placing situationist theory in the inextricable situation of the contemporary contestatory spectacle. Not, obviously, because film is necessarily more "spectacular" than writing (though this is a question of a domain that revolutionaries are nowhere near being able to dominate in the current context), but because seven years after the appearance of his book — well into a radically new period — he has made a film which is no more than that book and which is thus only a self-admiring glorification of an act of the past. But even if there is an inordinate proportion of flaunted self-satisfaction in this film, it isn't our intention to deny Debord the indisputable talent that remains to him and which can even still manifest itself in certain partially revolutionary and efficacious ways. The problem is not there. It is that Debord, in the activity of situationist theory where he holds a deserved author-ity, devotes himself less to the theory of negation than to maintaining a personal glory through the *art* of the negative, which society today integrates as a peripheral and entertaining art. This is an example of the path that a good manifesto and its authors must not follow.

As a preliminary to the drafting of a manifesto, there is a profound retardation to make up for in revolutionary theory. Notably in the mastery of phenomena particular, in their dimension or their novelty, to the "new epoch"; in the heretofore neglected interpretation of what is rising there. And in taking this route it is possible that we will discover new notions decisive for the struggles of the next few years.

A good manifesto, for example, ought not to talk to the revolutionary movement in the fashion of that frantic optimism which some feel obliged to adopt whenever they talk about revolution, insisting principally on the radical aspects, even inventing them for the occasion, and on the ineluctability of the final issue. This doctrinaire point of view only betrays the doubts of those who adopt it.

The manifesto will have to consider the *real* revolutionary movement; that is to say certainly the admirable element of what has already been accomplished, which justifies the very notion of a *revolutionary movement*, but solely in the sense that what has already been done *is going to be superceded*. It will also consider all the regrettable defects which compromise revolutionary develop-ment, its complicity with existing conditions. The correct analysis of a single step of the real movement is worth more than a hundred discourses on the timeless certainties of the final issue. The epoch when the mere arrogant declara-tion of those certainties had its efficacy is now over.

The manifesto will take *precise and trenchant* positions on the reality and the becoming of the revolutionary movement. It will have to locate and *name* this proletarian movement's really situationist tendencies, those which can in no way be considered such, and those which may become so and under what conditions. It will avoid that habit of contemporary revolutionary prose which sees an unadulterated confirmation of its theses in more or less everything that's happening. It will be necessary to *clarify* what has already been done and the present activity of consequential revolutionaries, in showing what the revolutionary proletariat is *necessarily* going to be led to do in the next few years. That is to say what questions struggles are necessarily going to depend upon, what forms they are necessarily going to take, before what *precise alternatives* the revolutionaries on one side and the dominant society on the other are going to be placed. Revolutionary theory can no longer content itself with presenting the final stage as the foreseeable negative of what exists; it is now necessary for it to conceive, in an ever-more-*practical* manner, all the eventualities of the intermediary periods and to advance diverse debated hypotheses on these periods.

We ought to put ourselves in a position to announce with certainty some foreseeable developments, to exclude others; to show what function catastrophism fills for power and for the contesters. Which are the catastrophes that one can reasonably show to be avoidable, which on the other hand are those that won't be avoided. We ought to foresee the principal socio-historic developments coming from all the aspects of the present breakdown of social functioning, that is to say to foresee the immediate context in which the proletariat is going to have to develop its struggles.

The project of a manifesto responds more to the necessity of presenting a series of simple positions on problems hitherto left in abeyance than to that of a more rational and striking presentation of points acquired from already existing theory. It will be a sort of guidebook for the revolutionary adventure of the next twenty years. Not an idyllic travel agency prospectus but a practical document mentioning the dangers and obstacles which have already begun to manifest themselves, and the *scientifically evaluated and situated* chances of success.

What will differentiate us from the pseudo-revolutionaries who today monopolize attention, in the manifesto and *in the activity that we are going to continue to develop*, is that we are going to talk about revolution as a *concrete and global* enterprise for the last quarter of this century and that we are going to say precisely under what conditions it can succeed as *total revolution*. From the conditions in which we conduct our activity, and because this activity is not directed by anyone, no one can say who will be the authors of the situationist manifesto *or manifestos*. One thing, however, is sure: our epoch really needs theoretical works, and it itself is going to create the forces necessary for the satisfaction of that need.

JEANNE CHARLES, DANIEL DENEVERT

"Notes pour une manifeste situationniste" is from *Chronique des Secrets Publics*, Volume 1 (June 1975).

ARMS AND THE WOMAN

One of the symptoms of the weakness of the revolutionary movement to-day is that it has not yet reached the point of giving birth to a qualitative and autonomous expression of *revolutionary women*. It is known that the degree of development attained by the forces of negation in existing society finds its unequivocal, decisive and obvious manifestation in the relations between revolutionary *men and women* and in the manner in which the direct and natural relation of the sexes is conceived.

The division of *roles* of the sexes in alienated society, inherited from feudal society and the first stages of industrial society, can be schematically defined in this way: *femininity* concentrates the *anti-historical* tendencies of alienated life (passivity, submission to nature, the superstition that follows from this, repetition, resignation), *masculinity* its *pseudo-historical* tendencies (a certain degraded taste for struggle, arrogance, pseudo-activity, innovation, confidence in the power of society, rationalism). Femininity and masculinity are the two *complementary* poles of the same alienation. In modern industrial society, these two poles *tend*, in losing their material bases, to blend into each other to constitute the specific traits of the modern proletarian, where the differences between the sexes are less and less marked.

In all epochs, and according to the nature of those epochs, men and women have never constituted two *pure* types. Whatever their sex, individuals unite, in various ways, the character traits and behavior of the two sexes. Nevertheless, femininity has up till now always been the dominant trait of the alienation of women, and masculinity that of men. But fundamentally, it is the traits of the old femininity which reappear at present in the generalized passivity of the reign of the modern economy, although femininity and masculinity, freed from their material roots, are recaptured and used indiscriminately by the two sexes, as modes of spectacular affirmation.

While in alienated society woman and man find themselves more and more on a plane of equality (except in the cases where patriarchy still prevails) because the woman cannot find in her male companion — who is as unarmed as she is — an admirable and all-powerful protector; in the modern revolutionary movement, in contrast, the woman begins by being sharply confronted with her old femininity in the face of the domination of a certain theoretical prestige. Because, for the individual who is *not involved* in theoretical activity, theory appears as an "ability to write," to "think," a product of intelligence, an individual creation full of mystery. This is the spectacle effect; the fetishism of theory for those who find themselves outside it. The woman often finds herself forced to admit that she has "not yet written anything," and that she has no active role in the elaboration of revolutionary theory, in apparent contrast to certain of the men she sees. In matters regarding theory, her first impulse is to rely on men, who seem to her "more qualified" than her. She ends up distrusting her own thought, paralyzed by external criteria. When she happens to penetrate unexplored terrains, she stops short, thinking that if it hasn't been done before, it must have been because it wasn't worth the trouble. Her thought, when in spite of everything she manages to have some, remains a dead letter: the woman never on her own follows through to the practical consequences of her thought. Often, she judges an individual very quickly, making a pertinent, perceptive critique, even before her male friend or friends; but in her passivity she stops there. When it comes to practical consequences, she hides behind men. Her reflections and her critiques are made in private, leaving masculinity to attend to *putting them into practice.*

But in this way she deprives herself of a direct grasp on her social environment; she never directly influences anything and thus cannot become a theorist. For theory is the critique of daily life; it is the operation of each individual conducted in this daily life; it is a succession of renewed and corrected *interventions* in relations with people (which are also the *effective terrain* of alienation) and, what amounts to the same thing, it is also a series of interventions in society. Theory is an undertaking of *revolutionary transformation* that implies that the individual theorist accept his own uninterrupted transformation. Theory lies therefore in the comprehension of and action on blocks (individual and social-historical).

If men have an *apparently* preponderant place in the revolutionary movement, it is because many among them enter the revolutionary struggle with the character traits of *masculinity* — that is to say, in reality with as few aptitudes as women, and with the same *unconscious complacence* regarding their character traits as women have regarding femininity — which can *create illusions*, since the practice of theory demands imagination, real struggle, confidence in oneself and in the power of the individual, aptitudes which the masculine character possesses in a degraded form. To convince oneself of this hidden misery of the modern revolutionary movement, it suffices to note that femininity would not be allowed to exist in it without the assent of masculinity, or at least would not be tolerated for long. Feminine passivity has its flip side in masculine activism. Up till now, it is primarily the passivity that has been noted, because it is the most glaring contradiction in a movement founded on the autonomy of individuals.

Women are only colonized by the spectacle of theory insofar as they are totally exterior to theory. And it is not the example or the *intervention* of men, themselves largely colonized by this *spectacle*, that can precipitate women's demystification, that can make them comprehend *in vivo* what theory is. Henceforth, the passivity of women must be criticized, not *superficially* because they don't write or don't know how to express themselves autonomously, but at the root, because they don't have any direct and practical efficacy; notably in their relations with others. Equally, it must no longer suffice for a man to "express himself" *abstractly*. His writings and his thought must directly have concrete effects. Masculinity and its activism must no longer have as a foil femininity and its passivity.

There is an obvious complacence present in the maintenance of these roles. The alienated individual is reluctant to root out what he has repressed; and since masculinity and femininity are complementary, they have all the solidity of *natural* and *inevitable* phenomena. In the refusal to combat these *roles*, there subsists in fact the *global* acceptance of alienated society. Those who claim to be revolutionaries say that they want to change the world and their own lives. But in reality these individuals hope that they will *be changed* by a revolution. They thus remain passive individuals, ready to *adapt* themselves, *if they have to*, but who *fundamentally* fear all change. They are quite the opposite of *situationists*.

The resolution of the deficiencies of revolutionary practice at the beginning of the new epoch now passes *directly* through the resolution of the deficiencies of revolutionary women; which is to say, also through the *supercession* of a certain limited masculine practice which has up till now accommodated itself to these deficiencies and their maintenance. It is an urgent objective for the *critique of daily life* to definitively destroy the inequality of the sexes in revolutionary activity; that is to say, to destroy the respective *roles* which both sexes establish in alienated life, the character structures of *femininity* and *masculinity* and the limitations that they impose on revolutionary experience.

There are two principal types of women in the revolutionary movement: the most numerous at present are the women provided with a protector. They are admitted into the revolutionary milieu with the traits of femininity, because they are presented by a man. The others present themselves: they are admitted as the result of a prestigious past which they have participated in, or for an ideology which they have assimilated well. These latter are admitted with the traits of masculinity, as men are.

Some of these women say absolutely nothing in public, contenting themselves with making remarks in private that they wouldn't otherwise dare to make; or they don't open their mouths except in response to the futile sort of questions that are believed to be the only ones that can be asked of them; or again, arbitrarily thrown into "theoretical discussions," anxiously watching out of the corner of their eye for the approval of their protector, they won't dare admit their ignorance of the subject, and entangle themselves in the confusion of their thoughts, or repeat what they've heard said, their difficulties in this domain seeming shameful to them; others openly display their insufficiencies, finding excuses for themselves in the difficulties they have in writing — but only in writing, as an inexplicable calamity — implying that they nonetheless *think* admirably; or perhaps they recognize in this a feminine defect, and fancy themselves protected, supposing that their honesty guards them from any more direct critique; still others express themselves by means of aggressive demonstrations toward men, to show that they aren't under any man's thumb and that they think autonomously. Each time, it is their colonization by the spectacle of theory which paralyzes women.

Thus, for the most part the only relations which remain to women are amorous ones. There they flaunt their sensitivity, ranting in private against theory as being something cold and abstract, and lauding "human relations." Women are often recognized as having greater sensitivity and subtlety when it comes to judging people. In addition, men, having a certain minimum of practical exigence, are considerably more prudent when it comes to critiques that will entail practical consequences. They prefer to admire their female companion for such a capacity, which they claim to possess only in a lesser degree — they had to repress it — and thus justify their relation with this woman: the passivity and public non-existence of the woman must be compensated by a greater hidden richness, and the monogamic justification of the couple is this complementarity of the man and the woman. If sensitivity is still an attribute of femininity, it is because theory is not understood for what it is, since men who are considered to be theorists are considered to lack sensitivity; whereas in fact theory includes the *practical application* of this sensitivity and this subtlety.

The modern revolutionary movement must destroy this opposition of pleasure/activity, sensitivity/lucidity, conception/execution, habit/innovation, etc. The femininity/masculinity opposition corresponds to a reified stage of human development.

The individuals colonized by the spectacle of a revolutionary theory are in fact colonized by the need to appear autonomous; they are subject to appearance. As long as theory continues to be understood as a product of intelligence, as the individual faculty of "thinking" and of "writing," and as such, as a possible source of personal prestige, men will continue to want to "express themselves" at all costs and women will lament not being able to imitate them.

It is now a matter of understanding theory for what it is. It is essential that women (and men) no longer accept one's acts being in contradiction with one's words, and no longer accept the existence of critiques without consequences. It is essential to restore to subjectivity all its rights by giving it practical follow-through. No one should be able to be lucid about others without being lucid about himself, or lucid about himself without being lucid about others. The modern revolutionary movement must become unlivable for masculinity and femininity. It must judge individuals *on their life*.

JEANNE CHARLES

"La critique ad mulierem" is from *Chronique des Secrets Publics*, Volume 1. This translation was first issued in June 1975 as a separate mini-pamphlet, which is still available.

FROM 'END OF SCIENCE'

There was no "Greek miracle"; the real nature of the Unity of wisdom of the first Greek philosophers is explained by its socio-historical context. The fundamental basis of the practical and spiritual emancipation subsequent to the Homeric mythology, in the 6th century B.C., lies essentially on the one hand in the development, amid domestic activity, of crafts and commerce at the instigation of the merchant and technician Solon, and on the other in the gradual formation of Athenian democracy at the expense of the Eupatrids, the landowner caste. The fact that at this period technics are not yet distinct from the *art of living* of the new caste of craftsmen is expressed in the unity of a "naturalist" knowledge directly derived from *technical activity* on nature (*tekhnē*). If pre-Socratic philosophy has to refer to a First Principle, this latter remains inherent in the *physis* itself. However, the industrialization of the crafts and the extension and institutionalization of slavery produce in the 5th and 4th centuries a more distinct social division of labor and a corresponding accentuation of separation in the act of knowing. Xenophon notes that in the cities "one sees a considerable specialization." And though not opposed to the accumulation of wealth, he writes: "What are called the mechanical arts carry a social stigma and are rightly despised in our cities. For these arts injure the bodies of those who work in or run them, in binding them to sedentary and confined life, and in some cases to spending entire days before fire. This physical degeneration also leads to a deterioration of the mind." (*Economics*.) In fact this atrophy of the mind, which was still thoroughly naive in the *physiologoi*, appears fully in Plato, the forefather of metaphysics in the strict sense of the word. In *Phaedo*, Socrates expounds the merits of discursive logic which approaches "each thing as much as possible with thought alone." This development of pure reason rejecting the "entire body" as impure, which characterizes the birth of *separate individualist thought*, is indissociable from the democratic ideal of a mercantile society divided into independent families. Even if Athenian democracy officially concerned the citizens alone, the socio-spiritual disintegration that its *egalitarian* principle gave rise to is perceptible in the century of Pericles in the slackening in the very heart of the relations between citizens and slaves. "In Athens the slaves are accorded an unbelievable license," says Xenophon. The same historian even mentions the local appearance of a form of remuneration tending toward wage-labor, certain slaves receiving, along with the strict necessities of their survival, a surplus in money. The *moralist-rationalist false consciousness* of the city of Athens, which while having need of a slave class no longer has the full conviction of its necessity, is also discernable in the philosophical efforts of Plato and Aristotle to *discursively justify* slavery: in feeling obliged to *demonstrate* that slaves are such "by nature," Aristotle simply takes the opposite moral view to those of his contemporaries who "claim that the law alone makes them so." In *The Republic*, Plato points out that law does not aim at the exceptional happiness of one class but "strives to realize the happiness of the entire city in uniting the citizens by the persuasion and constraint" of the State. The socio-historical process of disintegration of *unquestioned* royal power and of myth broke up the unity of knowledge; if the early philosophers to a large extent identified with the collective life of Hellenism, "after Socrates come the *sects*. Little by little philosophy gives over the reins to science" (Nietzsche). However, to retrospectively interpret pre-Socratic philosophy from the standpoint of an idyllic unitarism would be an error; one that Nietzsche himself, in *Philosophy in the Tragic Age of the Greeks*, doesn't always seem to avoid. In fact, Socrates and his disciples only clearly expressed the advanced state of separation between the mind and the senses, between Apollo and Dionysus, a separation that was already embryonic in Heraclitus, for whom "the eyes and ears are bad witnesses if the mind does not interpret what they say." But the falsehood that gives the vulgar the illusion of duration and immobility is not in the senses. The falsehood is only in the social use of their testimony. Moreover, Heraclitus himself, no doubt conscious of the originality and difficulty of his system, observes: "Among all those whose discourses I have heard, not a one has succeeded in understanding that wisdom is unlike all other things." In the period of the first Greek thinkers, the gods begin to definitively take refuge outside the world so that men can better *discern* all things.

JEAN-LOUIS MOINET

Translation of the first thesis of Jean-Louis Moinet's book *Fin de la Science* (1974), distributed by: Parallèles, 47 rue Saint-Honoré, Paris.

TROUBLE IS MY BUSINESS

A Short Guide to the
Anglo-American Situationist Image

"I would furthermore ask you to study this
theory from its original sources and not at
second hand; it is really much easier. . . .
The most amazing rubbish has been produced in this quarter."
—Engels to J. Bloch (21 September 1890)

Just as a new planet is discovered by observation
of its gravitational effects on other, visible ones,
so one could infer a great deal about the
Situationist International merely by studying the
reactions it has given rise to. In the poster *The
Blind Men and the Elephant* (January 1975) I
have gathered a number of such reactions, which
in their juxtaposition are even more revealing and
funny than they are individually.

> Each was partly in the right,
> And all were in the wrong.

Here, too, we will see the S.I. not as it is, but as it
has been presented spectacularly in the United
States and England. That is, we will see what the
S.I. is *not*, in its Anglo-American version.

To understand those who don't understand the
S.I., and who make sure that others don't, one
has to consider both the *ways* in which they mis-
represent it and their *motives* for doing so.

Just as ad men will start out with little hints leading up to the subject of an ad campaign, the
enemies of the situationists prepare the public
inversely by previews that tone down the expectations, seeming to refute in advance the theses
whose exposure they postpone as long as possible. First the silence and spiteful rumors, then the
grudging, contemptuous footnotes, then the extended chapters, articles and books where, without batting an eye, the authors act as if this was all
quite normal: if they hadn't discussed the S.I.
before it was just because it hadn't come to their
attention. "Many intellectuals hesitate to speak
openly of the S.I. because to speak of it implies
taking a minimum position: saying precisely what
one refuses of it and what one accepts of it. Many
of them believe, quite mistakenly, that to feign
ignorance of it in the meantime will suffice to
clear them of responsibility later" (*I.S.* 9).

Until recently at least, the majority of English-
language references to the S.I. have been apropos of its relation to the May 1968 movement in
France. This was not only because the
situationists participated directly in that movement but also because it was so *explicitly
situationist* and its form and location made it so
little susceptible to being subsumed under the
then-current ideologies (it had nothing to do with
racism, fascism, imperialism, etc.). The result of
this appropriate linking was that the S.I. partook
of the falsification of the May movement — so
much so that one could say as a general rule that
the falsification of the May movement in any
given book or article is in *direct proportion* to its
falsification of the S.I. "One learns most precisely how the system operates by observing
how it operates on its most precise enemies"
(*Double-Reflection*).

A common tactic of falsification is to separate the
S.I. from the insurgence of the masses. We learn
that the situationists are "only" theorists as opposed to being active; they are "academics,"
"Hegelians." This tendency runs up against the
problem that if these "utopian" thinkers are off in
some ivory tower, how do they exert the influence that causes them to be discussed in the first
place? Why is it that publications that formerly
suppressed any mention of the S.I. now find
themselves obliged to take up "situationist
themes" if they want to maintain any pretense of
being abreast of contemporary reality?
Moreover, those who contemptuously ridicule
the situationists — who systematically reject any
militant base through which they could exert their
influence bureaucratically — as being a miniscule
minority forget that this simply implies all the
more power to the *theory itself*.

Another image sees the S.I. as active, to be sure,
but on a *particular, limited terrain*. In this category belongs the notion that the situationists are
"a tendency in the student movement" or that
they are a cultural avant-garde. Here the imagination runs wild: they are "weird sort of
dadaists," they do "street theater," disrupt everything and in general act as sort of "nonsensi-
cal" court jesters. They are given credit for being
of the "radical movement," as its ultra-radical,
lunatic fringe; sort of Yippies in European terms,
perhaps. But the clown role doesn't really hold up
either: who ever heard of clowns (much less

Hegelian academics) being "universally despised by political organizations"? The "gadfly" image is often invoked. This gets closer to the truth of the S.I. — not, to be sure, its central truth, but its truth as seen through the narrow visers of the leftist groups: the S.I. represents the *bad conscience* of the left. It threatens the bureaucrats and ideologues with a loss of their constituency, the rank and file with a recognition of their self-demeaning militantism and obsolescence.

The leftist ideologue responds by finding in the S.I. "interesting theory" but "no practice," by which he expresses the fact that the S.I. came up with a lot of intriguing ideas but forgot to give him or the masses *precise instructions* as to what to do. And since *he* needs instructions he assumes that the masses do too. Rather than admit his confusion he *transfers* it to the masses: "Difficult theory? No, not at all — I've got it down pat. It's just that these guys never developed an adequate practice; like — well, if I wasn't so modest I could mention some people who have . . . But anyway, while we're waiting for some Practice to show up, let me take you on a quick run-through of these situationist theories. They do, after all is said and done, retain a certain undeniable, well, shall we say — *interest*. (I still haven't quite figured out how they do it.) And anyway, even if *I* can understand this stuff you probably can't and by explaining it to you I can demonstrate how abreast of the latest things I am — even though I'd like to caution you again that it's not really all that big a deal."

The "difficulty" for which situationist theory is often reproached — if we leave aside that element of it that is simply due to the complexity of the tasks of the modern revolutionary movement — is the difficulty of the present society trying to comprehend its necessary negation. That the ideologues find it difficult to place in the separate categories of bourgeois thought is simply a reflection of its irreconcilability with bourgeois society. The situationists have been seen as anarchists because they criticize marxists and vice-versa, as "right wing" because they criticize the left, or as primitivists "resisting progress" because they attack "modern society" and the technocrats. They are saddled with all sorts of one-sided ideological positions, then berated for inconsistency when they are found to contradict these fantasized dogmas. Similarly, they are credited — against the most explicit indications — with a "system" from which as a corollary various "omissions" are triumphantly noted: "feminist consciousness," "understanding of capital," "recognition" of the "positive aspects" of this or that, etc.

The types of falsification to which situationist theory has been subject naturally correspond to the diverse material and ideological positions of its enemies. An editor of *New Left Review* finds the notion of the spectacle "still in need of a scientific foundation" (*Student Power*, p. 9) because only such an "objective," sociologically neutered concept could be handled by him and his neo-stalinist colleagues without getting their hands burned. Or again, Vaneigem's well-known phrase about "refering explicitly to daily life" (*se référer explicitement à la vie quotidienne*) is revealingly mistranslated, and thus approved, by the psychologist David Cooper as "Those who talk of revolution . . . without making it real in their own lives . . . talk with a corpse in their mouths" (*The Death of the Family*, p. 97, ellipses his) — leaving out the part about class struggle and suggesting the "changing oneself" ideology. Or again, Bruce Brown, in *Marx, Freud, and the Critique of Everyday Life* (p. 32), cites the S.I. in such a way that the mutually explanatory "criticism in actions" and "theoretical critique" of modern society are represented respectively by "the struggles of the New Left" and "the critical intellectuals of the 'Freudo-Marxist' school" among whom he presumably counts himself. Or again, the British ultra-leftist journal *World Revolution* (April 1975), through the use of the amalgam technique and such gross falsifications as that the situationists hold that the working class has been integrated into capitalism, tries to slip the S.I. into a "modernism" lump where it can easily be dismissed. What annoys many of the ultra-leftist currents about the situationists is that the situationists are precisely not modernist, that their analysis of the new developments of capitalism and of its critique *at the same time* rediscovers and joins up with the old truth of the previously vanquished proletarian revolution. This irritates them because they want to hold onto this old truth *without any newness mixed in*, either from the situationists or from contemporary social reality.

It is worth noting that the current "anarchist revival" (and similar remarks could be made about several other trends, such as the interest in Reich or surrealism) is not really a revival of the classical anarchist movement but a confused attempt to characterize the new proletarian movement, which visibly surpasses all the other classical political perspectives. Thus, the sociologist Herbert Gombin's often perceptive article in *Anarchism Today*, though nominally about anarchism in modern France, effectively demonstrates that what is determinative in this "anarchism" is the situationist critique.

Among the more delirious reactions to the situationists is that of the "National Caucus of Labor Committees," according to whose paper *New Solidarity* (August 28 and September 6, 1974) the S.I. was "created by the C.I.A. from scratch in 1957." We won't give the big lie the benefit of a dignified refutation, and will pass by the various nefarious deeds the S.I. is credited with, from the sabotaging of the mini-bureaucrats in May 68 to the "detonation of riots" and of the Lip strike, in order to come a little closer to home. "In the U.S. Goldner and his Situationist International offshoot group Contradiction have been assigned the same kind of role: namely, to stop the Labor Committees from developing into a mass-based working-class party." Now, during the span of Contradiction (1970-72) none of us had ever so much as heard of these "Labor Committees" which we had been "assigned" to "stop." As for Goldner, "his" group met him by chance around a year after its formation. One or two meetings sufficed to demonstrate the more or less academic nature of his accord with the situationist theses, although we saw him occasionally over the next year in order to exchange some texts (he had translated sections of some of the S.I. books). Some time after the dissolution of Contradiction he informed me that he had joined the N.C.L.C., whereupon I naturally told him that that was the end of my relation with him. One can guess that Goldner, with the same naiveté that could see in the N.C.L.C. a "Luxemburgist organization" (it actually plays a similar spectacular role within the decomposed American left that P.L. did a few years before in the decomposing left — as the pure, uncompromising outcast group, promoting an image of violent militance and of a worker base calculated to intrigue and arouse the guilt of the rest of the predominantly student left; it is characteristic of the advance of the times that the newer group to fill this role must present a more sophisticated theoretical appearance and be from the start explicitly "anti-stalinist"), talked up the situationists within the group, perhaps with a view to the appearance of his translations in the N.C.L.C. publications. Sooner or later he must have run up against the contradictions between the group's radical bravado and its effectively stalinist practice and organization (all the methods without the means) and resigned, thus marking himself as a "CIA agent." (This same paranoid consciousness saw in *The Blind Men and the Elephant* the work of — the KGB!)

Certainly it is not through the "infiltration, penetration and dissolution of socialist and other workers' organizations" that the S.I. has influenced the workers of Lip or Contradiction dissuaded those of the U.S. from the outstretched arms of the N.C.L.C. "It is in an entirely different manner that the S.I. and the epoch pursue their dissolving action; but it will easily be understood that the leftists are the most infuriated by the matter: it is precisely in 'their public,' among the best individuals and groups that they would like to capture, that they meet again their old enemy, proletarian autonomy, at its first stage of affirmation. And they involuntarily render us this tribute of denouncing it as being *under our influence*." (*The Real Split in the International*.) The young Bakunin, a republican liberal, on being accused by his superiors of being "socialist," wrote for the first time to a socialist group requesting information on what that frightful doctrine might be. In the same way many of the more honest rank and file radicals are finding to their surprise that they are "situationist inspired" or that "situationist tendencies" have somehow infiltrated their ranks, their practice and their attempts to understand and improve it. Precisely as they begin to escape the petrification of one or another old leftist dogma with a purely student base, they will find that they are "petit-bourgeois intellectuals"; precisely as they begin to confront the real proletarianized world, the new tasks in all their concreteness and complexity, they will be called "utopians," "dreamers" who aren't dealing with the "needs of the people"; precisely as they begin to speak the truth, they will be accused of adopting "disruptive" or "situationist tactics." "Our enemies . . . do not even manage to understand that it is more often than not *by their blundering mediation* that these revolutionary elements whom they denounce and hunt down have themselves been able to learn that they were 'situationists'; and that in short this is how the epoch names *what they are*" (*Ibid.*).

But the falsifications of the avowed enemies of the S.I. are seen through more easily than the confusions disseminated by its self-proclaimed *partisans*. Many people's first exposure to explicitly "situationist ideas" comes by way of some pitiful excuse for a "scandal" produced by impatient pro-situationists who hardly have the vaguest idea of what they're doing. They take up and fetishize a formal element of situationist activity (detournement, "arrogance") without any content, or sloppily grab the first opportunity to propagate its fantasized content in exchange for abandoning its rigor and clarity. These excited appreciators of the S.I. — such as those who put out the Bay Area "End of Prehistory" radio programs August 1975, advertising themselves as "those who give free play to their most delirious fantasies" — never see the critical, experimental *method* of the S.I. but only certain half-baked programatic utopian conclusions. They hold their much flaunted anti-morality up against the most retrograde straw dogs (Christianity, militantism, etc.), without which contrast they would be nothing. They are only battening off a temporary monopoly of a few ill-digested notions from the S.I. The truth and coherence of situationist theory is such that even in distorted form it can arouse a certain interest. It is thus that the pro-situs can jump in to fill the void, to temporarily be the big fish in the theoretically small pond.

273

As yet, no publisher has taken up my proposal to translate the situationist books (which was mailed to some twenty publishing houses). Some more S.I. texts have since appeared in English, however. A pirate edition of the complete *Treatise*, under the title *The Revolution of Everyday Life*, is available from Paul Sieveking (c/o Box LBD, 197 Kings Cross Road, London W.C.1) or through Isaac Cronin or Chris Shutes (price: $5), and an authorized version of Van-eigem's book, published by Free Life Editions (41 Union Square West, NYC 10003), is due out sometime this year.

PROPOSAL

Ken Knabb will translate any or all of the situationist books when he can find a suitable publisher.

Conditions:

- Knabb must have final approval of the translation.

- If there is to be any annotation or commentary, he will provide it.

- In the case of an anthology of articles from the S.I. journal, he will make the selection. With this possible exception, the American editions must be un-abridged and follow the basic format of the French originals.

- All matters of the form and content of the texts must be subject to the final approval of their authors, with whom, if they so wish, Knabb is prepared to collaborate.

BUREAU OF PUBLIC SECRETS
P.O. Box 1044
Berkeley, California 94704

January 1975

An anthology of S.I. texts, *Leaving the 20th Century*, appeared early in 1975, edited by Christopher Gray (Free Fall Publications, Box 13, 197 Kings Cross Road, London W.C.1 — price: $3). The edition is sometimes sloppy (paragraphs are missing, articles are wrongly attributed, etc.), the selection is unrepresentative (not a single piece from the many where the S.I. explains its concrete activities, clarifies misunderstandings, etc.) and Gray's lengthy commentaries are not too

different from what one might expect to find in, say, *Ramparts* or *Rolling Stone*. That Gray was once briefly and for not much reason a member of the S.I. changes nothing: scarcely a single ex-member of the S.I. has shown himself capable of genuinely continuing the situationist project; if a few of them were once able to make some contributions, they have for the most part fallen back into nullity or, as in the case of Gray, worse.

Gray sees the S.I. in purely spectacular terms. He can't stop mentioning the journal's shiny metallic covers and exciting illustrations; an early S.I. article "seems one of the most brilliant single pieces of writing produced since the heyday of modern art"; the actual activities of the S.I. — even at its earliest period always characterized by their calculatedness — are ignored by him in favor of miscellaneous scandal-magazine type anecdotes, or treated as "stunts" pulled off by drunken fraternity boys. He never sees in the S.I. a serious theoretical effort, but only what he himself is capable of: a crude, impulsive *tantrum* against the society. Seeing the S.I. as a "lunatic fringe group," he can thus see the Motherfuckers as going it one better on such a terrain, or in the terrorist Angry Brigade, "destroying themselves at the same time as they took the critique of the spectacle to its most blood-curdling spectacular extreme," something resembling the Enragés.

The student insurgence of the sixties, precisely because it came from a sector enjoying certain margins of freedom not to be found in the factories, was able to carry certain enthusiasms and fantasies of easy "total revolution" more difficult to maintain among the workers, whose *different types of struggles* have for several years overshadowed their student harbingers. Gray is among those who identified with the superficial aspects of the earlier phase and who, now that these earlier aspects have been discredited and superceded or are simply no longer reported in the mass media *because they're now so commonplace*, bewail the absence of what once was and transfer their own impotence onto the movement they don't understand: "German and English universities occupied . . . Hippie ghettoes directly clashing with the police state . . . the sudden exhilarating sense of how many people felt the same way . . . the new world coming into focus. . . . Today — nothing. The Utopian image has faded from the streets. . . . Yet there were thousands and thousands of people there. What has happened to us all?" If we except the single culminating year 1968, there are in fact more, and more profound, revolts today than in the sixties; it is just that they are not the kind that welcome self-indulgent intellectual *speculators* like Gray — not even those who try to make up for it by patronizing the masses or by giving a preeminence to "the emotions and the body."

To be sure, the end of the sixties also marks the recuperation of a certain number of the earlier tentatives; but the point is then to precise in *what ways* this recuperation has taken place, due to *what mistakes* in the revolutionary movement. Gray, for his part, in a space that would almost suffice to reprint "Theses on the S.I. and Its Time," does not come up with a single useful observation on those "vital issues of organization and activity" regarding which he berates Debord and Sanguinetti for their silence. Like so many other pro-situs Gray wanted the S.I. to be God and ends up whining because it didn't hand him revolution on a silver platter, complete with immediate individual therapy. "After so many, many pages, let's try and be honest, just for a moment. . . . Everyone's life is a switch between changing oneself and changing the world. Surely they must somehow be the same thing and a dynamic balance is possible. I think the S.I. had this for a while, and later they lost it. I want to find it again. . . . It could connect, could come together." Almost sounds like a James Taylor record.

But the epoch is also producing those who will understand and supersede the S.I. And when the intrinsic conditions are fulfilled, the English-speaking proletariat will not miss its rendezvous with this "Gallic cock."

Letter from Afar

. . . But there are not only "personal" obstacles, there are also those linked to the conditions of the *present moment* of this epoch; conditions that inevitably determine our activity, expressing themselves for us in discouragement, hesitations, perplexity. In a very unwarranted but undeniable manner, we are so far only a *very small minority* to have on our hands *almost all the responsibility*, not, to be sure, for the situationist project itself, for which many people today feel more or less confusedly concerned, but for its *theoretical politics*, neglected by everyone else or envisioned according to the point of view of classical revolutionary ideologies.

. . . In general, most (revolutionaries) still understand too poorly what should be done and is worth doing, and how to do it. Most of the time we would be more interested in and capable of doing *this*, but it is rather *that* — requiring more abstract effort — which is going to seem more urgent and strategic to accomplish. For example, you have been able to hoist yourself into the avant-garde of the global struggle for a theoretico-practice, but it is in a zone of the world

where the first banalities — and above all how to make good use of them — are still almost unknown. You find yourself thus confronted with this contradiction: in order to make yourself understood and advance your project, you still have to continue to *first* get across the fundamental banalities up to an *irreversible threshold* (to be determined according to the scope and usages of the U.S.) before being able to speak exclusively at the better level you can and want to. One of the difficulties in this task is that you can't go about it as if you were still in the Europe of 1960-67 (as do Point-Blank and Diversion in different ways), but neither can you go about it as if you spoke simply in the Europe of 1974. You have to accomplish an enormous work of *classical propaganda* in addition to your more *up-to-date* tasks; but to do all this it is unthinkable to do it in two different manners (for example: a rudimentary language for the masses and a more refined one for more advanced revolutionaries); you therefore have to find the *style* of expression and action that effectively reconciles these two poles of your practice.

. . . There are a good *thirty* essential books lacking today, that is to say some thirty fundamental themes that up to the present have been developed nowhere. And there are at least that many hypotheses worth being seriously explored. To note only the latter, there are a dozen quite judicious perspectives and projects to be found in the S.I.'s Orientation Debate, and which have had no follow-up. (If no one does anything about them, I'll enjoy enumerating them publicly someday.) All these pages for theory that remain blank — that's the scandal of revolutionaries' "activity" to which I refer in *Misery of Theory*. . . .

Up till now, I have principally been able to develop — for myself and a little publicly — a sort of *theory of theory*. . . . Nothing is formally, much less definitively, fixed; I see there only a sort of platform enabling us to confront the uncertainty of our enterprise and to limit as accurately as possible the arbitrary element there is in each of our choices. . . .

(Later on, on the preliminary base of these developments, we will be able to apply ourselves to what is called a *strategy of agitations*; but if a politics of agitation would be impossible or ridiculous if we wanted to organize it from the point where we are now, nevertheless even a minimum public presence to our present activity already constitutes in itself an *agitation*.)

As is often lost sight of, the critique *of daily life* is not solely a critique of what the present social organization sets up positively or traces in negative in the daily life of individuals; it is also the critique of everything else that assures the functioning of this society, to which the daily life of individuals can't begin to accede short of a revolution. It is forgotten, for example, that if "Marx's thought is really a critique of daily life," in order to hold to such an affirmation it is completely irrelevant to know the relative richness or poorness of the life of the individual Marx. The question of its "richness" is sufficiently resolved in the fact that he was able to do what he did. Marx's thought is already a "critique of daily life" by the simple fact that he was able to *speak* of class society in an anti-ideological manner, in breaking with the methods and representations by which this society presents itself. I should say that I find myself in complete theoretical and practical opposition to that entire "situationist" current which holds as revolutionary *only* what brings an immediate "enrichment" to *its* daily life and which, setting out from this viewpoint, obviously never "enriches" anything. . . .

I envisage putting out a sort of periodic *Remarks*, in order to be able to settle all my accounts in one place; in order to avoid the scattered precisions (*mises au point*), a pain in the ass to realize and less effective because more often than not they are only known of *separately* by the people directly concerned, and not as composing part of the ensemble of a practice and of a precise strategy. . . .

Concerning the publication in Paris of the Orientation Debate:
It is desirable that the heritage of the S.I. — and by this mediation the heritage of the ensemble of revolutionary theory and of the old worker movement — belong more and more to the entire epoch; it is above all desirable that it find there more rapidly more *competent* inheritors; and we ourselves rarely know *where* such inheritors are. The publication of the *Débat* has the advantage of putting these eventual inheritors before the *raw truth* of an organization and no longer only before the interpretation of this truth (however correct that interpretation may be) in carefully weighed formulas, a reading of which, without the concrete evidence of the *Débat*, is inevitably abstract and exterior (*La véritable scission*).

With the *Débat* the reader finds himself now concretely confronted with the hesitations, the weaknesses, the questions left without response; as well as, to be sure, with qualities and perspectives utilizable for his own action. . . . This publication contributes toward reabsorbing the myth of the S.I., or of its leftovers, *back into concrete practical questions*. . . .

An objection that will inevitably be made . . . is that in putting it out we are, precisely because of

the glorious names attached to these texts, fostering a still more stupid use of them. Obviously we can't be unaware of the imbecilic use that will be made of them; but in voluntarily nourishing this imbecilic use we thus dialectically create the possibility of a better use, that is to say that we are going to force certain people to impose a better use of these texts to counter the stupid one. . . .

In publicly compromising this *aspect* of the truth of the S.I., we have compromised the "public" a little more with the truth of the S.I.

The choice of the title "Ex-Internationale . . .", which was adopted on my proposal, partakes of my theoretical tactic — developed in *Misery of Theory* — to consider the S.I. and its theoretico-practice *in the past*. It is good that, losing all encouraging external reference, each revolutionary feel alone before his task, that is, that he feel that he has to take responsibilities alone, without even the comfort of a label; which is the first step toward autonomy and the possibility of revolutionary associations *without militants*. In doing this, I am really only continuing what Debord began in smashing the S.I.; if Debord was in a good position to smash the S.I. from the inside against its unworthy members, he was in return in a rather poor position to destroy the myth of the S.I. at the exterior without thereby transfering the drawbacks of that myth onto his own person. As has already been noted by various revolutionaries, the myth of the S.I. could only be definitively smashed *from outside*.

In losing the S.I. as reference, this revolutionary epoch now finds itself alone with itself (conclusion of the theses on the S.I. and its time). . . .

Regarding eventual contacts with other revolutionaries, in order to limit the risks of engaging in false dialogues and of associating myself in spectacular political relations; in order not to feed the delirium of spectators of things revolutionary; in order to avoid wasting time; in order to avoid direct or indirect contact with personal enemies, I am refusing from now on to meet or correspond with anyone who has not already *openly implicated* himself in an activity. For me, it is no longer a matter of *finding out* if interlocutors are sincere or dishonest, courageous or cowardly, intelligent or not, liberated enough for our taste, what they think of themselves, of me, or what they think, period; but of judging, before even having to verify all that, *up to what point of practico-theoretical experimentation they have known how to conduct their own life*, that is to say up to what point they are *implicated in the revolution* as I am. . . .

(Daniel Denevert to Ken Knabb, February 1974)

Remarks on 'Remarks'

The responses to my pamphlet *Remarks on Contradiction and Its Failure* (March 1973) were invested with clarity, well expressing the complacency, the impotence, the lack of imagination, the stubborn clinging to illusions — in a word, the *ostrichism* — of the milieu I criticized therein.

A Point-Blank emissary in Paris announced that I was an imbecile, an asshole and "Point-Blank's number one enemy," and that if he ever ran into me he would smash my face. Others, less directly criticized, were nonetheless disconcerted that I had the nerve (they would say the stupidity) to criticize my own mistakes. Faced with an act so inconsistent with prevalent situationist bravado, they could only see there some weird sort of exhibitionistic masochism. The British group Piranha came up with the model of this genre: "So Knabb himself announces in his 'Remarks' that he is still a pro-situ! What a futile exercise! He seems determined to drown in his own shit." The members of Piranha of course, have no pro-situ taint. Oh, maybe they did a few years ago, but after reading *Real Split* they decided that they didn't anymore; or at least if they had any lingering doubts, they certainly weren't going to "announce" them. This element of *Remarks* was in fact precisely calculated to undermine this sort of complacency, particularly among the naive Americans previously more inclined to dismiss the whole business as some bizarre French affair, but now puzzling anxiously over critiques of the pro-situ to figure out just what this is all about and whether by chance it should happen to have something to do with them. They know that to be a pro-situ is a "bad thing" and so they are prepared to incorporate it into the ranks of their ideological no-nos — along with "ideology" for example. But first they must find out what it means! Gone, alas, are the days when all you had to do to become a situationist was to declare yourself one.

Some thought that what I wrote was perhaps true, but wondered why I would circulate a pamphlet on such a "specialized subject" to so many people. The blank incomprehension with which *Remarks* would mainly be received was not lost on me as I mailed it out to Contradiction's entire mailing list. But the critical, non-narrative form of the text that makes it relatively inaccessible to the passive makes it correspondingly more useful to those confronting similar problems in their own practice. *Remarks* and others of its genre that have begun to appear will be read more as the activities they discuss become less "specialized."

Others, in contrast, found many of the points discussed in *Remarks* trivial or banal. Well, many a promising project has smashed up on the ignorance of such trivialities. I know of no radical group, including the S.I., that has not made almost every mistake noted apropos of Contradiction (assuming the group is radical enough to even confront problems at this level).

The criticism of a text for its having "left out" something — except in the cases where this effectively constitutes a "lie by omission" — is the indication par excellence of the failure to grasp the process of the *negative*. Thus *Remarks* has been criticized for not presenting a balanced overall perspective on the movement; but that was not its purpose. It was primarily a critique, a correction of Contradiction's *orientation* toward the movement (and first of all of its very notion of such a unified "movement"), of the way we went about a certain task. Others worried that it wasn't padded with a bunch of stuff about "history," "the proletariat," etc.

But if some found it not situationist enough, others found it too much so. A certain sector of old soldiers (including some ex-members of Contradiction), shell-shocked from the exigencies of situationist practice, wants to repress the whole traumatic affair. This tendency, usually to be found rummaging around in the less taxing world of ultra-leftism, is disturbed that while I lay into things situationist, I don't throw out the method with the ideology. Just as some people see revolution as an unfortunate, accidental disturbance of an otherwise well-running society by "outside agitators," these people see in polemical debates and splits an unfortunate, accidental disturbance of an otherwise nicely progressing revolutionary movement.

Others want to invoke "the epoch" as the final explanation for the pure and simple failure of all the situationist groups. If they manifested themselves publicly in the past, they now denounce this past (including whatever meritorious elements there may have been) *in toto*; while others who in that period didn't manifest themselves at all now emerge, records spotless because blank, to spit contemptuously on all the rest. This is the key to the rage against my "dirty-judaical" activity. How dare I confront this experience! How dare I search out the points of *choice*. "What's the point of stating the failures of the past period?" says one, as if once one has noted one important error, all related moments in that necessarily very mixed and confused terrain which is that of present revolutionary experimentation can be dismissed as equally wrong or worthless. A diminishing force of cognition marks those who fail to concretely confront their failures. Even if still capable of partially perceptive formulations, their stubborn maintenance of a blind spot or an undialectical position inelutably cripples any subsequent theoretical effort.

Following the appearance of *Remarks* and the *Reich: How to Use* translation, certain people have naively fantasized me conducting "character-smashing sessions." But if the composition of *Remarks* was aided by a simultaneous personal experimentation, I have in many places explicitly refused to present such individual breakthroughs as being in themselves revolutionary. (In its December 1974 reprinting, I pointed out the one phrase in *Remarks* susceptible to being misconstrued in this way.) There's only one real character-smashing session: revolution. *Remarks* was an attempt not to come to terms with myself psychologically, but to seize a moment of history and *reverse it*.

Some Clarifications

Certain people have wondered why I and others take the risk of conducting our activity so openly, under our own names. We obviously recognize the appropriateness of clandestinity in the stalinist and fascist countries, or elsewhere to the extent that one's activities involve a significant element of illegality. But the particular theoretico-practical tasks we set ourselves — while benefiting considerably from the public *continuity* that enables the correction of misunderstandings or falsifications, the exposure of the coherent context of our activity, of concrete applications, etc. — entail a relatively small risk. While we are little known we will be ignored as harmless (the spectacle is to a large extent a victim of its own image of its opposition); to the extent that some of us become better known — which will simply be an incidental effect of the advance of the revolution — our suppression would also be known and would merely draw more attention to our theses without at all stopping their work. If some of our theses remain to an extent "occult" it is because of their intrinsic nature — rendered temporarily inaccessible to many by socially enforced ignorance — not because they are held secret by us in preparation for a coup d'état. In contrast to the leaders of a terrorist or neo-bolshevik group, we are not at all indispensable to "our" movement. The State can't control the revolution through anything it would do to us or get us to do, because the revolution is right where we want it: out of our control.

* * *

The situationists' breaks and exclusions have often been sarcastically identified with stalinist purges. In fact the two cases could hardly be more dissimilar. In the stalinist bureaucracies the Party disposes of all social life, whereas revolutionaries — as with the proletariat in general — do not even dispose fully of their own lives. Thus, to be purged from the Party is to be deprived of participation (however narrow it might be) in the ruling machine and in the material advantages such a position brings with it (not to mention the possibility of prison, torture, execution, exile, etc.); whereas to be excluded from a revolutionary group is to be deprived of nothing except perhaps a bit of stupid prestige. In the West, the same confusionist "freedom of expression" that makes open polarizations possible makes them necessary. There is no "right" to participate in an activity that conveys no privileges. The question of possible "injustices" or contested decisions resolves itself very simply: one who has something to say will make his presence felt beyond all attempts to ignore or denigrate him. It is obvious that a rebuffed or excluded individual who isn't able to engage in an autonomous activity thereby confirms the appropriateness of his separation from a collective activity supposedly arising from autonomous participants. Not to mention those whose ulterior activity takes a different *direction*.

* * *

The reader will not find the totality in this journal, but simply a certain number of formulations whose relation to the totality is calculated. Those who present everything each time assume a reader who is ignorant of everything else and incapable or undesirous of exploring more for himself, and this spectacular tactic is the best means of making sure that he stays that way. Although I and some others have devoted a particular attention to examining the *process* of modern revolutionary activity — and first of all have drawn attention to the very importance of this process, so scandalously neglected by everyone else — an element of the "narrowness" for which I have been reproached is merely the result of my beginning from where I find myself. The particular topics dealt with here are somewhat arbitrary and don't necessarily imply any lack of importance to those I haven't dealt with. Nothing is outside our project; but many truths are not worth saying because it wouldn't make any difference if they weren't true. "I rarely make mistakes, having never concealed that I have nothing to say on the numerous subjects in which I am ignorant, and habitually keeping in mind several contradictory hypotheses on the possible development of events where I don't yet discern the qualitative leap." (Guy Debord, in the "Orientation Debate.")

Papal Bull

In a pamphlet mainly directed against Daniel Denevert (see "Un Anti-Denevert" in the *Chronique*), Point-Blank mentions me as a would-be "pope of a sub-situ milieu." "Denevert's latest ally, Ken Knabb, has built a career on his organizational failure and on his commercial association with the statistician of the S.I., Jean-Pierre Voyer." Among popes, usually noted rather for their infallibility and organizational cunning, I am undoubtedly the first to have built a career on the exposure of my "organizational failure." This sort of spiteful paranoia can only see in any activity that contradicts its own the result of opportunistic, behind-the-scenes deals and intrigues.*

Jean-Pierre Voyer had in fact nothing to do, least of all economically, with the American publication of his pamphlet *Reich: How to Use*, which was financed by two friends and me, which "commercial association" has netted us a loss of about $200. (All the other publications I've been involved in have also been losses, with one exception: a print-shop worker liked Vaneigem's *Treatise* so well that he printed Contradiction's now out-of-print edition of Part I at less than cost.) My actual relation with Voyer hardly bears out Point-Blank's attempt to characterize me as one of his "followers." Shortly before the completion of my translation of his text, I first wrote to him regarding some questions about it. I published *Reich: How to Use* in June 1973, along with a comic poster announcing it, and reprinted extracts of one of his letters under the title "Discretion Is the Better Part of Value." Voyer proved, however, when I met him that fall, quite oblivious to the possible development or concrete application of many of his earlier theses, and I told him that his megalomaniac disengagement as a "pure theorist" from the real movement precluded any substantive relation between us. Voyer's "Encyclopedia" has since been published under the title *Introduction à la Science de la Publicité* (Champ Libre, 1975), which, although it contains incidentally several partially useful points, is scarred by a fetishism of its central concept and of Hegel, whose philosophy is not really detourned because not sufficiently devalorized.

---

* In the pamphlet *At Dusk: the Situationist Movement in Historical Perspective* — which appeared just before this journal was going to press — two ex-members of the now dissolved Point-Blank devote a large section to a critique of "the Knabbists." Their polemic against us maintains their old tradition of specious, infantile critiques, including the attribution to us of numerous positions and motives we have never expressed or had.

As for Daniel Denevert, I have maintained a particularly close correspondence and collaboration with him over the last two years, resulting in a better geographical coordination of our activities and above all a valuable exchange of ideas and experiences. But my relations with him and the other members of the C.R.Q.S. have never been formalized and are conducted in the framework described in the *Notice concerning the Reigning Society and Those Who Contest It*, put out in November 1974 by my Bay Area comrades and me. Although I have on occasion used the editorial 'we', the B.P.S. has always consisted only of me. If a certain degree of accord is manifested between some others and me, it stems not from fiat but from reality. The majority of the publications put out by the various *Notice* signers over the last three years, for example, have been completed before being shown to the others; and I did not even know of several of the projects most strikingly confirmative of my work until after they were published.

It is obviously not influence — which may be simply the influence of the truth or of an exemplary activity — that makes a hierarch, but its being exerted to reinforce its unilaterality or the image of its absence. It is a strange "pope" who continually throws people onto their own responsibility. In the final analysis, whatever one may say about the merit of one or another demystifying or educative tactic, it is the "underdog" who must take the principal initiative in suppressing his hierarchical dependence. Those who put the onus on the "leaders" only want better ones. Our movement does not depend on the good fortune of the cleverly self-negating leaders of leninist and anarchist mythology; people have to use their heads and *demystify themselves* of notions of the godlike qualities of revolutionary theorists, or of the converse mystification of considering them as "just" theorists who "don't do anything" but "only" write. Those who accuse us of "arrogance" and "manipulation" haven't thought about what they're saying; "turning people off with arrogance" is the last thing the manipulators ever do. It is invariably those people who tell us that *they* can understand us but that the masses aren't ready yet who call *us* "elitists." We treat others as if they were autonomous — just in case they are, and to make sure in any case that they are at least so from us.

First Things First

Various individuals, wishing to have the best of both worlds, approach us, letting us know *privately* how they agree with us and of the critiques they have of the various dubious milieus from which they come. It is invariably these people — the most worthless — who have the strange idea that they are the most valuable, that we should feel grateful for their *interest* because, after all, "If you can't talk to us, who *can* you talk to?" They suppose that they can find an interesting encounter, or even a place here, without rocking their own boat. Having compromised themselves in nothing, they are free, once, as is usual, they are rebuffed, to return none the worse to their previous milieu, where they can blather on about their "relation" with the situationists while maintaining an image of autonomy: we weren't able to "convince" them to "join" us, etc. An ex-member of the Venceremos Brigade (peace corps to Russia's neo-colony in the Caribbean), for example, approached Contradiction and explained to me how they had agreed to suppress various embarrassing details of life in Cuba in their glowing reports on it. Yet so far as I know he never expressed these interesting revelations publicly, apparently being too busy searching for some radical project to do.

The Bureau therefore automatically rejects anyone who approaches it without openly defending the theses he claims to agree with or without having settled accounts with his own situation — in the case of the more compromised milieus, denouncing and taking leave of them with the *maximum of noise and clarity*.

Easily Foreseeable Refusals

In addition to the routine rebuffing of diverse would-be dialoguers, from People's Churches and crypto-maoists to a rather wide range of media-freak nihilists, the following are among the concrete proposals I have refused with all the rudeness they merited:
- to "establish contact" with "the Italian Reichian organization";
- to contribute material for publication in the magazine *Guerrilla Art*;
- to provide information on the Bureau for a pro-fessional writer doing an article on "the current neo-Reichian movement" for the magazine *Human Behavior*.

The Bureau in Japan

In March 1974 Tommy Haruki addressed a letter to various anarchist or libertarian groups around the world, proposing to introduce them to comrades in Japan by way of the journal of CIRA-NIPPON ("Center of International Research of Anarchism") and adding, "Your expression of today's problems on anarchism would be very much desired also." I received a copy, to which I responded, in part, as follows.

... We think that anarchism remains an *abstract* opponent of the system because of its failure to seriously attempt to comprehend modern society or to develop a coherent revolutionary theory. For the most part, all that anarchists possess is a pathetic faith in the label "Anarchy." They are allergic to rigor; most of them make a virtue of parading their confusion and their inability to accomplish the smallest practical task. They justify the most stupid failures to take concrete *sanctions* against enemies, or to effect *decisions* in order to clarify and advance their own practice (e.g., to rebuff passive followers and spectators) by appealing to an abstract "anti-authoritarianism." So they end up with nothing but their frustrated good intentions.

I enclose a copy of some theses relative to anarchism from Guy Debord's book *The Society of the Spectacle* . . . which you may find useful.

We certainly agree with you that "what we need here and now is not an anthology of millenarian doctrines or revolutionary works in the past" and that "an interchange of today's information, inter-criticism, interaction of today's experiences" is essential; not with an eclectic aim of bringing together a mass of "ideologies," but as a step to precision, to *lucidity*, to the development of a more and more *coherent* theoretico-practice in the new revolutionary movement.

In this context, the present dialogue initiated by the "Center of International Research of Anarchism" is extremely minimal. Ultimately, for example, it would be of more interest to us to be in contact with *one* Japanese comrade who was in conscious practical accord with the Bureau's activities than with a hundred "libertarians" with whom all we had in common were a few vague sympathies. But it is natural that the first *internationalist* efforts of the new movement will begin from relatively confused bases, and necessarily pass through some rather banal mediations. . . .

Haruki saw to it that the Debord theses and most of my letter were published in the CIRA journal (*Anarchism* 4, August 1974, translated by H. Komizo), observing that the critiques applied perfectly to the Japanese anarchist milieu: "In this sense, an appearance of your criticism in their report . . . will be some bitter pill for them and all other libertarians of their ilk."

Haruki's address is: Manno Public Apartment No. 147, 2999 Manno-Hara-Shinden, Fujino-miya, Shizuoka, Japan.

「ビューロー・オブ・パブリック・シークレット」は、アナキストではなく情況主義者のグループであることを明らかにしておく。"過去の諸革命"は、さまざまな国家社会主義諸潮流の破壊的な結果を証明してみせたが、同時にアナキズムの無力性をも証明したと我々は考える。我々は、国家との如何なる妥協にも、華々しき商品制度と闘う革命的グループ内の位階制、またそれを隠

" BUREAU OF PUBLIC SECRETS "

KEN KNABB

日本の革命的アナキスト同志へ

ケン・ノブ

小溝　光・訳

Bureau News

Two of my pamphlets were published by the C.R.Q.S. in 1974, *Remarques sur le groupe Contradiction et son échec*, translated by Daniel Denevert (April), and *Double-Réflexion*, translated by Joël Cornuault (November), both with my collaboration. The *Chronique des Secrets Publics* reprinted an extract of a letter from me to Cornuault, "Remarques sur le style de Double-Reflection." On our side, Robert Cooperstein, Dan Hammer and I published in September 1974 a translation of Denevert's *Theory of Misery, Misery of Theory*. In the same pamphlet we also included the *Declaration concerning the C.R.Q.S.* and a section from Denevert's earlier pamphlet, *For the Intelligence of Some Aspects of the Moment*.

*

In November 1974 *Double-Reflection* was reprinted in England by Spontaneous Combustion (Box LBD, 197 Kings Cross Road, London W.C.1).

*

Extracts of a letter of mine of October 1973 to Jean-Pierre Voyer and others have been reprinted in Isaac Cronin's and Chris Shutes's recent journal, *Implications*.

*

Most of the B.P.S. publications — including the present journal — have been published in editions of 2000 copies.

*

Publications of the B.P.S. are on file at:
- Berkeley Public Library ("Boss Files," Reference Room), Shattuck and Kittredge, Berkeley.
- Tamiment Library, Bobst Library Building, 70 Washington Square South, New York City.
- "The Public Library," 197 Kings Cross Road, London.
- International Institute of Social History, Herengracht 262-266, Amsterdam.
The Bureau collection also includes — as its "Prehistory" — most of the publications of the C.E.M., 1044 and Contradiction. I have also distributed separately a number of copies of my *Introduction to the "Prehistory" Section of the Bureau Collection* (July 1973).

*

Addresses of 'Notice' comrades:
Tita Carrión, Robert Cooperstein: P.O. Box 950, Berkeley, CA 94701
Isaac Cronin, Dan Hammer: P.O. Box 14221, San Francisco, CA 94114
Gina Rosenberg, Chris Shutes: P.O. Box 4502, Berkeley, CA 94704

New address of the C.R.Q.S.:
Centre de Recherche sur la Question Sociale, B.P. 218, 75865 Paris CEDEX 18

AFFECTIVE DETOURNEMENT:
A CASE STUDY

In *Double-Reflection* (May 1974) I have sketched out the nature and limits of affective detournement. The present text is an examination of a period of experimentation (January-March 1973) during which many of the points in that pamphlet were first discovered or developed.

In the wake of the crises and breaking up of Contradiction, the inachievements "came home to roost." The situationist project, once I stopped participating in it, turned into a wistful infatuation which I hugged to myself like people cling to the memory of a lost love. In modern society the religious consolation tends to take the form of unofficial personal myths that hover half consciously as automatic neutralizers of the daily misery. My past radical activity, by being reduced to a memory, could only be worshipped. And so it joined the other elements of my own particular little compensatory world — music, books, etc. — as something whose power was undeniable since I was powerless. I had my own little fantasy of escape: If I could just hustle up enough money I would go to Paris; meanwhile my real everyday life became more and more reified, reduced to a narrower and narrower pattern centering around the needs of my economic and psycho-aesthetic survival.

The return to the Bay Area in December 1972 of some friends who had been in Paris helped to expose this misery. Even if these people were themselves far from a practical resolution, they were able to spark a new effort from me — one from a more or less vaneigemist perspective by zeroing in on the specific reification and lack of adventure in my life, the others, ex-comrades of Contradiction, by bringing back to consciousness the excitement of our old activities.

My first tentatives were inevitably diffuse and groping. But in all this I began from an understanding that any "personal" liberation was condemned to failure without ties to historical practice. Ideologically, at least, I had never abandoned my situationist perspectives. Thus, when I say that I experimented with such and such a "therapeutic" tactic, it should be understood that the particular tactics in themselves are of less significance than the context in which I aimed at detourning them.

I began to confront different concrete circumstances in rapid succession. It was generally the case that each concrete effort led to another one. Often the connection between them will seem obscure, but in fact the relation is quite direct and often even predictable, since in reality it is not a matter here of a series of accidental "problems" but of a series of interconnected and mutually reinforcing expressions of repression, of commodity fetishism.

I conducted an examination of my personal "psychogeography" — mapping out for example the repetitions in my daily movements in the city or within my own home — taking a bit out of context the early situationist experiments, on the principle that you discover how the society functions by learning how it functions against you. I started introducing arbitrary elements into my behavior, not with the passive surrealist notion of identifying the unpredictable with the marvelous, but in order to shake myself up — things like taking a walk to some place I would usually avoid, perhaps even because it was so banal.

I looked over Voyer's *Reich: mode d'emploi*, which I had read once a year before without thinking much of (owing to the fact that I was already going downhill). There was already an English translation of it but since it was such a sloppy one I decided to retranslate and publish it myself. However I was still searching for an "original" theoretical project through which I could pick up again the best strands of my old radical activity.

One legacy from the previous period was a real fetishism of books. From the regard for books as providing the one dependable consolation in a miserable life it was but a step to cling to and identify with the very mass of books themselves (complete sets of favorite authors, etc.) as providing a sort of objective character armor, a commodity bulwark against madness or more extreme pain. In themselves the books were just "goods," objects whose value depended on how I used them. But to me they were more than that; in the upside-down reality of my life they were magical, they had a life of their own. One evening, sitting around in my room depressed, I started writing down what my concrete choices were, which led to writing down what was in my way.

... I must observe the following with more attention: As I make resolves to change something about my life, to fight some rigidification, reification, commodification, that first resolve has a strong tendency to take a commodified *form*. For example, the intention to improve my house devolves into a list of *things* which I need to get. A concern over my sexuality devolves into — a new reading list (Reich, Stendhal, etc.). I have virtually played, over the last few weeks, with choosing the books and records to sell — an anti-commodity effort that turned into simply a different list in my head. This last gives me an idea. I will this evening do the same thing, but with so much more ruthlessness as to maybe change that situation qualitatively. (To be continued.)

Enough. Nearly two hundred miserable, piece of shit books later. It began to get a bit boring. But it is significant how, in a crude, primitive sort of way, I've come to identify my alienation with some of its most immediate *signs* (like the workers who destroyed cars, streetlights, etc., in France in 1961). That is, when exceptions are allowed for, I presently have an actually irrational impulse against my books, records, and house, as if they were enemies of mine. I have actually arrived at a point, as elementary as it might be with other people, where I would have very little problem (a positive enjoyment rather) in getting rid of it all if there were any particular reason to.

It's really funny. I get up and change the record. . . . I come back in here to continue this, and I can hardly stop thinking of books to get rid of. It's practically a compulsion, though a funny — not serious — one. It's almost, like I sort of mentioned above, that this is, for this particular banality, a first, predictable, necessary stage (a kind of overreaction against) in turning around to fight an alienation, a rigidity. Fuck these things! I actually feel like burning some of them! . . .

(Now, just to continue the path to zaniness, I follow Charlie Parker with Indonesian music. . . . It's very volatile! Look out!) Ah, this music is really crazy! Now, here is a little resolve: I resolve to abolish the list of books and records that I keep, except insofar as it is actually a question (fantastically esquisite wild music!) of remembering something I couldn't otherwise remember. This is a slightly inconvenient, uneconomic measure, but it's not so important. On the other hand, it is fun and necessary to break some of these little habits that not only reflect but also reinforce the commodification of my daily life. Here's another: the abolition of my calendar. If there's something really important that I might forget I can write a notice to myself. But for all the routine stuff, forget it, and if I forget it, tough shit!

Now somewhere in the above paragraph, dear reader, I changed to "Boogey Woogey Rarities" (the very name is a bit fantastic!). Now, I mention this because I feel better with myself than I have in a long time, and this reflects in a sort of companionship I am able to have with this music (particularly this kind of music). Maybe it's like the ideological superstructure or reflex corresponding to the real change at the base! Listen, reader (and I'm not being abstract here; I know the relatively few people that even might ever see this), my zaniness here is my greatest weapon. I enjoy now the thought that you will be laughing at (and hopefully with) me, but I also enjoy even more the thought that some of this will appear so ridiculous that you'll practically be made uncomfortable by it. I hope it rocks your wig! I know it does mine!
(20 January 1973)

I sold most of the books, but just for good measure, to prevent myself from living this experience merely as an intelligent business transaction, I took a few of them to a public park and burned them. I set up a little sign by the fire on which I wrote "Death to the commodity that dominates us!" or something like that, and walked away grinning.

I began to evaluate my relations with people — what I had to do with them, with what limitations, overdue critiques, etc. In the case of one — she happened to be the girl friend of another ex-Contradiction member — I concluded that she was really too much bullshit. Even though my relation with her was rather minimal, it had gone on a long time and had ramifications with some of my other friends. Rather than continue the fakery or merely try to avoid her, I wrote her a letter and sent copies to our common friends.

I should do you the justice of expressing my criticism to you, and my consequent decision to not see you, since I have already done so . . . to other people.

In all the time I have known you, I can hardly remember a moment when you expressed yourself, presented yourself to another, as a real person, as a subjectivity. I have almost never detected any *fundamental* (petty truths about unimportant, *external* particulars are obviously another matter) sincerity in your relations with other people. *You are always playing roles*. It's that simple. I could pick out any random conversation, for example, and remember embarrassing moments when you happened to say the "wrong thing" — not wrong because you were honestly expressing a mistaken opinion, but because you had misjudged what the "correct," sociable, or impressive thing to say might be.

My part, or that of others, in tolerating or contributing to these stupid, meaningless, non-superseding situations and relations is acknowledged; but that does not excuse you for your central part in them.

What function have the people with whom you have tried to surround yourself served? . . . I think you have used us to try and confirm an image of your independence, through a vague membership in a vague circle of fashionably "autonomous" people; as when, a month or two ago, you expounded to . . . me how "outside" of society something had made you feel — *you*, *outside* society! The only leaps you ever took (short skips into and out of women's lib, "revolution," and — law school) were about as adventurous, as chancy, as joining a bridge club or trying a new brand. You couldn't be more inside this sickening society.

The fact that, during the last half year, I visited with (I can hardly say *met*) you a half a dozen times is simply one of the most glaring measures of the degree of deadness of my life during that period; I was not deluded, I was simply *that* desperate for someone to talk to. That unimaginative. Well fuck that! I'll confine my conversations to walls if I can't do any better. . . .

Just one more point before I close. You're really selfish, in the petty, unenlightened sense. Any favors are for manipulative ends or are grudgingly given or both. No spontaneous generosity.

You've got a long way to go, baby.

(27 January 1973)

Whatever the accuracy or justifiability of this type of letter, the decision to write it, how strong to make it, or even whom to write it to, may have a somewhat arbitrary character, and exaggerations are common (the addressee often being made an absolute foil to what one wants). But the relief and lucidity resulting from the polarizing of a situation are often remarkable.

The next day the search for "what to do" was suddenly resolved. I wanted to confront the issues of the activities, the crises and the disappearance of Contradiction. Once conceived, nothing could have been more obvious, although in the previous six months I hadn't written so much as a line about Contradiction and had felt uncomfortable whenever I was reminded of it. That first day I wrote over forty pages of narration. I also decided to postpone the Voyer translation until I had publicly settled accounts with the hugely accumulated irresolutions of my old activity.

The next month was mainly devoted to writing my text on Contradiction. Typically I would write at home for a few hours until my mind began to get dull, then I would take a long walk and by the time I ended up at some cafe I would find myself refreshed and anxious to get back to my writing. (I also found that some plastic restaurant with straight clientel was often more conducive to critical thought than the more hip or sophisticated places where the roles and pretensions were so thick.) However I also continued a more "personal" research on myself, examining various character traits and affect blocks and experimenting with such techniques as neo-Reichian exercises and writing about myself in third person.

284

One evening I ate dinner with a couple friends and a friend of theirs. This latter guy was rather typical of that type on the margin of the situ milieu who is just close enough and just sophisticated enough to see which way the wind is blowing and affirm his wholehearted approval of whatever happens to be the latest situationist splash. He was thus running on at the mouth about Voyer, "character," "passionate subjectivity," etc. I asked him to give me one concrete example of what all this verbiage meant — i.e. a practical decision that he had implemented. Thrown into confusion, he ran on about "the concrete" — yes, that was really where it was at, etc. In a few days he, too, got a letter, with copies to mutual acquaintances.

> ...Your packaged, situationistically "in" remarks on things make me sick. ... The barrage of utter bullshit with which you dodged any coming to terms with yourself or our situation there ... cannot in any way be excused by any, say, appeal to nervousness towards me, that you "don't know me well enough," etc. If, after all this time, you don't know me well enough to know that you had better be up front with me or shut up, you're an imbecile. The only reason you could have had to be nervous (as opposed to honestly awkward) around me is that you have nothing to present but your pretensions, and with me you were (rightly) afraid that you wouldn't be able to fake them credibly enough.
>
> I have nothing in common with you that I don't have in common with *millions* of other people; who, moreover, don't make the pretensions you do about those things.
>
> To use a phrase you once hid behind without even knowing what it meant, you have no "comprehension of history"; you haven't the slightest idea how to make it, least of all how to make your own. All your reading of Hegel, Marx, Reich, Debord, ad nauseum, and your ability to talk and write spectacular Vaneigemese means ABSOLUTELY NOTHING. It's just a shell.
>
> Is there anything inside?
> (4 March 1973)

I had solved the question of this hanger-on and had put the unclear question of my relation with our friends on a more concrete basis. It was now their problem and to the extent that they (at first) responded defensively and uncomprehendingly, my independence from their sophisticated impotence was simply confirmed.

In general, a person who is always in the company of others is likely to dissipate his ideas, to lose the faculty of considering and concentrating. I have found that the strongest theoretical rushes often come from a decisive encounter (e.g. with a person or a pamphlet) *immediately followed by a few days of solitude*. Similarly, in the above case I had effectively thrown myself on my own at a point when my researches were coming to a head.

I set about a more deliberate experimental psychoanalytical program, inspired largely by the reading of *Character Analysis*. The more I experimented in the direction of adventure, the more I became aware of what a zombie I was — in the compulsive patterns of my thinking, gestures, etc.* I began to get a more precise idea of my "character" by fighting it, by inference, by a "triangulation" which pointed to a repressive psycho-physical formation which was the coherent source of the various apparently unconnected irrational symptoms. Only, whereas Reich treats character in a somewhat self-contained way, I took character to be in a dynamic with the society; not something which could be "dissolved" in itself, because it doesn't exist in itself, but rather as a sort of internal

---

* Cf. the numerous science-fiction stories where humanity is prey to some sort of psychological parasite. Often the protagonist, become temporarily "free," experiences a surge of intelligence and power: the parasite sustains itself by keeping man ignorant, unaware of his real capacities. Much of the fascination of such stories stems from the fact that they externalize as a *literally* alien force the domination of present humanity by the commodity (just as that related genre, the android story, presents literal machines which are virtually indistinguishable from humans).

correlative to the commodity-spectacle. I adopted the tentative formula: The anti-character struggle must *arm itself*, the revolutionary movement must *break its own blocks*.

I set pen and paper by my bed so I'd be ready to write down my dreams immediately upon waking. The next day, after writing them down I tried a free-associative analysis of them, noting where I felt blocks to various topics (e.g., suddenly feeling "tired," remembering other things "I need to do," receiving decoy insights). Some of these associations brought back the memory of childhood sexual fantasies, which I proceeded to reenact. Once I had slipped myself back in "under childhood," memories repressed for years succeeded one another.

The next evening, feeling the need to act a little in the "external" world to maintain and concretize my perspective amidst all this psychologizing, I snuck into the stupid movie *WR: Mysteries of the Organism* and wrote some graffiti that would be seen as the audience filed out after the show:

WATCHING 'WR' MAKES YOU ORGASTICALLY IMPOTENT

NOT THE SPECTACLE OF THE DISSOLUTION OF CHARACTER,
BUT THE DISSOLUTION OF CHARACTER AND THE SPECTACLE

With the intensification of my self-analysis, I began to feel more vibrant, a more erotic being (to the point of for the first time being able to affectively imagine homosexual pleasure, which for me was equivalent to having a more appreciative rather than repressive attitude toward my own body). I would sometimes see people going out of their way to meet me and I often started conversations with strangers without caring if anyone thought I was crazy. While normally rather unobservant of other people's gestures, I became pretty sensitive to them because I was more sensitive to my own, and I began to counter my typical trait of dominating, unilateral conversation. (Of course no matter how "open" you are, it still takes two, and some content, to make a dialogue; so most of these encounters didn't come to much after brief, sometimes exciting beginnings.)

One effect of my increased self-understanding was that I was better able to detect and combat psychological irrationalities in my text on Contradiction. For example, I found that in criticizing my own past I had a tendency to overemphasize Point-Blank, as providing a sort of absolute foil to me. It became obvious, when I honestly examined my feelings and even dreams, that I had an irrationally excessive attitude toward them: they were at once "threat" and concretized realization of numerous tendencies that I could see in myself. However poor their activity, its very existence was a reflection of my impotence.

This attitude was objectively reinforced by the fact that the paucity of genuinely situationist texts and activity in America lent a disproportionate apparent importance to the various confusionist manifestations which were identified in the popular mind with the S.I. As long as these manifestations were few and far between I could envision exhaustive critical denunciations of them, seeing myself as a restorer of the "purity" situationist theory formerly seemed to have when not very many people in America knew about it. The straw that broke the camel's back, shortly before, had been the *New Morning* special situationist issue. I wrote the following telegram to myself and pasted it on the wall in front of my desk.

ENOUGH IS ENOUGH! NO MORE!
THE LATEST SITUATIONIST REHASH IN THE NEW MORNING IS THE LAST STRAW STOP HENCE-FORTH I REFUSE TO JUMP ONTO THIS NAUSEATING HERE AND NOW STOP I ONLY RECONSTITUTE WITHIN MYSELF THE DELIRIUM BY IN THIS WAY TRYING TO COMBAT THE DELIRIUM WHICH RECONSTITUTES ITSELF WITHIN THE VERY POSITION WHICH CLAIMS TO COMBAT IT STOP I WILL REMEMBER THAT THIS LITTLE SIDE SHOW IS NOT AS SERIOUS AS IT WOULD LIKE TO THINK IT IS STOP IT IS SIMPLY ONE OF THE MORE BACKWARD MANIFESTATIONS OF AN INCREASING

RADICALISM IN THE SOCIETY STOP I HAVE NO THEORY TO DEFEND STOP I HAVE ONLY MYSELF TO DEFEND STOP THEREFORE I WILL DEAL WITH THIS SORT OF THING WHEN IT FORCES ITSELF ON MY ATTENTION BY DIRECTLY COMBATTING MY ACTIVITY STOP BETTER TO PUNCH THESE PEOPLE IN THE FACE OR LAUGH AT THEM THAN WASTE MY TIME AND ENERGY RUMINATING OVER HOW TO EXPOSE THEM STOP MAY THE SPIRIT OF BEETHOVEN TO WHICH I HAVE BEEN LISTENING WHILE TYPING THIS AND WHICH PERHAPS INSPIRED ME IN THE FIRST PLACE STAY WITH ME STOP THAT IS TO SAY WHEN I AM DOING SOMETHING *GRAND* THESE LITTLE NUISANCES WILL FALL INTO THEIR PROPER PLACE STOP POINT-BLANKISM IF I CAN'T BRING ABOUT YOUR DOWNFALL BY MY OWN PROJECTS THEN I'M A PRO-SITU STOP SINCERELY LUDWIG VAN KNABB
(18 February 1973)

The critique of Point-Blank in *Remarks on Contradiction*, which originally could have made a pamphlet by itself, was accordingly condensed to just enough to specify a few main tendencies in nascent American pro-situationist activity, as represented by those who were at the moment their most substantial and visible manifestors; and to kick up a little polarizing polemic.

Similarly, other elements of *Remarks* that would have expressed mere psychological compensation were eliminated or at least trimmed down. I avoided discussing certain matters the real purpose of which would have simply been to put a better face on my activities or to prove that I was capable of handling such and such a topic.

During the second week of March I was at fever pitch, with an energy I had not had since childhood. At every point I tried to pull the rug out from under myself. I particularly aimed at countering any defensive seriousness by constantly holding up to myself the absurdity and silliness of my ego. Sometimes, when no one else was around, I would walk down the street *singing* free-associations and laughing at myself. I was possessed, oscillating between a joyful lucidity and a fear of flipping into insanity. My character became almost tangible to me and reacted with physical symptoms as well as theoretical "bribes" (like the third-degree complementary team of torturer and "sympathetic" guy who regrets the unpleasantness, which could be dispensed with if one would only be "reasonable"). On the one hand, the critical-analytical tactics (daily dream analysis, etc.) began to become repetitive and lose their force and I began to lose the initiative necessary to continually supersede them. On the other, the bribes became almost more than I needed or could handle. The text on Contradiction, issuing from the released repression of so many events in our past, had begun to take on proportions that threatened to engulf me, like the projects in Contradiction that got so large that we ended up getting sick of them and unable to complete them. (The continuous addition of material to a text often also serves as a defensive buffer, surrounding and neutralizing the more daring and incisive formulations.) So insofar as I could grasp and control the situation, I took *Remarks* as the "pay" in exchange for the in-any-case inevitable characterological re-formation. Taking the long chronological narrative as raw material, I quickly rewrote the piece, this time concentrating not on the *history* of Contradiction but on what I had to say about it, the conclusions I could draw from it. I also applied many of the analytical techniques I had been using on myself to the writing of the pamphlet ("brainstorming," etc.).

With the completion and publication of *Remarks*, the characterological equilibrium — albeit perhaps somewhat loosened or "stretched" — had largely reestablished itself.

KEN KNABB

287

THE REALIZATION AND
SUPPRESSION OF RELIGION

Religion undoubtedly surpasses every other human activity in sheer quantity and variety of bullshit. If one considers in addition its role as accomplice of class domination throughout history, it is little wonder that it has brought upon itself the contempt and hatred of ever increasing numbers of people, in particular of revolutionaries.

The situationists recommenced the radical critique of religion, which had been abandoned by the Left, and extended it to its modern, secularized forms—the spectacle, sacrificial loyalty to leaders or ideology, etc. But their holding to a one-sided, undialectical position on religion has reflected and reinforced certain defects in the situationist movement. Developing out of the perspective that to be superseded, art must be both realized and suppressed, situationist theory failed to see that an analogous position was called for regarding religion.

Religion is the alienated expression of the qualitative, the "fantastic realization of man." The revolutionary movement must oppose religion, but not in preferring to it a vulgar amoralism or philistine common sense. It must take its stand on the other side of religion. Not less than it but more.

When religion is treated by the situationists, it is usually brought in only in its most superficial, spectacular aspects, as a straw man to be contemptuously refuted by those incapable of refuting anything else. Exceptionally, they may vaguely accept a Boehme or a Brotherhood of the Free Spirit into their pantheon of "greats" because they are mentioned favorably by the SI. But never anything that would challenge them personally. Issues deserving examination and debate are ignored because they have been monopolized by religion or happen to be couched in partially religious terms. Some may sense the inadequacy of such a dismissal, but are not sure how else to operate on such a taboo terrain and so they too say nothing or fall back on banalities. For people who want to "supersede all cultural acquirements" and realize the "total man," the situationists are often surprisingly ignorant of the most elementary features of religion.

It is not a matter of adding in a dose of religion to round out our perspective, to create a situationism "with a human face." One does not humanize a tool, a critical method. (The notion of "humanizing Marxism" only reveals the ideological nature of the Marxism in question.) It is a matter of examining the blind spots and dogmatic rigidities that have developed out of a largely justifiable critical assault on religion. It is precisely when a theoretical position has been victorious that it becomes both possible and necessary to criticize it with more rigor. The rough formula that was provocative in an earlier context becomes a basis for new ideologies. A qualitative advance is often accompanied by an apparently paradoxical retardation.

It is not enough to explain religion by its social role or historical development. The content that is expressed in religious forms must be discovered. Because revolutionaries haven't really come to terms with religion, it continually returns to haunt them. Because the critique of it has remained abstract, superficial, vulgar-materialist, religion continually engenders new forms of itself, even among those who were previously against it for all the correct "materialistic" reasons. The situationists can complacently observe that "all the Churches are decomposing" and not notice that we are also witnessing, precisely in the most industrially advanced countries, the proliferation of thousands of religions and neoreligions. Every new religious manifestation is a mark of the failure of radical theory to express the hidden, authentic meaning that is sought through those forms.

Religion includes many unlike and contradictory phenomena. Besides its purely apologetic aspects, it provides aesthetically appealing rituals; moral challenge; forms of contemplation that "recenter" one; organizing principles for one's life; communion rarely found in the secular world; etc. In exploding this agglomeration, the bourgeois revolution did not destroy religion but it served to some extent to separate out its diverse aspects. Elements of religion that were originally practical are thrown back on their own and required to be so once more or disappear.

The neoreligious trips and techniques are legion: modifications or combinations of traditional religions; therapies psychological and psycho-physical; self-help programs; contemplative techniques; psychedelics; activities taken up as "ways of life"; communitarian experiments. . . . Having been demystified, rationalized, commodified, these practices are to a certain extent taken up on the basis of their use value rather than being imposed as part of a monopolizing institutionalized system. The uses involved are, to be sure, widely varied, often escapist or trivial; and many of the old superstitions and mystifications remain even without the social rationale that formerly reinforced them. But this popular experimentation is not only a reflection of social decomposition, it is a major positive factor in the present revolutionary movement, the widespread expression of people trying to take their lives in their own hands. Situationist theory has oscillated between the vision of totally alienated people bursting out one fine day with the release of all their repressed rage and creativity, and that of microsocieties of revolutionaries already living according to the most radical exigencies. It has failed sufficiently to deal with the more ambiguous experiments on the margins between recuperation and radicality where contradictions are expressed and worked out; leaving them to the recuperation which apparently confirms its position. It is not a question of being more tolerant with these experiences, but of examining and criticizing them more thoroughly rather than contemptuously dismissing them.

As we develop a more radical, more substantial critique of religion, we can envisage interventions on religious terrains analogous to those of the early SI on artistic and intellectual terrains; attacking, for example, a neoreligion for not going far enough on its own terms, for not being, so to speak, "religious" enough, and not only from the classical "materialist" perspectives.

It is often forgotten that revolutionary theory is not based on preference or principle but on the experience of the revolutionary movement. The basis of the critique of "sacrifice," for example, is not that one should be egoistic on principle—that it is a bad thing to be altruistic, etc.—but stems from observation of the tendency for sacrifice and sacrificial ideology to be important factors in the maintaining of hierarchy and exploitation. It is merely a happy historical accident that there is a tendency for present revolutionary activity to be interesting and enjoyable; that being a tool of political manipulation is not only unpleasant but also unstrategic. The situationists were right to point out and affirm the playful aspects of radical struggles and the radical aspects of playful, apparently meaningless actions (vandalism, etc.). But the coincidence of these and other observations has led many people to the appealing if not quite logical conclusion that revolutionary activity is by definition pleasurable; or even that pleasure is by definition revolutionary. The problem is rather how to confront those situations where immediate pleasure does not automatically coincide with revolutionary needs: seeking ways to bring the two sides together (affective détournement) but not dissimulating the contradictions when this is not possible.

The same situationists who point out the stupidity of that leftism that reduces workers' struggles to purely economic issues, in their turn reduce revolution to purely "egoistic" issues when they insist that people are—or at least should be—only struggling "for themselves," "for the pleasure of it," etc. Their exhortations to "refuse sacrifice" substitute for any analysis or lead to false analyses. To denounce Maoism, for example, merely for its being based on "sacrifice" does not speak to the healthy, generous communitarian sentiments whose recuperation is at the source of much of Maoism's appeal. What is counterrevolutionary about Maoism is not sacrifice in itself, but the type of sacrifice and the use to which it is put. People have not only been willing, when necessary, to endure poverty, prison and other pains for revolution, they have often even done so joyously, foregoing material comfort as being relatively secondary, finding deeper satisfaction in the knowledge of the effectiveness and beauty of their acts. There are victories that are not visible to everyone, moments when one can see that one has "already won" a battle even though things may superficially seem the same as before.

It is necessary to distinguish between a principled devotion to a cause, which may involve some sacrifice of one's narrower egoistic interests, and degradation before a cause that demands the sacrifice of one's "better self"—one's integrity, honesty, magnanimity.

In emphasizing exclusively the immediate enjoyments to be found in revolutionary activity—out of naïve enthusiasm or with the aim of political or sexual seduction—the situationists have set themselves up for the complaints of those people who reject it on that basis, being disappointed in their expectations of entertainment.

It is understandable why antisacrifice has been such an uncriticized pillar of situationist ideology. First, it provides an excellent defense against accounting to oneself or others: one can justify many failings by simply saying that one wasn't passionately moved to do this or that. Secondly, the person who is a revolutionary solely for his own pleasure would presumably be indifferent or even counterrevolutionary when that happened to be more convenient; hence he is compelled, in order to prevent this embarrassing corollary from being noted, to postulate that revolutionary activity is always automatically pleasurable.

The very success of the SI contributed toward the apparent justification of an anachronistic pose deriving from the historical accident of its origins (out of the French cultural avant-garde, etc.) and even perhaps from the personalities of some of its determinative members. The aggressive situationist tone reflects the recentering of revolution in the real single individual engaged in a project that leaves nothing outside of itself. In contrast with the militant, the situationist is naturally quick to react against manipulation. Though such an attitude is quite the contrary of elitist, it is easily capable of becoming so in relation to those who lack this autonomy or self-respect. Having experienced the excitement of taking his history into his own hands (or at least having identified with those who have), he arrives at an impatience and contempt for the prevailing sheepishness. It is but a step from this quite understandable feeling to the development of a neo-aristocratic pose. This pose is not always a mark of the proverbial "hierarchical aspirations"; rather, frustrated by the difficulty of noticeably affecting the dominant society, the situationist seeks the compensation of at least noticeably affecting the revolutionary milieu, of being recognized there as being right, as having accomplished good radical actions. His egoism becomes egotism. He begins to feel that he merits an unusual respect for being so unusually antihierarchical. He haughtily defends his "honor" or "dignity" when someone has the effrontery to criticize him, and he finds in the SI and its approved forebears a style that goes well with this new manner of viewing himself.

An intuitive dissatisfaction with this egotistic style is at the source of much of the discussions expressed somewhat misleadingly in terms of "femininity" and "masculinity." There is nothing intrinsically "masculine," for example, about writing; women are going to have to learn how to do it if they don't want to remain impotent. What they don't have to learn is the pointless neoaristocratic posturing that has characterized predominantly male situationist expression.

Some situationists have not had any particular natural inclination for this posturing. But it has been difficult to isolate and therefore avoid it, since accusations of "arrogance," "elitism," etc., are often mistakenly aimed at precisely the most trenchant aspects of situationist practice. It is hard not to feel superior upon having some pseudocritique addressed to you that you've heard and refuted a hundred times before. Moreover, a false modesty may be misleading. There are some things you can't let pass. Although a revolutionary should not think that he (or his group) is essential to the movement and is therefore to be defended by any means, he must defend his actions insofar as he feels that they reflect important aspects of that movement. It is not a matter of secretly storing up modesty and other virtues that God will see and ultimately reward, but of participating in a global movement whose very essence is communication.

The situationist scene, providing a favorable field of play for vanity and in-group games, has attracted many people with very little to do with the revolutionary project; people who in other circumstances would have been fops, dandies, social intriguers, cultural dilettantes, hangers-on. It is true that the situationist movement has reacted against many of these elements with a vigor that was perhaps unexpected to them, and which has discouraged many others from thinking they could disport themselves there with impunity. But this has often been not because of their pretentious role, but because they did not maintain that role credibly enough.

Conversely, the situationist scene has tended to repel other in many ways serious individuals who felt this pretentious egoism to be an anachronism far removed from any revolution they would have been interested in. Seeing this pretentiousness apparently linked with the situationists' trenchant radicality, many people facilely rejected both at once, choosing other pursuits which, while more limited, at least avoided this repugnant posturing. The movement that counted on the radical appeal of antirole, antisacrificial activity ended up repelling people who had no desire to sacrifice themselves to the reactionary situationist role.

The egoist situationist has a rather philistine conception of human liberation. His egoism is only the inversion of self-abasement. He advocates "play" in a juvenile sense, as if the mere breaking of restrictions were automatically productive of pleasure. In evoking the child, he is sympathizing not only with his rebelliousness but also with his impatience and irresponsibility. His criticism of "romantic love" stems not only from a perception of its illusions and neurotic possessiveness, but also from a simple ignorance of love and its possibilities. It isn't so much the alienated human community that bothers him as the things that prevent him from participating in it. What he really dreams of, behind the situationist verbiage, is a cybernetized spectacular society that would cater to his whims in more sophisticated and varied ways. He is still a consumer, and a very conspicuous one, in his frantic insistence on "pleasure without limit," the gratification of an "infinite multiplication of desires." If he dislikes "passivity" it is not so much that being forced into it restricts his creative impulses as that he is an addict of nervous activity and doesn't know what to do with himself if he is not surrounded with lots of distractions. Of contemplation as moment of activity, or of solitude as moment of dialogue, he knows nothing. For all his talk about "autonomy," he lacks the courage to act without caring what others will think of him. It is not his life that he takes seriously, but his ego.

Critical theory does not present a fixed, "objective" truth. It is an assault, a formulation abstracted, simplified and pushed to the extreme. The principle is, "If the shoe fits, wear it": people are compelled to ask themselves to what extent the critique rings true and what they are going to do about it. Those who wish to evade the problem will complain about the critique as being unfairly one-sided, not presenting the whole picture. Conversely, the dialectically ignorant revolutionary who wishes to affirm his extremism will confirm the critique (as long as it's not against him) as being an objective, balanced assessment.

Much revolutionary theoretical nonsense stems from the fact that in a milieu where "radicality" is the basis of prestige, one has an interest in making ever more extremist affirmations and in avoiding anything that might be taken to reflect a weakening of one's intransigence toward the official bad things. Thus the situationists will look rather favorably on playful or erotic aspirations ("it's only necessary that they follow out their most radical implications," etc.) while dismissing moral aspirations with insults, although the ones are no more ambiguous than the others.

In exaggerated reaction against the general complicity of morality with the ruling society, situationists frequently identify with their enemies' image of them and flaunt their own "immorality" or "criminality." Such an identification is not only infantile, it is virtually meaningless these days when an irresponsible libertinism is one of the most widely accepted and extolled ways of life (though the reality usually lags far behind the image). It was the bourgeoisie that was denounced in the *Communist Manifesto* for having "left remaining no other nexus between man and man than naked self-interest." If we are to use the works of a Sade—that very picture of human alienation—or a Machiavelli, it is not as guidebooks for conducting our relations, but as unusually candid self-expressions of bourgeois society.

The egoist, antimoralist ideology has undoubtedly contributed to the quantity of bad faith and pointlessly acrimonious breaks in the situationist milieu. To be sure, situationists are often quite nice people; but this is virtually in spite of their whole ideological environment. I've seen situationists become embarrassed and practically apologize for having done some kind act. ("It was no sacrifice.") Whatever spontaneous goodness they have lacks its theory. Basic ethical vocabulary is inverted, confused and forgotten.

The fact that one can scarcely use a word like "goodness" without sounding corny is a measure of the alienation of this society and its opposition. The notions of the "virtues" are too ambiguous to be used without having been criticized and precised, but so are their opposites. Ethical concepts must not be left to the enemy without a fight; they must be contested.

Much of what makes people dissatisfied with their lives is their own moral poverty. They are encouraged on every side to be mean, petty, vindictive, spiteful, cowardly, covetous, jealous, dishonest, stingy, etc. That this pressure from the system removes much of the blame for these vices does not make it any less unpleasant to be possessed by them. An important reason for the spread of religious movements has been that they speak to this moral inquietude, inspiring people to a certain ethical practice that provides them with the peace of a good conscience, the satisfaction of saying what they believe and acting on it (that unity of thought and practice for which they are termed "fanatics").

The revolutionary movement, too, should be able to speak to this moral inquietude, not in offering a comfortingly fixed set of rules for behavior, but in showing that the revolutionary project is the present focus of meaning, the terrain of the most coherent expression of compassion; a terrain where individuals must have the courage to make the best choices they can and follow them through, without repressing their bad consequences but avoiding useless guilt.

The compassionate act is not in itself revolutionary, but it is a momentary supersession of commodified social relations. It is not the goal but it is of the same nature as the goal. It must avow its own limitedness. When it becomes satisfied with itself, it has lost its compassion.

What is the point of lyrical evocations of eventual revenge on bureaucrats, capitalists, cops, priests, sociologists, etc.? They serve to compensate for the lack of substance of a text and usually don't even seriously reflect the sentiments of the author. It is an old banality of strategy that if the enemy knows that he will inevitably be killed anyway, he will fight to the end rather than surrender. It is not of course a question of being nonviolent, any more than violent, on principle. Those who violently defend this system bring violence on themselves. Actually it is remarkable how magnanimous proletarian revolutions usually are. Vengeance is usually limited to a few spontaneous attacks against torturers, police or members of the hierarchy who have been notoriously responsible for cruel acts, and quickly subsides. It is necessary to distinguish between defense of popular "excesses" and advocacy of them as essential tactics. The revolutionary movement has no interest in vengeance; nor in interfering with it.

It is well known that Taoism and Zen have inspired many aspects of oriental martial arts: supersession of ego consciousness, so as to avoid anxiety that would interfere with lucid action; nonresistance, so as to turn the opponent's force against him rather than confront it directly; relaxed concentration, so as not to waste energy but to bring all one's force into sharp focus at the moment of impact. It is likely that religious experience can be drawn on in analogous fashion to enrich tactically that ultimate martial art which is modern revolutionary theoretico-practice. However, proletarian revolution has little in common with classical war, being less a matter of two similar forces directly confronting each other than of one overwhelming majority moving to become conscious of what it could be any time it realized it. In the more advanced countries the success of a movement has generally depended more on its radicality, and therefore its contagiousness, than on the number of weapons it could commandeer. (If the movement is widespread enough, the army will come over, etc.; if it isn't, weapons alone will not suffice, unless it be to bring about a minority coup d'état.)

It is necessary to reexamine the experiences of nonviolent religious or humanistic radical movements. Their defects are numerous and evident: Their abstract affirmation of "humanity" is an affirmation of alienated humanity. Their abstract faith in man's good will leads to reliance on moral influencing of rulers and on promotion of mutual "understanding" rather than radical comprehension. Their appeal to transcendent moral laws reinforces the ability of the system to do the same. Their victories gained by wielding the economy as a weapon are at the same time victories for the economy. Their nonviolent struggles still rely on the threat of force, they only avoid being the direct agents of it, shifting its use to "public opinion" and thus usually in the final analysis to the state. Their exemplary acts often become merely symbolic gestures allowing all sides to go on as before, but with tensions relaxed, consciences eased by having "spoken out," "been true to one's principles." Identifying with Gandhi or Martin Luther King, the spectator has a rationalization for despising others who attack alienation less magnanimously; and for doing nothing himself because, well-intentioned people being found on both sides, the situation is too "complex." These and other defects have been exposed in theory and have exposed themselves in practice for a long time. It is no longer a question of tempering the rulers' power hunger, cruelty or corruption

295

with ethical admonishments, but of suppressing the system in which such "abuses" can exist.

Nevertheless, these movements have at times achieved remarkable successes. Beginning from a few exemplary interventions, they have spread like wildfire and profoundly discredited the dominant system and ideology. At their best they have used—and often originated—quite radical tactics, counting on the contagious spread of the truth, of the qualitative, as their fundamental weapon. Their practice of community puts other radical milieus to shame, and they have often been more explicit about their goals and the difficulties in attaining them than have more "advanced" movements.

The situationists have adopted a spectacular view of revolutionary history in fixating on its most visible, direct, "advanced" moments. Often these moments owed much of their momentum to the long preparatory influence of quieter, subtler currents. Often they were "advanced" merely because accidental external circumstances forced them into radical forms and acts. Often they failed because they did not know very well what they were doing or what they wanted.

Revolutionary as well as religious movements have always tended to give rise to a moral division of labor. Unrealistic, quasi-terroristic demands intimidate the masses to the point that they adore rather than emulate the propagators and gladly leave full participation to those with the qualities and dedication apparently necessary for it. The revolutionary must strive to demystify the apparent extraordinariness of whatever merits he may have, while guarding against feeling or seeming superior because of his conspicuous modesty. He must be not so much admirable as exemplary.

Ongoing radical criticism has been a key factor in the situationists' subversive power; but their egoism has prevented them from pushing this tactic to the limit. Surrounded by all the verbiage about "radical subjectivity" and "masters without slaves," the situationist does not learn to be self-critical. He concentrates exclusively on the errors of others, and his facility in this defensive method reinforces his "tranquil" role. Failing to welcome criticism of himself, he cripples his activity; and when some critique finally does penetrate because of its practical consequences, he may be so traumatized as to abandon revolutionary activity altogether, retaining of his experience only a grudge against his criticizers.

In contrast, the revolutionary who welcomes criticism has a greater tactical flexibility. Confronted with a critique of himself, he may "aggressively" seize on its weakest points, refuting it by demonstrating its contradictions and hidden assumptions; or he may take a "non-resisting" stance and seize on its strongest points as a point of departure, transforming the criticism by accepting it in a profounder context than it was intended. Even if the balance of "correctness" is overwhelmingly on his side, he may choose to concentrate on some rather subtle error of his own instead of harping on more obvious ones of others. He does not criticize the most criticizable, but the most essential. He uses himself as a means of approaching more general questions. Embarrassing himself, he embarrasses others. The more concretely and radically a mistake is exposed, the harder it is for others to avoid similar confrontations with themselves. Even those who are at first gleeful at the apparent fall of an enemy into some sort of masochistic exhibitionism soon find their victory to be a hollow one. By sacrificing his image the revolutionary undercuts the images of others, whether the effect is to expose them or to shame them. His strategy differs from that of "subverting one's enemies with love" not necessarily in having less love, but in having more coherence in its expression. He may be cruel with a role or ideology while loving the person caught in it. If people are brought to a profound, perhaps traumatic, confrontation with themselves, he cares little that they momentarily think that he is a nasty person who only does these things out of maliciousness. He wishes to provoke others into participation, even if only by drawing them into a public attack on him.

We need to develop a new style, a style that keeps the trenchancy of the situationists but with a magnanimity and humility that leaves aside their uninteresting ego games. Pettiness is always counterrevolutionary. Begin with yourself, comrade, but don't end there.

Appendix

Kenneth Rexroth's *Communalism: From Its Origins to the Twentieth Century* (Seabury, 1974) contains a pithy exposition of ways in which the dialectic of religion has continually given rise to tendencies that have been thorns in the side of dominant society and religious orthodoxy, particularly in the form here of millenarian movements and intentional communities. Although Rexroth's anecdotal style often serves to concisely illustrate a point, much of his gossip about the foibles and delusions of the communalists, though amusing, obscures essential issues that he has not dealt with rigorously enough. He considers the communalist movements largely on their own terms—the nature of their communal life, the pitfalls they ran into, how long they endured. He is concerned more with whether the dominant society managed to destroy them than with whether they managed to make any dent in it. And indeed in many cases whatever subversive effect they had was only incidental. Many of the religious currents that exerted a more consciously radical force in social struggles, such as Gandhiism or the Quakers in the antislavery movement, did not of course take a communalist form and so are not treated here.

In the period following the defeat of the first proletarian assault, when most intellectuals debased themselves into Stalinism, reaction, or intentional historical ignorance, Rexroth was one of the few to maintain a certain integrity and intelligence. He continued to denounce the system from a profound if not coherently revolutionary perspective. In the "left wing" of culture, he criticized many aspects of the separation of culture and daily life, but without following this out to the most radical conclusion of explicitly and coherently attacking the separation as such. Since the society represses creativity, he imagines the "creative act" as being the means of a subtle subversion by the qualitative; but he conceives this creative expression largely in artistic, cultural terms. ("I write poetry to seduce women and overthrow the capitalist system.")

Rexroth has certainly had a determinative influence on a number of people—me, for one. But this influence, though healthy in many respects, has unfortunately not tended very much toward a lucid revolutionary theoretico-practice. He has failed to recognize many of the characteristics and expressions of the modern revolution, through lumping them too facilely with the failure of the old proletarian assault. Lacking a revolution, his social analyses range from perceptive insights to pathetic liberal complaining. He falls back on the notion of an "alternative society": individuals quietly practicing authentic community in the interstices of the doomed society; on the theory that even if this offers little chance of averting thermonuclear or ecological apocalypse, it's the most satisfying way to conduct your life while you're waiting for it. The proliferation of such individuals holding to radically different values is a practical rejection of commodity ideology, a living critique of the spectacle effect. It is one of the possible bases of the modern revolution. But these individuals must grasp the historical mediations through which these values could be realized. Otherwise they tend to devolve into a vulgar complacency as to their superiority to those who don't make such a break, and take pride in their irreconcilability to the system as they are integrated into it.

I highly recommend Rexroth's essay on Martin Buber in *Bird in the Bush* (New Directions, 1959).

[March 1977]

OPEN LETTER TO THE TOKYO "LIBERTAIRE" GROUP

Near the end of our meeting a couple weeks ago, Mr. Miura asked me to get in touch with you when I came to Tokyo again. In a moment of unthinking mere politeness I said that I would. I would therefore like to clarify my position. In fact when I come to Tokyo again I will not contact you because our one meeting, brief as it was, was enough: I have no interest in your group.

Contrary to your suggestion that while other anarchists perhaps had many of the faults that I criticized, you "Japanese anarchists" were somehow different, I must say that you are unfortunately quite typical, in no way different from anarchists in other countries. You rummage among the corpses of Proudhon, the male-chauvinist ideologue of small cooperative capitalism; of "our Bakunin," the proto-bolshevik; of World War I supporter Kropotkin; of the state-collaborating Spanish CNT (now once again trying to bureaucratically "organize" the struggles of the radical Spanish proletariat); and of various old oriental imitators thereof. You want to construct a mythical history for yourselves because you don't know how to make real history now.

Vaguely aware of your own impotence, you hope that it will go away if you join your individual impotences together. What actually happens is that what little creative energy you do possess is frittered away in the endless discussion and pursuit of such pointless, spectacular projects as a revived "Anarchist Federation."

Like most anarchists, you have developed a truly ludicrous collective unconsciousness as a defense against any challenge to your complacency. Confronted with a practical critique, you "never heard" of it, or "forgot" it, or are "too busy" for it. Only one of you even knew about my letter and the *Society of the Spectacle* theses in CIRA's *Anarchism* #4. Are Japanese anarchists' writings so boring that you don't even bother to read each other's publications?

I cannot yet read the Japanese in *Libertaire* magazine, but the incoherent ramblings in the English sections are pitiful enough. But perhaps that is only the responsibility of the two "editors." Perhaps the rest of you have no role in the magazine. (Or only a *subordinate* one?) When I thus asked you what other projects you had, some of you spoke vaguely of "support" for the Sanrizuka struggle but were unable to give any concrete details of what this "support" consisted of, or in what long-range strategical perspective you participated in it. Another simply said that he was "a worker," implying apparently that this excused him from doing any other activity because he was too busy.

300

What then is the purpose of his belonging to your group? What in fact is the purpose of your group?

It may be that I have judged you too much on the basis of the two or three people who talked most. It may be that one or two of you are more serious. If so, it is up to you to begin from the critiques you recognize, define your projects (however small but concrete), and act. This is just what it is impossible for you to do in "Libertaire." The collective toleration of endless bullshit neutralizes any concrete individual effort in a stew of contradictory, consequenceless "opinions." Your group is nothing but an obstacle to your real possibilities.

Down with the state! Down with musty anarchism!

Ken Knabb
Fujinomiya, 5 November 1977

A RADICAL GROUP
IN HONG KONG

One of the most essential and most difficult tasks of the modern revolutionary movement is communication between revolutionaries on either side of the Iron Curtain. A valuable contribution to this developing encounter has been made by the "70s," a libertarian group in Hong Kong opposed simultaneously to Western capitalism and the Chinese state-capitalist bureaucracy, and which is in contact with several anti-bureaucratic revolutionaries who have escaped from China. Over the last three years it has put out an English-language magazine, *Minus*, dealing with struggles in China and Hong Kong. It has also published two books: *The Revolution Is Dead, Long Live the Revolution*, an anthology of articles in English on the so-called "Cultural Revolution," and *Revelations That Move the Earth to Tears*, a Chinese-language collection of stories, poems and essays smuggled out of China.

In speaking of the "70s" here, I include also the loose grouping of people who though not formal members have some ongoing association with its projects, and who can all be contacted through the 1984 Bookshop (180 Lockhart Road, Wanchai, Hong Kong).

The 70s comrades have only partially developed a clear definition of themselves and their activity. Their Chinese-language magazine started out several years ago in an underground paper format, with imports of countercultural oddments already largely outmoded in the West. The first number of *Minus* contained the quaint admonition: "Remember: the alternative press is the only news source you can trust." One only has to remember how long most of the underground press uncritically glorified the Maoist regime; or how it played down and falsified May 1968 and suppressed any mention of the 1970 workers' uprising in Poland because its narrow "Third World"–Guevarist consciousness had no way of comprehending such struggles. Most of the original underground papers have collapsed as a result of the general recognition of their confusions and illusions, or have devolved into frankly reformist peddlers of "alternative" culture. *Minus* soon dropped its underground press characteristics, though it still maintains a membership in the "Alternative Press Syndicate."

The 70s's looseness of self-definition results in the usual defects of vague "affinity groups." Nonparticipants coast along with the projects of those with more initiative or "more experience." Internal differences are seldom polarized practically or publicly. Independent ideas, instead of leading to independent projects, get lost in lowest-common-denominator collective action, leading to boredom and dropping out. Their toleration of virtually anybody dilutes the clarity of their efforts. (E.g., they accept being interviewed by the French paper *Libération,* notorious for suppressing criticism of Maoism; which is thus free to distort their positions while beefing up its image as "covering all sides.") They run the risk, especially the actual escapees from China, of being swallowed up in the spectacular role of exotic revolutionaries, admired because they present no challenge. This is encouraged by their absence of clarity on their internal functioning, on their different tendencies and splits, and on their past experiments and the conclusions they have drawn from them. A large amount of their correspondence is simply fan mail from people who never offer any criticisms (nor expect to receive any) but who seek a "dialogue" consisting of the endless rehashing of ultraleftist banalities.

The 70s comrades' lack of clarity about their own practice reinforces their lack of clarity about the Chinese revolutionary movement's practice. Their publications have presented valuable information about events and life in China (Simon Leys's *Chinese Shadows* shows how farcical are the accounts of those visitors to China who naïvely derive their information from the tightly programmed tours); but they have rarely confronted tactical problems. They have reported on struggles against the bureaucracy, but they have not examined the errors and failures of those struggles in order to suggest how they could be different next time.

The theoretical vagueness of the 70s is reflected in the eclecticism of *The Revolution Is Dead.* Even leaving aside the three articles written from Leninist perspectives—whose analyses the 70s editors explicitly reject—several of the articles contain dubious formulations which are not criticized. Cajo Brendel's "Theses on the Chinese Revolution" are determinist and reductionist. His tedious comparison of the Chinese Communist Party with the Russian one reinforces the notion of the inevitability of the bureaucratic regime. He fails to formulate the *choices,* the contradictions that bear on revolutionary *possibilities.* He plays down the great Shanghai uprising of 1927 (see Harold Isaacs's *The Tragedy of the Chinese Revolution*) and reduces its crushing to a whim of Chiang Kai-shek's: "because he scorned Jacobinism, not because he feared the proletariat" (thesis #22). And all he sees during the sixties is a conflict between the "new class" (the managerial bureaucrats) and the old-line Party bureaucrats, in which "the ultimate victory of the 'new class' is the only logical perspective" (#60). The large-scale armed revolts touched off by the "Cultural Revolution," which burst the bounds of both bureaucratic factions, are mentioned only once, as "details": "every detail cannot be fitted into this analytical framework" (#58). An "analytical framework" in which the proletariat can't apparently play any role but that of a tool for one or another ruling class, or of a "detail," is a strange one to be taken up by a "libertarian communist."

Like many other commentators on China, K.C. Kwok takes the bureaucrats' rhetoric too seriously, accepting the issues as they define them, trying to follow the constantly shifting "lines" and figure out who is to the "left" or "right," etc. His "Everything Remains the Same After So Much Ado" is a confused hodgepodge resulting from the attempt to blend extensive, ill-digested borrowings from the Situationist International's "Explosion Point of Ideology in China" (also included in the book) with Yang Hsi-Kwang's "Whither China." "Whither China" and Li I-Che's "Concerning Socialist Democracy and Legality" are both important expressions of the development, under extremely difficult conditions, of an indigenous critique of the Chinese bureaucracy (comparable in this respect to Kuron and Modzelewski's "Open Letter to Polish Communist Party Members"). Nevertheless, their analyses are seriously distorted by their attempt to follow through with a radical antibureaucratic program while simultaneously holding up the Mao faction as a pillar of the revolution. Taken literally, the articles are merely expressions of the absurd contradictions of Maoist ideology pushed to the explosion point. To a large extent, however, the authors were consciously exploiting those contradictions. Li's article, originally a gigantic wall poster, was allowed to remain up in Canton a whole month because local officials couldn't be sure that this was not one more government-sponsored attack on "capitalist-roaders"; and when it was finally condemned and certain passages were singled out as "especially reactionary," Li was able to show that they were exact quotations of Mao.

(As a result of their writings, both Yang and Li have been sent to the prison camps. The 70s is involved in an international campaign for their release, along with that of those arrested during the Tiananmen riot.)

Yu Shuet's "Dusk of Rationality" and the two pieces by Wu Man contain valuable information and insights, but in both writers there are points where the analyses become vague and ideological. For example, Wu criticizes Mao because he "did not interpret Marxism through humanism in the endeavor to maintain its best qualities, but interpreted it as a tool for struggle with dialectics as the method" (p. 242). But Marx's dialectical method *is* often a useful tool for struggle. The problem lies in the appeal to an ideological *authority* implied by exegetical "interpretation," whether Maoist or "humanist." And Yu states that "in the past, the leadership of revolutions ignored the value of the individual" (p. 203). But in the context of the present revolution this is beside the point; when people eliminate external power over them, it doesn't matter if someone "ignores the value of the individual" —because he is not in a position to do anything about it. Of course it is natural that amidst the brutal reality of Stalinism, where even the most modest human values may become so mutilated as to be conceived only as vague, distant ideals, people cling desperately to such ideals. As Wu notes, the "altar of high ideals" found in the poems and stories of *Revelations That Move the Earth to Tears* "is something which they have created to take temporary shelter [in]" (p. 235). But as long as radical aspirations remains "ideals"—spectacular, separate from and "above" real life, expressed by an elite of artistic, ideological or religious specialists—this false dichotomy of "real" and "ideal" implicitly supports the bureaucracy by giving it credit for some sort of "realism." Similarly, Yu's reference to "rationality" is too ambiguous. If a vulgarized rationalism is taken up by the bureaucracy, this scarcely masks the delirious irrationality at the heart of Stalinism, the bureaucracy's need to falsify all aspects of life in order to cover up the big lie at its origin.

BUREAU OF PUBLIC SECRETS
October 1978

THE OPENING IN IRAN

The uprising in Iran is the most beautiful event since the Hungarian revolution of 1956. It has shaken all the ruling powers of the world and exposed their collusion. The Arab regimes are as alarmed as Israel. The Chinese bureaucracy was caught with its pants down: it supported the Shah and denounced his opposition (thus continuing the policy of Mao and Chou, who praised him for his "anti-imperialism"). As for the Russian bureaucracy, far from "stirring up trouble" in Iran, it has always aimed at maintaining a stable, highly policed regime there, as elsewhere on its borders, so as to prevent any contagion of rebellion from spreading to its own people. It has sold arms to the Shah and turned fugitive Iranian radicals over to SAVAK. Only when his downfall seemed likely did it cautiously begin hedging its bets. The saber rattling between Russia and the U.S. was strictly for the benefit of the spectators. American ambassador William Sullivan admitted: "We ran Laos, but in Iran, which is tremendously important to us, there's not much we, or anyone else, can do. Ironically all the major powers—the U.S., Britain, France, China and the Soviet Union—are alarmed by what's going on in Iran." (*New York Times*, 13 November 1978.)

The possibility that the mass insurgence might overflow bureaucratic or priestly mediation—this is what lies behind all the powers' horror of "chaos" or a "power vacuum" in Iran. The Iranian movement is not essentially a religious one; the partial margin of immunity granted religious expression simply provided an opening and a rallying point for it. Women who previously wore the veil as a symbol of defiance to the Shah are now defying Khomeini by refusing to wear it; his emissaries have had to report to him that the oil workers "do not respect religion"; and the momentum and contagion of the movement has already pushed even many of the religious to go beyond his dictates. The destruction of banks, stores and cinemas is not a reaction against "modernization" or "westernization," it is the same kind of reaction against *alienation* that is found in modern revolts in the West, from Watts to Gdansk.

The clergy, the bourgeoisie and the army all had, and still have, obvious contradictions with each other. But none could do without the other two. In spite of his intransigent rhetoric, Khomeini was negotiating behind the scenes and, like the National Front, had long taken care to keep the army as intact as possible, warning his followers against provoking it. Finally radical elements initiated the final battle without him and forced his hand. The army, on the verge of breaking up, had to give in to his government as the last hope for stemming the popular insurgence.

As in Portugal in the wake of the fall of the fascist regime, the political untenability of outside intervention plus the weakness and contradictions of the internal ruling forces in Iran may for a while leave spaces for partially free social experimentation. The strikers who have gone back to work only on their own terms; the people who have taken over and run their own towns, "answering only to themselves"—these represent potential dual-power situations that have not been brought completely under control. In spite of Khomeini's appeals, hundreds of thousands of arms seized by guerrilla groups or distributed among the people have not yet been turned in. And the autonomist movements of the Kurds, the Baluchis and the Azerbaijans are seizing their opportunity and may spread the insurgence to the already crisis-ridden bordering countries where overlapping sectors of those peoples live.

The rulers and commentators pretend to see in any radical action the work of communists or other leftists. In reality the Iranian "communist" party—the Tudeh Party—has long been discredited for its reformism and servility to Russian foreign policy. Though virtually wiped out by the Shah's police, it has nevertheless praised his "revolution from above" while denouncing the mass uprisings of 1963 and 1978. Recently it has called for a coalition government to work for the "normalization of the economy" and "put an end to the present crisis as quickly as possible."

As for the guerrilla groups and militant students, though largely disillusioned with the various "communist" regimes, they imitate the hierarchical organization and manipulative practice that led to those state-capitalist bureaucracies. Sixty years of Leninist-Stalinist counterrevolution have taught them nothing. They add to the ideological pollution with their wooden language and lower the consciousness of the "hard-working, patriotic workers" (who are thus applauded precisely for their alienation) with their chorus of "correct leadership," "progressive clergy," "people's army," "workers' states," and other such self-contradictions. But who struggles for the real power of the soviets?

A "popular" government cannot defend the revolution because it has to defend itself from the revolution. But once it has disarmed and demoralized the people, who can defend it from the reaction? Mossadeq set the stage for the CIA coup by using the army against strikers and demonstrators; Ben Bella set the stage for Boumédienne, who destroyed the pockets of self-management in Algeria; Allende (with the support of Castro) set the stage for Pinochet by attacking the workers and peasants who had armed themselves and seized factories and land.

The fundamental question in Iran is not which combination of forces will hold the state, but whether the workers will affirm themselves autonomously against it. If they don't speak for themselves the bureaucrats will speak for them. If they don't communicate their experiences and analyses (by seizing printing equipment or radio stations, for example) the mass media will continue to block out or falsify them. The only way to defend the revolution is to *extend* it. Even if it is defeated there will be that much more to undo. A reformist or bureaucratic movement will scarcely interest workers who already live in reformist or bureaucratic societies. Only a movement that strikes radically at the global system will strike a chord among them, win their support in resisting intervention, and inspire them to parallel revolt. "The next revolutions can find aid in the world only by attacking the world in its totality" (Situationist International).

Each time people begin to make their own history they rediscover the highest moments of the repressed attempts of the past. A revolt like that in Iran is an opening, it cuts through the organized confusion and enforced passivity and poses questions in concrete terms. It's the social moment of truth.

BUREAU OF PUBLIC SECRETS
12 March 1979

BANALITIES

The "free world" is not free and the "communist world" is not communist. The old proletarian movement failed to overthrow class society, notably by being deflected into reformist or totalitarian bureaucratic variants of classical capitalism. Everywhere people are still alienated from their own activity—what they are forced to produce returns as a power against them —and consequently alienated from each other. The modern development of capitalism has given rise to a new stage of this alienation: the spectacle, which monopolizes communication between people around what is presented to them, from "information" and vicarious adventures to images of exalted commodities or bureaucrats.

But this system has not resolved all its contradictions; over the last couple decades new struggles have arisen in all the regions of the world contesting various aspects of it and tending to reject bureaucratic mediation. The fundamental project ultimately implied by these struggles is the abolition of the state and all hierarchical power, of the commodity economy and wage labor. The technological preconditions for such a transformation already exist. The form of social organization capable of bringing it about has been prefigured in the workers councils that emerged in the revolutions repressed earlier in this century: democratic general assemblies of workers and others who rally to their project, assemblies that dissolve all external power and federate with each other internationally, electing delegates to carry out specific tasks who can be recalled at any moment.

Such a revolution cannot be furthered by manipulative methods that reproduce the dominant hierarchical relations. The task of revolutionaries is to contribute toward the self-consciousness, autonomy and coherence of radical struggles without themselves becoming a new "leadership" that would dominate those struggles. Because of this, and because "constructive" opposition tends to become integrated into the system, appropriate tactics are to a large extent "negative" or critical—attacking the institutions and ideologies that reinforce submission to the system, pointing out the shortcomings and possibilities of struggles against it—leaving people to choose their own way of responding to the situations thus exposed.

It's a matter of confronting the real world we live in; of linking theory and practice in experimental activity so as to resist the tendency of theory to petrify into ideology. Whatever of positive value has been expressed in art or religion can be realized only by superseding them as separate spheres, by bringing creativity and the search for fulfillment into play on the terrain of everyday life. "In a society that has destroyed all adventure the only adventure is in the destruction of the society."

BUREAU OF PUBLIC SECRETS
April 1979

THE RELEVANCE
OF REXROTH

1. Life and Literature

> REXROTH (*before reading his poetry*): "Well, what would you
> like tonight, sex, mysticism or revolution?"
> WOMAN IN AUDIENCE: "What's the difference?"[1]

Kenneth Rexroth was born in Indiana in 1905, descended from a
variety of abolitionists, socialists, anarchists, feminists and free-
thinkers. After an unusually enlightened upbringing he was orphaned
at the age of twelve. He spent most of his teenage years in Chicago,
where he worked as a newspaper reporter and helped run a jazz coffee
house, mingling with the musicians, artists, writers, radicals and
eccentrics who made up the bohemian world of the twenties. Almost
totally self-educated (he had only five years of formal schooling), he
read omnivorously, wrote poetry, did abstract painting, worked in
avant-garde theater and began teaching himself several languages. In
his late teens he hitched all over the country, spending summers in the
Far West working as a cowboy cook and wrangler and at various farm
and forestry jobs, and once worked his way to Paris and back.

He recounts these early adventures in *An Autobiographical Novel*.
The first impression you get is that it is mostly about other people—
Louis Armstrong, Alexander Berkman, Clarence Darrow, Eugene Debs,
Marcel Duchamp, Emma Goldman, D.H. Lawrence, Diego Rivera, Carl
Sandburg, Edward Sapir, Sacco and Vanzetti all turn up briefly, along
with an Indian woman who introduces him to sexual yoga, a member
of the Bugs Moran gang who later retires to Hollywood as a consultant
for gangster movies, a talkative poet who says he has belonged to "the
three most gossipy organizations in modern life, the Anglo-Catholics,
the Trotskyites, and the homosexuals," and a multitude of others—
anarchists, Communists, Wobblies, dadaists, surrealists, occultists,
prostitutes, crooks, cops, judges, jailers, hoboes, hillbillies, lumberjacks,
cowboys, Indians. . . . It's a fascinating book, not only for its account
of Rexroth's own incredible range of experiences, but for its evocation
of a radical-libertarian American subculture that passed away in the
early years of the century and for its glimpses of the 1920s bohemianism that foreshadowed the later worldwide counterculture. "What I

was witnessing was the development in a few places in Chicago, New York, and Paris of a culture pattern that was to spread all over the world. In another generation all professional people of any pretense to bohemianism in Sydney or Oslo did the things we did, but back in those days we all knew one another."[2]

An Autobiographical Novel leaves off in 1927, when Rexroth moved to San Francisco. (He said he liked it because it was accessible to the Western mountains, remote from New York cultural domination, and virtually the only major American city that was not settled by puritans but by "gamblers, prostitutes, rascals, and fortune seekers.")[3] In the thirties and forties he played an active role in a number of libertarian, civil rights and antiwar groups (during World War II he was a conscientious objector), and he was the leading spirit in the literary and cultural ferment that led to the postwar San Francisco Renaissance. During the fifties and sixties he wrote poems, plays, essays and social criticism, translated poetry from seven languages, presented book reviews and other programs over noncommercial radio KPFA, and pioneered the reading of poetry to jazz.

In 1968 he moved to Santa Barbara, California, where he taught courses in underground poetry and song. Apart from several extended visits to Japan, he lived there until his death in 1982.

* * *

I was fortunate enough to get to know him a little in the sixties, when I attended a class he was giving at San Francisco State College. He had been at odds with academia all his life (he called the universities "fog factories"), but by this time his stature was so undeniable and there was such a demand for "relevance" in education that he was allowed to create whatever course he wanted. His "class," which was certainly more instructive than any other I ever took, consisted simply of open-ended discussions of anything and everything, along with occasional other activities such as group dramatic performances.

He was generally pretty sympathetic to the recent countercultural developments in which most of us were involved, but he tempered our naïve enthusiasms with a healthy dose of humor and skepticism, made us aware of larger perspectives—comparing Bob Dylan with underground French singers we had never heard of, or declaring that the greatest psychedelic artist was some medieval mystic who had painted her own visions, or heartily approving the most radical antiwar actions while cautioning us against the manipulations of bureaucratic leftists. Occasionally, aroused by some social atrocity or some instance of personal meanness, he would lash out with a withering attack. Usually he just genially bantered with people. He rarely harped on his own views, but amid the give and take of conversation he would slip in a joke or an anecdote that would subtly undercut our illusions and put in a new light whatever we were talking about. Sometimes months or years later I would remember some seemingly offhand remark he had made and suddenly realize what his point was, and appreciate how modestly and tactfully he had made it.

His drawling, gravelly voice recalled W.C. Fields's, and in his public appearances he sometimes adopted a sort of Fieldsian oratorical manner to go along with it. "That reminds me of a time [*eyes rolled back nostalgically*] when I was talking to Lewis Mumford—a man with whom I usually agree [*muttered out of the side of his mouth*]—and he said . . ." This ironic showbiz persona was very entertaining, but I think he used it primarily to get his points across without too much solemnity: to the casual observer unaware of the irony he might seem to be merely a slightly pompous, name-dropping old "colorful character" recounting an amusing anecdote. He was no doubt aware of his own merits, but to me he never seemed to be caught up with himself—writing or talking, he was always dialoguing. So many writers call attention to every little finding they've come up with; Rexroth would toss off really original insights as if they were just well-known banalities, or attribute his own merits to others—many are the writers he praised for being mature, courageous, widely learned, at home in many cultures, etc., who were actually far less so than he himself. He was reputed to be pretty cantankerous at times, but to me what stands out is his geniality and magnanimity.

But I didn't know him well enough to say much about his personal life. This book deals mainly with his writings—and only with certain aspects of them. I wrote it for two reasons. I wanted to sort out for myself what I found valuable and what I disagreed with in a writer who has meant a lot to me; and I wanted to interest other people in reading him. I hope I succeed at least in the latter.

* * *

Some of Rexroth's earliest poems resemble the "cubist" poems of Gertrude Stein, Guillaume Apollinaire and Pierre Reverdy: they break up and restructure verbal elements like cubist painting does with visual elements. They also reflect his studies in primitive song and modern linguistics. He says that this sort of experimental eclecticism, which he shared with many other poets of the twenties, stemmed from the belief that "the current language of society had been debauched by the exploitative uses to which it had been put, and that it was necessary to find gaps in the structure of communication which were still fluent and through which the mind of the reader could be assaulted."[4] Eventually he came to feel that he could achieve the same effects within more accessible forms. Apart from those few early exceptions most of his poems are pretty straightforward and need little or no explication.

312

An academic critic once sarcastically referred to Rexroth, Gary Snyder and Philip Whalen as "members of the bear-shit-on-the-trail school of poetry."[5] Rexroth, of course, took this as a compliment. He often spent months at a time in the woods and mountains, and quite a few of his poems reflect his experiences there. In one of the most beautiful he is lying beside a waterfall reading *The Signature of All Things* by Jakob Boehme, the visionary mystic who "saw the world as streaming in the electrolysis of love."

> Through the deep July day the leaves
> Of the laurel, all the colors
> Of gold, spin down through the moving
> Deep laurel shade all day. They float
> On the mirrored sky and forest
> For a while, and then, still slowly
> Spinning, sink through the crystal deep
> Of the pool to its leaf gold floor. . . .
> The wren broods in her moss domed nest.
> A newt struggles with a white moth
> Drowning in the pool. The hawks scream,
> Playing together on the ceiling
> Of heaven. The long hours go by.[6]

So many of his love poems take place in nature that after a reading he was once asked, "Mr. Rexroth, don't you ever make love *in*doors?" In this one he and his lover are lying in a canoe lodged in a waterlily bed in a Midwestern stream.

> Let your odorous hair fall across our eyes;
> Kiss me with those subtle, melodic lips. . . .
> Move softly, move hardly at all, part your thighs,
> Take me slowly while our gnawing lips
> Fumble against the humming blood in our throats.
> Move softly, do not move at all, but hold me,
> Deep, still, deep within you, while time slides away,
> As this river slides beyond this lily bed,
> And the thieving moments fuse and disappear
> In our mortal, timeless flesh.[7]

Back in the city, Rexroth emceed the famous 1955 gathering at which Allen Ginsberg first read "Howl." As a defense witness at the obscenity trial that soon followed he dumbfounded the prosecutor by remarking that Ginsberg was simply carrying on a venerable tradition, going back to the Biblical prophets who came forth to denounce the iniquities of society. This is equally true of Rexroth's own "Thou Shalt Not Kill," a bitter antiestablishment diatribe written a couple years earlier upon the death of Dylan Thomas, which somewhat resembles and probably influenced Ginsberg's poem:

You are murdering the young men. . . .
You,
The hyena with polished face and bow tie,
In the office of a billion dollar
Corporation devoted to service;
The vulture dripping with carrion,
Carefully and carelessly robed in imported tweeds,
Lecturing on the Age of Abundance;
The jackal in double-breasted gabardine,
Barking by remote control,
In the United Nations . . .[8]

Besides these three main themes of "sex, mysticism and revolution," there are satirical epigrams (this one is on British cooking)—

How can they write or paint
In a country where it
Would be nicer to be
Fed intravenously?[9]

Elegies (this is from one in memory of his first wife, Andrée)—

I know that spring again is splendid
As ever, the hidden thrush
As sweetly tongued, the sun as vital—
But these are the forest trails we walked together,
These paths, ten years together.
We thought the years would last forever,
They are all gone now, the days
We thought would not come for us are here.[10]

Family scenes (in this one, which may seem strange to people raised in our increasingly illiterate age, he is fishing while one of his daughters sits nearby reading Homer)—

Mary is seven. Homer
Is her favorite author.
. . . She says, "Aren't those gods
Terrible? All they do is
Fight like those angels in Milton
And play tricks on the poor Greeks
And Trojans. I like Aias
And Odysseus best. They are
Lots better than those silly
Gods."[11]

And a variety of other genres too numerous to quote—lyrics to music (folk tunes, Elizabethan tunes, Erik Satie, Duke Ellington, Ornette Coleman); Buddhist meditations in Japan, recited to koto and shakuhachi ("The Silver Swan," "On Flower Wreath Hill"); feminine mystical-erotic poems which he pretended he had translated from a

314

young Japanese woman ("The Love Poems of Marichiko"); surreal Mother Goose rhymes and a subversive "Bestiary" for his children; reminiscences comic ("Portrait of the Author as a Young Anarchist"), erotic ("When We with Sappho") and nostalgic ("A Living Pearl"); memorials to repressed revolutions ("From the Paris Commune to the Kronstadt Rebellion"); open letters ("A Letter to William Carlos Williams," "Fundamental Disagreement with Two Contemporaries" addressed to Tristan Tzara and André Breton); and translations from Greek, Latin, French, Spanish, Italian, Chinese and Japanese (including several volumes of Oriental women poets).

What I think of as especially characteristic of Rexroth's poetry is the way he interrelates even the most disparate and seemingly incongruous topics. However immersed in nature, he always remains aware of the human world, and the juxtaposition of the two realms cuts through both nature sentimentality and civilized pettiness. Watching the constellations, he envisions the Spanish Civil War ("Requiem for the Spanish Dead"). Climbing in the mountains, he remembers Sacco and Vanzetti ("Climbing Milestone Mountain," "Fish Peddler and Cobbler"). Erotic relations interweave with evocations of the elegant mathematical relations that order the universe ("Golden Section," "Theory of Numbers"). Elegiac reveries drift from poetry to history to nature to society:

> The centuries have changed little in this art,
> The subjects are still the same.
> "For Christ's sake take off your clothes and get into bed,
> We are not going to live forever."
> "Petals fall from the rose,"
> We fall from life,
> Values fall from history like men from shellfire,
> Only a minimum survives,
> Only an unknown achievement.
> They can put it all on the headstones,
> In all the battlefields,
> "Poor guy, he never knew what it was all about."
> Spectacled men will come with shovels in a thousand years,
> Give lectures in universities on cultural advances, cultural lags. . . .
> This year we made four major ascents,
> Camped for two weeks at timberline,
> Watched Mars swim close to the earth,
> Watched the black aurora of war
> Spread over the sky of a decayed civilization.
> These are the last terrible years of authority.
> The disease has reached its crisis,
> Ten thousand years of power,
> The struggle of two laws,
> The rule of iron and spilled blood,
> The abiding solidarity of living blood and brain.[12]

I quote this fairly typical passage at some length to give you an idea of the tone and flow of his poetry; but it is difficult to convey just how widely he ranges and how complexly he interrelates without quoting whole pages. You can see this especially in the "philosophical reveries" gathered in his *Collected Longer Poems*. In the longest and most interesting one, "The Dragon and the Unicorn," which recounts a trip he took to Europe in the late forties, the chronological narration of his travels and encounters is interspersed with pointed cultural and political comments and with more abstract philosophical or mystical passages. The latter act as a counterpoint to the narrative, sometimes moving independently with no apparent relation to it; sometimes seeming to comment on it (a description of a bohemian gathering is followed by a discourse on the dilemma of isolated persons in a world of reification); sometimes clashing with it (a denunciation of some miserable social reality is followed by a vision of universal community). Rexroth notes that these passages of comment should be taken with a grain of salt—they are part of an internal dialogue and are often juxtaposed with complementary or contrasting viewpoints. In one place, for example, he declares: "The only Absolute is the Community of Love with which Time ends,"[13] but in another: "The Absolute as a community of love . . . I doubt if I believe it, but it seems to me a more wholesome metaphysical metaphor than most."[14]

To my taste Rexroth's philosophical reveries are much more interesting than the comparable works of T.S. Eliot and Ezra Pound —two poets he heartily disliked and whose influence he combatted all his life. At their best they may be "greater" poets (though even that is debatable), but Rexroth is certainly a saner and wiser one. He has none of Eliot's snobbery or neurotic prissiness, and even at his crustiest he is far less cranky, obsessive and self-indulgent than Pound. You can take his reflections seriously without having to make allowances for some absurd reactionary ideology.

During the reign of Eliot, Rexroth found most American poetry to be "dull academic stuff by petty people who lead dull, petty, academic lives. In the right circles it has been thought terribly unfashionable to write about anything so vulgar as love, death, nature—any of the real things that happen to real people."[15] Against this state of affairs he was constantly insisting on relevance, putting things back into perspective. Speaking of jazz poetry, he noted that despite its apparent innovativeness it simply "returns poetry to music and to public entertainment as it was in the days of Homer or the troubadours. It forces poetry to deal with aspects of life which it has tended to avoid in the recent past."[16] When Eliot pontificated on the need for "tradition" and disparaged William Blake as a naïve eccentric who made up his system from scratch, Rexroth observed: "Mr. Eliot's tradition goes back to Aquinas as interpreted in the pages of *L'Action Française*. Blake's goes back to the Memphite Theology and the Pyramid Texts."[17]

While academic poets followed Eliot's pseudoclassical doctrine that poetry should be "impersonal," Rexroth was writing poems that are classical in the truest sense, mature personal responses to the real issues of life—right in the tradition of Sappho, Petronius, Hitomaro, Tu Fu and the other classic poets he translated so superbly.

Rexroth sometimes played down his essays as mere "journalism" written to pay the rent while he pursued his primary work as a poet, but that is one point on which I have never taken him seriously. He is certainly one of my favorite poets, but as an essayist I think he is in a class by himself. I don't know any other so lively and so sane, so large-minded, so pithy and so bracing. He titles one of his collections *Assays* to recall Montaigne's original sense of the word *essai:* trial, test, experiment, attempt to come to grips with reality. One of the essays in that volume celebrates another writer he resembles in more ways than one: "Those guffawing, tobacco-spitting travel books that made Mark Twain's reputation in the first place and that gave Van Wyck Brooks fainting spells are fundamentally right. Always Mark Twain points out the human meaning of St. Peter's or the pyramids or the Pantheon."[18] This is just what Rexroth does. He is more sophisticated than Twain, and less corny, but he has the same gusto, the same worldly-wise irony, the same wry, skeptical, down-to-earth outlook he sums up in his essay on American humor:

> These are the key words of great—classic—epic—Homeric—humor. A sense of the consistent principle of incongruity on which Nature, for all our science and philosophy, really operates. The realization that the accepted, official version of anything is most likely false and that all authority is based on fraud. The courage to face and act on these two conclusions. The appreciation of the wonderful hilarity of the processes of human procreation and elimination. The acceptance of the prime fact that nobody made it that way—it just happened. . . . Life is all a great joke—but only the brave ever get the point.[19]

I don't want to give the impression that he was merely a cracker-barrel philosopher. Most self-educated people have a lot of blind spots, but Rexroth seems to have explored just about all the areas of human endeavor systematically, many of them deeply. The range of his reading was truly astonishing—histories, cookbooks, nature guides, geology surveys, ethnology reports, political polemics, theological treatises, the entire *Encyclopaedia Britannica* . . . He reviewed several thousand books over KPFA alone, and that was only a public-service sideline (a half-hour program every week for twenty years).

Yet he does not seem at all bookish. Whether he is writing about ancient Chinese science or American Indian songs or Van Gogh's paintings or "Rimbaud as Capitalist Adventurer," all this erudition is digested, connected, and grounded in personal experience. His essays

317

on jazz, for example, reveal a sound knowledge of its technical aspects (comparisons with classical music, etc.), but above all he zeroes in on its human history, its social roles, the lives of its creators, the conditions of its performance. He may reminisce about dancing at jazz clubs in the twenties, or recount a conversation with Charlie Parker or Charlie Mingus to debunk the Beats' jazz mystique, or (discussing the connection of music with the rhythms of sex and dance and work) throw in a passing remark like "Anybody who has ever worked on the range knows that not only does the true cowboy ballad swing in 'horse time,' but that you can change the pace of your horse by changing the rhythm of your song."[20]

Once in a while, particularly in the more ephemeral articles that he dashed off at the last minute, he will come out with some extravagant or even preposterous pronouncement. But by and large I think his opinions are pretty well founded. You won't agree with all of them (many are in any case just matters of taste), but what he says is almost always provocative. Criticizing the superficiality of Ionesco's satires, he says: "A satirical art which beats only dead dogs . . . leaves the audience with comfortable feelings of amused superiority."[21] Rexroth is more likely to puncture one of your own illusions and leave you realizing all you've still got to learn.

He said he tried to write like he talked, and he did. His autobiography and many of his essays were in fact not really "written" at all, but spoken ad lib, recorded and transcribed with minimal editing. Yet however he seems to digress, to hop around spontaneously from topic to topic, when he is done you realize how unerringly he has gotten to the heart of the matter. In his essay on Marcus Aurelius he wants to convey how far philosophy has declined since it related to real issues of life. Look how he brings this home in one droll, unforgettable image: "If a college student's mother died, his girl got pregnant, he acquired a loathsome disease, or he decided to become a conscientious objector, would he go to his philosophy professor for advice?"[22] He always brings things back to basics. His gist can usually be understood at first reading, even if you are unfamiliar with the books and ideas and events to which he refers; but there is always plenty more to sink your teeth into, and lots of intriguing hints for further explorations. I've read some of his essays so many times I practically know them by heart, yet each time I go back I discover things I hadn't noticed before. Even when his topic is something in which I have no particular interest, I still find him hard to put down. It's not just that he has an engaging style, it's that his breadth of vision puts whatever he is dealing with in a fresh perspective.

But he does have an engaging style, always recognizable yet as variegated as his topics. He can be free and easygoing ("a lot of Mozart sounds like a country boy whistling along his way to the swimming hole")[23] or as hard-boiled as Hammett or Chandler, of whose work he says: "The secret of this kind of writing is that it isn't buying anything and it isn't selling anything."[24] In a phrase he can evoke the Yiddish world of Isaac Singer ("those passionate arguments that used to sprinkle the whiskers with sour cream")[25] or epitomize the mordant, cynical style of Tacitus ("a style like a tray of dental instruments").[26] But he knows that "style never is just a matter of style, but the outward sign and garb of an inner spiritual state."[27] If he discusses a poet's prosody, it is not a mere academic exercise: he will show how it reflects a way of looking at things, a response to life. Denise Levertov's, for instance, is "a kind of animal grace of the word, a pulse like the footfalls of a cat or the wingbeats of a gull. It is the intense aliveness of an alert domestic love—the wedding of form and content in poems which themselves celebrate a kind of perpetual wedding of two persons always realized as two responsible sensibilities."[28] You never read very far in his aesthetic discussions without coming upon some worldly-wise social or moral or psychological connection. "The interiority of the characters [in Defoe's novels] is revealed by their elaborately presented outside. When they talk about their own motives, their psychology, their morals, their self-analyses and self-justifications are to be read backwards, as of course is true of most people."[29]

As a debunker of the imbecilities of mass culture Rexroth can be as entertaining as H.L. Mencken—

> This stuff [Maoist "proletarian literature"] is ridiculous and resembles nothing so much as nineteenth-century Sunday school stories of the little Roman boy who helped his sister escape from the lions, defied the millions of the emperor, ran errands for St. Paul and went to heaven.[30]

And just as scathing—

> Television is designed to arouse the most perverse, sadistic, acquisitive drives. I mean, a child's television program is a real vision of hell, and it's only because we are so used to these things that we pass them over. If any of the people who have had visions of hell, like Vergil or Dante or Homer, were to see these things it would scare them into fits.[31]

At his crustiest he in fact seems like nothing so much as a deeper and more radical Mencken. But while Mencken delighted in virtually indiscriminate verbal assaults for their own sake, Rexroth's debunking is always in the context of a positive vision. However outraged or pessimistic he may sometimes be, he is a world apart from that modern glib cynicism that has gotten so out of touch with any human fulfillment that it has nothing left but a dependent love-hate relation to the most delirious manifestations of cultural alienation. Always he relates to the real human life that goes on behind the façade of the inhuman system:

> Every day all states do things which, if they were the acts of individuals, would lead to summary arrest and often execution. . . . Most people except politicians and authors work out for themselves, in secret, ways of living which ignore organized society as much as possible. . . . What is called "growing up," "getting a little common sense," is largely the learning of techniques for outwitting the more destructive forces at large in the social order. The mature man lives quietly, does good privately, assumes personal responsibility for his actions, treats others with friendliness and courtesy, finds mischief boring and keeps out of it. Without this hidden conspiracy of good will society would not endure an hour.[32]

Whether or not most people do this, Rexroth is clearly implying his own personal ethic. He's been around enough to see through what he calls the Social Lie or the Great Fraud—to know that the "official version of anything is most likely false and that all authority is based on fraud." "An appreciable number of Americans really do believe the Great Fraud of the mass culture, what the French call the *hallucination publicitaire*. They only know what they read in the papers. They think it is really like the movies. . . . The art of being civilized is the art of learning to read between the lies."[33]

This is one of Rexroth's basic touchstones. Those who do read between the lies are at least to that extent his allies, whatever their other faults. "There is a lot of bullshit in Lawrence, Miller, or Patchen —but their enemies are my enemies."[34] He laughs at Henry Miller as a would-be deep thinker or visionary, but he appreciates him as a great picaresque autobiographer with an instinctive immunity to the Social Lie:

> Can you remember when you first started to read? Doubtless you thought that some day you would find in books the truth, the answer to the very puzzling life you were discovering around you. But you never did. If you were alert, you discovered that books were conventions, as unlike life as a game of chess. The written word is a sieve. Only so much of reality gets through as fits the size and shape of the screen, and in some ways that is never enough. . . . Most of the real difficulty of communication comes from social convention, from a vast conspiracy to agree to accept the world as something it really isn't at all. . . .
>
> Literature is a social defense mechanism. Remember again when you were a child. You thought that some day you would grow up and find a world of real adults—the people who really made things run— and understand how and why things ran. . . . Then, as the years went on, you learned, through more or less bitter experience, that there aren't, and never have been, any such people, anywhere. Life is just

a mess, full of tall children, grown stupider, less alert and resilient, and nobody knows what makes it go—as a whole, or any part of it. *But nobody ever tells.*

Henry Miller tells. Andersen told *about* the little boy and the Emperor's new clothes. Miller is the little boy himself. He tells about the Emperor, about the pimples on his behind, and the warts on his private parts, and the dirt between his toes. Other writers in the past have done this, of course, and they are the great ones, the real classics. But they have done it within the conventions of literature. They have used the forms of the Great Lie to expose the truth.[35]

I've never seen any other literary critic write anything quite like that. Rexroth is more knowledgeable and reliable than Miller, but he has the same innocent eye, the same lack of reverence for "Literature-with-a-capital-L," whether he is reviewing modern writers or reassessing key works of the past.

Most of his essays on the latter are collected in his two-volume *Classics Revisited.*[36] This is certainly a more relevant selection than most choices of the "hundred greatest books." To mention only one significant difference, most such lists are limited to Western works—a provincialism that is ridiculous in this day and age. Rexroth revisits most of the recognized Western classics, but he also introduces the reader to a number of others that are just as interesting, including basic Oriental works like the *Mahabharata,* the *Tao Te Ching,* and what he considers the world's two greatest novels, Lady Murasaki's *The Tale of Genji* and the Chinese *Dream of the Red Chamber.*

The ancient Middle Eastern story of *Gilgamesh* ("the first conscious self"), Herodotus's *History,* the *Bhagavad Gita,* the Finnish *Kalevala* ("the most ecological of epics"), the poetry of Tu Fu, the essays of Montaigne ("the inventor of the empiric ego"), *Don Quixote, The Tempest,* the memoirs of Casanova ("natural man living at the highest pitch"), Stendhal's *The Red and the Black* ("the first black comedy"), *War and Peace* and *Huckleberry Finn* are just a few of the other "basic documents in the history of the imagination" whose pertinence Rexroth reveals in these amazingly pithy little essays. East or West, ancient or recent, he cuts across historical and cultural distances to make the most far-ranging connections. Catullus's sensibility "is the material of the lyrics of Bob Dylan." The characters in *Njal's Saga* "are adult in a fashion unknown to Homer's Agamemnon or Proust's Swann." "Most of the great British ballads could be turned into Nō plays and vice versa." Baudelaire, of all people, arrives at a vision "not unlike Buddhism in its starkest form."

Part of the interest of these works is of course precisely their contrast to the present, the revelation of how people in other times and places lived and thought. But Rexroth always points out the things that remain the same amid all the differences: "Kerouac's *On the Road* differs vastly from *The Satyricon* in lack of insight, irony, and literary skill, but its characters are all drawn from the same unchanged class." Laclos's *Les Liaisons Dangereuses* "assumes a world like our celebrities, our international Jet Sets. . . . It is a description of people we know."

Some writers directly foreshadow our present condition: William Blake "could diagnose the early symptoms of the world ill because he saw them as signs that man was being deprived of literally half his being. . . . He is in fact concerned with the epic tragedy of mankind as it enters an epoch of depersonalization unequalled in history." Baudelaire "is the founder of the modern sensibility . . . . Some learn to cope with this sensibility. He was at its mercy, because he embodied it totally. He lived in a permanent crisis of the moral nervous system. His conviction that social relationships were one immense lie was physiological."

In other cases there may be no direct connection, but an illuminating parallel: "During the long war with Sparta, Athenian life became widely neurotic. A new type of interpersonal sickness came into being. The organs of reciprocity were crippled. Words for human relationships lost their meanings and turned into their opposites. Thucydides describes this derangement of communication at length in one of his greatest passages, a diagnosis of the internalization of madness of war which sounds like a description of contemporary America."

On the other hand, Whitman's *Leaves of Grass,* ostensibly a celebration of the America of his time, actually envisions "a social order whose essence is the liberation and universalization of selfhood." His people "all seem to be working for 'nothing,' participants in a universal creative effort in which each discovers his ultimate individuation. . . . Today we know that it is Whitman's vision or nothing."

Whether a work represents a turning point of the past or envisions a potential future, Rexroth's ultimate test is whether it remains true to the perennial human realities, whether it really "tells." Reviewing some new translations of the Greek tragedies, he says:

> They say our civilization is based on the Bible, Homer and the Greek tragedians. For my taste, the Bible is a dangerous book, because it can be, and with few exceptions has been, interpreted to give guarantees to life that life in fact never offers. Here in these plays, as in Homer, is life as it really is, men as we really are, when we beat our wives or cheat our grocer or plan our perfect societies or run for office or write our poems—but projected against the empty and splendid heavens, and made noble. Take away the costumes and the grand language, it is the same pride, the same doom haunting Orestes that haunts every Certified Public Accountant, every housewife, every automobile salesman. How much nicer people, and how much happier, they'd all be if they only knew it. Here is their chance to learn.[37]

322

2. Magnanimity and Mysticism

> HOFUKU (*pointing at mountains*): "Is not this Reality?"
> CHŌKEI: "It is, but it's a pity to say so."[1]

If I had to pick out a single text to exemplify what I like about Rexroth it would probably be his essay on the classic Chinese novels. In this passage he is characterizing the virtues of those vast, marvelous books:

> What are these virtues? First, an absolute mastery of pure narrative. Second, humanity. Third, as the synthesis of virtues one and two, a whole group of qualities that should have some one name—reticence, artistic humility, maturity, objectivity, total sympathy, the ability to reveal the macrocosm in the microcosm, the moral universe in the physical act, the depths of psychological insight in the trivia of happenstance, without ever saying anything about it, or them—the "big" things, that is. This is a quality of style. It is the fundamental quality of the greatest style. It does have a name, although it is not a term we usually think of as part of the jargon of literary criticism. The word is magnanimity. The antonym, I guess, is self-indulgence.[2]

He goes on to deplore the self-indulgence in one form or another of virtually all twentieth-century writers, from Proust and Henry James to Kerouac and on down. Then he singles out one notable exception, Ford Madox Ford's *Parade's End*, the only "completely adult major novel of my time":

> Ford didn't label his thesis; he probably didn't know he had one in that sense. His characters didn't philosophize about it. He didn't snoop around in their minds with a lot of jargon. Nobody's consciousness streamed. It all just happened, like it does, and you were left with that —the brutal and the silly and the beautiful facts. It is so easy to be artistic. It is so hard to be mature.[3]

Variations on this theme recur throughout Rexroth's writings. In great drama, he says, "psychological and moral depth must be there, but there only to be discovered by those in the audience who themselves have such depth. These qualities cannot be written on the surface or they destroy the integrity of the action."[4] Whereas he agrees with Ford that "Dostoievsky was guilty of the worst possible taste in making his characters discuss the profundity of the very novel in which they were taking part."[5] "The troubled souls of Dostoievsky's novels are not grown men. They talk endlessly about things that adults learn it is better to keep quiet about. Tragedy ceases to be impressive when it is so garrulously articulate, and at last even to be believable."[6]

323

Rexroth has a special fondness for certain writers who embody a quiet, modest, unselfconscious wisdom—the biographer-fisherman Izaak Walton, the amateur naturalist Gilbert White, the antislavery Quaker John Woolman—while he detests the vanity of artists who glory in their supposedly special role:

> Michelangelo was surely
> A noisy man, and terribly
> Conceited. After all, nothing
> Ever happened to him that
> Doesn't happen to all of us.
> If you have a tragedy to
> Portray, you should be humble
> About it, you are serving
> The bread of communion.[7]

In his essay on Julius Caesar's writings he says: "Masterfully concealed in *The Gallic War* and *The Civil War* is a philosophy of human relationships that only maturity can comprehend or even recognize. The masterful concealment, of course, is an essential part of the maturity."[8] The same thing might be said of Rexroth's own writings. For my purposes in this book I have tended to cite his most explicit pronouncements, but if you read him through you will see that he usually deals with the "big things" with a light touch, and often leaves them implicit, to be discerned between the lines.

But if ever he does reveal his life philosophy, and even sum up its central themes in a single word, it is in that essay on the Chinese novels. Which continues:

During the Second World War I knew a little Quaker from a farm in Indiana who traveled around the country at his own expense and got up in First Day meetings to recite Webster's definition of magnanimity. He had "come with this concern to thee, because thee might find it helpful." This is the definition:

"**magnanimity**, *n.; pl. –ties. (F. magnanimité, L. magnanimitas.) 1. Quality of being magnanimous; that quality or combination of qualities in character enabling one to encounter danger and trouble with tranquility and firmness, to disdain injustice, meanness, and revenge, and to act and sacrifice for noble objects. 2. A deed or a disposition characterized by magnanimity. 3. Grandiose temperament; extravagance of soul. Rare.*"

Having said that the little old Quaker sat down and next week appeared at another meeting. It certainly did help me, probably more than any other words in those hideous years.

No artist belongs in the very first rank who is the victim of his creations. Only this special kind of nobility guaranteed the independence of the primary creators. Homer has it, but Dante does not. It is a kind of courage, like Johnson's famous "Courage, Sir, is the first of virtues, because without it, it is sometimes difficult to exercise the others."[9]

It is the courage to endure the inevitable "ruin of all bright things," to face the fact that "love does not last forever, friends betray each other, beauty fades, the mighty stumble in blood and their cities burn."[10] The "message" of Homer, as Rexroth approvingly paraphrases it, is that the universe has no inherent meaning, everything is ephemeral, the only values are those that people create in relation with each other. "The thing that endures, that gives value to life, is comradeship, loyalty, bravery, magnanimity, love, the relations of men in direct communication with each other. From this comes the beauty of life, its tragedy and its meaning, and from nowhere else."[11]

This may sound rather "existential," but nothing is more foreign to Rexroth than what he calls the *"angst* for *angst's* sake" of the "paralyzed rabbit metaphysics of existentialism." "I do not respond to the 'existentialist dilemma' at all. Its inventor, Søren Kierkegaard, has always seemed to me a sick man who treated his girl friend wretchedly. A man 'badly in need of help' as the head-shrinkers say. . . . I do not look on my Being every hour as a dreadful meeting with reality. I like it."[12]

If Rexroth often evokes the "tragic sense of life," at other times his works reveal a more mystical consciousness. These two attitudes would seem to contradict each other, but he appears to treat them as complementary, equally valid perspectives—sometimes contrasting them, as in the dialectic of his philosophical reveries, sometimes combining them, as in his plays, which have tragic Greek themes but which, like Japanese Nō plays, culminate not in a dramatic climax but in a transcendent resolution of karmic entanglements.[13]

He describes his point of view as "a religious anarchism" or an "ethical mysticism," and in one place, in lieu of elaborating, he refers the reader to some of his major influences: "For better statements, I refer you to the work of Martin Buber, Albert Schweitzer, D.H. Lawrence, Boehme, D.T. Suzuki, Piotr Kropotkin, or, for that matter, to the Gospels and the sayings of Buddha, or to Lao Tze and Chuang Tze."[14] This may seem a rather eclectic list, but it does give a good idea of the different facets of his "religious" philosophy. Which might be summed up in his lines:

> What is taken in
> In contemplation is poured out
> In love.[15]

In his autobiography Rexroth describes an experience he had when he was four or five years old, sitting on the curb in front of his house in early summer:

An awareness, not a feeling, of timeless, spaceless, total bliss occupied me or I occupied it completely. I do not want to use terms like "over-whelmed me" or "I was rapt away" or any other that would imply the possession of myself by anything external, much less abnormal. On the contrary, this seemed to me to be my normal and natural life which was going on all the time and my sudden acute consciousness of it only a matter of attention.[16]

In their deepest and most enduring form such "mystical" experiences are often associated with meditation and spiritual discipline; but Rexroth implies that the same awareness comes to all of us at moments, though we may scarcely know what is happening, and it is strangely easy to forget as we once again become caught up in the compulsive turmoil of the world.

The peace which comes from the habit of contemplation ... is not rare nor hard to find. It offers itself at moments to everyone, from early childhood on, although less and less often if it is not welcomed. It can be seized and trained and cultivated until it becomes a constant habit in the background of daily life. Without it life is only turbulence, from which eventually meaning and even all intensity of feeling die out in tedium and disorder.[17]

"At the core of life," he says in his essay on the *Tao Te Ching,* "is a tiny, steady flame of contemplation."[18] Even without knowing anything about it, people instinctively return to this "quiet center." It is always there, even amid the most turbulent situations; but some scenes are especially conducive.

Whoever wrote the little psalms of the *Tao Te Ching* believed that the long calm regard of moving water was one of the highest forms of prayer. ... Many sports are actually forms of contemplative activity. Fishing in quiet waters is especially so. Countless men who would burst out laughing if presented with a popular vulgarization of Zen Buddhism, and who would certainly find it utterly incomprehensible, practice the contemplative life by flowing water, rod in hand, at least for a few days each year. As the great mystics have said, they too know it is the illumination of these few days that gives meaning to the rest of their lives.[19]

Rexroth's nature poems are full of such experiences. In this one he is lying under the stars:

> My body is asleep. Only
> My eyes and brain are awake.
> The stars stand around me
> Like gold eyes. I can no longer

> Tell where I begin and leave off.
> The faint breeze in the dark pines,
> And the invisible grass,
> The tipping earth, the swarming stars
> Have an eye that sees itself.[20]

Sometimes, as above, the experiences are described more or less explicitly. More often they are simply hinted at:

> When I dragged the rotten log
> From the bottom of the pool,
> It seemed heavy as stone.
> I let it lie in the sun
> For a month; and then chopped it
> Into sections, and split them
> For kindling, and spread them out
> To dry some more. . . .

Late that night, as he steps out of his cabin to look at the stars—

> Suddenly I saw at my feet,
> Spread on the floor of night, ingots
> Of quivering phosphorescence,
> And all about were scattered chips
> Of pale cold light that was alive.[21]

This was no doubt a real sequence of events, but at the same time it seems to suggest a parallel inner settling and illumination—and it does this in a manner truer to the "unselfing" character of the process than if he had said *I had* such and such experiences. As in many of the great Chinese and Japanese poems, a state of mind is conveyed through the lucidity of what at first appears as merely an objective nature scene. The outer landscape corresponds to the inner one, the macrocosm to the microcosm.

In a manner almost reminiscent of Whitman, Rexroth evokes the vastest connections and reflections—

> The immense stellar phenomenon
> Of dawn focuses in the egret
> And flows out, and focuses in me
> And flows infinitely away
> To touch the last galactic dust. . . .
> My wife has been swimming in the breakers,
> She comes up the beach to meet me, nude,
> Sparkling with water, singing high and clear
> Against the surf. The sun crosses
> The hills and fills her hair, as it lights
> The moon and glorifies the sea

And deep in the empty mountains melts
The snow of Winter and the glaciers
Of ten thousand thousand years.[22]

In his last poems, mainly written in Japan, these moments of
"cosmic consciousness" are expressed in increasingly Buddhist terms—
above all in terms of the ultimate vision of the Avatamsaka (Flower
Wreath) Sutra:

the Net of Indra,
The compound infinities of infinities,
The Flower Wreath,
Each universe reflecting
Every other, reflecting
Itself from every other . . .[23]

Rexroth's work seems to reflect a significant Zen influence, but
actually he was quite critical of many aspects of Zen and professed a
greater affinity with other forms of Buddhism. He lambasted popularized Western Zen as an irresponsible, pretentious fad, but he also
criticized traditional Japanese Zen for its complicity with military regimes, from the samurai to World War II, and he seems to have had
little taste for the cultism and guru worship too often found in Zen as
well as in other Oriental religious disciplines. He would no doubt have
granted that Zen meditation is one of the most effective ways to
cultivate the peace of contemplation "until it becomes a constant habit
in the background of daily life." But he seemed to feel that too urgent
a striving for enlightenment may miss the point. Buddha's last words
are said to have been: "The combinations of the world are unstable by
nature. Monks, strive without ceasing." Rexroth, in a more Taoist
frame of mind, advises:

The combinations
Of the world are unstable
By nature. Take it easy.[24]

The truest illumination, he says, arises as a side-effect of a way of
life, not as an experience sought for its own sake.

I believe that an ever-increasing capacity for recollection and transcendence is developed by a kind of life rather than by manipulation.
Buddhism is certainly pure religious empiricism. It has no beliefs, only
the simply and purely defined religious experience which becomes for
the experiencers an always accessible and ever-abiding present reality.
The foundation for this is neither nervous-system gymnastics nor
theological notions. It is the Noble Eightfold Path, whose culmination
is the "unruffledness"—Nirvana—which underlies reality.[25]

328

He didn't think much of the idea of using of psychedelics as a short cut to mystical vision—at most he conceded that they had given many young people their first hint of the "interiority" repressed by middle-class American culture. In this context he often quoted St. John of the Cross: "Visions are symptoms of the defect of vision." For Rexroth the transcendent religious experience is not a vision of some different, supernatural world, but a reawakened awareness of this one.

> The real objects are their own transcendental meaning. . . . The holy is in the heap of dust—it is the heap of dust. . . . True illumination is habitude. We are unaware that we live in the light of lights because it casts no shadow. When we become aware of it we know it as birds know air and fish know water.[26]

People tend to describe such moments of awareness in terms of their own diverse religious beliefs, but the actual experiences seem to be pretty much the same, and are also found among nonreligious people. Though beyond rational conceptualization, they do not necessarily imply anything supernatural. Rexroth is quite clear about this distinction. He is refreshingly free of New Age gush and too perceptive to be taken in by the superstitions and pseudosciences so widely believed in even today. Recalling the otherwise intelligent people of his own generation who swallowed astrology or Reichian orgone boxes, he observes: "Anyone who had taken a course in high school physics would have known that this stuff was arrant nonsense but the trouble was that these people had lost belief in high school physics along with their belief in capitalism or religion. It was all one fraud to them."[27]

He is almost equally skeptical about the scientific pretensions of modern psychology and psychoanalysis. In his amusing article "My Head Gets Tooken Apart" he describes a time when he was paid by an Institute of Personality Assessment and Research to participate in a three-day investigation of "the creative personality." After a hilarious account of the battery of tests, interviews and questionnaires he is put through, he concludes:

> What did it all mean? Nothing. . . . This unvarnished hokum with which our society intimidates itself is far less effective—far less scientific—than the varnished hokum of other days and peoples. Any Sioux medicine man, any kind and attentive priest, any properly aged grandmother, any Chinese herbalist, could have found out more in a half hour than these people did in three days. . . . I for one would, if I had my rathers, far rather trust myself to the boys in horns and bearskins who painted the Altamira cave.[28]

Some of the traditional practices, he implies, may at least possess a kernel of intuitive insight into the basic human situations. Hokum or not, people are instinctively drawn to whatever seems to express the

329

psychological or spiritual archetypes, the perennial inner conflicts and relations and aspirations. "What is sought in Alchemy or the Hermetic Books or the Memphite Theology, or irrational fads like flying saucers, is the basic pattern of the human mind in symbolic garb."[29] And that basic pattern is found there because it came from other basically similar minds:

> What the Gnostics projected onto the screen of their profound ignorance as a picture of the universe was in reality a picture of their own minds. Its mythology is a symbolic portrayal, almost a deliberate one, of the forces which operate in the structuring and evolution of the human personality . . . an institutionalized panorama of what Jung has called the Collective Unconscious. . . . (This notion, as Jung has pointed out, does not involve any mysterious undersoul shared by all men—it is a collective picture because all men respond to life in much the same way, because they all have the same physiological endowment.) We can operate upon our minds by the manipulation of symbols if not on the cosmos.[30]

For Rexroth there is no question of believing in the objective validity of any occult or religious system; what he is interested in is the "interiority," the "values that cannot be reduced to quantities,"[31] which may find expression in such forms. Insofar as religion is an attempted explanation of objective reality, it is progressively outmoded by advances in mankind's knowledge; but it may, he says, have a continued relevance to inner, subjective realities:

> Ideally, religion is what would be left after man *knew* everything. . . . As the speculative constructions of religion fall away as explanations of "reality" they assume the character of symbolic masks of states of the soul. If they persist in the practices of a cult, we say they have been etherialized. It is precisely their irrationality which keeps dogma and ritual alive. If they can be reduced to "common-sense" explanations or denials they die away. Only the mysteries survive, because they correspond to the processes of man's internal life, outward visible signs of inner spiritual realities.[32]

Rexroth liked to say, "Religion is something you do, not something you believe." He had a fond interest in traditional folk-religious rituals and festivals of all sorts, to the point of extolling even their most threadbare modern vestiges. "I don't care if it takes Daddy a year to pay off the bills for the First Communion Party or the Bar Mitzvah or the wedding. For a moment there has been at least a token acknowledgment that even the poorest and most humdrum life is of transcendent importance, that no individual human being is insignificant."[33] In this spirit he himself participated in various religious communions—Buddhist, Vedantist, Quaker, and even Catholic.

> What attracted me [to Catholicism] was not its Christianity, but its paganism. . . . The liturgical life of the Church moved me because it echoes the most ancient responses to the turning of the year and the changing seasons, and the rhythms of animal and human life. For me the Sacraments transfigured the rites of passage . . . . In the rites of passage—the fundamental activities and relationships of life—birth, death, sexual intercourse, eating, drinking, choosing a vocation, adolescence, mortal illness—life at its important moments is ennobled by the ceremonious introduction of transcendence; the universe is focused on the event in a Mass or ceremony that is itself a kind of dance and a work of art.[34]

Needless to say, he was opposed to practically everything about the Catholic Church except its traditional rituals; but like many people he seems to have taken part in those religious practices that appealed to him and simply ignored the aspects that didn't. "Today we have large sections of our most literate population voluntarily adopting the religious behavior and beliefs of more primitive communities for purely pragmatic, psychologistic, personal reasons."[35] His Catholicizing was mostly within Anglo-Catholic communions, which offer the rituals while rejecting the central dogmatic authority of the Roman Church.

However that may be, it has always puzzled me how someone like Rexroth could have anything to do with any Christian church. It is one thing to practice some type of meditation or take part in some ritual or festival that everyone understands is simply an arbitrary form to focus one's life or celebrate communion; it is another to seem to lend credibility to repugnant institutions and to sick dogmas that are still widely believed. As Rexroth himself says in a different mood:

> For thousands of years men of good will have been trying to make Judaism and Christianity morally palatable to sane and civilized men. No other religions have ever required such efforts at etherialization. . . . Why do people bother? If they must have a religion, the basic texts of Taoism, Buddhism, Confucianism need no such reworking. It may be necessary, particularly of the Buddhist documents, to trim off the exotic rhetoric, but it is not necessary to make them mean exactly the opposite of what they say.[36]

Whatever his personal taste in rituals, Rexroth's writings on religion are usually lucid enough. As always he is seeking what might be relevant, suggestive, exemplary. In his study of the nineteenth-century radical Catholic Lamennais, for example, it is Lamennais's "spiritual sensibility" that interests him, "not the details of his changing theology and philosophy." "His doctrines changed, his life did not, and so it is his life and the literary, one might say, poetic, expression of that life consistency which is important."[37]

One thing for sure, there's nothing puritanical or unworldly about

Rexroth's mysticism. He says that the theme of his poems in *The Phoenix and the Tortoise* is

> the discovery of a basis for the recreation of a system of values in sacramental marriage. The process as I see it goes something like this: from abandon to erotic mysticism, from erotic mysticism to the ethical mysticism of sacramental marriage, thence to the realization of the ethical mysticism of universal responsibility—from the Dual to the Other. These poems might well be dedicated to D.H. Lawrence, who died in the attempt to refound a spiritual family.[38]

Like he said, there is a lot of bullshit in Lawrence—mushy rhetoric, corny primitivism, dated sexual polemics, even vaguely fascistic tendencies. What remains important is his struggle to get back to the primal realities, to restore the vital, organic connections; beginning with the most intimate one. Writing of Lawrence's love and nature poems, Rexroth says: "Reality streams through the body of Frieda, through everything she touches, every place she steps . . . everything stands out lit by a light not of this earth and at the same time completely of this earth . . . . Beyond Holy Matrimony lies the newly valued world of birds, beasts, and flowers—a sacramentalized, objective world. 'Look, we have come through'—to a transformed world, with a glory around it everywhere like ground lightning." And of his death poems: "Lawrence did not try to mislead himself with false promises, imaginary guarantees. Death is the absolute, unbreakable mystery. Communion and oblivion, sex and death, the mystery can be revealed—but it can be revealed only as totally inexplicable."[39]

Rexroth's own love poems manifest a Lawrencian reverence for sex as an ultimate, unfathomable mystery:

> Invisible, solemn, and fragrant,
> Your flesh opens to me in secret.
> We shall know no further enigma.
> After all the years there is nothing
> Stranger than this. We who know ourselves
> As one doubled thing, and move our limbs
> As deft implements of one fused lust,
> Are mysteries in each other's arms.[40]

Ever so delicately he evokes the fleeting timelessness of the communion of lovers:

> The future   is long gone by
> And the past   will never happen
> We have   only this
> Our one forever
> So small   so infinite

So brief   so vast
Immortal   as our hands that touch
Deathless   as the firelit wine we drink
Almighty   as this single kiss
That has no beginning
That will never
Never
End[41]

Kabbalism or Tantrism or the *Song of Songs,* he likes to invoke the mysticisms that play on the connection or parallel between human and divine love, that see sex as a sacramental communion, or even as a mode of contemplation:

Love is the subjective
Aspect of contemplation.
Sexual love is one of
The most perfect forms of
Contemplation, as far as it
Is without ignorance, grasping,
And appetite.[42]

This is what he means by "from the Dual to the Other":

For the undeveloped heart,
The news or even the sight
Of the destruction of thousands
Of other human beings
May assume only the form
Of a distant cry . . . .
However, as the dual,
The beloved, is known and
Loved more and more fully, all
The universe of persons
Grows steadily more and more real.[43]

One of Rexroth's deepest influences was Martin Buber, the Jewish "philosopher of dialogue." Buber, he says, is "practically the only religious writer a non-religious person could take seriously today."[44] Religious he certainly is, but in a special way that has led his philosophy jokingly but not altogether inaccurately to be called "Zen Judaism." After an early occasion when he felt that his preoccupation with a special "religious experience" had led him to fail to respond fully to someone who had come to him for help, Buber wrote:

Since then I have given up the "religious" which is nothing but the exception, extraction, exaltation, ecstasy; or it has given me up. I possess nothing but the everyday out of which I am never taken. The mystery is no longer disclosed, it has escaped or it has made its dwelling here where everything happens as it happens. I know no fulness but each mortal hour's fulness of claim and responsibility. . . . If that is religion then it is just *everything*, simply all that is lived in its possibility of dialogue.[45]

Buber sees the most fundamental reality neither in subjective experience nor in the objective world, but in the "realm of the between." "In the beginning is relation." "All real living is meeting." In his great *I and Thou* he distinguishes two basic types of relation: I–It and I–Thou. I–It is a subject-object relation of using or experiencing; the It (or He or She) is only a "thing among things," susceptible to comparison and categorization. The I–Thou relation is unique, mutual, total, and inevitably temporary. "Egos appear by setting themselves apart from other egos. Persons appear by entering into relation to other persons."[46]

Rexroth stresses that Buber's view is not a sentimental preaching of "sharing" or "togetherness" ("our current Togetherness is simply the massing of frightened cyphers"), nor an advocacy of collectivism as opposed to individualism. "Individualism understands only a part of man, collectivism understands man only as a part."[47] Both Buber and Rexroth sharply distinguish collectivity (a collection of units) from genuine community (an ensemble of persons in direct living relations with each other).

Rexroth criticizes Buber on three main points: when he becomes an apologist for Zionism (although Buber's Zionism at least was never belligerent: he worked arduously for a genuine rapprochement between Jews and Arabs); when he concludes his study of libertarian communalist currents (*Paths in Utopia*) with too much wishful thinking as to the promise of the early Israeli kibbutzim; and when, in the last part of *I and Thou*, he arrives at the notion of God as the "eternal Thou." Rexroth objects to the repugnant aspects of Buber's biblical God; but more generally he distrusts any sort of "metaphysical greed" for some absolute relation. "Any art which has a happy ending in reserve in Infinity is, just to that degree, cheating. . . . It seems to me that the fullest realization of the self comes in the acceptance of the limits of contingency. It is harder, but more ennobling, to love a wife as another human being, fugitive as oneself, than it is to carry on imaginary conversations with an imaginary Absolute."[48] More fundamentally, however, acceptance of ephemeral, contingent relations is the very essence of Buber's standpoint; the notion of an "eternal Thou" is not really a necessary implication of his philosophy. "However Martin Buber might disagree doctrinally, take away his God and nothing important in his philosophy has changed. It remains a philosophy of joy, lived in a world full of others."[49]

A vital part of Buber's work is his presentation of Hasidism, a popular mystical movement that arose in the Jewish communities of eastern Europe in the eighteenth century. Rexroth discusses at length the history and nature of Hasidism, and how it differs in some ways from Buber's sophisticated reinterpretation of it; but what stands out regardless is a "holy good humor" and an affirmation of community all too rare in religious movements. Buber's *Tales of the Hasidim* somewhat resemble Zen or Taoist or Sufi anecdotes, but they have a more communal and ethical character. Like the latter, they often reveal a decisive event in a person's life, but this is generally not so much an experience of enlightenment as a moment of inner moral "turning." There is no definitive spiritual attainment; each new situation, each new encounter, calls for one's whole being. The Hasidic tales take place in the context of a quite orthodox traditional Judaism, full of superstitions, antiquated social relations and unappealing religious forms; yet in spite of all this,

> what comes through most is joy and wonder, love and quiet, in the face of the continuously vanishing world. It is called God's Will, but the movement of the universe . . . is accepted on very similar terms to those of the *Tao Te Ching*. Song and dance, the mutual love of the community—these are the values; they are beautiful precisely because they are not absolute. And on this foundation of modesty and love and joy is raised a moral structure which heals and illuminates as hardly any other Western European religious expression does.[50]

Rexroth is always enthusiastic about these ethical or "world-affirming" mysticisms, always quick to praise and encourage any tendencies toward joining contemplation and community, toward integrating religious life with ordinary life in the world. Mysticism has, of course, more often been used to provide a justification for ignoring ethical responsibilities and social realities. The experience of transcendent unity has been taken to imply that all the suffering and turmoil in the world is only illusory and need not concern us. The paradoxical statements of mysticism (transcendence of duality, "All is one," etc.) may be appropriate figures of speech to hint at an indescribable experience, they may even be true in a certain sense, but it is confusing different levels of reality to conclude that they are also true in the ordinary sense. The simplest refutation of this sort of transcendental sophistry is to note that even those who preach it take some aspects of worldly life quite seriously (notably the money they charge).

Rexroth never falls for it. Whenever it appears he is quick to denounce it. "The real reason for the popularity of the Occult Ancient East was pointed out long ago by Kipling: 'Ship me somewhere East of Suez . . . where there ain't no ten commandments.' If your religion is just exotic enough, you don't need to bother about responsibility. You can get away with anything."[51] Nor does Rexroth buy the notion that one must first "heal oneself" before acting in the world. As he often noted, the great mystics of the past are virtually unanimous in insisting that the two go together. "The Catholic contemplative, the Sufi, the Buddhist monk, follow counsels of perfection—illumination comes as the crown of a life of intense ethical activism, of honesty, loyalty, poverty, chastity, and above all charity, positive, out-going love of all creatures. The good life creates the ambience into which spiritual illumination flows like a sourceless, totally diffused light."[52] A classic statement of priorities by one of the greatest Western mystics: "If a person were in such a rapturous state as St. Paul once entered, and he knew of a sick man who wanted a cup of soup, it would be far better to withdraw from the rapture for love's sake and serve him who is in need" (Meister Eckhart).[53] The same is implied, but with a significant additional nuance that Rexroth especially appreciates, in the Mahayana ideal of the bodhisattva:

> A bodhisattva, in case you don't know, is one who, at the brink of absorption into Nirvana, turns away with the vow that he shall not enter final peace until he can bring all other beings with him. He does this, says the most advanced Buddhist thought, "indifferently" because he knows that there is neither being nor not-being, neither peace nor illusion, neither saved nor saviors, neither truth nor consequence. This is the reason for that benign, world-weary expression on the faces in Far Eastern religious art.[54]

But a farseeing compassion ultimately implies opposing the social system that prevents it from being fulfilled. Rexroth adds a modern supplement to the bodhisattva vow:

> While there is a lower class,
> I am in it. While there is
> A criminal element,
> I am of it. Where there is
> A soul in jail, I am not free.[55]

3. Society and Revolution

> *"It seems somewhat ridiculous to talk of revolution . . . .*
> *But everything else is even more ridiculous, since it implies*
> *accepting the existing order in one way or another."*
>
> —Situationist International[1]

Rexroth grew up in the final years of the old revolutionary movement. World War I not only demonstrated the bankruptcy of the old social order, it revealed the superficiality of the movement against it, as virtually all the supposedly antiwar and internationalist leftist organizations rallied to their respective nation-states. The end of the war brought a wave of upsurges in Europe, but all were soon crushed or neutralized. The one apparent exception, the 1917 Russian revolution, ultimately turned out to be the most disastrous defeat of all. The Bolsheviks took over, repressed the libertarian forces that had made the revolution, and imposed a new variant of the old system: bureaucratic state-capitalism. The "Communist" bureaucracy became the new ruling class; the state became the sole, all-owning capitalist.

> Bolshevism is not communism or even socialism in any sense in which those words were understood before 1918. It is a very primitive form of state capitalism. It is a method of forcing a backward, semi-colonial country through the period of capital accumulation which the major capitalist nations went through in the early years of the 19th century.[2]

The Bolshevik counterrevolution was not only a disaster for Russia; its example poisoned and ultimately destroyed the entire international revolutionary movement for decades to come. The Bolsheviks' power and prestige as the supposed leaders of the only "successful" revolution enabled them to dominate, manipulate and sabotage radical movements everywhere else "until there was no one left who was not completely centered on the Kremlin, either as a mindless Stalinist hatchet man or a psychopathic anti-Bolshevik." "Many thousands have turned to reaction, religion, or plain folly because to them Socialist revolution meant Bolshevism."[3]

Meanwhile in western Europe and America the system arrived at various accommodations with the reformist socialist parties and labor unions (New Deal, popular fronts, welfare statism).

The socialist and trade union movements in the West have functioned in reality—not just as governors to insure that steam is let off when the pressure gets too high, not just as what are now called "fail safe" devices, though they certainly are that—but as essential parts of the motive organization of capitalism, more, in other words, like carburetors that insure there will be just the right mixture of fuel and air for each new demand on the engine.[4]

In certain countries where this did not work well enough social crises were repressed through the imposition of fascism (a hybrid of totalitarian state-capitalism and traditional monopoly capitalism). Caught between Bolshevism, reformism and fascism, the genuinely radical elements were isolated and in many cases simply wiped out. The last and greatest manifestation of the old movement, the Spanish anarchist revolution of 1936–1937, was jointly destroyed by all three.

> The generation of revolutionary hope was over. The conscience of mankind went to school to learn methods of compromising itself. The Moscow trials, the Kuo Min Tang street executions, the betrayal of Spain, the Hitler-Stalin Pact, the extermination of whole nations, Hiroshima, Algiers—no protest has stopped the monster jaws from closing. As the years go on, fewer and fewer protests are heard. The spokesmen, the intellects of the world, have blackmailed themselves and are silent.[5]

A whole generation of writers, artists and intellectuals was shell-shocked, mentally and morally maimed, and sunk into demoralization and compromise.

> How many stopped writing at thirty?
> How many went to work for *Time*?
> How many died of prefrontal
> Lobotomies in the Communist Party?
> How many are lost in the back wards
> Of provincial madhouses?
> How many on the advice of
> Their psychoanalysts, decided
> A business career was best after all?
> How many are hopeless alcoholics?[6]

Rexroth was one of the few exceptions. In the twenties he was an active member of one of the most exemplary organizations of the old movement, the anarcho-syndicalist IWW (Industrial Workers of the World); in the early thirties he carried on similar work independently. When there ceased to be any significant revolutionary movement, he set in for the long retrenchment—establishing contacts among persons who had maintained integrity and radicality, initiating reassessments of perspectives, continuing to speak out and act where possible.

338

He had seen through the Bolshevik pretenses as early as 1921, when Trotsky and Lenin crushed the libertarian revolt of the Kronstadt soviet; but while clearly opposing all forms of "Communism" he did not, like so many others of his generation, react into supporting Western capitalism.

> I am far better aware of
> The evils of Stalinism
> Than you are, you ex-Trotskyite
> Warmonger. But it won't get you
> Anywhere to tell me I should
> Welcome the beast who devours me
> Just because a bigger lion
> Is eating somebody else on
> The other side of the arena.[7]

As for the limits of reformist politics: Hitching through Montana in 1927, Rexroth and Andrée get a ride with a well-to-do man of the world with an unusually cynical opinion of politicians. Rexroth asks if he doesn't think there are a few honest exceptions, such as Robert La Follette and Burton Wheeler (radical reform senators from Wisconsin and Montana). The man answers by describing the backstop in a baseball field: "It catches the balls the catcher misses, and all the fouls that go off in that direction, so that nobody in the box seats gets hurt. That's the function of guys like La Follette and Wheeler, and believe me, they know it if you don't."[8] The next day they find out that their companion is Senator Wheeler.

The failures of Bolshevism and reformist socialism to bring about a truly radical social change confirmed Rexroth's anarchism. It had become more evident than ever that capitalism cannot be eliminated by state programs and that any state bureaucracy, no matter how supposedly radical, naturally tends to perpetuate its own power. Capitalism and the state are simply interlinked aspects of the same system:

> Labor power on the market,
> Firepower on the battlefield,
> It is all one, merely two
> Aspects of the same monster.[9]

The state is basically a protection racket. The fact that it incidentally provides a few beneficial services merely camouflages its essential role as enforcer of the money-commodity economy, without which most of the artificially maintained conflicts of interest that now provide a pretext for the state would lose their rationale. "The state does not tax you to provide you with services. The state taxes you to kill you. The services are something which it has kidnapped from you in your organic relations with your fellow man, to justify its police and war-making powers."[10] Rexroth quotes Herbert Read to the effect that "anarchism possibly may sound impractical, but certainly less impractical than the modern capitalist nation-state would sound if described to someone in another civilization; and it is obvious that nothing else will work; any form of State is bound to fail from now on, and fail disastrously."[11]

During World War II Rexroth was a conscientious objector (doing alternative service as an attendant in a psychiatric ward). He was not an advocate of strict nonviolence in every situation, but he does seem to have been absolutely opposed to all wars between modern nation-states, considering them worse than any of the evils they claim to be fighting. During the war he formed the antiwar Randolph Bourne Council (named in memory of a libertarian writer who wrote on the theme "War is the health of the state") and worked to aid Japanese-Americans who were being harassed and sent to concentration camps. (He came up with scams through which many were enabled to escape incarceration altogether.)

After the war Rexroth and a few others organized the San Francisco Anarchist Circle (later renamed the Libertarian Circle).

> Every week we had an educational meeting, each time devoted to a single topic. The Andalusian Agricultural Communes, the Shop Stewards' Movement in revolutionary Germany, communalist groups in the United States, the Kronstadt revolt, Nestor Makhno and his Anarchist society and army in the Russian Civil War, the I.W.W., Mutualist Anarchism in America, and individuals: Babeuf, Bakunin, Kropotkin, Alexander Berkman, Emma Goldman, Voltairine de Cleyre and the Anarchist Woman's Movement. . . . The place was always crowded and when the topic for the evening was Sex and Anarchy you couldn't get in the doors. . . . There was no aspect of Anarchist history or theory that was not presented by a qualified person and then thrown open to spontaneous discussion. . . . Our objective was to refound the radical movement after its destruction by the Bolsheviks and to rethink all the basic principles, i.e., in other words to subject to searching criticism all the ideologists from Marx to Malatesta.[12]

The ultimate influence of the Libertarian Circle seems to have been as much cultural as political. Flourishing from 1946 into the early fifties, it was perhaps the first major focus of the postwar ferment that came to be called the San Francisco Renaissance. Some of its participants went on to found Pacifica radio station KPFA, several experimental theater groups and numerous little magazines; others included many of the poets and artists who were to be influential in the Bay Area over the next two decades.

Rexroth was in the thick of all this. In addition to his vital role in the Libertarian Circle, he hosted weekly discussion, seminars and readings in his own home, and in numerous articles, interviews and KPFA broadcasts he lambasted the cultural and political establishments and heralded the new dissident tendencies. At a time when most commentators were complacently declaring that the age of experiment and revolt was over, he began to see new signs of hope. In his pioneer article "Disengagement: The Art of the Beat Generation" (1957) he wrote: "The youngest generation is in a state of revolt so absolute that its elders cannot even recognize it. . . . Critically invisible, modern revolt, like X-rays and radioactivity, is perceived only by its effects at more materialistic social levels, where it is called delinquency."[13]

Rexroth and the other San Francisco Renaissance poets are themselves sometimes loosely called Beats, but as he emphatically reiterated in numerous articles, neither he nor most of the others had much in common with the media-created beatnik stereotypes. His critiques of Jack Kerouac's sentimentality, self-indulgence and general mindlessness were particularly caustic. (In retaliation, most of the current spate of memoirs, biographies and histories of the "Beat Era" dismiss Rexroth with a few snide remarks or spiteful rumors; while academia generally continues to treat him as a nonperson contemptuously pigeonholed as "the father of the Beats.")

The emergence of the civil rights movement was more to his taste. In a 1960 article he praises the spontaneity and direct personal action of the first protesters, and warns them against attempts by bureaucratic "organizers" to take over and institutionalize them:

> The brutal reactionary tendencies in American life were being challenged, not on a political basis, Left versus Right, but because of their patent dishonesty and moral violence. . . . The programs are used up . . . . power and program are not the question: what matters is the immediate realization of humane content, here, there, everywhere, in every fact and relationship of society. . . . This means personal moral action. I suppose, if you wish to call it that, it means a spiritual revolution. . . . The Montgomery bus boycott . . . demonstrated something that had always sounded like sheer sentimentality. It is better, braver, far more effective and far more pleasurable to act with love than with hate. When you have won, you have gained an unimpeachable victory. . . . Furthermore, each moral victory converts or neutralizes another block of the opponents' forces.[14]

This spontaneous direct action was indeed a good beginning, to clear the air of decades of compromises and confusions. (The "Left versus Right" schema, for example, has long been a virtually meaningless pretense of opposition between virtually indistinguishable frauds.) But Rexroth's wholesale rejection of "programs" is obviously too simplistic. In the aftermath of the destruction of the old revolutionary movement this sort of attitude was understandable: people were rightly suspicious of mindless subservience to doctrinaire programs

341

and organizations; it was necessary to reassess perspectives from scratch and remain open to diverse possibilities. During this earlier period Rexroth's strategy of fostering dialogue and creative community without worrying too much about a consistent theory did indeed prove very fruitful—no one else played such a vital role in laying the foundations for the San Francisco Renaissance of the fifties, which in turn was one of the pivotal points of departure for the more widespread contestation of the sixties. But that new contestation posed new tactical and theoretical questions which Rexroth, persisting in his previous empirical eclecticism, failed to address in any very coherent way.

In 1960 he accepted an offer to do a weekly column for the San Francisco *Examiner* (a Hearst paper). He seems to have had a policy of accepting virtually any congenial assignment as long as he was given complete independence—publishers had to accept a piece exactly as he wrote it or not at all. He said that newspapers and popular magazines offered him more freedom than the sectarian political journals and academic quarterlies: "They are interested in lively, engaging copy, and within reason, the more controversy the better."[15] This may be true as far as it goes, but what if what one has to say does not seem "within reason"? Even with a carte-blanche policy there are always subtle pressures to self-censorship. There is always the implied threat that one's contract could be discontinued (as, in fact, Rexroth's ultimately was after he wrote a controversial article on the American police in 1967).

But granting that he did accept this dubious position, he didn't do a bad job with it. The style of his columns is slightly adjusted to the more popular audience, but he is virtually as outspoken as in his other writings and his range of topics is if anything even broader. Reviewing a book about the San Francisco Bay, he says: "You can know all about what Henry James really meant, or the art of the fugue, but if you are not at home in the world under your feet and before your eyes, you are actually uncivilized."[16] In this sense his columns probably helped to civilize thousands of local readers. They certainly provide a wealth of material on the Bay Area scene of the time, including many topics not treated in such detail elsewhere in his writings, from the live arts to local politics, architecture and city planning.

Whatever his topic, he is always trying to foster the qualities of a vital, diversified community. In general he encourages local participation, experimentation and autonomy, though he sometimes urges centralized coordination in areas where consistent planning is needed. Of a free theater performance in the park he says: "Let's hope this is an entering wedge, and that eventually we will have all sorts of musical and dramatic activity in the parks. I can think of few better ways to raise the muscle tone of a flabby community. Sooner or later out of the spectators will come participants."[17] It is amusing to see how cogently he addresses different groups in their own terms—challenging

342

those who claim to be Christians to emulate Christ and go to the poor, the outcast, the hopeless (to help them, not to convert them), or telling Chinatown merchants they would make even more money if they turned Grant Avenue into a mall, revived the Chinese opera and offered more authentic Oriental goods, instead of going for the fast tourist buck.

There is, of course, a certain irony in some of his proposals. Within their limits they may be more desirable—and even in some cases more "practical"—than prevalent policies, but he knows that ultimately they are not enough. Some of them would face too much resistance from entrenched political and economic interests; others are "zero-sum" (an improvement in one area would be at the expense of another). "The brutal fact is that the real problems—ecological, economic, social, moral, ethical, religious, sexual, intersexual—cannot be solved within the context of this society or any society at present known."[18]

Most of these columns, however, are simply personal reactions to day-to-day issues, with only vague implications of a larger social critique. After being fired from the *Examiner* Rexroth shifted to a more explicitly political series of monthly columns for the San Francisco *Bay Guardian* (1967–1972) and *San Francisco* magazine (1967–1975). In these increasingly pessimistic articles he blasts the corruption and collusion of politicians, governments, businesses and mass media, and bewails the mindless destruction of every vestige of human and ecological community. Most of his denunciations are only too justified; but they don't add up to a coherent analysis that goes below the surface to elucidate radical possibilities. As usual with merely reactive muckraking, the result is merely oppressive, encouraging a retreat to the "personal" as the only terrain still partially free from the global madness.

Rexroth had perceptively discerned the first signs of a new revolt at a time when most commentators were blind to such a possibility; but he saw this revolt in largely cultural or spiritual terms. When more overtly confrontational struggles arose he tended to dismiss them as mere symptoms of social collapse and clung to his previous strategy of subtle moral and artistic subversion. This can be seen even in the one such struggle for which he does show a certain enthusiasm, the May 1968 revolt in France.

> Probably the most significant thing about the explosion in France is the revelation of the moral bankruptcy of the establishment. Neither the General nor the leaders of the Communist Party had the faintest idea of what it was all about. De Gaulle had no explanation except the sublimely comic one that it was all due to the Communists. The Communists, with just enough insight to be really scared, indiscriminately denounced the revolt—both of the rank and file leaders of the striking workers and of all the youth—with savage, unbridled abuse.

... Whatever the temporary settlement in France, this rejection of the immense, deadly system of false values which has ruled the age of commerce and industry will not stop.[19]

This is true enough as far as it goes; the problem is that he does not go any farther. It is typical that he recognizes the May revolt as a rejection of a system of false values but scarcely examines it as an attempt to supersede a system of social organization. He never analyzes its origins, its goals, its innovative tactics or its conflicting tendencies—all matters of greater significance than the "revelation" of a moral bankruptcy that had long been obvious.

Rexroth rightly criticized the New Left for its lack of coherent strategy, but he himself hardly seems to have had any strategy at all beyond vaguely encouraging "personal moral action" or occasional ad hoc collective action on specific issues. After the demise of the Libertarian Circle he and his San Francisco Renaissance friends never seem to have developed their social critique, or even to have presented in any very sustained or explicit way whatever libertarian perspective they still had. Since these people were in many ways deservedly influential, their failure to tackle the new theoretical and strategical issues contributed to the political naïveté of the sixties counterculture. In the absence of a coherent libertarian perspective, the old ideologies naturally returned to fill the void. Militant fractions of the New Left soon degenerated into the most dreary or delirious rehashes of old leftism; to which most of the rest reacted in disgust and turned in more reformist or apolitical directions.

The debacle of New Left politics in the late sixties in turn reinforced Rexroth's emphasis on the more cultural aspects of the movement. *The Alternative Society* (1970) reflects this slant. Although it contains articles on a variety of social topics, nearly half the book is about recent developments in underground poetry and song; the alternative society turns out to be the youth counterculture, or at least its most profound tendencies: the "subculture of secession." "It is a mistake to talk about protest songs, protest poetry. Protest assumes a possibility for correction. It occurs from within a culture. As the long tale of horror has gone by, protest has changed to alienation, alienation to total secession."[20] This is not so much a geographical secession (though it may include the formation of separate communities) as a fundamental reorientation of life values, a reorientation that has persisted, though less visibly, while superficial hippie fashions have come and gone.

As they strive for a new community, honest morality, sane goals in life, and their passing fads and follies drop away, the youth who are seceding from our crazy, lethal social order are converging with those predecessors—Mennonites, Brethren, Amish, Hutterites, Quakers—

344

who withdrew from the madness and horror of the Wars of Religion and the collapse of the society of the Middle Ages.[21]

In *Communalism: From Its Origins to the Twentieth Century* (1974) Rexroth examines these and other previous alternative societies, from the early Christians through the heretical sects and millenarian movements of the Middle Ages to the secular utopian communities of the last two centuries.

Until we arrive at the latter, almost all of them are religious. In this regard Rexroth's book is a rich exposition of the social dialectic of religions, which have of course usually functioned to reinforce the ruling order, but which when pushed to their most radical implications have sometimes tended to undermine it. Even such apparently tame tendencies as lay monasticism may represent a potential threat: "Organized monasticism was a method of quarantining the Christian life. This is why the Church has always insisted that monasticism be celibate. . . . Lay monasticism, a community of families holding all things in common, living a life modeled on that of the apostles, unavoidably becomes a counter-culture."[22] This threat becomes more obvious in the connection of heretical groups like the Brotherhood of the Free Spirit with millenarian revolts, and in the emergence of religiously inspired anarcho-communist groups like the Diggers in the English Revolution.

Nevertheless all of these alternative communities, even the later, more consciously radical and secular ones, have had an ambiguous relation to the dominant society. To a certain extent they may have provided refuges from it and exemplified different values and possibilities; but by coexisting with it they inevitably entangled themselves in compromises and confusions, and usually soon fell apart from their own contradictions. Rexroth's book is a very interesting account of the successes, failures, foibles and follies of these groups; but his analysis is too narrowly empirical. By treating the alternative communities mainly in terms of their internal organizational problems and individual survival (he regards the Hutterites, for example, as the most "successful" since they are the only ones who have maintained a fully communalist life for hundreds of years) he avoids facing their limited relevance to present-day contestation. Charismatic leaders, cohesive religious beliefs and hard work may, as he concludes, have been vital factors for small utopian groups struggling to survive within a world of scarcity and hostility, but they hardly have anything to do with the project of a global postscarcity society.

Whether or not such a society is likely, he knows that we have reached a point where it is both possible and necessary:

It is either utopia or catastrophe. . . . The symptoms of the collapse of the civilization are all about us, and they are far more pronounced

345

than they were in the last years of the Roman Empire. Yet not all of these symptoms are necessarily pathological. The contemporary world is being pulled apart by two contrary tendencies—one toward social death, one toward the birth of a new society.[23]

But when he attempts to analyze the nature of this conflict he sometimes lapses into confusions and non sequiturs:

> It is in the freer areas of the social interpersonal relations of individuals, away from factory or governmental bureaucracy, that the revolutionary developments are most apparent. Effective attack on the State and the economic system requires power, and the State, which is simply the police force of the economic system, has, so far, all the effective power. Demonstrations or Molotov cocktails are equally powerless before the hydrogen bomb. This is why the important changes are taking place in what the youth revolt calls "life style."[24]

His treatment of "power" here is rather muddled. It is true that it is generally futile to fight the state on its own terms, but this does not mean that the only alternative is to limit oneself to changes in lifestyle and interpersonal relations. Where was all the state's power in France in May 1968? or in Portugal in 1974? or in Poland in 1980? or in East Europe in 1989? And of what relevance then was the hydrogen bomb? In all these cases the system has survived not so much by physical repression as by cooption, by divide-and-rule tactics, by manipulating oppositional movements into reformist compromises.

> All over the world we are witnessing an instinctive revolt against dehumanization. Marxism proposed to overcome the alienation of man from his work, from his fellows, and from himself by changing the economic system. The economic system has been changed, but human self-alienation has only increased. Whether it is called socialism or capitalism, in terms of humane satisfactions and life-meaning it is the same East and West. So today the present revolt is not primarily concerned with changing political or economic structures but is a head-on attack on human self-alienation as such.[25]

The economic system may have been modified in various ways, but it has never anywhere been radically superseded as envisaged by Marx. (As Rexroth notes elsewhere, "Marxism" has about as little to do with Marx as Christianity has with Christ.) The debacle of "Communist" state-capitalism and the long-evident inadequacy of reformist socialism have demonstrated the obsolescence of statist leftism, but not of the original antistate-anticapitalist project of Marx and the anarchists. Modern revolt is rightly contesting every form of alienation instead of limiting itself to the narrowly political and economic struggles of the old left, but it can hardly hope to successfully attack alienation "as

346

such" without sooner or later eliminating its political and economic foundations.

Rexroth sees his alternative society as a "new society within the shell of the old," but he never envisions just how it might break the shell and actually supersede the old society. He seems only to have a vague hope that a "saving remnant" of people quietly practicing authentic community in the interstices of the doomed system might somehow keep the flame alive. Even if this offers little chance of averting thermonuclear or ecological apocalypse, he feels that it's the most satisfying way to live while you're waiting for it.

> If the alternative society becomes a society of ecological Bodhisattvas we will have reached the final confrontation—mutual aid and respect for life, full awareness of one's place in the community of creatures—these are the foundations for an alternative society. . . . They're not likely to win; the time is gone, but at least they can establish a Kingdom in the face of Apocalypse, a garrisoned society of the morally responsible which will face extinction with clean consciences and lives as happily lived as possible.[26]

Rexroth was speaking out on the threats to the ecology decades before most people had ever heard of the word, and it becomes more obvious every day that he was only too right about their seriousness. A viable global ecological balance is a delicate matter—once it is upset beyond a certain degree it becomes impossible to reverse the trend. There are now numerous well-known ecological abuses which if not promptly corrected could soon pass the point of no return. Even those that are stopped now may continue to have delayed effects for years. And of course most are still scarcely curbed at all, and are unlikely to be so as long as the system exists in which powerful interests can derive short-term profits from them.

> It is my opinion that the situation is hopeless, that the human race has produced an ecological tipover point and is rushing toward extinction, a species death that will be complete within a century. This is quite without any consideration of the hydrogen bomb . . . . But assuming there is a possibility of changing the society's "course in the darkness deathward set," it can only be done by infection, infiltration, diffusion and imperceptibly, microscopically, throughout the social organism, like the invisible pellets of a disease called Health.[27]

This brings us back to poetry and song, which Rexroth sees as among the most effective means of such "infection."

Underground song, he says, goes back at least as far as the medieval Goliardic lyrics of wine, women and satire (popularized in Carl Orff's *Carmina Burana* and more recently recorded in the original versions). In France he traces its development from the sexual mysticism of the troubadours and the bohemian underworld of François Villon through the nineteenth-century *poètes maudits* and *cafés-chantants* to Georges Brassens and other post–World War II singers, who are "responsible for the greatest renaissance of song in modern times" and for "the replacing of the acquisitive appetite with the lyric sensibility." Brassens, he says, "speaks for the hardcore unassimilables with complete self-awareness. He knew that he and behind him his ever-growing following could not, and never would be assimilated, and he knew why, and he said so in every song, whatever that song was about. With him the counter-culture comes of age."[28]

In America Rexroth traces a parallel evolution from the traditional ballads, folksongs and blues to the countercultural singers of the sixties. He distinguishes authentic folksongs—the "natural expression of an organic community"[29]—from pseudofolk protest songs, most of which he considers laughably corny, if not worse: expressions of the Social Lie. Some of his own poems, of course, contain explicit radical statements, but he always rejected the notion that the arts should be subordinated to "progressive" demands. He felt that lyrics that communicate genuine personal vision are ultimately more subversive than explicit propaganda. Poetry, he says, "produces a deeper and wider and more intense response to life. The presumption is not that we will be better men—that's up to us—but that deeply familiar with poetry, we will respond to life, its problems, and its people, its things, objects, everything, in a much more universal way, and that we will use much more of ourselves."[30] His further presumption is that this deepened response to life, by running counter to alienation and conditioning, tends to undermine the established order:

> The counterculture as a culture, as a way of life—you can't catch up with it, it's in the bloodstream of society. You can't pin it down. Its effect is continuously corrosive. . . . Joni Mitchell's stuff . . . involves and presents a pattern of human relationships which is unassimilable by the society . . . . the kind of love it sings of can't exist in this society. The song gets out like a bit of radioactive cobalt. It just foments subversion around itself as long as it is available.[31]

If only it were so easy! It is hard to determine the ultimate effects of a work of art, but it seems doubtful to me if any lyrics, whether by Brassens or Mitchell or anyone else, are all that unassimilable. At most they have probably played a modest role in preserving a spark of human spirit amid the dehumanizing pressures around us. Rexroth's remark on William Blake's poems points to this salutary role while at the same time revealing its limits: "This is the art of providing the heart with images of its alienation. If the individual or society can project the dilemmas which reason cannot cope with, they can be controlled if not mastered. This was Blake's function. He saw the oncoming Business Civilization and prepared a refuge, a symbolic fortress or haven."[32]

Moreover, it is necessary to distinguish between the counterculture "as a way of life" and as simply a new style in the arts. Insofar as the sixties counterculture consisted of audacious experiments in different modes of life and consciousness, it was indeed very "corrosive." But it is misleading to present its artistic expressions as its central factor. A few poems and songs may have had a significant influence, but for the most part they were merely diluted and belated reflections of the adventures that were really going on.

Rexroth's thesis seemed to be confirmed more in the "Communist" countries. He could point out how a mere visit of Allen Ginsberg to Prague or Joan Baez to East Berlin threw the bureaucrats into a nervous panic. But this was because virtually any sort of nonconformity threatened the ideological monopoly on which the Stalinist bureaucracies' power depended. In the more flexible Western systems a work of art can be extreme indeed and still be assimilated as part of the show—its very extremism may serve to support the system's pretension of offering total freedom of expression (as long as it is not realized in action, but remains a spectacle).

But here is the *reductio ad absurdum* of Rexroth's thesis:

On the whole my own taste runs to poet singers who get to the root of the matter, who speak for fundamental changes in the sensibility in human relationships and therefore in language. Dylan at his best, Donovan, Leonard Cohen, Joni Mitchell . . . there are countless people like this all over the world, more perhaps in France than elsewhere. Much of the entertainment that went on night and day in the Theatre Odéon during the 1968 May revolt had nothing overtly to do with the, after all passing, revolt in the streets, the evils of the regime, or the betrayals of the political Left. People sang songs that attacked the evil at its source by presenting an alternative kind of human being.[33]

Whatever subversive effect poetry and song may sometimes have, Rexroth's argument falls rather flat if, when a rare opportunity arises where everything is in question and people have a brief chance to change history, he can think of nothing more to do than go on singing. There was more poetry in the act of taking over the Odéon than in whatever songs may have been sung there. In a situation like May 1968, where millions of people have been shaken out of their usual sleepwalking existence and are getting a taste of real life, the point is no longer to "present" visions of alternative human relations, but to fulfill them.

The whole organization of modern society works against this, not only the obvious political and economic constraints, but the subtler, all-pervading cultural pacification that turns people into addicts of passive consumption. Our lives are dominated by a constant barrage of spectacles—news, ads, stars, vicarious adventures, images of revolt . . . The situationists have shown that this is not merely a superficial feature of modern life, but reflects a qualitatively new stage of capitalist alienation. "The spectacle is not a collection of images, but a social relation among people, mediated by images" (Guy Debord, *The Society of the Spectacle*).[34]

In this new context the role of the arts becomes more ambiguous—whatever their creative or seemingly radical aspects, they too tend to become part of the show, to reinforce the passivity of the spectator:

> The relation between authors and spectators is only a transposition of the fundamental relation between directors and executants. . . . The spectacle-spectator relation is in itself a staunch bearer of the capitalist order. The ambiguity of all "revolutionary art" lies in the fact that the revolutionary aspect of any particular spectacle is always contradicted and offset by the reactionary element present in all spectacles. [Debord and Canjuers][35]

Rexroth does not really confront this new development, which to a great extent weakens his case for the subversiveness of art. Basically he still accepts the traditional roles of art, he just wants it to fulfill those roles better and more widely, to be more authentic and relevant. He stresses the need for art to be vital communication, but this communication remains a special activity done only by certain people within certain forms and circumstances.

Even those avant-garde tendencies that have sought to overcome the spectacle aspect of art by encouraging audience participation (in Happenings, for example) do so within limitations of space and time and content that turn such participation into a farce. As the situationists concluded, the true fulfillment of art ultimately implies going beyond the boundaries of art, bringing creativity and adventure into the critique and liberation of every aspect of life; and first of all into challenging the submissive conditioning that prevents people from creating their own adventures. This does not mean that all literary and artistic works are totally irrelevant or reactionary; but it is doubtful if even the best of them are as intrinsically subversive as Rexroth seems to hope.

But if Rexroth's strategy of subtle cultural subversion is in some respects dubious, he is certainly right to encourage the fullest possible creativity and community here and now, to insist that "humane satisfactions and life-meaning" must not be postponed to some utopian future. The means may not be identical with the goal, but they must at least be consistent with it. The values that Rexroth stood for are vital to any genuine social liberation precisely because they are meaningful and satisfying for their own sake. As he put it in one of

his most moving poems, written in 1952 for the funeral of an old
friend:

> We believed we
> Would see with our own eyes the new
> World where man was no longer
> Wolf to man, but men and women
> Were all brothers and lovers
> Together. We will not see it.
> We will not see it, none of us.
> It is farther off than we thought.
> ... It does not matter.
> We were comrades together.
> Life was good for us. It is
> Good to be brave—nothing is
> Better. Food tastes better. Wine
> Is more brilliant. Girls are more
> Beautiful. The sky is bluer . . . .
> If the good days never come,
> We will not know. We will not care.
> Our lives were the best. We were the
> Happiest men alive in our day.[36]

Farewell, wonderful old mentor!

[Fall 1990]

NOTES

[Information added in the present reprinting is in square brackets.]

Abbreviations

A   *Assays* (New Directions, 1961)

AN   *An Autobiographical Novel* (Doubleday, 1966) [The expanded edition (New Directions, 1991) retains the same pagination.]

AS   *The Alternative Society: Essays from the Other World* (Herder & Herder, 1970)

BB   *Bird in the Bush: Obvious Essays* (New Directions, 1959)

C   *Communalism: From Its Origins to the Twentieth Century* (Seabury, 1974)

CLP   *Collected Longer Poems* (New Directions, 1968)

CR   *Classics Revisited,* with Afterword by Bradford Morrow (New Directions, 1986)

CSP   *Collected Shorter Poems* (New Directions, 1966)

ER   *The Elastic Retort: Essays in Literature and Ideas* (Seabury, 1973)

MCR   *More Classics Revisited,* edited by Bradford Morrow (New Directions, 1989)

MS   *The Morning Star* (New Directions, 1979) [Now incorporated in *Flower Wreath Hill: Later Poems* (New Directions, 1991).]

SE   *World Outside the Window: Selected Essays,* edited by Bradford Morrow (New Directions, 1987)

SFE   San Francisco *Examiner* columns

SFM   *San Francisco* magazine columns

SP   *Selected Poems,* edited by Bradford Morrow (New Directions, 1984)

WEE   *With Eye and Ear* (Herder & Herder, 1970)

CHAPTER ONE

1. Rexroth often used this question (referring to his three main poetic themes) as an icebreaker when he was giving a reading of his poetry. The response quoted here was his favorite.

2. AN 169.

3. AN 366.

4. "Poetry and Society," *The Coast*, Spring 1937, p. 35. On cubist poetry see the introduction to Rexroth's translations of Pierre Reverdy's *Selected Poems* (New Directions, 1969), reprinted in SE 252–258.

5. "Smokey The Bear Bodhisattva," WEE 212.

6. "The Signature of All Things," CSP 177/SP 42–43.

7. "Floating," CSP 144/SP 29–30.

8. "Thou Shalt Not Kill," CSP 268–269/SP 95–96.

9. "Observations in a Cornish Teashop," CSP 331.

10. "Andrée Rexroth," CSP 154/SP 34.

11. "Homer in Basic," CSP 317. [If you haven't ever read Homer, or if it's been a while since you have, please treat yourself to the superb Robert Fitzgerald translations.]

12. "August 22, 1939," CSP 97–98/SP 5–6. (The date is the anniversary of Sacco and Vanzetti's execution in 1927.)

13. Introduction to CLP.

14. AN 152.

15. SFE, 17 July 1960. Rexroth's views on modern American poetry are summed up in his book *American Poetry in the Twentieth Century* (Herder & Herder, 1971).

16. "Jazz Poetry," SE 71.

17. "Poets, Old and New," A 208. (*L'Action Française* was a fascist journal greatly admired by Eliot.)

18. "Mark Twain," A 97.

19. "Would You Hit a Woman with a Child, or Who Was that Lady I Seen You with Last Night?" BB 88–89.

20. "Some Thoughts on Jazz as Music, as Revolt, as Mystique," BB 25–26. See also "What's Wrong with the Clubs" (A 75–81/SE 191–196).

21. SFE, 6 March 1960.

22. "Marcus Aurelius, *The Meditations*," CR 80.

23. "The Authentic Joy of Philip Whalen," WEE 211.

24. "The Younger Generation and Its Letters," *New Republic*, 15 February 1954.

25. "The Lost Vision of Isaac Bashevis Singer," WEE 192.

26. "Tacitus, *Histories*," CR 76.

27. "Franz Kafka, *The Trial*," MCR 141/WEE 21–22.

28. "Poets, Old and New," A 235.

29. "Daniel Defoe, *Robinson Crusoe*," MCR 57/ER 60.

30. "Modern Chinese Literature," *Chicago Review* xvii:1 (1964), p. 169.

31. Interview in Lawrence Lipton's *The Holy Barbarians* (Messner, 1959), pp. 295–296.

32. Introduction to Tolstoy's *The Kingdom of God Is Within You* (Farrar, Straus & Giroux, 1961), pp. v–vi; reprinted in MCR 124–125/WEE 160–161.

33. "Greek Tragedy in Translation," WEE 143.

34. BB viii.

35. "The Reality of Henry Miller," BB 156–157. Compare the later, more critical essay "Henry Miller: The Iconoclast as Everyman's Friend" (WEE 188–191).

36. The unreferenced quotations on pages 321–322 are from the respective essays in CR and MCR/ER, except for that on Thucydides, which is from the essay on Euripides's *Hippolytus* (MCR 11/ER 15).

37. "Greek Tragedy in Translation," WEE 143–144.

CHAPTER TWO

1. Quoted in R.H. Blyth's *Zen in English Literature and Oriental Classics* (Hokuseido, 1942), pp. 79–80.

2. "The Chinese Classic Novel in Translation: The Art of Magnanimity," BB 215.

[In case you're interested, what are generally considered the five greatest Chinese novels are now each available in both abridged and complete translations: *The Dream of the Red Chamber* (a.k.a. *The Story of the Stone*), a wonderful novel of manners with Taoist undertones; *Out-*

laws of the Marsh (*The Water Margin* or *All Men Are Brothers*), a larger-than-life series of picaresque adventures; *Monkey* (The Journey to the West), a satirical Buddhist fantasy; *Three Kingdoms* (*The Romance of the Three Kingdoms*), a historical novel full of military strategy and political intrigue; and the erotic *Chin P'ing Mei* (*The Golden Lotus* or *The Plum in the Golden Vase*).]

3. *Ibid.*, BB 216

4. SFE, 10 July 1960.

5. "Ford Madox Ford, *Parade's End*," MCR 139–140/ER 127.

6. "Dostoievsky, *The Brothers Karamazov*," CR 184.

7. "The Dragon and the Unicorn," CLP 185–186/SP 64. See CR and MCR/ER for essays on Walton, White and Woolman.

8. "Julius Caesar, *The War in Gaul*," CR 67.

9. "The Chinese Classic Novel in Translation," BB 216–217.

10. "The Hasidism of Martin Buber," BB 139/SE 99.

11. "Unacknowledged Legislators and Art pour Art," BB 18.

12. SFE, 20 November 1960.

13. Rexroth's four plays are collected in *Beyond the Mountains* (New Directions, 1951).

14. Introduction to *The Signature of All Things* (New Directions, 1950).

15. "The Dragon and the Unicorn," CLP 157.

16. AN 338.

17. SFE, 13 September 1965.

18. "Lao Tzu, *Tao Te Ching*," MCR 7/ER 10.

19. "Izaak Walton, *The Compleat Angler*," CR 143–144.

20. "The Lights in the Sky Are Stars," CSP 238.

21. "The Signature of All Things," CSP 178–179/SP 44.

22. "The Phoenix and the Tortoise," CLP 90–91/SP 23–25.

23. "On Flower Wreath Hill," MS 45.

24. *Ibid.*, MS 41.

25. AN 338. Rexroth's most extensive discussion of Buddhism is in his introduction to *The Buddhist Writings of Lafcadio Hearn* (Ross-Erikson, 1977), reprinted in SE 303–319.

26. Introduction to CLP.

27. AN 119.

28. "My Head Gets Tooken Apart," BB 71–72.

29. "The Holy Kabbalah," A 43.

30. "Gnosticism," A 141–142/SE 141–142.

31. "The Bollingen Series," WEE 203.

32. "The Holy Kabbalah," A 42–43.

33. SFE, 25 December 1960.

34. AN 335, 252.

35. "The Hasidism of Martin Buber," BB 109/SE 79.

36. *Ibid.*, BB 136–137/SE 97–98.

37. "Lamennais," ER 186–187.

38. Introduction to *The Phoenix and the Tortoise* (New Directions, 1944).

39. Introduction to Lawrence's *Selected Poems* (New Directions, 1947; Viking, 1959), pp. 11, 14, 23; reprinted in BB 189, 192, 203/SE 16, 18, 25. Compare the later, more critical essay "D.H. Lawrence: The Other Face of the Coin" (WEE 34–39).

40. "Inversely, as the Square of Their Distances Apart," CSP 148/SP 32.

41. "This Night Only" (to Satie's *Gymnopédie #1*), CSP 338.

42. "The Dragon and the Unicorn," CLP 268.

43. *Ibid.*, CLP 178.

44. "The Hasidism of Martin Buber," BB 106/SE 77.

45. Martin Buber, *Between Man and Man*, translated by Ronald Gregor Smith (Macmillan, 1965), p. 14.

46. Martin Buber, *I and Thou*, translated by Walter Kaufmann (Scribner's, 1970), p. 112. The other two quotations are from the earlier translation by Ronald Gregor Smith (Scribner's, 1958), pp. 18, 11.

47. "The Hasidism of Martin Buber," BB 130–131/SE 93–94.

48. *Ibid.*, BB 139–140/SE 99–100.

49. *Ibid.*, BB 112/SE 81.

50. *Ibid.*, BB 141–142/SE 101.

51. *Ibid.*, BB 110–111/SE 80.

52. SFE, 30 August 1964.

53. Raymond Blakney, *Meister Eckhart: A Modern Translation* (Harper, 1941), p. 14.

54. "The World of the Shining Prince," ER 143.

55. "The Dragon and the Unicorn," CLP 233 (adapted from Eugene Debs).

CHAPTER THREE

1. *Situationist International Anthology,* edited and translated from the French by Ken Knabb (Bureau of Public Secrets, 1981), p. 63.

2. SFE, 29 December 1966.

3. AN 128.

4. "The Institutionalization of Revolt, the Domestication of Dissent," SE 201.

5. "Kenneth Patchen, Naturalist of the Public Nightmare," BB 96–97.

6. "Thou Shalt Not Kill," CSP 272/SP 99.

7. "The Dragon and the Unicorn," CLP 235–236.

8. AN 355–356.

9. "The Dragon and the Unicorn," CLP 207.

10. Interview in Lipton's *The Holy Barbarians,* pp. 293–294.

11. Introduction to *The New British Poets* (New Directions, 1949), p. xxvi.

12. *Excerpts from a Life,* edited by Ekbert Faas (Conjunctions, 1981), pp. 57–58. This small book, published in a limited edition, contains episodes from Rexroth's continuation of his autobiography into the thirties and forties. [It has since been incorporated into the expanded edition of *An Autobiographical Novel* (New Directions, 1991), where a slightly edited version of the cited passage can be found on p. 518.]

13. "Disengagement: The Art of the Beat Generation," AS 2/SE 42.

14. "The Students Take Over," A 110–111, 102, 104/SE 123, 115–118.

15. BB vii.

16. "His Corner of the World," *New York Times Book Review,* 27 October 1957.

17. SFE, 21 July 1963.

18. SFM, December 1970.

19. SFM, July 1968. On the May revolt, which situationist theories and tactics contributed toward provoking, see *Situationist International Anthology,* pp. 225–256, 343–352.

20. "Back to the Sources of Literature," AS 164.

21. SFE, 9 January 1966.

22. C 30.

23. C xv, xvii–xviii.

24. C xi–xii.

25. C xii.

26. "Facing Extinction," AS 185–186.

27. SFM, July 1969.

28. "Back to the Sources of Literature," AS 153.

29. *Ibid.,* AS 160.

30. "The Poetry of the Far East in a General Education," in *Approaches to the Oriental Classics,* edited by William de Bary (Columbia University Press, 1959), p. 197.

31. Interview in *The San Francisco Poets,* edited by David Meltzer (Ballantine, 1971), pp. 42–44; reprinted as *Golden Gate: Interviews with Five San Francisco Poets* (Wingbow, 1976), pp. 52–54. This is vintage Rexroth: perhaps his best interview, certainly his funniest.

32. "Poets, Old and New," A 208–209.

33. "Back to the Sources of Literature," AS 165.

34. Guy Debord, *The Society of the Spectacle* (Paris, 1967; translation: Black & Red, 1977), thesis #4.

35. Guy Debord & Pierre Canjuers, "Preliminaries Toward Defining a Unitary Revolutionary Program," in *Situationist International Anthology,* pp. 307–308.

36. "For Eli Jacobson," CSP 244–245/SP 89–91.

BIBLIOGRAPHY

All Rexroth's poetry and plays and most of his translations are available from New Directions, along with the *Autobiographical Novel,* the *Selected Essays* and the two *Classics Revisited* volumes. Most of the other prose books are out of print.

Fantasy Records issued two LPs of Rexroth's jazz poetry, *Poetry Readings in the Cellar* (with Lawrence Ferlinghetti, 1959) and *Poetry and Jazz at the Blackhawk* (1960), both long out of print. *A Sword in a Cloud of Light,* a cassette of a 1977 reading with jazz and koto-shakuhachi accompaniment, is available from Watershed Tapes (P.O. Box 50145, Washington, DC 20004).

The most comprehensive study of Rexroth is Morgan Gibson's *Revolutionary Rexroth: Poet of East-West Wisdom* (Archon, 1986), which incorporates but substantially reworks material from his earlier book, *Kenneth Rexroth* (Twayne, 1972). Despite his title Gibson says relatively little about Rexroth's political radicality and social criticism; but his discussion of the poetry and plays, with particular emphasis on their Oriental aspects, is reliable and often insightful. His bibliography lists a large number of other writings about Rexroth.

James Hartzell and Richard Zumwinkle's *Kenneth Rexroth: A Checklist of His Published Writings* (UCLA Library, 1967) is essential for those interested enough to search the larger libraries for Rexroth's hundreds of uncollected articles. (Nearly all of them can be found in the library of the University of California at Berkeley.) A much larger bibliography is in progress, but will not be completed for several years.

Linda Hamalian has completed a biography of Rexroth and is preparing an expanded edition of his autobiography, which will incorporate *Excerpts from a Life* and other material on his later years. Rexroth's correspondence with James Laughlin is soon to be published by Norton.

[Unfortunately Hamalian's biography, *A Life of Kenneth Rexroth* (Norton, 1991), turned out to be extremely hostile and uncomprehending.]

In addition to the out-of-print books—which should certainly all be reissued—completed manuscripts exist for two books that have never been published at all: *The Poetry of Pre-Literate Peoples* (an anthology) and *Camping in the Western Mountains* (a guidebook from the thirties). There also remains an enormous amount of uncollected Rexroth material—columns, articles, reviews, introductions, interviews, letters, radio tapes, paintings—much of which would be worth bringing out in book form. I have compiled a 200-page anthology of the *Examiner* and *San Francisco* columns, but have not yet found a suitable publisher.

THE WAR AND
THE SPECTACLE

The orchestration of the Gulf war was a glaring expression of what the situationists call *the spectacle*—the development of modern society to the point where images dominate life. The PR campaign was as important as the military one. How this or that tactic would play in the media became a major strategical consideration. It didn't matter much whether the bombing was actually "surgical" as long as the *coverage* was; if the victims didn't appear it was as if they didn't exist. The "Nintendo effect" worked so well that the euphoric generals had to caution against too much public euphoria for fear that it might backfire. Interviews with soldiers in the desert revealed that they, like everyone else, depended almost totally on the media to tell them what was supposedly happening. The domination of image over reality was sensed by everyone. A large portion of the coverage consisted of coverage of the coverage. The spectacle itself presented superficial debates on the new level of instant global spectacularization and its effects on the spectator.

Nineteenth-century capitalism alienated people from themselves and from each other by alienating them from the products of their own activity. This alienation has been intensified as those products have increasingly become "productions" that we passively contemplate. The power of the mass media is only the most obvious manifestation of this development; in the larger sense the spectacle is everything from arts to politicians that have become autonomous *representations* of life. "The spectacle is not a collection of images; it is a social relation among people, mediated by images" (Debord, *The Society of the Spectacle*).

Along with arms profits, oil control, international power struggles and other factors which have been so widely discussed as to need no comment here, the war involved contradictions between the two basic forms of spectacle society. In the *diffuse spectacle* people are lost amid the variety of competing spectacles, commodities, styles and ideologies that are presented for their consumption. The diffuse spectacle arises within societies of pseudoabundance (America is the prototype and still the unchallenged world leader of spectacle production, despite its decline in other regards); but it is also broadcast to less developed regions—being one of the main means by which the latter are dominated. Saddam's regime is an example of the rival *concentrated spectacle,* in which people are conditioned to identify with the omnipresent image of the totalitarian leader as compensation for being deprived of virtually everything else. This image concentration is normally associated with a corresponding concentration of economic power, state capitalism, in which the state itself has become the sole, all-owning capitalist enterprise (classic examples are Stalin's Russia and Mao's China); but it may also be imported into Third World mixed economies (such as Saddam's Iraq) or even, in times of crisis, into highly developed economies (such as Hitler's Germany). But for the most part the concentrated spectacle is a crude stopgap for regions as yet incapable of sustaining the variety of illusions of the diffuse spectacle, and in the long run it tends to succumb to the latter, more flexible form (as recently in eastern Europe and the USSR). At the same time, the diffuse form is tending to incorporate certain features of the concentrated one.

The Gulf war reflected this convergence. The closed world of Saddam's concentrated spectacle dissipated under the global floodlights of the diffuse spectacle; while the latter used the war as a pretext and a testing ground for implementing typically "concentrated" methods of control—censorship, orchestration of patriotism, suppression of dissent. But the mass media are so monopolized, so pervasive and (despite token grumbling) so subservient to establishment policies that overtly repressive methods were hardly needed. The spectators, under the impression that they were expressing their own considered views, parroted the catch phrases and debated the pseudoissues that the media had instilled in them day after day, and as in any other spectator sport loyally "supported" the home team in the desert by *rooting* for it.

This media control was reinforced by the spectators' own internalized conditioning. Socially and psychologically repressed, people are drawn to spectacles of violent conflict that allow their accumulated frustrations to explode in socially condoned orgasms of collective pride and hate. Deprived of significant accomplishments in their own work and leisure, they participate vicariously in military enterprises that have real and undeniable effects. Lacking genuine community, they thrill to the sense of sharing in a common purpose, if only that of fighting some common enemy, and react angrily against anyone who contradicts the image of patriotic unanimity. The individual's life may be a farce, the society may be falling apart, but all complexities and uncertainties are temporarily forgotten in the self-assurance that comes from identifying with the state.

War is the truest expression of the state, and its most powerful reinforcement. Just as capitalism must create artificial needs for its increasingly superfluous commodities, the state must continually create artificial conflicts of interest requiring its violent intervention. The fact that the state incidentally provides a few "social services" merely camouflages its fundamental nature as a *protection racket*.

When two states go to war the net result is as if each state had made war on its own people—who are then taxed to pay for it. The Gulf war was a particularly gross example: Several states eagerly sold billions of dollars' worth of arms to another state, then massacred hundreds of thousands of conscripts and civilians in the name of neutralizing its dangerously large arsenal. The multinational corporations that own those states now stand to make still more billions of dollars restocking armaments and rebuilding the countries they have ravaged.

Whatever happens in the Middle East in the complex aftermath of the war, one thing is certain: The first aim of all the states and would-be states, overriding all their conflicting interests, will be to crush or coopt any truly radical popular movement. On this issue Bush and Saddam, Mubarak and Rafsanjani, Shamir and Arafat are all partners. The American government, which piously insisted that its war was "not against the Iraqi people but only against their brutal dictator," has now given Saddam another "green light": to slaughter and torture the Iraqis who have courageously risen against him. American officials openly admit that they prefer continued police-military rule in Iraq (with or without Saddam) to any form of democratic self-rule that might "destabilize" the region—i.e., that might give neighboring peoples the inspiration for similar revolts against their own rulers.

In America the "success" of the war has diverted attention from the acute social problems that the system is incapable of solving, reinforcing the power of the militarist establishment and the complacency of the patriotic spectators. While the latter are busy watching war reruns and exulting at victory parades, the most interesting question is what will happen with the people who saw through the show.

* * *

The most significant thing about the movement against the Gulf war was its unexpected spontaneity and diversity. In the space of a few days hundreds of thousands of people all over the country, the majority of whom had never even been at a demonstration before, initiated or took part in vigils, blockades, teach-ins and a wide variety of other actions. By February the coalitions that had called the huge January marches—some factions of which would normally have tended to work for "mass unity" under their own bureaucratic guidance—recognized that the movement was far beyond any possibility of centralization or control, and agreed to leave the main impetus to local grassroots initiative. Most of the participants had already been treating the big marches simply as gathering points while remaining more or less indifferent to the coalitions officially in charge (often not even bothering to stay around to listen to the usual ranting speeches). The real interaction was not between stage and audience, but among the individuals carrying their own homemade signs, handing out their own leaflets, playing their music, doing their street theater, discussing their ideas with friends and strangers, discovering a sense of community in the face of the insanity.

It will be a sad waste of spirit if these persons become ciphers, if they allow themselves to be channeled into quantitative, lowest-common-denominator political projects—tediously drumming up votes to elect "radical" politicians who will invariably sell them out, collecting signatures in support of "progressive" laws that will usually have little effect even if passed, recruiting "bodies" for demonstrations whose numbers will in any case be underreported or ignored by the media. If they want to contest the hierarchical system they must reject hierarchy in their own methods and relations. If they want to break through the spectacle-induced stupor, they must use their own imaginations. If they want to incite others, they themselves must *experiment*.

Those who saw through the war became aware, if they weren't already, of how much the media falsify reality. Personal participation made this awareness more vivid. To take part in a peace march of a hundred thousand people and then see it given equal-time coverage with a prowar demonstration of a few dozen is an illuminating experience—it brings home the bizarre unreality of the spectacle, as well as calling into question the relevance of tactics based on communicating radical viewpoints by way of the mass media. Even while the war was still going on the protesters saw that they had to confront these questions, and in countless discussions and symposiums on "the war and the media" they examined not only the blatant lies and overt blackouts, but the more subtle methods of media distortion—use of emotionally loaded images; isolation of events from their historical context; limitation of debate to "responsible" options; framing of dissident viewpoints in ways that trivialize them; personification of complex realities (Saddam = Iraq); objectification of persons ("collateral damage"); etc. These examinations are continuing and are giving rise to a veritable industry of articles, lectures and books analyzing every aspect of media falsification.

The most naïve see the falsifications as mere mistakes or biases that might be corrected if enough members of the audience call in and complain, or otherwise pressure the mass media into presenting a somewhat wider range of viewpoints. At its most radical this perspective is expressed in the limited but suggestive tactic of picketing particular media.

Others, aware that the mass media are owned by the same interests that own the state and the economy and will thus inevitably represent those interests, concentrate on disseminating suppressed information through various alternative media. But the glut of sensational information constantly broadcast in the spectacle is so deadening that the revelation of one more lie or scandal or atrocity seldom leads to anything but increased depression and cynicism.

Others try to break through this apathy by adopting the manipulative methods of propaganda and advertising. An antiwar film, for example, is generally assumed to have a "powerful" effect if it presents a barrage of the horrors of war. The actual subliminal effect of such a barrage is, if anything, prowar—getting caught up in an irresistible onslaught of chaos and violence (as long as it remains comfortably vicarious) is precisely what is exciting about war to jaded spectators. Overwhelming people with a rapid succession of emotion-rousing images only confirms them in their habitual sense of helplessness in the face of a world beyond their control. Spectators with thirty-second attention spans may be shocked into a momentary antiwar revulsion by pictures of napalmed babies, but they may just as easily be whipped into a fascistic fury the next day by different images—of flag burners, say.

Regardless of their ostensibly radical messages, alternative media have generally reproduced the dominant spectacle-spectator relation. The point is to undermine it—to challenge the conditioning that makes people *susceptible* to media manipulation in the first place. Which ultimately means challenging the social organization that produces that conditioning, that turns people into spectators of prefabricated adventures because they are prevented from creating their own.

BUREAU OF PUBLIC SECRETS
2 April 1991

RENÉ VIÉNET'S
"CAN DIALECTICS BREAK BRICKS?"
— Pacific Film Archive, Berkeley, 19 March 1992, 7:30 p.m. —

"Imagine a kung fu flick in which the martial artists spout Situationist aphorisms about conquering alienation while decadent bureaucrats ply the ironies of a stalled revolution. This is what you'll encounter in René Viénet's outrageous refashioning of a Chinese fisticuff film. An influential Situationist, Viénet stripped the sound-track from a run-of-the-mill Hong Kong export and lathered on his own devastating dialogue. . . . A brilliant, acerbic and riotous critique of the failure of socialism in which the martial artists counter ideological blows with theoretical thrusts from Debord, Reich and others . . . Viénet's target is also the mechanism of cinema and how it serves ideology." —PFA Program Note

Since Guy Debord has permanently withdrawn all his films from circulation, *Can Dialectics Break Bricks?* is virtually the only available example of a situationist use of cinema. Viénet's film is a far lesser creation than any of Debord's, but still well worth seeing for its consistent use of the situationist technique of *détournement*—the diversion of already existing cultural elements to new subversive purposes. Other filmmakers have used aspects of this technique, but only in confused and half-conscious ways, or for purely humorous ends à la Woody Allen's *What's Up, Tiger Lily?*

Viénet's film is even funnier, but its humor comes not so much from its satire of an absurd film genre as from its undermining of the spectacle-spectator relation at the heart of an absurd society. In both its social-critical content and its self-critical form, it presents a striking contrast to the reformist whining and militant ranting that constitute most supposedly radical media. By turning the persuasive power of the medium against itself (characters criticize the plot, their own role in it, and the function of spectacles in general), it constantly counteracts the viewers' tendency to identify with the cinematic action, reminding them that the real adventure—or lack of it—is in their own lives.

A VHS copy of *Can Dialectics Break Bricks?* (1973, 90 minutes, French with English subtitles) is available from Drift Distribution, 709 Carroll St. #3-R, Brooklyn, NY 11215.

An extensive account of Debord's films, Thomas Levin's "Dismantling the Spectacle: The Cinema of Guy Debord," can be found in *On the Passage of a Few People Through a Rather Brief Moment in Time: The Situationist International, 1957–1972* (ed. Elisabeth Sussman, MIT Press, 1989).

Los Angeles 1965/1992

The Los Angeles rebellion was a rebellion against the commodity, against the world of the commodity in which worker-consumers are hierarchically subordinated to commodity value. . . . The looting of the Watts district was the most direct realization of the distorted principle: "To each according to his false needs"—needs determined and produced by the economic system which the very act of looting rejects. But once the vaunted abundance is taken at face value and directly *seized* instead of being eternally pursued in the rat race of alienated labor and increasing but unmet social needs, real desires begin to be expressed in festival, in playful self-assertion, in the *potlatch* of destruction. . . .

The Los Angeles blacks are better paid than any others in the United States, but they are also the most segregated from the flaunted affluence of California. Hollywood, the pole of the global spectacle, is in their immediate vicinity. They are promised that, with patience, they will join in America's prosperity, but they come to see that this prosperity is not a fixed level but an endless ladder. The higher they climb, the further they get from the top. . . . If they keep quiet their *survival* is guaranteed; capitalism has become sufficiently concentrated and entrenched in the state to distribute welfare to the poorest. But by the very fact that they lag behind in the advance of socially organized survival, the blacks pose the problems of *life*; what they are really demanding is not to survive but to *live*. . . .

The rational world produced by the industrial revolution has liberated individuals from their local and national limitations and linked them on a global scale; but it irrationally separates them once again, in accordance with a hidden logic that finds its expression in insane ideas and grotesque value systems. Estranged from their own world, people are everywhere surrounded by strangers. The barbarian is no longer at the ends of the earth, he is *here*, made into a barbarian by his forced participation in the collective hierarchical consumption. . . . But the repulsive absurdity of certain hierarchies, and the fact that the entire world of the commodity is directed blindly and automatically to their protection, leads people to see—the moment they engage in a negating practice—that every hierarchy is absurd.

SITUATIONIST INTERNATIONAL
December 1965

Excerpts from the *Situationist International Anthology* (Bureau of Public Secrets, P.O. Box 1044, Berkeley, CA 94701). Reprinted May 1992. No copyright.

WATTS 1965
The Decline and Fall of the
Spectacle-Commodity Economy

August 13–16, 1965, the blacks of Los Angeles revolted. An incident between traffic police and pedestrians developed into two days of spontaneous riots. Despite increasing reinforcements, the forces of order were unable to regain control of the streets. By the third day the blacks had armed themselves by looting accessible gun stores, enabling them to fire even on police helicopters. It took thousands of police and soldiers, including an entire infantry division supported by tanks, to confine the riot to the Watts area, and several more days of street fighting to finally bring it under control. Stores were massively plundered and many were burned. Official sources listed 32 dead (including 27 blacks), more than 800 wounded and 3000 arrests.

Reactions from all sides were most revealing: a revolutionary event, by bringing existing problems into the open, provokes its opponents into an unhabitual lucidity. Police Chief William Parker, for example, rejected all the major black organizations' offers of mediation, correctly asserting: "These rioters don't have any leaders." Since the blacks no longer had any leaders, it was the moment of truth for both sides. What did one of those unemployed leaders, NAACP general secretary Roy Wilkins, have to say? He declared that the riot "should be put down with all necessary force." And Los Angeles Cardinal McIntyre, who protested loudly, did not protest against the violence of the repression, which one might have supposed the most tactful policy at a time when the Roman Church is modernizing its image; he denounced "this premeditated revolt against the rights of one's neighbor and against respect for law and order," calling on Catholics to oppose the looting and "this violence without any apparent justification." And all those who went so far as to recognize the "apparent justifications" of the rage of the Los Angeles blacks (but never their real ones), all the ideologists and "spokesmen" of the vacuous international Left, deplored the irresponsibility, the disorder, the looting (especially the fact that *arms and alcohol* were the first targets) and the 2000 fires with which the blacks lit up their battle and their ball. But who has defended the Los Angeles rioters in the terms they deserve? We will. Let the economists fret over the $27 million lost, and the city planners sigh over one of their most beautiful supermarkets gone up in smoke, and McIntyre blubber over his slain deputy sheriff; let the sociologists bemoan the absurdity and intoxication of this rebellion. The role of a revolutionary publication is not only to justify the Los Angeles insurgents, but to help elucidate their perspectives, to explain theoretically the truth for which such practical action expresses the search.

In Algiers in July 1965, following Boumédienne's coup d'état, the situationists issued an "Address" to the Algerians and to revolutionaries all over the world which interpreted conditions in Algeria and the rest of the world *as a whole*. Among other examples we mentioned the movement of the American blacks, stating that if it could "assert itself incisively" it would unmask the contradictions of the most advanced capitalist system. Five weeks later this incisiveness was in the streets. Modern theoretical criticism of modern society and criticism in acts of the same society already coexist; still separated but both advancing toward the same realities, both talking about the same thing. These two critiques are mutually explanatory, and neither can be understood without the other. Our theory of "survival" and of "the spectacle" is illuminated and verified by these actions which are so incomprehensible to American false consciousness. One day these actions will in turn be illuminated by this theory.

Until the Watts explosion, black civil rights demonstrations had been kept by their leaders within the limits of a legal system that tolerates the most appalling violence on the part of the police and the racists—as in last March's march on Montgomery, Alabama. Even after the latter scandal, a discreet agreement between the federal government, Governor Wallace and Martin Luther King led the Selma marchers on March 10 to stand back at the first police warning, in dignity and prayer. The confrontation expected by the demonstrators was reduced to a mere spectacle of a potential confrontation. In that moment nonviolence reached the pitiful limit of its courage: first you expose yourself to the enemy's blows, then you push your moral nobility to the point of sparing him the trouble of using any more force. But the main point is that the civil rights movement only addressed legal problems by legal means. It is logical to make legal appeals regarding legal questions. What is irrational is to appeal legally against a blatant illegality as if it was a mere oversight that would be corrected if pointed out. It is obvious that the crude and glaring illegality from which blacks still suffer in many American states has its roots in a socioeconomic contradiction that is not within the scope of existing laws, and that no future *judicial* law will be able to get rid of this contradiction in the face of the more fundamental laws of this society. What American blacks are really daring to demand is the right to really live, and in the final analysis this requires nothing less than the total subversion of this society. This becomes increasingly evident as blacks in their everyday lives find themselves forced to use increasingly subversive methods. The issue is no longer the condition of American blacks, but the condition of America, which merely happens to find its first expression among the blacks. The Watts riot was not a *racial* conflict: the rioters left alone the whites that were in their path, attacking only the white policemen, while on the other hand black solidarity did not extend to black store-owners or even to black car-drivers. Martin Luther King himself had to admit that the revolt went beyond the limits of his specialty. Speaking in Paris last October, he said: "This was not a race riot. It was a class riot."

The Los Angeles rebellion was a rebellion against the commodity, against the world of the commodity in which worker-consumers are *hierarchically* subordinated to commodity standards. Like the young delinquents of all the advanced countries, but more radically because they are part of a class without a future, a sector of the proletariat unable to believe in any significant chance of integration or promotion, the Los Angeles blacks take modern capitalist propaganda, its publicity of abundance, *literally*. They want to possess *now* all the objects shown and abstractly accessible, because they want to *use* them. In this way they are challenging their exchange-value, the *commodity reality* which molds them and marshals them to its own ends, and which has *pre-selected everything*. Through theft and gift they rediscover a use that immediately refutes the oppressive rationality of the commodity, revealing its relations and even its production to be arbitrary and unnecessary. The looting of the Watts district was the most direct realization of the distorted principle: "To each according to their *false* needs"—needs determined and produced by the economic system which the very act of looting rejects. But once the vaunted abundance is taken at face value and directly *seized*, instead of being eternally pursued in the rat-race of alienated labor and increasing unmet social needs, real desires begin to be expressed in festive celebration, in playful self-assertion, in the *potlatch* of destruction. People who destroy commodities show their human superiority over commodities. They stop submitting to the arbitrary forms that distortedly reflect their real needs. The flames of Watts *consummated* the system of consumption. The theft of large refrigerators by people with no electricity, or with their electricity cut off, is the best image of the lie of affluence trans-formed into a truth *in play*. Once it is no longer bought, the commodity lies open to criticism and alteration, whatever particular form it may take. Only when it is paid for with money is it respected as an admi-rable fetish, as a symbol of status within the world of survival.

Looting is a *natural* response to the unnatural and inhuman soci-ety of commodity abundance. It instantly undermines the commodity as such, and it also exposes what the commodity ultimately implies: the army, the police and the other specialized detachments of the state's monopoly of armed violence. What is a policeman? He is the active servant of the commodity, the man in complete submission to the commodity, whose job it is to ensure that a given product of human labor remains a commodity, with the magical property of having to be paid for, instead of becoming a mere refrigerator or rifle —a passive,

366

inanimate object, subject to anyone who comes along to make use of it. In rejecting the humiliation of being subject to police, the blacks are at the same time rejecting the humiliation of being subject to commodities. The Watts youth, having no future in market terms, grasped another *quality* of the present, and that quality was so incontestable and irresistible that it drew in the whole population—women, children, and even sociologists who happened to be on the scene. Bobbi Hollon, a young black sociologist of the neighborhood, had this to say to the *Herald Tribune* in October: "Before, people were ashamed to say they came from Watts. They'd mumble it. Now they say it with pride. Boys who used to go around with their shirts open to the waist, and who'd have cut you to pieces in half a second, showed up here every morning at seven o'clock to organize the distribution of food. Of course, it's no use pretending that food wasn't looted. . . . All that Christian blah has been used too long against blacks. These people could loot for ten years and they wouldn't get back half the money those stores have stolen from them over all these years. . . . Me, I'm only a little black girl." Bobbi Hollon, who has sworn never to wash off the blood that splashed on her sandals during the rioting, adds: "Now the whole world is watching Watts."

How do people make history under conditions designed to dissuade them from intervening in it? Los Angeles blacks are better paid than any others in the United States, but they are also the most *separated* from the California superopulence that is flaunted all around them. Hollywood, the pole of the global spectacle, is right next door. They are promised that, with patience, they will join in America's prosperity, but they come to see that this prosperity is not a fixed state but an endless ladder. The higher they climb, the farther they get from the top, because they start off disadvantaged, because they are less qualified and thus more numerous among the unemployed, and finally because the hierarchy that crushes them is not based on economic buying power alone: they are also treated as *inherently* inferior in every area of daily life by the customs and prejudices of a society in which all human power is based on buying power. Just as the human riches of the American blacks are despised and treated as criminal, monetary riches will never make them completely acceptable in America's alienated society: individual wealth will only make a *rich nigger* because blacks as a whole must *represent poverty* in a society of hierarchized wealth. Every witness noted the cry proclaiming the global significance of the uprising: "This is a black revolution and we want the world to know it!" *Freedom Now* is the password of all the revolutions of history, but now for the first time the problem is not to overcome scarcity, but to master material abundance according to new principles. Mastering abundance is not just changing the way it is shared out, but *redefining its whole orientation*. This is the first step of a vast, all-embracing struggle.

The blacks are not alone in their struggle, because a *new proletarian consciousness* (the consciousness that they are not at all the masters of their own activities, of their own lives) is developing in America among strata which in their rejection of modern capitalism resemble the blacks. It was, in fact, the first phase of the black struggle which happened to be the signal for the more general movement of contestation that is now spreading. In December 1964 the students of Berkeley, harassed for their participation in the civil rights movement, initiated a strike challenging the functioning of California's "multiversity" and ultimately calling into question the entire American social system in which they are being programmed to play such a passive role. The spectacle promptly responded with exposés of widespread student drinking, drug use and sexual immorality—the same activities for which blacks have long been reproached. This generation of students has gone on to invent a new form of struggle against the dominant spectacle, the *teach-in*, a form taken up October 20 in Great Britain at the University of Edinburgh during the Rhodesian crisis. This obviously primitive and imperfect form represents the stage at which people *refuse to confine their discussion of problems* within academic limits or fixed time periods; the stage when they strive to pursue issues to their ultimate consequences and are thus led to practical activity. The same month tens of thousands of anti–Vietnam war demonstrators appeared in the streets of Berkeley and New York, their cries echoing those of the Watts rioters: "Get out of our district and out of Vietnam!" Becoming more radical, many of the whites are finally going outside the law: "courses" are given on how to hoodwink army recruiting boards (*Le Monde*, 19 October 1965) and draft cards are burned in front of television cameras. In the affluent society disgust is being expressed for this affluence and *for its price*. The spectacle is being spat on by an advanced sector whose autonomous activity denies its values. The classical proletariat, to the very extent to which it had been provisionally integrated into the capitalist system, had itself failed to integrate the blacks (several Los Angeles unions refused blacks until 1959); now the blacks are the rallying point for all those who refuse the logic of this integration into capitalism, which is all that the promise of racial integration amounts to. Comfort will never be comfortable enough for those who seek what is not on the market, what in fact the market specifically eliminates. The level attained by the technology of the most privileged becomes an insult, and one more easily grasped and resented than is that most fundamental insult: reification. The Los Angeles rebellion is the first in history to justify itself with the argument that there was no air conditioning during a heat wave.

The American blacks have their own particular spectacle, their own black newspapers, magazines and stars, and if they are rejecting it in disgust as a fraud and as an expression of their humiliation, it is because they see it as a *minority* spectacle, a mere appendage of a general spectacle. Recognizing that their own spectacle of desirable consumption is a colony of the white one enables them to see more quickly through the falsehood of the whole economic-cultural spectacle. By wanting to participate really and immediately in the affluence that is the official value of every American, they are really demanding the egalitarian *actualization* of the American spectacle of everyday life— they are demanding that the half-heavenly, half-earthly values of the spectacle be put to the test. But it is in the nature of the spectacle that it cannot be actualized either immediately or equally, *not even for the whites.* (The blacks in fact function as a perfect spectacular object-lesson: the threat of falling into such wretchedness spurs others on in the rat-race.) In taking the capitalist spectacle at its face value, the blacks are already rejecting the spectacle itself. The spectacle is a drug for slaves. It is designed not to be taken literally, but to be followed from just out of reach; when this separation is eliminated, the hoax is revealed. In the United States today the whites are enslaved to the commodity while the blacks are negating it. The blacks are asking for *more than the whites*—this is the core of a problem that has no solution except the dissolution of the white social system. This is why those whites who want to escape their own slavery must first of all rally to the black revolt—not, obviously, in racial solidarity, but in a joint global rejection of the commodity and of the state. The economic and psychological distance between blacks and whites enables blacks to see white consumers for what they are, and their justified contempt for whites develops into a contempt for passive consumers in general. The whites who reject this role have no chance unless they link their struggle more and more to that of the blacks, uncovering its most fundamental implications and supporting them all the way. If, with the radicalization of the struggle, such a convergence is not sustained, black nationalist tendencies will be reinforced, leading to the futile interethnic antagonism so characteristic of the old society. Mutual slaughter is the other possible outcome of the present situation, once resignation is no longer tolerable.

The attempts to build a separatist or pro-African black nationalism are dreams giving no answer to the real oppression. The American blacks have no fatherland. They are *in their own country* and they are *alienated.* So are the rest of the population, but the blacks are aware of it. In this sense they are not the most backward sector of American society, but the most advanced. They are the negation at work, "the bad aspect that makes history by setting the struggle in motion" (*The Poverty of Philosophy*). Africa has no special monopoly on that.

The American blacks are a product of modern industry, just like electronics or advertising or the cyclotron. And they embody its contradictions. They are the people that the spectacle paradise must simultaneously integrate and reject, with the result that the antagonism between the spectacle and human activity is totally revealed through them. The spectacle is *universal,* it pervades the globe just as the commodity does. But since the world of the commodity is based on class conflict, the commodity itself is hierarchical. The necessity for the commodity (and hence for the spectacle, whose role is to *inform* the commodity world) to be both universal and hierarchical leads to a universal hierarchization. But because this hierarchization must remain *unavowed,* it is expressed in the form of unavowable, because *irrational,* hierarchical value judgments in a world of *irrational rationalization.* It is this hierarchization that creates *racisms* everywhere. The British Labour government has come to the point of restricting nonwhite immigration, while the industrially advanced countries of Europe are once again becoming racist as they import their subproletariat from the Mediterranean area, developing a colonial exploitation within their own borders. And if Russia continues to be anti-Semitic it is because it continues to be a hierarchical society in which labor must be bought and sold as a commodity. The commodity is constantly extending its domain and engendering new forms of hierarchy, whether between labor leader and worker or between two car-owners with artificially distinguished models. This is the original flaw in commodity rationality, the sickness of bourgeois reason, a sickness which has been inherited by the bureaucratic class. But the repulsive absurdity of certain hierarchies, and the fact that the entire commodity world is directed blindly and automatically to their protection, leads people to see—the moment they engage in a negating practice—that every hierarchy is absurd.

The rational world produced by the Industrial Revolution has rationally liberated individuals from their local and national limitations and linked them on a global scale; but it irrationally separates them once again, in accordance with a hidden logic that finds its expression in insane ideas and grotesque values. Estranged from their own world, people are everywhere surrounded by strangers. The barbarians are no longer at the ends of the earth, they are among the general population, made into barbarians by their forced participation in the worldwide system of hierarchical consumption. The veneer of humanism that camouflages all this is inhuman, it is the negation of human activities and desires; it is the humanism of the commodity, the solicitous care of the parasitical commodity for its human host. For those who reduce people to objects, objects seem to acquire human qualities and truly human manifestations appear as unconscious "animal behavior." Thus the chief humanist of Los Angeles, William Parker, could say: "They started acting like a bunch of monkeys in a zoo."

When California authorities declared a "state of insurrection," the insurance companies recalled that they do not cover risks at that level —they guarantee nothing beyond survival. The American blacks can rest assured that as long as they keep quiet they will in most cases be allowed to *survive*. Capitalism has become sufficiently concentrated and interlinked with the state to distribute "welfare" to the poorest. But by the very fact that they lag behind in the advance of socially organized survival, the blacks pose the problems of *life;* what they are really demanding is not to survive but to *live*. The blacks have nothing of their own to insure; their mission is to destroy all previous forms of private insurance and security. They appear as what they really are: the irreconcilable enemies, not of the great majority of Americans, but of the alienated way of life of the entire modern society. The most industrially advanced country only shows us the road that will be followed everywhere unless the system is overthrown.

Certain black nationalist extremists, to show why they can accept nothing less than a separate nation, have argued that even if American society someday concedes total civil and economic equality, it will never, on a personal level, come around to accepting interracial marriage. This is why *this American society itself must disappear*— in America and everywhere else in the world. The end of all racial prejudice, like the end of so many other prejudices related to sexual inhibitions, can only lie beyond "marriage" itself, that is, beyond the *bourgeois family* (which has largely fallen apart among American blacks)—the bourgeois family which prevails as much in Russia as in the United States, both as a model of hierarchical relations and as a structure for a stable *inheritance of power* (whether in the form of money or of social-bureaucratic status). It is now often said that American youth, after thirty years of silence, are rising again as a force of contestation, and that the black revolt is their Spanish Civil War. This time their "Lincoln Brigades" must understand the full significance of the struggle in which they are engaging and totally support its universal aspects. The Watts "excesses" are no more a political error in the black revolt than the POUM's May 1937 armed resistance in Barcelona was a betrayal of the anti-Franco war. A revolt against the spectacle—even if limited to a single district such as Watts —calls *everything* into question because it is a human protest against a dehumanized life, a protest of *real individuals* against their separation from a community that would fulfill their *true human and social nature* and transcend the spectacle.

SITUATIONIST INTERNATIONAL
December 1965

Newly translated and reissued July 1992 by the Bureau of Public Secrets.

STRONG LESSONS
FOR ENGAGED BUDDHISTS

Have you learned lessons only of those who admired you,
and were tender with you, and stood aside for you?
Have you not learned great lessons from those who reject you,
and brace themselves against you? or who treat you with
contempt, or dispute the passage with you?
—Whitman, "Stronger Lessons"

In the middle of the Vietnam war Thich Nhat Hanh and a few other Buddhist monks, nuns and laypeople broke with the 2500-year tradition of Buddhist apoliticism and founded the Tiep Hien Order in an effort to relate Buddhist ethical and meditational practice to contemporary social issues. Members of the order organized antiwar demonstrations, underground support for draft resisters, and various relief and social service projects. Though the movement was soon crushed in Vietnam, Nhat Hanh has carried on similar activities from exile in France, and the idea of "socially engaged Buddhism" has spread among Buddhists around the world. One of its main expressions in the West, the Buddhist Peace Fellowship, defines its purpose as being "to bring a Buddhist perspective to contemporary peace, environmental, and social action movements" and "to raise peace, environmental, feminist, and social justice concerns among Western Buddhists."

The emergence of engaged Buddhism is a healthy development. Despite the bullshit that Buddhism shares with all religions (superstition, hierarchy, male chauvinism, complicity with the established order), it has always had a core of genuine insight based on the practice of meditation. It is this vital core, along with its freedom from the enforced dogmas characteristic of Western religions, that has enabled it to catch on so readily even among the most sophisticated milieus in other cultures. People engaged in movements for social change might well benefit from the mindfulness, equanimity and self-discipline fostered by Buddhist practice; and apolitical Buddhists could certainly stand to be confronted with social concerns.

So far, however, the engaged Buddhists' social awareness has remained extremely limited. If they have begun to recognize certain glaring social realities, they show little understanding of their causes or possible solutions. For some, social engagement simply means doing some sort of volunteer charitable work. Others, taking their cue perhaps from Nhat Hanh's remarks on arms production or Third World starvation, resolve not to eat meat or not to patronize or work for companies that produce weapons. Such gestures may be personally meaningful to them, but their actual effect on global crises is negligible. If millions of Third World people are allowed to starve, this is not because there is not enough food to go around, but because there are no profits to be made by feeding penniless people. As long as there is big money to be made by producing weapons or ravaging the environment, someone will do it, regardless of moral appeals to people's good will; if a few conscientious persons refuse, a multitude of others will scramble for the opportunity to do it in their place.

Others, sensing that such individual gestures are not enough, have ventured into more "political" activities. But in so doing they have generally just followed along with the existing peace, ecological and other so-called progressive groups, whose tactics and perspectives are themselves quite limited. With very few exceptions these groups take the present social system for granted and simply jockey within it in favor of their particular issue, often at the expense of other issues. As the situationists put it: "Fragmentary oppositions are like the teeth on cogwheels: they mesh with each other and make the machine go round —the machine of the spectacle, the machine of power."[1]

A few of the engaged Buddhists may realize that it is necessary to get beyond the present system; but failing to grasp its entrenched, self-perpetuating nature, they imagine gently and gradually modifying it from within, and then run into continual contradictions. One of the Tiep Hien Precepts says: "Possess nothing that should belong to others. Respect the property of others, but prevent others from enriching themselves from human suffering or the suffering of other beings."[2] How is one to prevent the exploitation of suffering if one "respects" the property that embodies it? And what if the owners of such property fail to relinquish it peacefully?

If the engaged Buddhists have failed to explicitly oppose the socio-economic system and have limited themselves to trying to alleviate a few of its more appalling effects, this is for two reasons. First, they are not even clear about what it is. Since they are allergic to any analysis that seems "divisive," they can hardly hope to understand a system based on class divisions and bitter conflicts of interest. Like almost everyone else they have simply swallowed the official version of reality, in which the collapse of the Stalinist state-capitalist regimes in Russia and East Europe supposedly demonstrates the inevitability of the Western form of capitalism.

Secondly, like the peace movement in general they have adopted the notion that "violence" is the one thing that must be avoided at all

---

1. *Situationist International Anthology* (Bureau of Public Secrets, 1981), p. 124.

2. *The Path of Compassion: Writings on Socially Engaged Buddhism* (Parallax Press, 1988), p. 152.

cost. This attitude is not only simplistic, it is hypocritical: they themselves tacitly rely on all sorts of state violence (armies, police, jails) to protect their loved ones and possessions, and would certainly not passively submit to many of the conditions they reproach others for rebelling against. In practice pacifism usually ends up being more tolerant toward the ruling order than toward its opponents. The same organizers who reject any participant who might spoil the purity of their nonviolent demonstrations often pride themselves on having developed amicable understandings with police. Small wonder that dissidents who have had somewhat different experiences with the police have not been overly impressed with this sort of "Buddhist perspective."

It is true that many forms of violent struggle, such as terrorism or minority coups, are inconsistent with the sort of open, participatory organization required to create a genuinely liberated global society. An antihierarchical revolution can only be carried out by the people as a whole, not by some group supposedly acting on their behalf; and such an overwhelming majority would have no need for violence except to neutralize any pockets of the ruling minority that may violently try to hold on to their power. But any significant social change inevitably involves *some* violence. It would seem more sensible to admit this fact, and simply strive to minimize violence as far as possible.

This antiviolence dogmatism goes from the dubious to the ludicrous when it also opposes any form of "spiritual violence." There is, of course, nothing wrong with trying to act "without anger in your heart" and trying to avoid getting caught up in pointless hatred and revenge; but in practice this ideal often just serves as an excuse to repress virtually any incisive analysis or critique by labeling it as "angry" or "intellectually arrogant." On the basis of their (correct) impression of the bankruptcy of traditional leftism, the engaged Buddhists have concluded that all "confrontational" tactics and "divisive" theories are misguided and irrelevant. Since this attitude amounts to ignoring virtually the entire history of social struggles, many richly suggestive experiences remain a closed book to them (the anarchist experiments in social organization during the 1936 Spanish revolution, for example, or the situationist tactics that provoked the May 1968 revolt in France), and they are left with nothing but to "share" with each other the most innocuous New-Agey platitudes and to try to drum up interest in the most tepid, lowest-common-denominator "actions."

It is ironic that people capable of appreciating the classic Zen anecdotes fail to see that sharp wakeup tactics may also be appropriate on other terrains. Despite all the obvious differences, there are certain interesting analogies between Zen and situationist methods: both insist on practical realization of their insights, not just passive assent to some doctrine; both use drastic means, including rejecting pointless dialogue and refusing to offer ready-made "positive alternatives," in order to pull the rug out from under habitual mindsets; both are therefore predictably accused of "negativity."

One of the old Zen sayings is: *If you meet a Buddha, kill him.* Have the engaged Buddhists succeeded in "killing" Thich Nhat Hanh in their minds? Or are they still attached to his image, awed by his mystique, passively consuming his works and uncritically accepting his views? Nhat Hanh may be a wonderful person; his writings may be inspiring and illuminating in certain respects; but his social analysis is naïve. If he seems slightly radical this is only in contrast to the even greater political naïveté of most other Buddhists. Many of his admirers will be shocked, perhaps even angered, at the idea that anyone could have the nerve to criticize such a saintly person, and will try to dismiss this leaflet by pigeonholing it as some bizarre sort of "angry leftist ideology" and by assuming (incorrectly) that it was written by someone with no experience of Buddhist meditation.

Others may grant that some of these points are well taken, but will then ask: "Do you have any practical, constructive alternative, or are you just criticizing? What do you suggest that we do?" You don't need to be a master carpenter to point out that the roof leaks. If a critique stirs even a few people to stop and think, to see through some illusion, perhaps even provokes them to new ventures of their own, this is already a very practical effect. How many "actions" accomplish as much?

As for what you should do: the most important thing is to stop relying on others to tell you what you should do. Better make your own mistakes than follow the most spiritually wise or politically correct leader. It is not only more interesting, it is usually more effective, to pursue your own experiments, however small, than to be a digit in a regiment of digits. All hierarchies need to be contested, but the most liberating effect often comes from challenging the ones in which you yourself are most implicated.

One of the May 1968 graffiti was: *Be realistic, demand the impossible.* "Constructive alternatives" within the context of the present social order are at best limited, temporary, ambiguous; they tend to be coopted and become part of the problem. We may be forced to deal with certain urgent issues such as war or environmental threats, but if we accept the system's own terms and confine ourselves to merely reacting to each new mess produced by it, we will never overcome it. Ultimately we can solve survival issues only by refusing to be blackmailed by them, by aggressively going beyond them to challenge the whole anachronistic social organization of *life.* Movements that limit themselves to cringing defensive protests will not even achieve the pitiful survival goals they set for themselves.

BUREAU OF PUBLIC SECRETS
October 1993

You've Lived the Life — Now See the Movie!

GUY DEBORD'S
"The Society of the Spectacle"

90 minutes. French videocopy with English subtitles by Keith Sanborn
Pacific Film Archive, Berkeley, Wednesday, 22 May 1996, 7:30 p.m.

If we ever get out of this mess, future generations will look back on Guy Debord as the person who contributed to that liberation more than anyone else in this century.

Guy Debord (1931–1994) was the most influential figure in the Situationist International, a small experimental group that played a key role in catalyzing the May 1968 revolt in France. *The Society of the Spectacle* (1973) is Debord's film adaptation of his own 1967 book. As passages from the book are read in voiceover the text is illuminated, via direct illustration or various types of ironic contrast, by clips from Russian and Hollywood features (*Potemkin, Ten Days That Shook the World, For Whom the Bell Tolls, Shanghai Gesture, Johnny Guitar, Mr. Arkadin,* etc.), TV commercials, publicity shots, softcore porn, street scenes, and news and documentary footage, including glimpses of Spain 1936, Hungary '56, Watts '65, France '68, and other revolts of the past. Intertitle quotes from Marx, Machiavelli, Clausewitz or Tocqueville occasionally break the flow.

Leaving aside the question of aesthetic merit (in which regard Debord's films are incidentally among the most brilliantly innovative works in the history of the cinema), *The Society of the Spectacle* is certainly the most important radical film ever made. Not just because it is based on the most important radical book of the twentieth century, but because it unfortunately has no real cinematic competition. Many films have provided a few insights into this or that aspect of modern society, but Debord's is the only one that presents a consistent critique of the whole global system. Many radical filmmakers have given lip service to Brecht's notion of encouraging spectators to think and act for themselves rather than sucking them into passive identification with hero or plot, but Debord is virtually the only one who has actually realized this goal. Aside from a few Debord-influenced works (notably Viénet's *Can Dialectics Break Bricks?* and Cronin and Seltzer's *Call It Sleep*), his films are the only ones that have made a coherent use of the situationist tactic of *détournement:* the diversion of already existing cultural elements to new subversive purposes. Détournement has been widely imitated, but usually without real understanding. It does not mean merely randomly juxtaposing incongruous elements, but (1) creating out of those elements a new coherent whole that (2) criticizes both the existing world and its own relation to that world. Some artists, filmmakers, and even ad designers have used superficially similar juxtapositions, but most are far from fulfilling (1), much less (2).

The Society of the Spectacle is neither an ivory tower "philosophical" discourse nor a helplessly impulsive "protest," but a ruthlessly lucid examination of the most fundamental tendencies and contradictions of the society we live in. This means that it needs to be reread (and reseen) many times, but it also means that it remains as pertinent as ever while countless radical and intellectual fads have come and gone. As Debord noted in his later *Comments on the Society of the Spectacle* (1988), in the intervening decades the spectacle has become more all-pervading than ever, to the point of repressing virtually any awareness of pre-spectacle history or anti-spectacle possibilities: "Spectacular domination has succeeded in raising an entire generation molded to its laws."

Bureau of Public Secrets, P.O. Box 1044, Berkeley, CA 94701

Undermining the Society of the Spectacle

"So many things we wanted have not been attained; or only partially and not like we thought. What communication have we desired, or experienced, or only simulated? What true project has been lost? . . . Whether dramatic or documentary, the cinema functions to present a false, isolated coherence as a substitute for a communication and an activity that are absent."

*

"Official news is elsewhere. The society sends back to itself its own historical image as a merely superficial and static history of its rulers. . . . All existing equilibrium, however, is brought back into question each time unknown people try to live differently. But it's always far away. We learn of it through the papers and newscasts. We remain outside it, confronted with just another spectacle. We are separated from it by our own nonintervention."

*

"The very principle of the spectacle—nonintervention—is linked to the alienation of the old world. Conversely, the most pertinent revolutionary experiments in culture have sought to break the spectator's psychological identification with the hero so as to draw him into activity by provoking his capacities to revolutionize his own life."

*

"The relation between authors and spectators is only a transposition of the fundamental relation between those who give orders and those who carry them out. . . . The spectacle-spectator relation is in itself a staunch bearer of the capitalist order. The ambiguity of all 'revolutionary art' lies in the fact that the revolutionary aspect of any particular spectacle is always contradicted and offset by the reactionary element present in all spectacles."

*

"Revolution is not 'showing' life to people, but bringing them to life. A revolutionary organization must always remember that its aim is not getting its adherents to listen to convincing talks by expert leaders, but getting them to speak for themselves, in order to achieve, or at least strive toward, an equal degree of participation. The cinematic spectacle is one of the forms of pseudo-communication (developed, in lieu of other possibilities, by the present class technology) in which this aim is radically unfeasible. . . . In appearance a film-club discussion is an attempt at dialogue, at social encounter, at a time when individuals are increasingly isolated by the urban environment. But it is in fact the negation of such dialogue since the people have not come together to *decide* on anything."

*

"The spontaneous acts we can see everywhere forming against power and its spectacle must be warned of all the obstacles in their path and must find a tactic taking into account the enemy's strength and means of cooption. This tactic, which we are going to popularize, is *détournement*."

*

"Détournement: the reuse of already existing artistic elements in a new ensemble. . . . The two fundamental laws of détournement are the loss of importance of each detourned autonomous element—which may go so far as to completely lose its original sense—and at the same time the organization of another meaningful ensemble that confers on each element its new scope and effect. Détournement has a peculiar power which obviously stems from the double meaning, from the enrichment of most of the terms by the coexistence within them of their old and new senses. It's practical because it's so easy to use and because of its inexhaustible potential for reuse."

*

"The only interesting venture is the liberation of everyday life, not only in the perspectives of history but for ourselves and right away. This entails the withering away of alienated forms of communication. The cinema, too, has to be destroyed."

Excerpts from Guy Debord articles and filmscripts included in the *Situationist International Anthology* (Bureau of Public Secrets, P.O. Box 1044, Berkeley, CA 94701)

SITUATIONIST BIBLIOGRAPHY

Since 1968 dozens of books and innumerable pamphlets, journals, leaflets, etc., by non–SI members have appeared that can be considered more or less situationist in the broad sense of the term, in that, well or poorly, they have adopted the SI's perspectives and methods. This bibliography, however, mentions only the main publications of the SI itself, the pre- and post-SI works of some of its members, and some of the books about the SI.

Pre-SI Texts

Guy Debord (ed.), *Potlatch: 1954–1957* (Lebovici, 1985) is currently out of print. Gérard Berreby (ed.), *Documents relatifs à la fondation de l'Internationale Situationniste: 1948–1957* (1985; Éditions Allia, B.P. 90, 75862 Paris cedex 18), a huge (650 8″×11″ pages) and lavishly illustrated collection, includes not only all the issues of *Potlatch* but numerous other texts from Cobra, the Lettrist International and the Movement for an Imaginist Bauhaus, along with Asger Jorn's *Pour la forme* and Jorn and Debord's *Fin de Copenhague*. Another early Jorn-Debord collaboration, Debord's *Mémoires* (1958), which consists entirely of detourned elements, has recently been reprinted (Pauvert, 1993). Except for the half dozen pre-SI articles in the *SI Anthology*, virtually none of these texts have been translated.

Guy Debord's Films

Hurlements en faveur de Sade (Films Lettristes, 1952). 90 minutes.
Sur le passage de quelques personnes à travers une assez courte unité de temps (Dansk-Fransk Experimentalfilmskompagni, 1959). 20 minutes.
Critique de la séparation (Dansk-Fransk Experimentalfilmskompagni, 1961). 20 minutes.
La Société du Spectacle (Simar Films, 1973). 90 minutes.
Réfutation de tous les jugements, tant élogieux qu'hostiles, qui ont été jusqu'ici portés sur le film "La Société du Spectacle" (Simar Films, 1975). 25 minutes.
In girum imus nocte et consumimur igni (Simar Films, 1978). 80 minutes.

All are 35mm, B&W. *Oeuvres cinématographiques complètes: 1952–1978* (Champ Libre, 1978; Gallimard, 1994) contains illustrated scripts for all six films. Translations of the first five are available in *Society of the Spectacle and Other Films* (Rebel, 1992). *In girum* has been translated by Lucy Forsyth (Pelagian, 1991).

In 1984 Debord removed all his films from circulation in France as a protest against the reaction of the French press and public to the assassination of his friend and publisher, Gérard Lebovici. Shortly before Debord's suicide in November 1994 (he had a painful terminal illness) he and Brigitte Cornand made a 60-minute "antitelevisual" video, *Guy Debord, son art et son temps,* which was shown January 1995 on a French cable channel along with *La Société du Spectacle* and *Réfutation de tous les jugements.* Information on the video can be obtained from Brigitte Cornand, c/o Canal +, 85/89 Quai André Citroën, 75711 Paris cedex 15. It is not clear at this time if Debord's films will ever become available again, but needless to say numerous videocopies of the three televised works are now in circulation around the world. A videocopy of *La Société du Spectacle* with English subtitles is available from Keith Sanborn, c/o Ediciones la Calavera, P.O. Box 1106, Peter Stuyvesant Station, New York, NY 10009.

French SI Books

Internationale Situationniste: 1958–1969 (Van Gennep, 1970; Champ Libre, 1975). 700 pages, illustrated. Reissue of all twelve French journals in the original format. Selections translated by Christopher Gray in *Leaving the Twentieth Century: The Incomplete Work of the Situationist International* (Free Fall, 1974; long out of print). Ken Knabb's *Situationist International Anthology* (Bureau of Public Secrets, 1981) is more accurate and comprehensive.

Raoul Vaneigem, *Traité de savoir-vivre à l'usage des jeunes générations* (Gallimard, 1967). Translated as *The Revolution of Everyday Life* by John Fullerton and Paul Sieveking (Practical Paradise, 1972); and by Donald Nicholson-Smith (Rebel/Left Bank, 1983; revised 1994).

Guy Debord, *La Société du Spectacle* (Buchet-Chastel, 1967; Champ Libre, 1972; Gallimard, 1992). Translated as *The Society of the Spectacle* by Fredy Perlman and John Supak (Black & Red, 1970; revised 1977); and by Donald Nicholson-Smith (Zone, 1994).

René Viénet, *Enragés et situationnistes dans le mouvement des occupations* (Gallimard, 1968). Includes numerous documents and illustrations. Translated as *Enragés and Situationists in the Occupation Movement, May '68* (Autonomedia/Rebel, 1992).

Guy Debord and Gianfranco Sanguinetti, *La véritable scission dans l'Internationale* (Champ Libre, 1972). Analysis of post-1968 SI crises. Translated by Michel Prigent and Lucy Forsyth as *The Veritable Split in the International* (Piranha, 1974; revised: Chronos, 1990).

Débat d'orientation de l'ex-Internationale Situationniste (Centre de Recherche sur la Question Sociale, 1974). Internal documents, 1969–1971. Not translated except for the selections in the *SI Anthology.*

SI Publications in Other Languages

Most of the more original and important SI texts appeared in French. (The *SI Anthology* is drawn entirely from French texts except for the piece by the Italian section on pp. 338–339.) SI publications in other languages often represented the more artistic and opportunistic tendencies (notably in Italy, Germany, Scandinavia and the Netherlands) that were repudiated early in the SI's history. In the later period, what would have become the British section never got off the ground and the American and Italian sections scarcely lasted much longer, coming as they did right in the middle of the post-1968 crises that were soon to lead to the SI's dissolution.

The American section's main publications were Robert Chasse's pamphlet *The Power of Negative Thinking* (New York, 1968; a critique of the New Left, actually published shortly before Chasse joined the SI) and one issue of a journal, *Situationist International* #1 (New York, 1969; notably including critiques of Marcuse, McLuhan, Bookchin, Baran and Sweezy, etc.). The journal has been reissued by Extreme Press. After their December 1969 resignation/exclusion, Chasse and Bruce Elwell produced an extensive critical history of the American section, *A Field Study in the Dwindling Force of Cognition* (1970), which the SI never answered.

The Italian section published one issue of a journal, *Internazionale Situazionista* #1 (1969), and carried out a number of interventions in the crises and struggles in Italy. None of the Italian texts have been translated into English, but there is a complete French edition, *Écrits complets de la Section Italienne de l'Internationale Situationniste (1969–1972)*, translated by Joël Gayraud and Luc Mercier (1988; Contre-Moule, Cedex 2461, 99246 Paris-Concours).

The Scandinavian section published three issues of the Danish journal *Situationistisk Revolution* (1962, 1968, 1970). Some of its other activities are described in *I.S.* #10, pp. 22–26.

Most of the major SI writings have been translated into English, German, Greek, Italian and Spanish; some have also been translated into Arabic, Chinese, Danish, Dutch, Korean, Japanese, Polish, Portuguese, Swedish, and by now probably several other languages.

Post-SI Works

Guy Debord, *Préface à la quatrième édition italienne de "La Société du Spectacle"* (Champ Libre, 1979; reprinted in the Gallimard edition of *Commentaires*). Translated by Lucy Forsyth and Michel Prigent as *Preface to the Fourth Italian Edition of "The Society of the Spectacle"* (Chronos, 1979).

—*Considérations sur l'assassinat de Gérard Lebovici* (Lebovici, 1985; Gallimard, 1993). Not translated.

—(with Alice Becker-Ho), *Le "Jeu de la Guerre": Relevé des positions successives de toutes les forces au cours d'une partie* (Lebovici, 1987). Account of a board game with strategical commentaries. Not translated.

—*Commentaires sur la société du spectacle* (Lebovici, 1988; Gallimard, 1992). Translated by Malcolm Imrie as *Comments on the Society of the Spectacle* (Verso, 1990).

—*Panégyrique, tome premier* (Lebovici, 1989; Gallimard, 1993). Translated by James Brook as *Panegyric, Volume I* (Verso, 1991). The first and only installment of Debord's "memoirs."

—*"Cette mauvaise réputation..."* (Gallimard, 1993). Not translated.

—*Des contrats* (Le Temps Qu'il Fait, 1995). Debord's film contracts. Not translated.

Some Debord letters are included in the two volumes of published Champ Libre *Correspondance* (1978 & 1981).

Gianfranco Sanguinetti (pseudonym Censor), *Rapporto veridico sulle ultime opportunità di salvare il capitalismo in Italia* (Milan, 1975). Translated into French by Guy Debord as *Véridique rapport sur les dernières chances de sauver le capitalisme en Italie* (Champ Libre, 1976). Not translated into English.

—*Del terrorismo e dello stato* (Milan, 1979). Translated by Lucy Forsyth and Michel Prigent as *On Terrorism and the State* (Chronos, 1982).

Raoul Vaneigem (pseudonym Ratgeb), *De la grève sauvage à l'autogestion généralisée* (Éditions 10/18, 1974). Partially translated by Paul Sharkey as *Contributions to the Revolutionary Struggle* (Bratach Dubh, 1981; Elephant, 1990).

—(pseudonym J.F. Dupuis), *Histoire désinvolte du surréalisme* (Paul Vermont, 1977). Translated by Donald Nicholson-Smith as *A Cavalier History of Surrealism* (AK, 1997).

—*Le livre des plaisirs* (Encre, 1979). Translated by John Fullerton as *The Book of Pleasures* (Pending Press, 1983).

—*Le mouvement du Libre-Esprit* (Ramsay, 1986). Translated by Randall Cherry and Ian Patterson as *The Movement of the Free Spirit* (Zone, 1994).

—*Adresse aux vivants sur la mort qui les gouverne et l'opportunité de s'en défaire* (Seghers, 1990). Not translated.

—*Avertissement aux écoliers et lycéens* (Mille et Une Nuits, 1995). Not translated.

René Viénet, *La dialectique peut-elle casser des briques?* (1973). 90-minute kungfu film with altered soundtrack. A videocopy with English subtitles (translation: Keith Sanborn), *Can Dialectics Break Bricks?*, is available from Drift Distribution (709 Carroll St. #3-R, Brooklyn, NY 11215).

Of the various above-mentioned translations, Nicholson-Smith's versions of *The Revolution of Everyday Life* and *The Society of the Spectacle* are the most fluent, but rather free. Such liberties may be appropriate in the case of Vaneigem's relatively "lyrical" work, but they sometimes obscure the rigorous dialectical structure of Debord's text. The Black & Red version sticks closer to the original, but contains numerous errors. Considering the central importance of Debord's book, the serious reader might do well to study both versions together.

At the opposite extreme, the translations published by Chronos are clumsily overliteral, often to the point of unreadability. The various other translations fall somewhere in between, generally sufficing to give a pretty good idea of the originals, but all containing inaccuracies and stylistic infelicities. Those of Debord's *Comments* and *Panegyric* are among the most accurate; that of Viénet's *Enragés and Situationists* contains quite a few careless errors.

Books About the SI

Jean-Jacques Raspaud and Jean-Pierre Voyer's *L'Internationale Situationniste: protagonistes, chronologie, bibliographie (avec un index des noms insultés)* (Champ Libre, 1971) is a handy reference to the French journal collection. Jean-François Martos's *Histoire de l'Internationale Situationniste* (Lebovici, 1989) recounts the SI's development and perspectives largely in the situationists' own words. Anselm Jappe's *Guy Debord* (French translation from the original Italian, Via Valeriano, 1995) covers most of the same material thematically, with particularly extensive treatment of the Marxian connection that is usually slighted in the more cultural studies. Pascal Dumontier's *Les situationnistes et Mai 68* (Lebovici, 1990) is a competent account.

Elisabeth Sussman (ed.), *On the Passage of a Few People Through a Rather Brief Moment in Time: The Situationist International, 1957–1972* (MIT/Institute of Contemporary Art, 1989), an illustrated catalog of the 1989–90 exhibition on the SI in Paris, London and Boston, includes several previously untranslated SI texts along with an assortment of scholarly articles devoted almost exclusively to the early artistic-cultural aspects of the SI's venture. Greil Marcus's *Lipstick Traces: A Secret History of the Twentieth Century* (Harvard, 1989, illustrated) concentrates even more on the presituationist ventures of the 1950s, which the author relates rather impressionistically to other extremist cultural movements such as Dada and early punk. Iwona Blazwick (ed.), *An Endless Adventure, an Endless Passion, an Endless Banquet: A Situationist Scrapbook* (Verso/ICA, 1989, illustrated) includes an assortment of texts illustrating the (for the most part rather confused) influence of the SI in England from the 1960s through the 1980s. The first half of Sadie Plant's *The Most Radical Gesture: The Situationist International in a Postmodern Age* (Routledge, 1992) is a fairly competent summary of the main situationist theses; the second half will be of interest primarily to those who are so ill-informed as to imagine that the situationists had some resemblance to the post-modernists and other fashionably pretentious ideologists of confusion and resignation. Stewart Home (ed.), *What Is Situationism? A Reader* (AK, 1996) presents an assortment of views, mostly hostile and uncomprehending, as is Home's own previous book, *The Assault on Culture* (Aporia/Unpopular, 1988). Simon Ford's *The Realization and Suppression of the Situationist International: An Annotated Bibliography 1972–1992* (AK, 1995) lists over 600 texts, mostly in English, about or influenced by the SI. Ken Knabb's *Public Secrets* (Bureau of Public Secrets, 1997) includes some relevant material.

Publishers and Distributors

Éditions Champ Libre was renamed Éditions Gérard Lebovici in memory of its founder-owner, who was assassinated in 1984. (The assassins were never identified.) Besides the books mentioned here it has published many other situationist-influenced authors along with a wide range of works of related interest. After yet another change of name and address, it is now Éditions Ivrea, 1 Place Paul Painlevé, 75005 Paris.

Guy Debord recently shifted from Champ Libre/Lebovici to Éditions Gallimard (5 rue Sébastien-Bottin, 75007 Paris), which has reprinted most of his books.

Most situationist texts in English are available from:

- Left Bank Distribution, 1404 18th Ave., Seattle, WA 98122
- Perennial Books, Box B14, Montague, MA 01351
- AK Distribution, P.O. Box 40682, San Francisco, CA 94140
- AK Distribution, 33 Tower Street, Edinburgh EH6 7BN, Scotland

NOTES ON THE TEXTS

Do We Need Snyder for Poet-Priest?
May 1970. 100 copies. Leaflet distributed at a Gary Snyder poetry reading in Berkeley.

In This Theater ...
August 1970. Originally issued as a tiny illustrated pamphlet (including the two *Alice in Wonderland* pictures that appear on the cover of this book). A few dozen copies were circulated as a sort of announcement of the formation of "1044" by Knabb and Ron Rothbart.

Ode on the Absence of Real Poetry Here This Afternoon
October 1970. 150 copies. Read at an open poetry reading in Berkeley.

Bureaucratic Comix
January 1971. 500 copies. 18″ × 22″ poster. Reprinted (1000 copies) by Create Situations (New York). Reprinted in *Neon Lights* #1 (Manchester, England).

Critique of the New Left Movement
Excerpts from unpublished drafts by Contradiction (John Adams, Isaac Cronin, Dan Hammer, Ken Knabb, Michael Lucas and Ron Rothbart), representing about half of the selection that we put together for limited circulation when the project was abandoned in April 1972.

That fuller selection is included in the *Bureau Prehistory,* a 90-page photocopy collection of the complete publications of the Council for the Eruption of the Marvelous (1970), 1044 (1970) and Contradiction (1970–72), available from me for $10.

On the Poverty of Hip Life
April 1972. Excerpts from unpublished Contradiction draft (see above).

Remarks on Contradiction and Its Failure
March 1973. Pamphlet. 750 copies. Reprinted (1000 copies) December 1974. Translated into French by Daniel Denevert (CRQS, 1974).

"Reich: How To Use" (comic)
June 1973. 2000 copies. 11″ × 17″ poster. Publicity for:

Reich: How To Use (Voyer)
July 1973. Foldout. 6000 copies. Translation of Jean-Pierre Voyer's *Reich: mode d'emploi* (Champ Libre, 1971). Reprinted in *Sexzine* (London) and in

Anarchy #42 (New York, 1995). Voyer's text has also been translated into Dutch, German, Greek, Italian and Spanish. His address is Institut de Préhistoire Contemporaine, B.P. 20-05, 75221 Paris cedex 05, France.

I have taken the opportunity to make a number of minor improvements in my original translation of this and the following text. (Unless otherwise indicated, all the other texts in this book are reproduced exactly as they originally appeared, except that I have corrected a few typos.)

Discretion Is the Better Part of Value

July 1973. Leaflet. 200 copies. Translation of excerpts from a Voyer letter elaborating on some points in his Reich article.

Double-Reflection

May 1974. Pamphlet. 2400 copies. Reprinted by Spontaneous Combustion (London, 1974). Translated into French by Joël Cornüault (CRQS, 1974) and reprinted anonymously in Paris (1978). Translated into German by the Agentur für die Selbstaufhebung des Proletariats (Berlin, 1984). Translated into Greek by Tákes Athanarópoulos (Elefteros Typos Bookshop, Athens, ca. 1985).

Theory of Misery, Misery of Theory

Translation of Daniel Denevert's *Théorie de la misère, misère de la théorie* (Paris, November 1973). This and the two following texts were originally translated by Robert Cooperstein, Dan Hammer and Ken Knabb and issued as a single pamphlet (September 1974, 2000 copies). Our translations were accurate, but somewhat overliteral. I have retranslated all three texts here in an effort to render the sometimes rather dense passages as clearly as possible.

To Clarify Some Aspects of the Moment

Translation of chapter 3 of Daniel Denevert's *Pour l'intelligence de quelques aspects du moment* (originally published anonymously in Paris, January 1972).

Declaration Concerning the Center for Research on the Social Question

Translation of *Déclaration à propos du Centre de Recherche sur la Question Sociale,* signed by Françoise [Nadine] Bloch, Jeanne Charles [Françoise Denevert], Joël Cornuault, and Daniel Denevert (Paris, April 1974).

Notice Concerning the Reigning Society and Those Who Contest It

November 1974. 2000 copies. 9″ × 25″ poster signed by Tita Carrión, Robert Cooperstein, Isaac Cronin, Dan Hammer, Ken Knabb, Gina Rosenberg and Chris Shutes. Distributed with a second poster listing publications available from the signers and from the CRQS. Reprinted in Cronin and Shutes's journal *Implications* (December 1975). Translated into French, Spanish and Italian by the Agence pour l'auto-suppression du prolétariat (Lille, France, 1977).

386

The Blind Men and the Elephant

January 1975. 2000 copies. 18" × 23" poster. Collection of quotes about the SI, along with excerpts from Debord and Sanguinetti's *La véritable scission dans l'Internationale* and a proposal to translate the situationist books. An expanded collection of the quotes can be found in the *SI Anthology*.

Bureau of Public Secrets #1

January 1976. 2400 copies. Only issue of BPS journal.

"The Society of Situationism," "Notes Toward a Situationist Manifesto" and the review of Gray's *Leaving the 20th Century* were reprinted in England by Spontaneous Combustion.

"The Society of Situationism" was translated into French by Daniel Denevert, Françoise Denevert and Ken Knabb (1976, photocopy circulation) and reprinted by Jean-François Labrugère (Grenoble). Partially translated into Japanese in *Anarchism* #19 (Tokyo, 1978). Translated into German in *Subversion* #8 (Berlin, 1985) by the Agentur für die Selbstaufhebung des Proletariats. Translated into Greek in *De Bello Civili* #1 (Thessaloniki, 1991).

"Affective Detournement: A Case Study" was translated into French by Daniel Denevert and Ken Knabb (1976, photocopy circulation).

The "Arms and the Woman" translation, first issued separately in June 1975 (2000 copies), was reprinted by Lust for Life (Oregon, 1976); in *Anarchist Review* #3 (England, 1977); by the London School of Economics Anarchist Group (ca. 1978); in *Red Menace* #5 (Toronto, 1980); and in *Not Bored* #7 (Michigan, 1984), and was the basis for translations into Japanese (Tommy Haruki, 1978) and Swedish (*Praxis* #1, Stockholm, 1980). The text was also translated directly from the original French into German, Dutch and Spanish.

The excerpt from the Moinet book was reprinted in *Extraphile* #4 (Virginia, 1994).

The Realization and Suppression of Religion

March 1977. Pamphlet. 2500 copies. Reprinted in *Anarchy* #15 (Missouri, 1988). Translated into French by Grégoire Palamas (Nantes, 1978); by Christian Camous (Paris, 1978); and by Joël Guigné and Jimmy Lallement in *Essais* #34 (Angers/Angoulême, 1979). In 1984 I prepared a corrected French version (photocopy circulation), and this version was polished and published by Jean-François Labrugère (Grenoble, 1986).

I also reprinted the Appendix on Kenneth Rexroth as a separate leaflet and distributed it at one of Rexroth's last public appearances (San Francisco International Poetry Festival, June 1980).

Open Letter to the Tokyo "Libertaire" Group

November 1977. English and Japanese versions (translated by Tommy Haruki) mailed to a couple dozen Japanese anarchist groups. The English version was reprinted in that month's issue of *Libertaire*.

A Radical Group in Hong Kong

October 1978. Leaflet. 1000 copies. The last half was reproduced in the introduction to a Canadian reprinting of *China: The Revolution Is Dead, Long Live the Revolution* (Black Rose Books, Montreal, 1979).

The Opening in Iran

March 1979. 11" × 17" poster with detourned map of Iran. 3000 copies, of which several hundred were distributed to radical Iranian students in the United States. Translated into Greek by Thanásis Papadjímas (Thessaloniki, 1979). Translated into French by Éditions du Ténia Armé (Paris, 1979); by La Bande des Dialecticiens (Brussels, 1980); and by Jean-François Labrugère, Jean Martaguet and Ken Knabb (Grenoble, 1980).

Banalities

April 1979. Printed on back of a price list of BPS publications. A few hundred copies were circulated with the Iran poster.

The Relevance of Rexroth

Fall 1990. 88-page book. 5000 copies were printed, of which around 500 have been sold and 1000 given away. Provisional translation into French (1993; 100 copies) by Ken Knabb and Jean-François Labrugère (B.P. 144, 38002 Grenoble cedex, France). Revised translation published by Atelier de Création Libertaire (Lyon, 1997).

The War and the Spectacle

April 1991. 4-page leaflet. 16,000 copies. Reprinted in *Anarchy* #29 (Missouri); *Fifth Estate* (Detroit); *God Speaks Through Me* #4 (Butt Cheese Productions, Illinois); *Retrofuturism* #15 (Iowa); the Aggressive School of Cultural Workers (Iowa); *Loompanics Unlimited Catalog* and *Loompanics' Golden Records* anthology (Washington); *Version 90* #3 (Massachusetts); *Linha Imaginòt* #6 (Toulouse, France); and *News from Nowhere* #1 (San Francisco). Partial reprintings in *Open Eye* #1 (London); *The Thistle* (Massachusetts); and *War After War* (City Lights, San Francisco). Copied onto various computer networks. Translated into Polish in *Rewolta* #7 (Warsaw). Translated into Greek (two versions, one in Athens, another by the *Bello Civili* group in Thessaloniki). Translated into Japanese (Tommy Haruki). Translated into French (Labrugère, J.-P. Piotaix, Knabb). The latter was partially reprinted in *Irak: les révoltes inconnues* (Montreal, 1992).

On Viénet's film "Can Dialectics Break Bricks?"

March 1992. 300 copies. Leaflet publicizing a showing of René Viénet's 1973 film. Reprinted in *Anarchy* #35 (Missouri) and *Extraphile* #4 (Virginia).

Around this same time I reprinted 500 copies of "For a Revolutionary Judgment of Art" (Guy Debord's 1961 article on Godard's *Breathless*) for distribution at Berkeley showings of Godard's film. The text, not reproduced here, can be found in *SI Anthology*, pp. 310–314.

Los Angeles 1965/1992

May 1992. Leaflet. 2000 copies. Excerpts from the SI's 1965 article on the Watts riot. Translated into Japanese by Tommy Haruki.

Haruki, incidentally, has translated several other SI articles and has recently completed a Japanese version of *The Society of the Spectacle*. His current address is: Agora—Tommy Haruki, Nishi-machi 17-2, Fujinomiya, Shizuoka 418, Japan.

Watts 1965: The Decline and Fall of the Spectacle-Commodity Economy

July 1992. 4-page leaflet. 10,000 copies. New translation of the complete SI article, "Le déclin et la chute de l'économie spectaculaire-marchande" (Paris, 1965). Reprinted in *Anarchy* #34 (Missouri) and *Extraphile* #3 (Virginia). The earlier *SI Anthology* version of the article was reprinted in *Media Blitz* #2 (New York) and partially by Notes from Nowhere (Massachusetts).

(There have been dozens of reprintings of various other *SI Anthology* articles, which I haven't bothered to list here. A number of them have also recently been copied onto the World Wide Web computer network.)

Strong Lessons for Engaged Buddhists

October 1993. Leaflet. 4000 copies. Distributed at Thich Nhat Hanh appearances in Berkeley and San Francisco and mailed to all Buddhist Peace Fellowship chapters. Reprinted (1994–96, 5000 copies) for subsequent Bay Area appearances of Nhat Hanh, the Dalai Lama, Gary Snyder, and Robert Aitken (Zen teacher and BPF co-founder). Reprinted in *No* #10 (Liverpool); in *Extraphile* #2 (Virginia); and in *Turning Wheel: Journal of the Buddhist Peace Fellowship* (Berkeley, summer 1994). Copied onto the World Wide Web.

On Debord's film "The Society of the Spectacle"

May 1996. 500 copies each. Two leaflets publicizing a showing of Debord's 1973 film.

Situationist Bibliography

Slightly corrected and updated from the third printing of the *SI Anthology* (July 1995).

SELECTED RESPONSES

*"I have paid you a rare compliment; I have assumed that
you mean what you say."*
　　　　　　　　　　　　　　　　　　　—Nero Wolfe

Although the theoretical output of the Knabbist axis amounts to very little in
terms of conceptual presentation, they have achieved a certain preeminence
within the American situationist movement by virtue of their sheer prolificacy,
their ability to maintain at least the appearance of a continuing project. . . . In
Double Reflection, "theory" appears as *meta*-theory, as, in a restricted sense,
a theory of theory and theorizing about theorizing. This deliberate narrowing
of the scope of critical inquiry marks a retreat from an historical plane of
analysis. . . . The "critical" undertakings of the Bureau of Public Secrets and
his allies find their culmination in the project of a "Phenomenology (*sic*) of the
Subjective Aspect of Practical-Critical Activity." . . . This trivialization of theory
appears not only in Knabb's crude parody of the Hegelian system but in his
simplistic psychologization of "practical-critical activity." In the Knabbist
cosmos, which is surprisingly impervious to historical change, the theorist
becomes the "experiencing subject," who develops endlessly through a sequence
of subjective "moments," arriving finally at an ultimate goal of "realization." This development, although erratic, is hardly dialectical: Knabb, in his
Hegelian mimicry, does not even attempt a parallel construction to the latter's
Phenomenology. His pseudo-phenomenology does not involve the subject's
interpretation of the world as it appears to him; there is no movement analogous to the progression of naive consciousness from sense-certainty to perception to understanding. . . . In his poster, *The Blind Men and the Elephant,*
Knabb himself wishes to play the role of curator of the situationist movement;
since everyone outside of himself and his associates is unable to interpret the
situationist project, Knabb takes upon himself the task of explaining the S.I.
and of translating its texts. . . . It is, of course, no accident that Point-Blank
formed a primary object of the Knabbists' scorn; we, and later Diversion,
constituted the most formidable threat to their hegemonic ambitions. . . . If we
recognize the failure of Point-Blank, it is certainly not out of a capitulation to
our former antagonists. Our present interests lie outside the situationist
movement.

　　　　　　　　　—David Jacobs & Chris Winks, *At Dusk: The Situationist
　　　　　　　　　Movement in Historical Perspective* (Berkeley, August 1975)

* * *

Using their names in public is presumably a device for demystifying activity,
for teaching the elementary but generally poorly appreciated lesson that it is
from for-real individuals that theory and practice come. Furthermore, their

public self-presentation over time provides a certain sort of "continuity," provides data for others to use in studying and creating situationist activity and theory. . . . The "Notice" poster discouraged idle readers from writing the "Notice Comrades" idly, encouraging them to "show us" their agreement by their own public work. . . . They've taken on a difficult task, attacking one manifestation of a central problem. Namely that to the extent that a radical generates some temporary successes, there will be others who enjoying the successes, will, if anything, become relatively content because of the successes and will appreciatively expect more of the same, from others; while the leaders, personally feeling the sterility of the followers, will tend to see in the evolving relationship a justification for the maintenance of their role . . . . Early in this century this process was so poorly appreciated that the revolutionary movement decimated itself without even taking the crudest anti-hierarchical formal organizational measures. Now it is fairly clear that the destruction of this process requires the destruction of the whole spectacle. Which is difficult for seven individuals to accomplish in front of an audience all too interested in participation in the show. . . . The Notice Comrades, dealing with the above, employ an enriched technique of invitation to join-in-the-fun. Namely, they insult the passive reader . . . and along with their insults, they offer to him, perhaps intentionally, certain defects just waiting for him to attack publicly.

> —"Diverse Comments on the Public Activity of the Bay Area 'Notice Comrades' " (article in anonymous pamphlet, New England, July 1976)

* * *

This pamphlet is in favour of the humanization of daily life and "the realization of religion." The super-reform of the detestable and unpalatable; the call for compassion and magnanimity in a world of loathing is just a bad joke. . . . Just as Spartacus slave revolt shocked the world of antiquity (1st century BC Italy), into producing a millenarian adventist Messiah (Jesus the Toad of Nazareth), and saddled Judas Iscariot with the wicked debt for his "sacrifice," so the fierce and nasty revolutionary project since the 1960's has been arousing similar messianic cults—Knabb's is one. Cruelty is less harmful than indulgence and fake compassion. Such "compassion" in the face of roles and ideology can only be complicity and commiseration. CLASS WAR MUST BE WARLIKE. Our enemies know well how to exploit our humanity and sympathy. Death to all exploiters, no forgiveness!!

> —Michael Bradley & Michel Prigent,
> *The Catalyst Times* #0 (London, July 1977)

* * *

The notion of behindism as originally treated in *Double-Reflection* was acceptable as an attempt to describe and comprehend what the author considered to be "a permanent organizational problem of our epoch." If it already manifested a rather dubious concern to distinguish a somewhat more sincere, well-intentioned form of followerism from other more crude forms, it was nevertheless worth reading; it did not pretend to be anything but a tentative contribution to an ongoing discussion, one way among others of approaching a certain problem. The most serious drawback of this notion stemmed from the author's assumption that "practical-critical activity" was sufficiently established and perfectly studiable as such, without seeing that the notion of behindism had only manifested itself within a *particular sector* of the social practice of theory and within a *narrow* conception of the notion of theory. . . . *There's no such thing as "theoretical activity";* it is nothing but a *representation* which tends to justify the role of petty specialists in revolution while reinforcing the paralysis of their direct imitators. . . . The very term "theorist" reflects the fetishism of language, which is dominated by the logic of the division of labor and which recreates that logic. . . . The Bay Area comrades' perspective tended to reinforce the image of the model-theorist that the behindist already had in his head. . . . It was necessary to *criticize* the theoretical model that this notion implied. It takes two for there to be a behindist—the other party has to go along with the relation. Behindism is a phenomenon that can persist only in the context of *illusionistic* relations between individuals, accompanying an enterprise whose objectives are *abstract* and insufficiently defined. When the task, and therefore the obstacles that must be overcome, become clear, the behindist can only conquer or give up, he can't settle for half-measures.

—Daniel Denevert, "Sur le fond d'un divorce" (Paris, October 1977)

* * *

No anarchist do refute or cast a diatribe toward Proudhon, Bakunin, Kropotkin and Spanish C.N.T. like you except a Marxist, an ultra-nationalist and an ignorant liberalist. . . . You know "When you are in Rome you must do as a Roman do." It is at least an etiquette over the world. Surely you have done it in the bad manner like some Japanese "anarchists."

—Yoshiharu Hashimoto, "A Reply to a Situationist,"
in *Libertaire* (Tokyo, November 1977)

* * *

The hierarchy of the American situationists was divided along traditional lines: At the top sat Knabb, the "reluctant" pope, encouraging "autonomy" or intervening benevolently according to which action seemed more likely to maintain both the *family* of dependent social relations and a modicum of public production. . . . Knabb's *Double-Reflection* is central to a comprehension of the American situationists. In it he concentrated and solidified their image of revolutionary practice as a series of acquirable techniques transmitted hierarchically through a supervised apprenticeship which created a community with its own standards of conduct and criteria of judgment. . . . Knabb's recent text *The Realization and Suppression of Religion* is a strikingly self-conscious moment of this superficial reformation which openly rejects the objective determinants of the anti-statist struggle—even going so far as to adopt the viewpoint of the enlightened spectator, in order to better lure him into the camp. . . . He gently strokes those people who have had the good sense to ignore society and go off on their own . . . and leaves open the role of "theorist" for himself should these people seek a little advice on the social context of their struggles. Those of us who know Knabb personally can recognize that each time he broadens his conception of serious struggles it more and more closely conforms to his own narrow private life and preoccupations. He can never set aside the manipulative tactics he appears to bemoan because beneath the humble exterior, its "flip-side," lies a bottomless arrogance based on a belief in an absolute truth—himself.

—Isaac Cronin, "The American Situationists: 1972–77" (Berkeley, February 1978)

* * *

The recent publication by Ken Knabb called "Situationist International Anthology" needs a few critical words in order to cut to size this pretentious creep. But above all what is striking when one picks up this anthology is the way it is edited. The English speaking reader can only read what Knabb has selected. In so doing he has put his stamp on this anthology, shaping it to his own ideological perspectives. It is no more than a knabbization. One day when the whole of the review called *Internationale situationniste* is made available in English, as it stands in French, no more, no less, everyone will be able to notice that Knabb's anthology is but a poor rendering of the original texts, today it is no more than a boring morass in the hands of this editor. . . . what this Saint forgets to tell his readers is of his own contradictions, his own mistakes, his own confusion, in fact his own stupidity that he has dished out in numerous neo-pamphlets over a period of more than ten years. . . . anyone with a bit of critical insight can see that Knabb is a jerk and a Berkeley pseud. Here are a few examples of this knabbery, in fact all of it could be included in his *Blind Men and the Elephant.* It is shameful on his part to have brushed all his false consciousness under his California carpet, so there is nothing left for us but to pull the rug from under his editor's feet. Knabb in his *Realization and Suppression of religion,* published in 1977, went so far as to say: "when religion is treated by the situationists, it is usually brought in only in its most superficial, spectacular aspects," this is a lie, pure hogwash. How can this student in revolution say such a thing and include for example Vaneigem's text *Basic banalities* which deals extensively with God, religion, and modern alienation. . . . Maybe the Reverend Knabb should have gone to Jonestown (Guyana), in fact the massacre orchestrated by that other swine-priest called Jones contradicted Knabb's intervention mania, it was another irony of history and it fell on Knabb's thick head! And yet he continues to distribute his magnificent piece on religion. And of course there is no mention of all this in his anthology, it is disgusting. Knabb should try to intervene armed with his "new Bible," in Salt Lake City or try the terrain of all Christian Revivalists, the repugnant Billy Graham included. . . . A couple of years earlier, he went so far as to admit in his *"Bureau of Public Secrets"* (a sort of dishrag) that he had been a book fetishist, at last he has another fetish "his anthology with his name on the front" and he is even known in the Library of Congress, why not send a copy to Reagan?! . . . Mr. Knabb in his journal called *League of Secret Misery,* once more gave us another gem to laugh at, and goddamit did we laugh, he had sent himself a telegram, today he can do the same, congratulating himself on his new venture. It is pitiful. . . . At the time of the fall of the *last* shah of Iran, our Saint issued a poster called "The Opening in Iran" (Freudian slip no doubt!). Anyone with a bit of common sense would have realized that which was to come in that part of the world, was a nightmare.

... Knabb in fact took his ready-made schema out of his suitcase and started applying it to Iran, the result was a disaster that did not help a critique of religion in that country.

—Michel Prigent, "Biography of the Anthologer" (London, April 1982)

* * *

In the U.S.A. the Situationist International is mostly known, if it is known at all, as a small group of dadaist provocateurs that had something to do with the May 1968 uprising in France. The name has been batted around in reference to punk, because Sex Pistols Svengali Malcolm McLaren was supposedly connected with the situationists. . . . The situationists were, ah, sort of like the Yippies, one hears. Or New York's Motherfuckers. . . . Or the Frankfort School . . . the ideas were similar, right? *Situationist International Anthology*—the result of years of work by Ken Knabb, an American student of the group— makes clear that the Situationist International was something considerably more interesting: perhaps the most lucid and adventurous band of extremists of the last quarter century. . . . It is exhilarating to read this book—to confront a group that was determined to make enemies, burn bridges, deny itself the rewards of celebrity, to find and maintain its own voice in a world where, it seemed, all other voices of cultural or political resistance were either cravenly compromised or so lacking in consciousness they did not even recognize their compromises. . . . The *Situationist International Anthology* does not present the complete text of the situationist journal, and it has no illustrations. But the translations are clear and readable—sometimes too literal, sometimes inspired. Entirely self-published, the anthology is a better job of book-making than most of the books published today by commercial houses. There are virtually no typos; it is well indexed, briefly but usefully annotated, and the design, binding, and printing are all first class. In other words, Knabb has, unlike most other publishers of situationist material in English, taken the material seriously, and allowed it to speak with something like its original authority. . . . The writing in the *Situationist International Anthology* makes almost all present-day political and aesthetic thinking seem cowardly, self-protecting, careerist, and satisfied. The book is a means to the recovery of ambition.

—Greil Marcus, *Village Voice Literary Supplement* (New York, May 1982)

* * *

Marx rightly noted that it was in the most democratic state of his time, the United States of America, that the citizens were the most religious. . . . If the world of the commodity is a religious world, the fact that the state is liberated from religion leads the citizens to become all the more submissive to religion. . . . Thus it is not surprising that it was an American, and specifically a Californian, Ken Knabb, who is to our knowledge the first person to have pointed out (in his 1977 pamphlet *The Realization and Suppression of Religion*, which has since been translated into French) the insufficiencies of the situationist critique regarding religion.

—Jean-Pierre Voyer, *Revue de Préhistoire Contemporaine* #1
(Paris, May 1982)

* * *

In 1978, after visiting the "70's" in Hong Kong, the American situationist Ken Knabb wrote a critique of the group entitled "A Radical Group in Hong Kong." . . . Despite our vastly differing positions, we find most of Knabb's criticisms well-founded. In the libertarian tradition of adversion to critique, anti-critique and self-critique (about which even Bakunin must turn in his grave), the "70's" never "cared" to reply (some of the group's overseas contacts even wrote to the group expressing their disgust for Knabb's doing so!).

—International Correspondence, "Open Letter on Our Split from 'Undercurrents'/'Minus' " (Hong Kong, July 1982)

* * *

Anyone who cannot read French and is now interested in the Situationist International owes Ken Knabb some kind of debt. It was Knabb who single-handedly introduced the SI's writings to the United States. (In 1974, of course, Christopher Gray's *Leaving the Twentieth Century: The Incomplete Work of the SI* introduced them to the United Kingdom. But Gray's book wasn't well-translated or very representative in its selections; furthermore it wasn't adequately distributed in the U.S.) . . . I'm sorry to have to report that by and large [Knabb's other publications] suck. . . . *The Relevance of Rexroth* looks like a poetry magazine but reads like a doctoral dissertation, which has got to be one of the most unpoetic things around. . . . Knabb's book wants the truth to be known about Rexroth—that he is under-rated and that more of his books should be brought back into print—but it also wants to criticize him, on precisely the grounds that the situationists made their own. Rexroth didn't understand the spectacle, Knabb claims, and thus Rexroth didn't understand the May 1968 revolt in France. But who cares if he did or he didn't? . . . The second thing Knabb sent me that, ah, sucked was the little thing called "The War and the Spectacle," which he wrote, reproduced and distributed in April, 1991. (Why so late, Ken? The ground war was over on 28 February.) It begins with the sentence, "The orchestration of the Gulf war was a glaring expression of what the situationists call *the spectacle*—the development of modern society to the point where images dominate life," which has got to be one of the all-time great turn-offs. Not only is the tone appropriate to grade schoolers, and not only is the definition of what "the spectacle" is simplistic, but the whole concept seems to be that recent events prove that the situationists were *right*. . . . Rest in peace, Ken: the situationists were indeed right. And so, in a way, are you when you write, "The point is to undermine [the spectacle-spectator relation]—to challenge the conditioning that makes people *susceptible* to media manipulation in the first place." But *how*?

—Bill Brown, "Ken Knabb, R.I.P.," in *Not Bored* #19 (Rhode Island, June 1991)

* * *

Many on the left . . . distrust interaction with the outside world for fear that it may corrupt the purity of their means. One of their greatest fears is cooptation and inclusion of their activities and beliefs in the structure of the status quo. The article from *Anarchy* (see "War and the Spectacle") in this issue of *The Thistle* echoes this concern with its warning that the spark of the protests against the war risk being smothered by organized political movements to do "irrelevant" things like register people to vote. . . . We abjure participation in structured, hierarchical organizations at the risk of distorting our view of the world and foiling our attempts to achieve far-reaching progressive change.

—Grant Emison, *The Thistle* (Massachusetts, 28 August 1991)

* * *

Ken Knabb gets at the essence of Rexroth through his ideas, quoting a few poems but mainly choice passages of prose. Knabb also gets at the way Rexroth talked, the way he "bantered with people" or slipped into an "ironic showbiz persona . . . to get his points across without too much solemnity." Yes, that is exactly the way he was at times. . . . Knabb insightfully connects Rexroth's chief themes, sex, mysticism, and revolution, showing how Rexroth persistently interrelated these and other apparently incongruous topics: civilization and nature, sex and mathematics, personal intimacies and history, visionary contemplation and birthday parties, verse rhythm and riding a horse, for instance. Knabb is especially insightful in his shrewd analysis of Rexroth's revolutionary theory and practice, his Buddhist anarchism, his communitarian personalism, his affinities with Martin Buber. . . . Knabb's main disagreement with Rexroth is that he offered insufficient guidance for the massive revolts of the late 1960's, when he had decided that personal freedom, poetry, song, and the arts generally subverted the oppressive society more than social action. Knabb argues that even the arts of rebellion have been co-opted in the "barrage of spectacles" that maintain the status quo, a thesis that is developed further in his *Situationist International Anthology* and other publications. Rexroth might well have welcomed such intelligent criticism, but who can say what his precise response would have been? My dissatisfaction about Knabb's book is that it is too short to offer full explanations for Rexroth's ideas. . . . Like Eliot Weinberger, Knabb thinks that Rexroth's writings require little explication: but few critics have read as widely as they have, and I know of no one, in or out of academia, who has read more widely than Rexroth. The point of many of his allusions may be clear, but the processes of his imaginative thinking are not so easily grasped. More, not less, explication of his work is needed.

—Morgan Gibson, *Poetry Flash* (Berkeley, January 1992)

* * *

The development of the radical critique of religion has been hitherto unsatisfactory, with the exception of Ken Knabb's *The Realization and Suppression of Religion*. Rarely, if at all, more than a vulgar materialism, such contributions to the critique as exist almost always fail to get to the root of the matter, overlooking the *content* of religion in order to attack the *form*. The fact, however, that religion has certain characteristics and plays a certain role within a given social form *does not limit it to that*. . . . [Knabb's pamphlet] stands alone within the radical milieu as an attempt to grasp what it is in religion that speaks to the human heart. He calls for a discovery of "the content that is expressed in religious form," and criticises the previous development of the critique for its failure to meet the mark. . . . On a practical and personal level for Knabb, the notion of the revolutionary movement as "focus of meaning" takes the form of "affective detournement" . . . . I understand this as theory that is practiced, a kind of self-applied Reichian psychoanalysis. Not that this is "changing the world by changing oneself"; Knabb states explicitly that "any 'personal' liberation is condemned to failure without historical practice." But his striving for a sort of "authenticity" under the "character-armour" does seem to have a "mystic" quality about it; I was reminded, while reading Knabb's "Affective Detournement: A Case Study," of the Spanish Christian mystic St. John of the Cross, who would "Desire nothing in order to desire everything/Love nothing in order to love everything."

—Trevor Carles, "Notes on Religion," in
Lantern Waste #1 (Petersham, Australia, September 1992)

* * *

Loved your "Strong Lessons"—really good. The lack of analysis—the simple-mindedness (not to put too fine a point on it)—of the Buddhist Peace Fellowship's work has been driving me bonkers. . . . By chance, I spoke with [a BPF board member] after getting your leaflet and mentioned it to him, whereupon he told me he'd organized a meeting to discuss it! . . . I hope there'll be a substantive response.

—Nelson Foster (Zen teacher and BPF co-founder), November 1993

* * *

We have circulated your latest broadside around the city and it has created quite a stir. One Buddhist group has been rocked to the core. Apparently this group is trying to expel the members who brought your statement up for discussion. These tainted members also sent copies to their associates in NYC and a ruckus arose there.

—Left Bank Books worker (Seattle, May 1994)

INDEX

407